COUNTRY LIVING
MAGAZINE

Guide to Rural England

THE NORTHEAST
OF ENGLAND

County Durham, Northumberland, Tyne and Wear, Yorkshire

By Peter Long

© Travel Publishing Ltd

Published by:
Travel Publishing Ltd
7a Apollo House, Calleva Park
Aldermaston, Berkshire RG7 8TN
ISBN13 9781904434719
© Travel Publishing Ltd
Country Living is a registered trademark of The National
Magazine Company Limited.

First Published: 2003
Second Edition: 2006
Third Edition: 2008

COUNTRY LIVING GUIDES:

East Anglia	Scotland
Heart of England	The South of England
Ireland	The South East of England
The North East of England	The West Country
The North West of England	Wales

PLEASE NOTE:

All advertisements in this publication have been accepted in good faith by Travel Publishing and they have not necessarily been endorsed by *Country Living* Magazine.

All information is included by the publishers in good faith and is believed to be correct at the time of going to press. No responsibility can be accepted for errors.

Editor:	Peter Long
Printing by:	Scotprint, Haddington
Location Maps:	© Maps in Minutes ™ (2008) © Collins Bartholomews 2008 All rights reserved.
Walks:	Walks have been reproduced with kind permission of the internet walking site: www.walkingworld.com
Walk Maps:	Reproduced from Ordnance Survey mapping on behalf of the Controller of Her Majesty's Stationery Office, © Crown Copyright. Licence Number MC 100035812
Cover Design:	Lines & Words, Aldermaston
Cover Photo:	Bridge over the River Wharfe, Grassington, Yorkshire © www.picturesofbritain.co.uk
Text Photos:	Text photos have been kindly supplied by the Pictures of Britain photo library © www.picturesofbritain.co.uk and © Bob Brooks, Weston-super-Mare

Foreword

From a bracing walk across the hills and tarns of The Lake District to a relaxing weekend spent discovering the unspoilt hamlets of East Anglia, nothing quite matches getting off the beaten track and exploring Britain's areas of outstanding beauty.

Each month, *Country Living Magazine* celebrates the richness and diversity of our countryside with features on rural Britain and the traditions that have their roots there. So it is with great pleasure that I introduce you to the *Country Living Magazine Guide to Rural England* series. Packed with information about unusual and unique aspects of our countryside, the guides will point both fair-weather and intrepid travellers in the right direction.

Each chapter provides a fascinating tour of the North East of England area, with insights into local heritage and history and easy-to-read facts on a wealth of places to visit, stay, eat, drink and shop.

I hope that this guide will help make your visit a rewarding and stimulating experience and that you will return inspired, refreshed and ready to head off on your next countryside adventure.

Susy Smith

Susy Smith
Editor, Country Living magazine

PS To subscribe to *Country Living Magazine* each month, call 01858 438844

Introduction

This is the third edition of *The Country Living Guide to Rural England - the North East* and we are sure that it will be as popular as its predecessors. Regular readers will note that the page layouts have been attractively redesigned and that we have provided more information on the places, people, and activities covered. Also, in the introduction to each village or town we have summarized and categorized the main attractions to be found there which makes it easier for readers to plan their visit. Peter Long, a very experienced travel writer has, of course, completely updated the contents of the guide and ensured that it is packed with vivid descriptions, historical stories, amusing anecdotes and interesting facts on hundreds of places in Yorkshire, Northumberland and Durham.

The advertising panels within each chapter provide further information on places to see, stay, eat, drink, shop and even exercise! We have also selected a number of walks from walkingworld.com (full details of this website may be found to the rear of the guide) which we highly recommend if you wish to appreciate fully the beauty and charm of the varied rural landscapes and coastlines of the North East of England.

The guide however is not simply an "armchair tour". Its prime aim is to encourage the reader to visit the places described and discover much more about the wonderful towns, villages and countryside of Yorkshire, Northumberland and Durham. In this respect we would like to thank all the Tourist Information Centres who helped us to provide you with up-to-date information. Whether you decide to explore this region by wheeled transport or on foot we are sure you will find it a very uplifting experience.

We are always interested in receiving comments on places covered (or not covered) in our guides so please do not hesitate to use the reader reaction forms provided at the rear of this guide to give us your considered comments. This will help us refine and improve the content of the next edition. We also welcome any general comments which will help improve the overall presentation of the guides themselves.

For more information on other titles in the *Country Living Rural Guide* series and the full range of travel guides published by Travel Publishing please refer to the order form at the rear of this guide or log on to our website (see below).

Travel Publishing

Contents

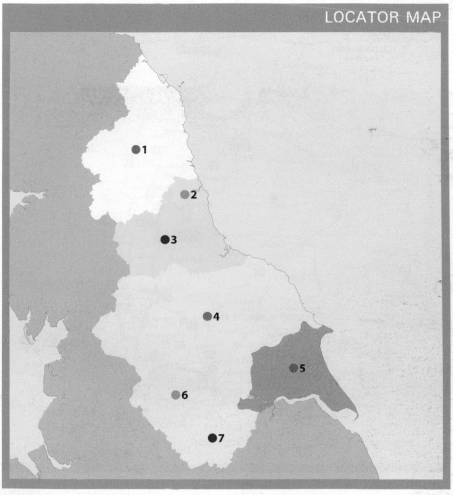

LOCATOR MAP

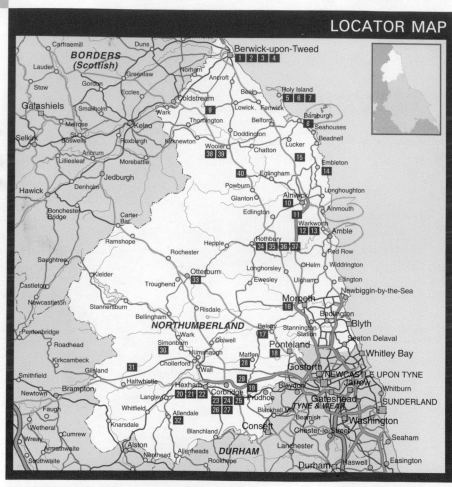

LOCATOR MAP

ADVERTISERS AND PLACES OF INTEREST

🏛 historic building   🏛 museum and heritage   🏚 historic site   ✥ scenic attraction   ❦ flora and fauna

1| Northumberland

Stretching from the edge of the Cheviots to the east coast, and from Berwick-upon-Tweed in the north to the River Blyth in the south, east Northumberland is an area of quiet villages and small market towns, majestic castles, and what many people consider to be the finest coastline in England. Designated as the North Northumberland Heritage Coast, the area boasts a wealth of historical attractions such as Bamburgh Castle, Lindisfarne and the Farne Islands.

For all its beauty, it's a quiet coastline, and you can walk for miles along the dunes and beaches without meeting another soul. No deck chairs or noisy ice cream vans here – just a quietness broken occasionally by the screeching of gulls. Coquet Island is a renowned bird sanctuary where the visitor can see puffins, roseate terns, razorbills, cormorants and eiders.

Lindisfarne, a small island lying between Bamburgh and Berwick, is perhaps the most evocative place of all on the coast. It was to here that St Aidan and a small community of Irish monks came from Iona in AD 635 to found a monastery from which missionaries set out to convert northern England to Christianity.

The region has withstood a tempestuous past and has been the focus of fierce fighting, nowhere more so than the border town of Berwick, whose strategic location made it a

📖 stories and anecdotes 🐦 famous people 🎨 art and craft 🎭 entertainment and sport 🚶 walks

prime target in the endless skirmishes between the English and the Scots. The Border Reivers, or mosstroopers, rustled, pillaged and fought among themselves, incurring the wrath of both English and Scottish kings. All along the coastline can be seen superb castles such as those of Norham, Etal, Chillingham and Edlingham. Some have been converted into grand mansions for the great families of the area, while others are now no more than ruins.

Inland from the coast the land is heavily farmed, and there is a pleasant landscape of fields, woodland, country lanes and farms. The villages, with their ancient parish churches and village greens, are especially fine. The village green was essential in olden times, as the Scots constantly harried this area, and the villagers needed somewhere to guard their cattle after bringing them in from the surrounding land.

The area to the south east around Ashington was once coalmining country, though the scars are gradually being swept away. The industry is remembered in a museum of mining at Woodhorn. Even here, however, an earlier history is evident, as the former Woodhorn church is one of the most interesting in Northumberland.

Legacies of the past can be explored at Segedunum Roman fort, Wallsend - so called because this was where Hadrian's Wall ended. It is now the beginning - or end - of the Hadrian's Wall Path National Trail.

West Northumberland, where the North Pennines blend into the Cheviots, is an exhilarating mixture of bleak grandeur, beauty and history. Stretching north towards the Scottish border, are the 398 square miles of the Northumbrian National Park and the Kielder Forest Park. The forest covers 200

Hadrian's Wall

square miles and contains Europe's largest man-made lake, Kielder Water, opened by the Queen in 1982. To the south is Hadrian's Wall, that monumental feat of Roman civil engineering built on the orders of Emperor Hadrian in AD 122. The best-known Roman monument in Britain and the best-known Roman frontier in Europe, it stretches for some 70 miles from Wallsend in the east to Bowness-on-Solway in the west, and in 1987 was declared a UNESCO World Heritage Site. To see the Wall twisting across the moorland is an awe-inspiring sight, and no visitor to Northumberland should miss it. Towards the east of the area, the hills slope down towards a stretch of fertile land with little towns like Rothbury and Wooler, which in themselves deserve exploration. But up on the high ground a person could walk for miles without meeting another soul. The highest point, at 2,650 feet, is The Cheviot itself, a few miles from the Scottish border.

Berwick-upon-Tweed

🏛 Barracks 🏛 Bridges 🏛 Town Hall

🏛 Holy Trinity Church 🏛 Museums

🏛 Berwick Castle

Berwick-upon-Tweed is one of England's most beguiling towns. It is unique in being completely encircled by an Elizabethan town wall, which can still be walked along, the 1.5 mile circuit providing fine views of the town and the Northumberland coastline. The River Tweed serves as the border between Scotland and Northumberland along much of its length, but a few miles to the west of Berwick, the border takes a curious lurch north, and curls up and over the town to the east before reaching the coast. So, while Berwick is on the north bank of the Tweed, it's well and truly within Northumberland.

For centuries, this former Royal burgh of Scotland was fought over by the Scots and the English, and changed hands no less than 14 times until it finally became part of England in 1482. But even now, Scotland exerts a great influence. The local football team, Berwick Rangers, plays in the Scottish League, and in 1958 the Lord Lyon, who decides on all matters armorial in Scotland, granted the town a coat-of-arms – the only instance of armorial bearings being granted in Scotland for use in England.

But for many years after becoming English, the town was a curious anomaly. In the 16th century Berwick was declared a 'free burgh',

---

A must for visitors to Berwick-upon-Tweed is a trip to Bridge Street located in the old part of town down by the River Tweed. Popular with both visitors and locals alike, the diversity of shops and businesses, mostly privately-owned and run, has won great acclaim. Among these is The Irving Gallery, an exciting new gallery showing and selling paintings and drawings, prints, photographs and cards.

Artists regularly featured include Mark Irving, Kate Philp, Peter Podmore, Derek Jones, Mary Ann Rogers, Walter Holmes, Mick Oxley, Michael Ewart, Eddie Sanderson, Daphne Harrison, Sarah Riseborough, Ruud Spil, Jane McCracken, Jonathan Lloyd and Amanda Brumwell. The Gallery also offers a quality bespoke framing service and has space available for workshops, talks and demonstrations.

Gallery hours are 10.30am to 5.00pm (sometimes closed on Thursdays).

THE IRVING GALLERY

25 Bridge Street, Berwick-upon-Tweed, Northumberland TD15 1ES
Tel: 01289 332789

🎭 stories and anecdotes 🕊 famous people 🎨 art and craft ✏ entertainment and sport 🚶 walks

FOOD GLORIOUS FOOD

13 Woolmarket, Berwick-upon-Tweed,
Northumberland TD15 1DH
Tel: 01289 304442
e-mail: Karen@fgfdeli.co.uk
website: www.fgfdeli.co.uk

Food Glorious Food provides an excellent service for the citizens of Berwick-upon-Tweed and for the many visitors to this historic town. Owner Karen Cummins' shop, a prime example of a local independent delicatessen, is stocked with all kinds of high-quality foodstuffs from top local and national producers. A fine selection of cheese includes the superb organic Godminster Cheddar, and other choices run from made-to-order sandwiches to cooked and cured meats, home baking, pickles, chutneys, sauces, preserves, coffees, teas and fresh orange juice. Brands in stock include Hawkshead Relish – world-renowned purveyors of pickles and mustards; Atkins & Potts; Paddy & Scotts; and Jules & Sharpie's 'hot preservaments'. And for those who like to present their food with style, the shop stocks the lovely Susie Watson ceramics. This outstanding food shop is open from 8.30 to 4.30 Monday to Saturday.

THE GREEN SHOP

30 Bridge Street, Berwick-upon-Tweed, Northumberland TD15 1AQ
Tel/Fax: 01289 305566

Green is the name and green is the philosophy of **The Green Shop**, which since opening in 1993 has adhered to ethical, environmentally aware and Fair Trade policies and principles. In the heart of Berwick, Ross and Pauline's shop is filled with shelf upon shelf and row upon row of food, clothes and crafts from the region, the UK and around the world – fresh, pre-packed and frozen

food and dry goods – fruit, vegetables, meat and dairy products, organic wines, beers and spirits, cotton clothing, essential oils, seeds, toiletries and cosmetics, most of the last being locally sourced and produced without animal testing.

Awards have come in abundance to this splendid shop, including Best Independent Retailer in a readers' poll in the

Tweeddale Press and the Eastern Borders Development Association, as well as organic certification from the Biodynamic Agricultural Association.

neither in Scotland nor in England, a situation that lasted right up until 1885. Its ambiguous status was such that when war was declared on Russia in 1853, it was done in the name of 'Victoria, Queen of Great Britain, Ireland, Berwick-upon-Tweed and all the British Dominions'. When peace was announced in 1856, no mention was made of Berwick. So technically, the town remained at war with Russia.

The situation was rectified in 1966, when a Soviet official made a goodwill visit to the town and a peace treaty was signed. During the ceremony, the Berwick mayor told the Soviet official that the people of Russia could at last sleep easy in their beds.

Berwick's original medieval walls were built in the 13th century by Edward I. They were subsequently strengthened by Robert the Bruce when he recaptured the town in 1318, and finally rebuilt by Italian engineers at the bequest of Elizabeth I between 1558 and 1569, though the work was never completed. They are regarded as being the finest preserved fortifications of their time in Europe.

Berwick's strategic location led it to become an important military town. For many years the garrison soldiers were billeted in local taverns and private houses, but this placed a heavy financial burden on the townspeople. Complaints to the government led to the building of **Berwick Barracks** between 1717 and 1721. Designed by Nicholas Hawksmoor, they were the first purpose-built barracks in Britain, and within them you'll find the **King's Own Scottish Borderers Museum**. Here visitors will learn about a Scottish regiment that was raised in 1689 by the Earl of Leven, and which is still in existence today.

Housed in the clock tower of the barracks is the **Berwick-upon-Tweed Borough**

Berwick Barracks

Museum and Art Gallery, which explores the history of the town. The museum contains a remarkable collection given to the town by Sir William Burrell, who lived in nearby Hutton Castle. Famous for collecting the works of art that can now be seen in the Burrell Art Gallery in Glasgow, Burrell also donated 300 works of art, sculpture and pottery to Berwick. The **Gymnasium Gallery**, opened in 1993, displays regularly changing exhibtions of contemporary art.

Berwick's Bridge Street is being promoted as the best shopping street in North Northumberland and the Scottish Borders. The street is home to a number of specialist shops – basically a collection of businesses whose owners have a real passion for what they do and a real interest in their customers. A visitor from London described it as the Covent Garden of the North and decided to

DELI UPON TWEED

18 Hide Hill, Berwick-upon-Tweed,
Northumberland TD15 1AB
Tel: 0115 937 6010
e-mail: info@deliupontweed.co.uk
website: www.deliupontweed.co.uk

Alison and John Webber's passion for quality food is evident the moment you step inside **Deli upon Tweed**, which they opened in August 2007. Behind the large and enticing window displays in a traditional stone building, their shop is stocked with a wide variety of superb foodstuffs, much of it sourced locally. An average of 30 cheeses is always on display, along with cooked and cured meats (award-winning locally produced glazed hams); Patchwork Pâtés; Carrols heritage potatoes; home-baked cakes and tarts both sweet and savoury; jams, chutneys, dressings, oils and vinegars, herbs and spices; Doddington ice creams in 10 flavours (don't miss the award-winning heather honey); apple juice; coffees; and always, gluten-free products. To take away, they offer bespoke sandwiches, soups, jacket potatoes, salad pots and picnic food. Shop hours are 8.30 to 5.30 Monday to Saturday.

stay another day in the town after discovering the street.

Three distinctive bridges linking the town centre with the communities of Tweedmouth and Spittal span the Tweed estuary. The oldest of these is the 17th-century **Berwick Bridge**, a handsome stone bridge with 15 arches, completed in 1626. The **Royal Tweed Bridge** is the most modern, having been completed in 1928 with a concrete structure built to an iron bridge design. The enormous 126 feet high, 28-arch **Royal Border Bridge**, carrying the East Coast mainline railway, was built between 1847 and 1850 by Robert Stephenson.

The Berwick skyline is dominated by the imposing **Town Hall** with its clock tower and steeple that rise to 150 feet, and which is often mistaken for a church. Built between 1754 and

1761, this fine building has a façade as elaborate as its well-documented history. From the lofty steeple's bell chamber a curfew still rings out each evening at 8pm. On the ground floor, markets were held in the Exchange and shops and cells existed where now a gift shop and coffee house stand. Guided tours in the summer enable visitors to explore the upper storeys, where there are civic rooms and the former town gaol. A small **Cell Block Museum** is also located there.

Facing Berwick Barracks is **Holy Trinity Church** – one of the few Commonwealth churches in England. It was built between 1650 and 1652, during the Commonwealth of Oliver Cromwell, to replace a dilapidated medieval church that stood on the same site.

On the northwest side of the town you will find all that remains of **Berwick Castle**. Built in the 13th century, it was demolished in 1850 to make way for the railway station, and the platform now occupies the site of the former Great Hall. The ruins are in the care of English Heritage.

Around Berwick-upon-Tweed

TWEEDMOUTH
1 mile S of Berwick off the A1

Tweedmouth and Spittal, on the English side of the Tweed estuary, are largely suburbs of Berwick. In mid-July a ceremony is held in Tweedmouth, dating back to 1292, to celebrate the fact that the River Tweed, one of the best salmon rivers in Britain, reaches the sea here. The local schools hold a ballot to elect a 'Salmon Queen', and her crowning marks the beginning of Feast Week, which centres round a church service and involves lots of festivities, including a traditional salmon supper.

HORNCLIFFE
4 miles W of Berwick off the A698

🏛 Union Suspension Bridge

The village of Horncliffe, five miles upstream of Berwick, can only be reached by one road that leads into and out of the village, making it feel rather remote. Many visitors are unaware of the existence of the river, but there is nothing more pleasant than wandering down one of the paths leading to the banks to watch the salmon fishermen on a summer's evening.

Not far from the village the River Tweed is spanned by the **Union Suspension Bridge** linking Scotland and England. It was built in 1820 by Sir Samuel Browne who also invented the wrought-iron chain links used in its construction. The graceful structure, 480 feet long, was Britain's first major suspension bridge to carry vehicular traffic, and although not carrying a major road, it is still possible to drive over it.

NORHAM
6 miles SW of Berwick on the B6470

🏛 Station Museum 🏰 Norham Castle

🎭 Blessing of the Nets

Norham is a neat, historical village that sits on the banks of the Tweed. Up until 1836, the town was an enclave of the County Palatinate of Durham, surrounded by Northumberland on the south, east and west, and Scotland on the north. **Norham Castle** (English Heritage) was built in the 12th century by the Bishop of Durham and stands on a site of great natural strength, guarding a natural ford over the river. It withstood repeated attacks in the 13th and 14th centuries and was thought to be impregnable. However, in 1513, it was

Norham Castle

stormed by the forces of James IV on his way to Flodden and partially destroyed.

Although it was later rebuilt, the castle was again destroyed by the Scots in 1530, and had lost its importance as a defensive stronghold by the end of the 16th century.

Norham's **Station Museum** is located on the former Tweedmouth to Kelso branch line. The museum features the original signal box, booking office, porter's room and model railway.

Each year in Norham an unusual ceremony takes place. **The Blessing of the Nets** is held at midnight on 13th February to mark the beginning of the salmon fishing season. The service is held by lantern light, with the clergyman standing in a boat in the middle of the river.

DUDDO
7 miles SW of Berwick on the B6354

🏚 Duddo Stones

Close to the village are the **Duddo Stones**, one of Northumberland's most important ancient monuments. This ancient stone circle, which now consists of five upright stones more than seven feet high, dates back to around 2000 BC. The stones stand on private ground and can only be reached from the village by foot.

TILLMOUTH
9 miles SW of Berwick on the A698

🏚 Twizel Castle 🏚 St Cuthbert's Chapel

The village of Tillmouth lies along the banks of the River Till, a tributary of the Tweed, which is crossed by the 15th-century Twizel Bridge, although a more modern structure now carries the A698 over the river. Up until the building of the 1727 Causey Arch in County Durham, the old Twizel Bridge, with a

span of 90 feet, had the largest span of any bridge in Britain. There are some lovely walks here and a well-signed footpath leads to the ruins of **Twizel Castle** and the remains of **St Cuthbert's Chapel** on the opposite bank, dating from the 18th or 19th centuries, but incorporating some medieval stonework.

LOWICK
8 miles S of Berwick on the B6353

Lowick is a quiet farming community, which contains only a few shops and a couple of pubs. About a mile east of the village are the earthworks of a former castle. The Norman church was replaced by the present St John the Baptist Church.

LINDISFARNE, OR HOLY ISLAND
10 miles SE of Berwick off the A1

🏛 Priory and Castle 📖 Lindisfarne Gospels
🐾 Pilgrims' Way 🐾 St Cuthbert's Way

Northumberland's northern coastline is dominated by Holy Island, also known by its Celtic name of Lindisfarne. The island is accessible only at low tide, via a three-mile long causeway linking it with the mainland at Beal. Tide tables are published locally and are displayed at each end of the road. There are refuges part way along for those who fail to time it correctly.

As you cross, note the 11th-century **Pilgrims' Way**, marked by stakes, still visible about 200 metres south of the modern causeway. This route was in use until comparatively recent times.

The island was given to St Aidan in AD 635 by Oswald, King of Northumbria. St Aidan and his small community of Irish monks came from Iona to found a base from which to convert northern England to Christianity. This led to the island being called one of the cradles of English Christianity. St Cuthbert came here to teach and the island became a magnet for pilgrims. When he died in AD 687 he was buried in the church. St Cuthbert's island can be reached at low tide from the island and was used by the saint during times of solitude. A cross marks the site of his tiny chapel.

These early monks are also remembered for producing some of the finest surviving examples of Celtic art – the richly decorated **Lindisfarne Gospels**, dating from the 7th century. When the island was invaded by Vikings in the 9th century, the monks fled taking their precious gospels with them. These have, miraculously, survived and are now in the safety of the British Museum. Facsimiles are kept on Lindisfarne and can be seen in the 12th-century parish church on the island. The monks also took with them St Cuthbert's bones, and wandered around for over 100 years before eventually finding a safe resting place for them in Durham.

During the 11th century a group of Benedictine monks settled here. The ruins of their great sandstone **Lindisfarne Priory** (see panel below) with its Romanesque-style great pillars can still be explored. The Priory is one of the holiest Anglo-Saxon sights in England; crossing the dramatic causeway to Holy Island, you journey into a significant site of Britain's spiritual heritage. Few places are as beautiful or have such special significance. When St Cuthbert's corpse was found undecayed in AD 698, the Priory became one of the most sacred shrines in Christendom. For over 1,300 years it has been a place of pilgrimage, and remains so today. Here you

Lindisfarne Priory

Lindisfarne, Northumberland TD15 2SJ
Tel: 01289 389200

Lindisfarne Priory is one of the Holiest Anglo-Saxon sites in England. When you cross the dramatic causeway to Holy Island, you journey into our spiritual heritage. Few places are as beautiful or have such special significance. The corpse of St Cuthbert was found undecayed in AD 698, and this became one of the most sacred shrines in Christendom. For over 1,300 years it has been a place of pilgrimage and still is today.

Here you can learn about the Monastery's fantastic wealth, and walk in the grounds where brutal Viking raiders plundered the priory, forcing Monks to refuge on the mainland. It is advisable to have a tide table with you when you visit Lindisfarne - at high tide the causeway linking Holy Island to the Northumbrian coast is submerged, cutting off the Island.

There is a sculpture on show entitled 'Cuthbert of Farne' which was created by local artist Fenwick Lawson. This sculpture depicts a comtemplative Cuthbert reflecting on his religious life and desire for solitude. His interlaced hands echo the stillness and peace he sought. The Museum is lively and atmospheric and explains what life was like more than a millenium ago. Open daily except Christmas and New Year, the facilities include parking, toilets, gift shop, souvenir guide and exhibition.

stories and anecdotes 　 famous people 　 art and craft 　 entertainment and sport 　 walks

CELTIC CRAFTS

Marygate, Holy Island, Berwick-upon-Tweed,
Northumberland TD15 2SJ
Tel: 01289 389033
e-mail: info@celticcrafts.uk.com
website: www.celticcrafts.uk.com

For anyone who appreciates the intricate, beautiful and unique designs of the Celtic tradition they will find **Celtic Crafts** on Holy Island an undiluted delight. Housed in one of the oldest buildings on the island (dating from 1606), it is an attractive outlet for items of Celtic inspiration, including jewellery, goblets and chalices, glassware and china, designer knitwear and other goods sourced from small workshops throughout the British Isles. The jewellery range includes a superb collection of engagement and wedding rings in gold, silver or platinum, some set with precious or semi-precious stones. Many of the pieces are inspired by the Lindisfarne Gospels, dating from the 7th century. Some are exclusive to Celtic Crafts, notably the St Cuthbert Cross in silver or gold, with a garnet in the middle. More familiar items include books,

postcards, CDs, T-shirts... and the famous and very moreish creamy fudge. Above the retail outlets are two floors of comfortable, stylish holiday accommodation, with two bedrooms directly above and a modern kitchen and living area on the top floor.

PILGRIM'S COFFEE HOUSE

Falkland House, Marygate, Holy Island,
Berwick-upon-Tweed, Northumberland TD15 2SJ
Tel: 01289 389109 website: www.pilgrimscoffee.com

The pilgrimage ends here folks!

Set on the idyllic island of Lindisfarne, **Pilgrim's Coffee House** offers a unique coffee experience.

Highly trained baristas will create some of the best coffee you will ever taste; complemented by scrumptious homemade cakes and scones.

Try a Gingerbread Latte and a giant slice of carrot cake. Indulge in gifts for all the family with our Pilgrim's range.

Enjoy our warm friendly atmosphere inside, or relax in the tranquillity of our walled garden outside.

Pilgrim's has recently finished a mobile coffee van that will refresh tourists where other places cannot. The van will be in the Pilgrim's colours, so keep an eye out if you are walking on the island

Believe us; Pilgrim's is **worth** missing the tide for!

Visitors to the craft shop and coffee house should remember that Holy Island is tidal!

🏚 historic building   🏛 museum and heritage   🏛 historic site   ✿ scenic attraction   🌱 flora and fauna

can learn about the monastery's fantastic wealth, and walk in the grounds where Viking raiders plundered the Priory, forcing the monks to find refuge on the mainland. One recent addition is a sculpture entitled 'Cuthbert of Farne', created by local artist Fenwick Lawson and depicting a contemplative Cuthbert, hands folded in prayer. The Museum displays are lively and atmospheric, and explain what life was like more than a millennium ago. The Priory is open daily except for Christmas and New Year. **Lindisfarne Castle** (National Trust) was established in Tudor times as yet another fortification to protect the exposed flank of Northumbria from invasion by the Scots. In 1902 it was bought by Edward Hudson, a magazine publisher, who employed the great Edwardian architect Sir Edward Lutyens to rebuild and restore it as a private house. The house and its small walled garden are open to the public during the summer months.

Holy Island village is a community of around 170 people who work mainly in farming and the tourist trade. Some are also employed in the island's distillery, noted for excellent traditional mead, which can be purchased locally. Much of the island is also a nature reserve, with wildflowers and a wide variety of seabirds. St Mary's Church in the village has some fine Saxon stonework above the chancel arch.

The island is the finishing point for the 62-mile **St Cuthbert's Way**, a long-distance footpath that opened in 1996. The trail begins at Melrose, across the Scottish border, and along the way passes through the Northumberland National Park and the Cheviot Hills.

Lindisfarne Castle

BAMBURGH
16 miles SE of Berwick on the B1340

🏰 Castle	🏛 Grace Darling Museum
🐦 Farne Islands	🔦 Longstone Lighthouse

'King Ida's Castle huge and square' was Sir Walter Scott's description of **Bamburgh Castle** (see panel on page 14), a magnificent structure aggressively perched on a rocky outcrop 150-feet high above the North Sea strand, dominating the Northumbrian landscape. Sir Walter was thinking of the Saxon king, Ida the Flame-Bearer, who built the first fortress here in AD 547. Ida's grandson, Ethelfrith the Destroyer, gave the settlement to his wife, Bebba, from whom the castle derives its name – 'Bebban-burgh'.

King Ida's castle was built of wood. It was the Normans who erected the mighty red sandstone keep that still dominates the battlemented courtyards today. Bamburgh is epic in scale, even by the standards of this coastline and its abundance of spectacular castles.

The present stone castle sprawls across eight acres and its 10-foot thick walls were crucial in repulsing many attacks in the lawless days of medieval Northumbria. But, by the

Bamburgh Castle

Bamburgh, Northumberland NE69 7DF
Tel: 01668 214515 Fax: 01668 214060
e-mail: bamburghcastle@aol.com
website: www.bamburghcastle.com

Standing on a rocky outcrop overlooking miles of beautiful sandy beach, **Bamburgh Castle** dominates the Northumbrian landscape. The castle became the passion of the 1st Baron Armstrong who, in the 1890s, began its renovation and refurbishment. This love of Bamburgh was passed down through the family to the late Lord Armstrong, who personally oversaw the completion of his ancestor's dream.

Today Bamburgh Castle is still the home of the Armstrong family, and visitors are able to enjoy what has been described as the finest castle in all England. The public tour includes the magnificent King's Hall, the Cross Hall, reception rooms, the Bakehouse and Victorian Scullery, as well as the Armoury and Dungeon. Throughout, these rooms contain a wide range of fine china, porcelain and glassware, together with paintings, furniture, tapestries, arms and armour.

The Armstrong Museum, occupying the former Laundry Building, is dedicated to the life and work of the first Lord Armstrong. An inventive engineer, shipbuilder and industrialist, he left a great legacy to the modern age and Tyneside in particular.

The castle is open daily from mid March to the end of October, between 11am and 5pm, and teas and light refreshments are available from The Clock Tower.

time of the Wars of the Roses, even those sturdy walls could not withstand Edward IV's new-fangled cannon. Bamburgh became the first English castle to succumb to artillery fire.

By the late 1500s, much of the castle stood in ruins. Various attempts were made over succeeding centuries to rehabilitate the vast building – most notably in the early 1700s when the philanthropist Dr John Sharp *'repaired and rendered habitable the gret Norman square tower'*, set up a Charity School where *'20 poor maidens were lodged, clothed and educated till they be fit for service'*, opened a free surgery and dispensary for local people, and provided free accommodation in the castle's many gloomy chambers for sailors who had been shipwrecked off this notoriously dangerous stretch of coast.

The castle's most significant benefactor was William George, 1st Lord Armstrong, the very model of a Victorian self-made millionaire. A solicitor-turned-engineer, he amassed a huge fortune from his inventive improvements of hydraulic engines, armaments and shipbuilding. He devoted a large part of his immense wealth to building a spectacular mansion, Cragside, near Rothbury; then spent another considerable fortune on restoring Bamburgh Castle. The castle became his passion and, in the 1890s, he began an ambitious programme of renovation and refurbishment. Lord Armstrong commissioned the fashionable London architect Charles Ferguson to re-create a medieval castle that also incorporated all the latest Victorian state-of-the-art amenities. At the time, Ferguson's lavish restoration offended medieval purists – they preferred Norman ruins. Today, you can't help but be impressed by the impeccable craftsmanship. Bamburgh Castle is still home to the Armstrong family, and visitors are able to enjoy what has been described as the finest castle in all England. The public tour includes the magnificent King's Hall, the Cross Hall, reception rooms, the Bakehouse and Victorian Scullery, as well as the

Bamburgh Beach

Armoury and Dungeon. The rooms contain a wide range of fine china, porcelain and glassware, together with paintings, furniture, tapestries, arms and armour. The castle is open daily from mid-March to the end of October between 11am and 5pm; teas and light refreshments are available from The Clock Tower.

The village was the birthplace of Grace Darling, the celebrated Victorian heroine, who, in 1838, rowed out with her father from the **Longstone Lighthouse** in a ferocious storm to rescue the survivors of the steam ship *Forfarshire,* which had foundered on the Farne Islands rocks. She died of tuberculosis only four years later, still only in her twenties, and is buried in the churchyard of St Aidan's. The **Grace Darling Museum**, in Radcliffe Road, contains memorabilia of the famous rescue.

Just offshore are the **Farne Islands**. This small group of 28 uninhabited islands of volcanic Whin Sill rock provides a major breeding sanctuary for migratory seabirds including puffins, guillemots, razorbills, arctic

and sandwich terns and kittiwakes. They are the home to a large colony of Atlantic Grey seals, which can often be seen from the beach on the mainland.

The islands have important Christian links, as it was on Inner Farne that St Cuthbert died in AD 687. A little chapel was built here in his memory and restored in Victorian times. According to legend, the nearby Tower House was built in medieval times by Prior Castell on the site of Cuthbert's cell. Boat trips to the Farne Islands leave from the harbour in Seahouses. Landings are permitted on Inner Farne and Staple Island, times are restricted for conservation reasons and advance booking is necessary at busy times of the year.

WAREN MILL
15 miles SE of Berwick on the B1342

Waren Mill is a small village situated on Budle Bay, a large inlet of flats and sand where vast numbers of wading birds and wildfowl come to feed. Caution should be taken when walking on the flats, as sections quickly become cut off at high tide.

FORD & ETAL ESTATE

Heatherslaw Mill, Cornhill-on-Tweed,
Northumberland TD15 2PX
Tel: 01890 820338   Fax: 01890 820384
e-mail: tourism@ford-and-etal.co.uk
website: www.ford-and-etal.co.uk

FFor anyone visiting North Northumberland, nothing embodies the essence of this wonderful part of the world than the twin estate villages of **Ford and Etal**.

These villages and their neighbours – Branxton, Milfield, Crookham, Heatherslaw – in the valley of the River Till (the only tributary of the Tweed in England) offer an amazing range of sights, delights and pleasures to appeal to the widest variety of interests: castles, stately homes, churches, a corn mill, an art gallery, a battlefield, a plant nursery, a nature reserve, a quaint railway, a river and marvellous walks.

The heart of the 16,500-acre estate is at Heatherslaw, where the Visitor Centre includes a video presentation of the working of the estate and the long history and rich tradition of the region. Heatherslaw Corn Mill is a lovingly restored watermill on the banks of the Till, using the original 1830s machinery to produce high-quality stoneground flour from locally grown wheat. Mill produce is sold in the mill shop, along with locally baked bread, cakes and biscuits. Teas and light meals are available in the Heatherslaw Tearoom. Heatherslaw Light Railway is a 15inch gauge steam railway running through pleasant countryside to Etal, two miles away – a leisurely return trip of 50 minutes.

Etal is a charming village with picturesque cottages and the only pub in the county with a thatched roof. The village is overlooked by 14th-century Etal Castle, where the Visitor Centre tells the story of the castle, border warfare and the Battle of Flodden (the last and bloodiest battle fought in Northumberland, in 1513; the battlefield lies a few hundred yards from the village of Branxton. Etal's old electricity generator now houses the bespoke furniture maker Taylor & Green, and at nearby Letham Hill, the Errol Hut Smith and Woodwork Shop produces excellent wrought ironwork and fine furniture and wood turning.

In the model village of Ford, the old water garden of the Castle contains a specialist plant nursery. Lady Waterford Hall, named after the estimable Louisa Ann, Marchioness of Waterford, creator of the village, is now a gallery showcasing her life sized murals. Other places of interest in the village include the Horseshoe Forge, John Martin's Rare Books, a post office and village shop serving teas and coffees. This is wonderful walking and cycling country, and other outdoor pursuits are catered for by the gliding centre at Milfield, the Kimmerston Riding Centre, Ford Moss Nature Reserve (an SSSI) and the Maelmin Heritage Trail at Milfield. There's always something going on in and around the estate, and the excellent website gives details of local accommodation, news, events and seasonal attractions.

BELFORD

14 miles S of Berwick off the A1

🦆 Greensheen Hill   📖 St Cuthbert's Cave

Belford is an attractive village of stone houses whose broad main street contains some interesting old shops and a fine old coaching inn, reflecting the fact that this was once an important town on the Great North Road. Today, it is an ideal holiday base, standing on the edge of the Kyloe Hills, where there are some fine walks, and close to the long golden beaches and rocky outcrops of the coast.

St Cuthbert's Cave, to the north of the town, is only accessible by foot. It is completely natural, and concealed by a great overhanging rock surrounded by woodland. It is believed that the saint's body lay here on its much interrupted journey across Northumbria. From the summit of nearby **Greensheen Hill** there are superb views of the coast and of the Cheviots to the west.

FORD AND ETAL

12 miles SW of Berwick off the B6354

🏰 Etal & Ford Castles   🏛 Heritage Trail
🏰 Church of the Blessed Virgin Mary
🏛 Heatherslaw Corn Mill

The twin estate villages of Ford and Etal (see panel opposite) were built in the late 1800s. Set beside the River Till, **Etal** is a picturesque village of attractive white-painted cottages and a pub, the Black Bull, which is the only hostelry in Northumberland with a thatched roof. Another singularity here is the green for quoits, a Northumbrian game traditionally played with horseshoes.

At one end of the single street is **Etal Castle** (English Heritage), which was fortified in the early 1300s by the Manners family, sending a clear message to their bitter enemies, the Herons, who had built their castle at nearby Ford a few years earlier. Etal Castle was captured and partially destroyed in 1497 by King James IV of Scotland on his way to Flodden. The ruins, which occupy a lovely position on a steep bank above the river, now contain a visitor centre and exhibition telling the story of the castle, border warfare and the Battle of Flodden. Etal's **Church of the Blessed Virgin Mary** was built in 1858 by Lady Augusta Fitz-Clarence in memory of her husband and daughter.

Ford is also a 'model' village, created in the 1860s by the estimable Louisa Ann, Marchioness of Waterford, who had been a bridesmaid to Queen Victoria. She was a noted beauty and also an accomplished artist who had studied with the Pre-Raphaelite artist John Ruskin. After the death of her husband, she devoted her time to decorating the village school (which she had built) with some quite remarkable murals depicting Old Testament scenes. She used local families and the school children as models thus creating a pictorial gallery of life and work in the area at that time. The school is no longer used and is now open to the public as the **Lady Waterford Gallery**.

Other elements of Lady Waterford's legacy include the Horseshoe Forge, built as a blacksmith's shop, a fountain surmounted by a marble angel, and the Jubilee Cottage, built in 1887 to commemorate Queen Victoria's Golden Jubilee.

The Marchioness lived at **Ford Castle** which was originally built in 1282 and greatly extended in the following century. Like Etal Castle, it was badly damaged by the Scots on their way to Flodden, converted into a comfortable mansion in the 1760s, and again

📖 stories and anecdotes   🦜 famous people   🎨 art and craft   🎭 entertainment and sport   🚶 walks

Alnwick Castle

Alnwick, Northumberland NE66 1NQ
Tel: 01665 510777
e-mail: enquiries@alnwickcastle.com
website: www.alnwickcastle.com

Owned by the Percy family since 1309, **Alnwick** is one of the finest castles in the British Isles. Originally built to defend England's northern border from the Scottish armies, the castle is the family home of the Duke and Duchess of Northumberland. With magnificent views over the River Aln and surrounding countryside, the castle is a few minutes walk from the centre of the historic market town of Alnwick.

Within the massive stone walls, the beautifully kept grounds contain fascinating exhibitions. Discover the history of the Northumberland Fusiliers since 1674 in the Abbot's Tower. Marvel at the richness of Northumberland's archaeological past in the Postern Tower, and listen to life as a member of the Percy Tenantry Volunteers (1798-1814) in the Constable's Tower.

At the heart of the castle is the keep. Pass through the medieval towers and enter a wonderful family home. State Rooms, refurbished in the mid-19th century by the Fourth Duke,

contain paintings by Canaletto, Van Dyck and Titian. Finely carved wooden panels adorn the walls, windows and ceilings. A children's quiz helps your family learn more about Alnwick Castle.

There are various events held throughout the spring and summer, including Birds of Prey displays, horse driving trials and an International Music Festival. Noted as a location for *'Harry Potter'*, *'Elizabeth'* and *'Robin Hood, Prince of Thieves'* Alnwick Castle is open daily from 1st April to 31st October.

altered by the Marchioness in the 1860s. The castle itself is not open to the public, but its old walled garden is now a nursery selling a wide range of plants.

At **Heatherslaw**, between the two villages, is the Heatherslaw Railway, a 15 inch gauge steam railway that runs between Etal Castle and **Heatherslaw Corn Mill**, a water-powered working watermill dating back to 1830, which still uses its original machinery to produce flour. About two-and-a-half miles southwest is the small village of Milfield, where there is a 16th-century tower house known as Coupland Castle. Scattered around this area are standing stones and mysterious examples of rock art, all of which can be explored following the **Maelmin Heritage Trail** from Milfield. The trail includes a full scale replica henge, and a Mesolithic hut built for the BBC programme *Meet the Ancestors*.

Alnwick

| 🏰 Castle 🏰 St Michael's Church |
| 🏰 Hotspur Tower 🏛 Museums |
| 🏛 Hulne Priory 🏛 Abbey 🌱 Gardens |

Alnwick (pronounced 'Annick') is one of Northumberland's most impressive towns. It still retains the feel and appearance of a great medieval military and commercial centre, being an important market town since the granting of its charter in 1291. The town is dominated by the huge fortress of **Alnwick Castle** (see panel opposite), set in beautiful parklands designed and landscaped in the 18th-century by Capability Brown and Thomas Call. Alnwick Castle began, like most of Northumberland's castles, as a Norman motte and bailey. In the 12th century this was replaced by a stone castle, which was greatly added to over the centuries. In 1309, the castle came into the possession of Henry de Percy, who strengthened the fortifications. Henry's great grandson was made an earl, and the castle was then passed down 11 generations of Earls. When the male Percy line died out, it passed through the female line to Sir Hugh Smithson, who took the Percy name and was created Duke of Northumberland. When the Duke inherited the castle in 1750 it was falling into disrepair and he commissioned the renowned Robert Adam to restore the castle into a residence fit for a Duke. The superb ceilings and fireplaces can still be seen today. Further sweeping changes were made in the 1850s and 1860s, when the 4th Duke commissioned the Victorian architect Anthony Salvin to transform the castle into a great country house with all modern comforts while recapturing its former medieval glory. Visitors can admire the Italian Renaissance-style State Rooms and treasures that include

paintings by Titian, Tintoretto, Canaletto and Van Dyck, collections of Meissen china and exquisite furniture. The castle is open daily from 1st April to 31st October.

There is also an impressive archaeological museum and extensive archive collections, as well as the **Northumberland Fusiliers Museum** housed in The Abbot's Tower.

The castle is still the home of the Percys, and is a favourite location for making films, including *Robin Hood, Prince of Thieves* and the *Harry Potter* films, where it doubles as Hogwart's School.

Bailiffgate Museum brings the people and places of North Northumberland to life using six specially-themed areas to showcase the unique heritage of this historic region. Housed in the former St Mary's church, dating back to 1836, the museum features interactive exhibits and specially-commissioned film and archive footage, paintings, drawings and events throughout the year.

The present Duke and Duchess of Northumberland have transformed the 12-acres of castle grounds with a £14-million restoration and **Alnwick Garden** attracted more than 300,000 visitors in its first year of opening. There are flower beds brimming with some 15,000 plants, a scented Rose Garden containing over 2,000 shrub roses, and the European-inspired Ornamental Garden. The breathtaking centrepiece is the Grand Cascade, a wonderful tumbling mass of water culminating in a series of fountains that spray 350 litres of water six metres into the air every second. Other delights include the bamboo Labyrinth, Woodland Walk and The Treehouse, high in the trees outside the walls of the main garden. Continuing developments are underway to create a state-of-the-art Pavilion and Visitor Centre, more gardens, an

ALNWICK LODGE

West Cawledge Park, Alnwick, Northumberland NE66 2HJ
Tel: 01665 604363/603377
e-mail: bookings@alnwicklodge.com
website: www.alnwicklodge.com

Alnwick Lodge enjoys a picturesque setting close to the A1 trunk road, one mile south of the historic town of Alnwick. The Lodge and surrounding grounds have been home to Peter Smith since 1976, joined by Evelyn in 1994. During this period West Cawledge Park has been tastefully transformed from a dilapidated Northumbrian Farm Stead into Alnwick Lodge. Sixteen well-equipped guest bedrooms, all with en-suite facilities, are individually designed, decorated and furnished to a high standard, and range from singles to doubles, twin, family and an exclusive suite. The antiques in the rooms are for sale. Locally sourced produce, including eggs fresh from the orchard, feature in the splendid breakfasts that start the day; packed lunches and evening meals are available if ordered in advance.

The Lodge Offers

*   Superb accommodation for private guests (children and well behaved pets are welcome).

*   A unique location to host wonderful house parties, tailored to your own requirements.

*   A base for corporate events, wedding parties, cycling, golfing, fishing, shooting, carriage driving and equestrian events.

West Cawledge Park was owned by the Duke of Northumberland, in the mid-18th century the 4th Duke transformed Alnwick Castle into one of England's great country castles that is still their home. The magnificent state rooms with their wonderful paintings, china, furniture, and of course Harry Potter, can be visited daily from Easter until October.

The Castle is just one of the many attractions in the area that bring visitors from near and far to Alnwick, others include the new Alnwick Water Garden, the ruins of Alnwick Abbey, the wonderful Northumbrian coast with Warkworth, Dunstanburgh, Bamburgh and Lindisfarne Castles only a short drive away.

The culture past and present needs plenty of time to explore, there's no finer base to discover these and other attractions than Alnwick Lodge.

Treehouse, Alnwick Gardens

Scotsman was used, but today the game is played using a more conventional football.

St Michael's Church overlooks the River Aln, and dates from the 1400s. It was unusual in a place as lawless as Northumberland at that time to build a church as large and as splendid as St Michael's.

The popular and colourful Alnwick Fair, dating back to the 13th century, takes place each June.

orchard and a grotto. The garden shop sells a wonderful array of gifts, gardening goods and plants, and the garden is accessible throughout to visitors with disabilities.

Hulne Park landscaped by the great Northumbrian-born Capability Brown, encompasses the ruins of **Hulne Priory,** the earliest Carmelite Foundation in England dating from 1242.

Alnwick town itself is worthy of an afternoon's exploration around its evocatively-named ancient narrow streets of Pottergate, Fenkle Street, Green Batt, Bondgate Without and Bondgate Within. A road leads through the narrow arch of **Hotspur Tower**, the one surviving part of the town's fortifications, built by the second Duke of Northumberland in the 15th century. All that's left of the once mighty **Alnwick Abbey** is its 15th-century gatehouse, situated just beyond Canongate Bridge.

Each year on Shrove Tuesday the town is host to an annual tradition that begins with the Duke throwing a ball over the castle wall into the town and ends when the ball is retrieved from the river. Traditionally the head of a

Around Alnwick

LESBURY
3 miles E of Alnwick on the A1068

Lesbury is a long straggling village on the River Aln, which is tidal up to this point. There's an old stone bridge over the river and a small Norman church with a square tower topped by a pyramidal roof. The church was restored by Anthony Salvin in 1846 when some fine stained glass windows from the AK Nicholson studios were installed. The vicar here in the mid-1600s was Patrick Mackilwyan who is featured in Fuller's *Worthies*. During the Plague of 1665, he visited the afflicted in their tents outside the village despite being 97 years old at the time. Mackilwyan died at the age of 101 and left an epitaph declaring that *'Of friends and books, good and few are best.'*

ALNMOUTH
3 miles E of Alnwick off the A1068

Alnmouth is a small, unspoilt seaside resort at the mouth of the River Aln, with fine sandy

WALK | 1

Alnmouth to Foxton Circular

Distance: *4.0 miles (6.4 kilometres)*

Typical time: *90 mins*

Height gain: *35 metres*

Map: *Explorer 332*

Walk: *www.walkingworld.com ID:1560*

Contributor: *Julia Ewart*

ACCESS INFORMATION:

Follow the A1068 Coastal Route to Hipsburn roundabout. Turn down to Alnmouth and head into the village. Turn left down beside the friary to the Alnmouth Common/Beach Car Park. Car park charges apply in high season only, not evenings.

DESCRIPTION:

The walk takes us along from where the River Aln meets the sea, hence the village name of Alnmouth, and the port that was built in 1208 for grain shipment. We then head to the neighbouring village of Lesbury to cross the river and walk back down the banks again, before leaving for a detour to Foxton Hall, a very grand golf course for the elite. We head back down the coastal path where we meet the Alnmouth Golf Course, the second oldest links course in the country and originally the 'Alnmouth Working Mens Golf Course. The Commons of Alnmouth are still run by the village 'Burges', whose job it is to maintain and upkeep the commons.

ADDITIONAL INFORMATION

Alnmouth is on the main Alnwick to Newcastle bus route; check for times with Arriva 0870 608 2608. Sprinter trains stop at Almouth Station (actually at Hipsburn 1.5 miles away); check Rail Enquiries.

FEATURES:

River, Sea, Pub, Toilets, Play Area, Wildlife, Birds, Great Views, Café, Gift Shop, Food Shop, Good for Kids, Mostly Flat, Public Transport, Restaurant.

WALK DIRECTIONS:

1 | From the end of the car park follow the sign for the village and toilets, along the path over the dunes to the golf course and onto the road.

2 | Turn left and follow the road around to the junction. Keep left, walking along Riverside Road, above the mouth of the River Aln and around to a small harbour. Walk along past the children's play area to some stables, where the road bears right. Turn left and walk down Lovers Lane to Duchess Bridge along the path beside the river.

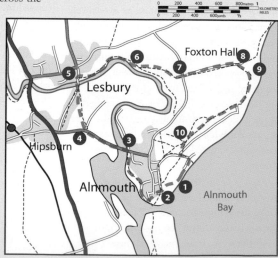

3 | At the bridge, go up the steps, through a gate and cross the road, to turn left onto the pedestrian bridge. Walk along the footpath at the side of the road to just past the entrance to the cricket ground.

4 | Turn right at the public footpath signpost for Lesbury. Follow the path up the side of the cricket ground, then follow waymark up the side of the hedge to a gate. Go through the kissing-gate, then another, then bear left a bit and down to meet a tarmac track. Turn right and go down the track, crossing the footbridge over the river.

5 | At the end of the bridge, turn right and head for the little footbridge over a stream. The footpath is signed to Alnmouth and Foxton Hall. Follow the footpath along the riverbank, keeping below some wooden fencing, until you reach a stile.

6 | Over the ladder-stile, our path veers slightly left through the field, to the next stile. Cross over the stile and follow the path up through the field to another stile. Cross this stile and head for the telegraph post. Turn left at the post and go up the bank to the next stile.

7 | Cross the stile, then the road (carefully) and walk down the road to Foxton Hall Golf Course.

8 | Just in front of the hall, turn right and walk along the path, then cross in front of the green to the path in the rough. Continue along this path till it meets the coastal path.

9 | Turn right and follow the coastal path as it runs alongside Foxton, then between the two courses for a while, before reaching a defence armoury from the war.

10 | Fork left at this point and go down the hill alongside the golf course to the road. Turn left and walk up to the old lifeboat houses, one dated 1850. Back at Alnmouth Common Car Park and the end of the walk, have a look at the information board about the common. If you're lucky, the ice cream man may be in the car park!

beaches and two golf courses. The village's origins go back to the 8th century and it was the main seaport for the town of Alnwick in the Middle Ages. John Paul Jones, the Scot who founded the American navy, bombarded the port during the American War of Independence.

Alnmouth's great days as a port ended on Christmas Day 1806 when a mighty storm deposited so much water that the River Aln broke its banks and formed a new channel. The new channel however was much shallower and ships exporting coal and wool were unable to navigate the new course. The port went into decline, but some measure of relief came about 40 years later when the East Coast railway was built. This opened up a new role for the town as a seaside resort for those wishing to escape smoky Newcastle in order to enjoy the wonderful beaches that stretch for several miles down the coast.

The village is the starting point for many excellent walks along superb stretches of coastline both southwards, past extensive dunes to Warkworth, and north to the former fishing village of Boulmer.

WARKWORTH
6 miles SE of Alnwick on the A1068

| 🏛 Castle | 🏛 The Hermitage |
| 🏛 St Lawrence's Church | |

At the southern end of Alnmouth Bay, on the River Coquet, lies **Warkworth Castle** (English Heritage). The site has been fortified since the Iron Age, though the first stone castle was probably built by one 'Roger, son of Richard', who had been granted the castle by Henry II in the 12th century.

What can be seen now is mainly late 12th and 13th century, including the great Carrickfergus Tower and the West Postern

DILLY DILLY

20 Castle Street, Warkworth,
Northumberland NE65 0UW
Tel: 01665 713333
e-mail: shop@dillydilly.net website: www.dillydilly.net

Close to Warkworth Castle, at the southern end of Alnmouth Bay, **Dilly Dilly** is filled with lovely things to enhance the home. The shop is owned and personally run by Christine Shield and her youngest daughter, Jilly, who share a passion for all things British. They buy from British makers and offer a selection of the best home-produced items, from leather goods to stoneware and earthenware for the home or conservatory, pewter giftware, wooden pieces for coffee tables or desks, and linen and canvas products for the kitchen, garden or workshop. They are proud to be the sole stockists in the region of chinaware from the Burleigh Pottery, founded in the Victorian era.

Their cosy, welcoming shop was built as a private home in the 17th century and retains many original features in keeping with the surrounding conservation area. Shop hours are 10.30 to 5 Tuesday to Saturday, 11 to 5 Sunday, closed Monday.

NEW BARNS BUTCHERS, RESTAURANT & TEA ROOM

New Barns Farm, Warkworth, nr Morpeth,
Northumberland NE65 0TR
website: www.newbarnsfarmbutcher.co.uk

Peter Forsyth and Robert Edmondson represent four generations who have farmed here in a picturesque setting just outside Warkworth. **New Barns Butchers** are top-quality traditional family butchers selling a wide variety of home-reared or locally sourced meats every day of the week. They rear Old Spot, Tamworth and Saddleback pig for the superb cuts and joints, for the sausages – traditional, Continental and gluten-free – and the traditionally dry- or sweet-cured bacon. The matured beef and the lamb are all Northumberland-bred, and the honey-roast and breaded ham comes from a top local supplier. Other great things to eat include wonderful home-made pies (steak; chicken & mushroom; chicken & leek; lamb & apricot) and handmade 6oz and 10oz steak burgers, gluten-free, with no artificial flavours or

preservatives. The same quality determines what's on offer in the restaurant, where the mouthwatering choice includes breakfast, light lunches, quiches, pâtés, terrines and ready-meals to take away, as well as fresh cakes, scones and biscuits. A full Sunday lunch is served from 12 to 4. The farm can provide outside catering for a variety of occasions, and the beautiful location makes it an ideal venue for wedding parties and other celebrations.

Towers, built by Roger's son, Robert. The castle came into the ownership of the Percys in 1332 and the family lived here up until the 1500s. The family crest can be seen on the Lion Tower. The castle is a delightful sight in spring when the grass mound on which it stands is covered with thousands of daffodils.

Warkworth Castle

The most famous of all the Percys, Harry (known as Hotspur) was brought up here. In 1399 the family played an important role in placing Henry Bolingbroke on the throne as Henry IV.

An unusual and interesting walk is signposted to **The Hermitage**, along the riverside footpath below the castle, where a ferry takes you across the river to visit the tiny chapel hewn out of solid rock. It dates from medieval times and was in use until late in the 16th century.

Warkworth is an interesting and beautiful village in its own right. An imposing fortified gatehouse on the 14th-century bridge, now only used by pedestrians, would enable an invading army to be kept at bay north of the Coquet. **St Lawrence's Church** is almost entirely Norman, though its spire – an unusual feature on medieval churches in Northumberland – dates from the 14th century.

AMBLE
7 miles SE of Alnwick on the A1068

Coquet Island

Amble is a small port situated at the mouth of the River Coquet, once important for the export of coal, but now enjoying new prosperity as a marina and sea-fishing centre,

with a carefully restored harbour. It is a lively place, particularly when the daily catches of fish are being unloaded.

A mile offshore lies **Coquet Island**. It was here that St Cuthbert landed in AD 684. The island's square-towered lighthouse was built in 1841 on the ruins of a 15th-century monastery known as Cocwadae. Parts of the monastic building have survived, including a Benedictine cell dating from the 14th century.

Coquet Island had a reputation in former times for causing shipwrecks, but is now a celebrated bird sanctuary, noted for colonies of terns, puffins and eider ducks. Managed by the Royal Society for the Protection of Birds, the island can be visited by boat trips departing from Amble quayside throughout the summer.

DRURIDGE BAY
12 miles SE of Alnwick off the A1068

Country Park Chibburn Preceptory

Druridge Bay Country Park is set just behind the sand dunes and grasslands of Druridge Bay. The park includes Ladyburn Lake, where there is sailing and windsurfing, plus walking trails, a visitors' centre and picnic area. The whole area was once a huge open-cast coal mine before it was landscaped and opened as a park in 1989. Nearby are the ruins of medieval **Chibburn Preceptory** – a small medieval house and chapel, which belonged to the Knights Hospitaller.

CRASTER
5 miles NE of Alnwick off the B1339

🌱 Howick Hall   🌱 Arnold Memorial Site

Craster is a small, unpretentious fishing village with a reputation for the best oak-smoked kippers in the country. At one time, herring were caught around this coast in vast quantities, but a combination of over-fishing and pollution resulted in a decline in numbers, so the fish now have to be imported. During the kipper curing season, visitors can peer into the smoking sheds where the herring are hung over smouldering piles of oak chips.

South of Craster is **Howick Hall**, built in 1782, and having long associations with the Grey family whose family lineage includes many famous public figures – most notably the 2nd Earl Grey, the great social reformer

and tea enthusiast. The gardens are open to the public in spring and summer and are noted for their beauty, particularly in the rhododendron season.

Craster Quarry was closed in 1939, and is now a small nature reserve called the **Arnold Memorial Site**. It was this quarry that supplied London and other large cities with its kerbstones. This is the starting point for a pleasant walk along the coastal footpath to Dunstanburgh castle.

EMBLETON
6 miles NE of Alnwick on the B1339

🏛 Dunstanburgh Castle

The dramatic ruins of **Dunstanburgh Castle** stand on a cliff top east of the village, on a site that was originally an Iron Age fort. The fabric of the castle as seen today was built in 1313 by Thomas, Earl of Lancaster, and in the Wars of the Roses it withstood a siege from troops led by Margaret of Anjou, Henry VI's Queen. The damage caused by the siege was never repaired, and the castle remains ruinous to this day.

The castle can't be reached by road, but a path from the village passing through Dunstan Steads, a mile southeast of Embleton, will bring you to it. The castle, plus the whole coastline to the north as far as Brunton Burn, is owned by the National Trust.

To the north of Embleton is the

Craster Harbour

SPITALFORD COTTAGE

Embleton, Alnwick,
Northumberland NE66 3DW
Tel: 01665 576291
e-mail: cottage@spitalford.co.uk
website: www.spitalford.co.uk

On the Northumberland coastal route (B1339) on the edge of Embleton village, **Spitalford Cottage** offers a unique holiday experience and an ideal base for exploring the region. The house was built in 1269 for Eleanor de Montfort, sister of Henry III, and a careful modernisation programme has retained original features such as beams and inglenooks while offering all the expected up-to-date amenities. On the ground floor are a magnificent open-plan kitchen/dining room and a sitting area with a wood-burning stove. A handsome spiral staircase leads up to the two superbly appointed en suite bedrooms, one with a super king size bed, the other with twin beds. The house stands in a large, attractive garden, and an adjoining field is home to Ruby and Tallulah, two friendly kune kune pigs who like to meet the guests. Among the many local attractions are beaches and castles and the lovely gardens at Howick Hall.

village of **Newton-by-the-Sea**, where there are some attractive 18th-century fisherman's cottages built around three sides of a square.

BEADNELL
10 miles NE of Alnwick on the B1340

🏛 St Ebba's Chapel ᚹ St Aidan's Dunes

Beadnell is a small fishing village with a harbour and some important 18th-century lime kilns that are now owned by the National Trust. Running eastwards from the harbour into the sea is Ebb's Nook, a narrow strip of land on which stands the scant remains of 13th-century **St Ebba's Chapel**, dedicated to the sister of King Oswald, King of Northumbria. This is a delightful stretch of coast, and keen walkers can follow the coastline either by shore path or along the

Sunset at Beadnell Bay

B1340 past **St Aidan's Dunes** (owned by the National Trust) to Seahouses.

SEAHOUSES
13 miles NE of Alnwick on the B1340

Seahouses is a lively fishing port and small resort with an interesting harbour, magnificent beaches and sand dunes stretching for miles on either side of the town. It is conveniently situated for viewing the Farne Islands, which lie between two and five miles off the coast, and visitors can take a boat trip departing from the harbour to see them at close hand.

CHATHILL
8 miles N of Alnwick off the A1

🏛 Preston Tower

Close to Chathill is **Preston Tower**, built by Sir Robert Harbottle, Sheriff of

Northumberland, in 1392. The outside walls are seven feet thick, while inside are fine tunnel-vaulted rooms, which have changed little over the centuries. Two turret rooms have been simply furnished in the style of the period and there are displays depicting the Battle of Flodden and life in the Borders at the start of the 15th century.

ELLINGHAM
7 miles N of Alnwick off the A1

🏛 St Maurice's Church   🏛 Hall

Ellingham (pronounced 'Ellin-jam') is a small agricultural village centred around **St Maurice's Church**, whose Norman details were all but swept away in a restoration of 1862. It features a central tower instead of the more usual west one. **Ellingham Hall** stands at the end of a quiet lane beyond the village.

THE PACK HORSE INN

Ellingham, Chathill, Northumberland NE67 5HA
Tel: 01665 589292
e-mail: enquiries@packhorseinn-ellingham.co.uk
website: www.packhorseinn-ellingham.co.uk

If you enjoy good food at a reasonable price, then **The Pack Horse Inn** in the quiet village of Ellingham is the place to eat. This delightful early-18th century traditional hostelry serves no bought-in or pre-prepared food. Everything is freshly prepared each day using the best, locally-sourced ingredients. So you may well find dishes such as Seahouses smoked salmon or Bamburgh Bangers on the menu which changes almost on a daily basis to ensure the freshest, most interesting seasonal food is available. The two qualified chefs, Stuart Reid and Tim Holmes, are passionate about food and are always willing to vary dishes on the menu to suit a customer's requirements and to take into account individual likes and dislikes, or food intolerances - just ask. Meals are served daily from 12 noon until 2pm, and again from 6.30pm to 9pm. In good weather, enjoy your refreshments on the terrace in the beer garden. If you are planning to stay in this scenic corner of the county, the Pack Horse has 5 guest bedrooms, all attractively furnished and equipped with colour TV and hospitality tray. There is also an adjoining self-contained cottage which sleeps four people.

🏛 historic building   🏛 museum and heritage   🏛 historic site   🌢 scenic attraction   🌿 flora and fauna

EGLINGHAM
6 miles NW of Alnwick on the B6346

St Maurice's Church   The Ringses

St Maurice's Church dates from about 1200, and was built on a site granted to the monks of Lindisfarne in AD 738 by King Ceowulf of Northumbria. In 1596 it was attacked by the Scots, and part of the chancel had to be rebuilt in the early 17th century.

A few bumps in a field not far away indicate where the village once stood, and a mile to the southwest is a small hill fort with the quaint name of **The Ringses**.

CHILLINGHAM
11 miles NW of Alnwick off the B6348

Castle   Ros Castle

Chillingham is a pleasant estate village best known for the herd of wild, horned white cattle that roam parkland close to Chillingham Castle. Descendants of the cattle that once roamed Britain's forests, they are the only herd of wild white cattle in the country. Chillingham village was built by the Earls of Tankerville and contains many Tudor-style houses.

Chillingham Castle is beautifully sited within a 365-acre park. Begun in 1245, the castle belonged for many years to the Grey family who fought many battles with the Scots and the Percys of Alnwick. Sadly, the castle fell into ruin in the 1930s, but was bought in the 1980s by Sir Humphrey Wakefield, a descendant of the Grey family, and has been splendidly restored. Attractions include the impressive Grand Hall, a jousting course, dungeon and torture chamber. The castle and surrounding gardens are open to the public from May to September. Two signposted walks have been laid out through Chillingham Woods, giving superb views over the surrounding countryside.

The nearby church is worth visiting to see the ornate 15th-century tomb of Sir Ralph Grey and his wife, Elizabeth. This splendid monument is regarded as the finest surviving example of its kind in England.

Just outside the village is the National Trust-owned hill fort **Ros Castle**, once a vital beacon site visible as far afield as the Scottish hills and Holy Island. The whole area was thrown into chaos in 1804 when an over-enthusiastic warden lit the beacon by mistake.

EDLINGHAM
5 miles SW of Alnwick on the B6341

Castle   Corby's Crags

Edlingham mustn't be confused with the villages of Eglingham and Ellingham, both a few miles to the north. Here at Edlingham the moorland road crosses **Corby's Crags** affording visitors one of the finest views in Northumberland. The panorama encompasses the Cheviot Hills in the north, while to the south a rolling landscape of heather moors and crags stretches as far as Hadrian's Wall.

Chillingham White Cattle

On a clear day it's possible to catch a glimpse of the high peaks of the Pennines.

Edlingham Castle was built in the 12th century, but abandoned in 1650 when parts of it collapsed. The ruins were originally thought to be of a simple Northumbrian tower house, but excavations in the late 1970s and early 1980s showed it as having been much more substantial than that.

LONGFRAMLINGTON
9 miles SW of Alnwick on the A697

🏃 Devil's Causeway

Longframlington derives its name from its principal family, the de Framlingtons, who are recorded as the 12th-century benefactors of Brinkburn Priory. The route of the **Devil's Causeway**, a Roman road between Hadrian's Wall and the Scottish border, can easily be traced west of the village, along what is now a farm lane past Framlington Villa.

There are few shops here but the village retains the traditional craftsmanship of a Northumbrian pipe maker. The workshop, where you can see the production of these unique and beautiful musical instruments, is open to the public.

Morpeth

🏛 Clock Tower 🏛 Town Hall 🏛 Chantry

🏛 St Mary's Church 🏛 Newminster Abbey

🐿 Emily Davison

The county town of Morpeth seems far removed, both in spirit and appearance, from

River Wansbeck, Morpeth

the mining areas further down the Wansbeck valley. An attractive market town, Morpeth was once a stopping point on the A1 from Newcastle and Edinburgh, before the days of bypasses, and some fine inns were established to serve the weary travellers.

The Normans built a castle here that stood in what is now Carlisle Park. It was destroyed by William Rufus in 1095. A second castle was built close by, but was demolished by King John in 1215. It was subsequently rebuilt, but was mostly destroyed yet again by Montrose in 1644, though substantial ruins remain. Known as Morpeth Castle, it is now a restored gatehouse, managed by the Landmark Trust and is open once a year.

The third – which isn't really a castle but has the appearance of one – was built by John

Dobson in 1828 as the county gaol and courthouse. Still standing, it is now private apartments and self-catering accommodation.

The **Clock Tower** in the middle of Oldgate has been raised in height several times. It probably dates from the early 1600s although medieval stone was used in its construction. In its time it has served as a gaol and a place from where the nightly curfew was sounded. Its bells were a gift from a Major Main, who was elected MP for the town in 1707. He had intended them for Berwick, but they didn't elect him, so, as a local saying goes, 'the bells of Berwick still ring at Morpeth'. The Clock Tower is one of only a handful of such buildings in England. The **Town Hall** was built in 1714 to designs by Vanbrugh, and the handsome bridge over the Wansbeck was designed by Telford.

Not to be missed is the 13th-century **Morpeth Chantry** on Bridge Street. Originally the Chapel of All Saints, over the years it has served as a cholera hospital, a mineral water factory and a school where the famous Tudor botanist William Turner was educated. Nowadays, it houses the museum of the Northumbrian bagpipe – a musical instrument that is unique to the county. An ingenious sound system brings the pipes to life and they are set in the context of bagpipes around the world – from India to Inverness. The town's tourist information centre is also located here, as are a craft centre, a silversmith's and a mountain sports shop.

St Mary's Church, lying to the south of the river, dates from the 14th century. It has some of the finest stained glass in Northumberland. In the churchyard is the

THE PLOUGH INN

Mitford, nr Morpeth,
Northumberland NE61 3PR
Tel: 01670 512587

Set beside the River Wansbeck, the delightful village of Mitford has the ruins of a castle, an exceptionally fine parish church, and an outstanding hostelry, **The Plough Inn**. It's owned and run by Helen Shand, a welcoming host who has always wanted to run a pub and now presides over one of the best. The inn has two bars, each with its open fire, as well as a pleasant beer garden. Quality beers, real ales, fine wines and spirits are all available as well as tea and coffee.

The Plough is well-known locally for the quality of the appetising home-made food it serves which is traditional in essence but with a modern twist. The lunch and dinner menus, which change every 3 months, offer a good choice of dishes, including a vegetarian option. There's also a separate menu for children and for Sunday lunch.

On Tuesday evenings, the pub hosts a Quiz Night, starting at 8.30pm, and on the first Sunday evening of the month, all local folk musicians are invited to "bring your fiddle, mouth organ, banjo or penny whistle to give us a tune!"

grave of suffragette **Emily Davison**, who ran among galloping horses and was killed under the hooves of *Anmer*, the King's horse, during the 1913 Derby meeting. Her funeral attracted thousands of people to Morpeth. About a mile west of the town are the remains of **Newminster Abbey**, a Cistercian foundation dating from the 12th century. It was founded by monks from Fountains Abbey in Yorkshire.

Around Morpeth

ASHINGTON
5 miles E of Morpeth on the A197

🏃 Wansbeck Riverside Park

Ashington is a sprawling town around the River Wansbeck, built to serve the mining industry. The two-mile-long **Wansbeck Riverside Park**, which has been developed along the embankment, offers sailing and angling facilities, plus a four-mile walk along the mouth of the River Wansbeck. The famous footballing brothers Bobby and Jackie Charlton were born in Ashington in the 1930s.

WOODHORN
6 miles E of Morpeth on the A197

🏛 St Mary's Church   🏛 Colliery Museum

🏃 Queen Elizabeth Country Park

At Woodhorn, close to Ashington, stands the fascinating late Anglo-Saxon **St Mary's Church**, said to be the oldest church building in Northumberland. The outside was heavily restored in 1843, though the inside is almost wholly pre-Norman. Notable among its treasures is a 13th-century effigy of Agnes de Velence, wife of Hugh de Baliol, brother of the Scottish king, John Baliol. The **Woodhorn Colliery Museum**, which is linked to the **Queen Elizabeth Country Park** by a short

light railway, offers interesting displays of mining life and the social history of the area. Turning the Pages is an award-winning interactive exhibition on the Lindisfarne Gospels.

NEWBIGGIN BY THE SEA
7 miles E of Morpeth on the A197

🏛 St Bartholomew's Church

Newbiggin by the Sea is a fishing village and small resort enjoying an attractive stretch of coastline with rocky inlets and sandy beaches, now much improved after the ravages of the coal industry.

   St Bartholomew's Church has a particularly interesting 13th-century interior. The village has the oldest operational lifeboat house in Britain, built in 1851.

LONGHORSLEY
6 miles N of Morpeth off the A697

Longhorsley is noted for being the home of Thomas Bell, inventor of self-raising flour. He called it Bell's Royal, but the name was later changed to Bero.

   Born at Blackheath in London, Emily Davison spent a lot of time in the village. A plaque on the wall of the post office, her former home, commemorates her death under the feet of the king's horse at Epsom in 1913. Her suffragette activities are remembered by the local Women's Institute each year when flowers are placed on her grave in Morpeth.

KIRKHARLE
11 miles W of Morpeth off the B6342

🏛 Hall   🏃 Kirkharle

The village of **Kirkharle** was where Lancelot Brown, later known as 'Capability' Brown, was born in 1716. England's greatest landscape gardener earned the sobriquet 'Capability' from his habit of telling clients that their grounds had excellent 'capabilities' of improvement. He made the most of those capabilities in the superb landscapes he created at Blenheim, Kew, Stowe, Chatsworth, Warwick Castle and, it is believed, also at Wallington Hall. Despite his pre-eminence there is no national exhibit celebrating his life and work, but at the Laundry Court Coffee House in Kirkharle, there's an interesting exhibit commemorating the local boy who made good.

Just to the north of Kirkharle is **Wallington Hall**, lying deep in the heart of the Northumbrian countryside. It is a National Trust property dating from 1688. The two great families associated with the place – the Blacketts and the Trevelyans – have each made their own mark on what must be one of the most elegant houses in Northumberland. In the Great Hall is a famous collection of paintings about Northumbrian history, and one of the rooms has an unusual collection of dolls' houses.

BELSAY
7 miles SW of Morpeth on the A696

🏛 Hall ⚴ Bolam Lake Country Park

Belsay Hall (see panel below) was built for Sir Charles Monck on an estate that already

had a castle and a Jacobean mansion. Set in 30 acres of landscaped gardens, Belsay Hall is Greek in style and contains the architecturally splendid Great Hall. Two miles west is the **Bolam Lake Country Park**, with a 25-acre lake, trails and picnic areas

BEDLINGTON
5 miles SE of Morpeth off the A189

Bedlington, formerly known as the county town of Bedlingtonshire, was a district of the County Palatine of Durham until 1844, when it was incorporated into Northumberland. The town became the centre of a prosperous mining and iron-founding community and has two important links with railway history. The rolled-iron rails for the Stockton and Darlington Railway were manufactured here, and it is also the birthplace of the great locomotive engineer, Sir Daniel Gooch. One of the greatest engineers of his day, Sir Daniel was the locomotive superintendent on the Great Western Railway, and the man who first linked up North America and Europe via a telegraph line.

There is an attractive country park at Humford Mill, with an information centre and nature trails. At Plessey Woods, southwest of

Belsay Hall Castle and Gardens

Belsay, near Ponteland, Northumberland NE20 0DX
Tel: 01661 881297 Fax: 01661 881043

Belsay Hall Castle and Gardens is one of the best English Heritage properties in the area. The Grade I listed hall was built for Sir Charles Monck on an estate that already had a castle and Jacobean mansion, and they all stand in 30 acres of beautifully landscaped gardens. There is a magnolia garden, terraces, rhododendrons, a winter garden and croquet lawn, and a quarry garden. In addition, there's free parking, a tea room (summer only) and various small exhibitions.
Opening Times: Daily 24 March-30 September 10-6; 1-31 October 10-4; 1 November-31 March 10-4 (except Tue and Wed); closed 24-26 December and 1 January.

🎭 stories and anecdotes 🦜 famous people 🎨 art and craft 🎦 entertainment and sport ⚴ walks

the town, another country park extends along the wooded banks of the River Blyth, around Plessey Mill, with trails and a visitor centre.

BLYTH
12 miles NE of Newcastle on the A193

🏛 High Light Lighthouse 🏛 Plessey Wagonway

Blyth is a small industrial town at the mouth of the River Blyth. Much of the town's industrial heritage is linked to the Northumberland coalfields – their rapid decline in recent years is a loss from which the area is only slowly recovering. The oldest part of the town is set around an 18th-century lighthouse called the **High Light**. Blyth claims its own piece of railway history with one of the country's earliest wagonways, the **Plessey Wagonway**, dating from the 17th century and built to carry coal from the pits to the riverside.

As well as coal mining and shipbuilding, the town was once a centre of salt production, and in 1605 it is recorded that there were eight salt pans in Blyth. The town's industrial landscape and coastline was the inspiration for several paintings by JS Lowry. The building that is now the headquarters of the Royal Northumberland Yacht Club was a submarine base during the Second World War.

PONTELAND
7 miles NW of Newcastle on the A696

🏛 St Mary's Church 🌱 Kirkley Hall Gardens

Though this small town has largely become a dormitory town for Newcastle-upon-Tyne, resulting in a lot of recent development, it still retains a character of its own. **St Mary's Church** – much altered, but essentially 12th-century, stands opposite the attractive Blackbird Inn, housed in a 13th- and 14th-century fortified house. Within the gardens of the Old Vicarage is a 16th-century vicar's pele.

A few miles north of Ponteland are **Kirkley Hall Gardens**, which are open to the public. There are 35,000 different species of labelled plant here, and it is home to the national collections of beech, dwarf willow and ivy.

PRUDHOE

9 miles W of Newcastle on the A695

 Castle

The romantic ruins of **Prudhoe Castle** are in the care of English Heritage. King William the Lion of Scotland unsuccessfully attacked the castle in 1173 and 1174, and the threat of further attacks led Henry II to agree to the building of a new stone castle. Completed in the 12th century, it was one of the finest in Northumberland, and was later provided with a moat and drawbridge, a new gatehouse and a chapel. There is an impressive oriel window above the altar of the chapel. A Georgian manor house in the courtyard houses an exhibition that tells the history of the castle.

MICKLEY SQUARE

10 miles W of Newcastle on the A695

Cherryburn

A signpost at Mickley Square points the visitor to **Cherryburn** (National Trust). The house is noted as the birthplace of Thomas Bewick (1753-1828), the well-known illustrator and wood-engraver, famous for his portrayal of birds, animals and country life. The house contains an exhibition of his woodcuts and there are frequent demonstrations of the printing techniques used in his time. Bewick is buried in the churchyard at nearby Ovingham.

NORTH ACOMB FARM SHOP

Stocksfield, Northumberland NE43 7UF
Tel: 01661 843181
website: www. northacombfarmshop.co.uk

For some 30 years, Robin and Caroline have sold produce from their family-run working farm in beautiful Tyne valley near Stocksfield. Listed by Les Routiers, their **North Acomb Farm Shop** is everything a farm shop should be. Robin and Caroline pride themselves on offering the finest meat, freshest dairy products and vegetables.

The shop has gained a great reputation for its certified Aberdeen Angus Beef, home-bred succulent lamb and traditionally-fed pork. Free range geese, ducks and quinea fowl are available at christmas, along with a choice of local game in season. Then there are the farm fresh and free range chickens and traditional turkeys, home-made sausages and blackpudding to our own recipes, home-cured bacon and gammon. Farm-made cheeses, free range eggs, home-churned butter, cream, milk and ice cream are also available along with farm fresh vegetables, chutneys and accompaniments. Home-made meals, cakes, pies and desserts made to Caroline's and Robin's own recipes are ready for the freezer.

You will also find a range of carefully selected items in the delicatessen and a few well-chosen gift items and greetings cards, all with a rural flavour.

Hadrian's Wall

Hadrian's Wall and the National Park

🏛 🚶 Hadrian's Wall Path

This is the land of the Border Reivers, or mosstroopers, bands of marauding men from both sides of the Border who rustled, pillaged and fought among themselves, incurring the wrath of both the English and Scottish kings. A testament to their activities is the fact they gave the word 'blackmail' to the English language. The Pennine Way passes over the moorland here, dipping occasionally into surprisingly green and wooded valleys. There are also less strenuous walks, circular routes and cycle tracks laid out, with maps and leaflets available from the park visitor centres, at Rothbury, the quaintly-named Once Brewed, and Ingram. Here you can also learn about the history of the area as well as things to see.

Three main valleys penetrate the National Park from the east – Harthope Valley, Breamish Valley and Coquetdale. Harthope Valley is accessed from Wooler, along the Harthope Burn. Part of it is called Happy Valley, and is a popular beauty spot. There are a number of circular walks from the valley floor up into the hills and back again.

Breamish Valley is the most popular of the valleys, and it's here that the Ingram Visitors' Centre is located. Again, there are trails and walkways laid out.

Coquetdale is the gentlest of the three, and is popular with anglers. It winds up past Harbottle towards Alwinton and Barrowburn, but in so doing passes through the Otterburn Training Area, where up to 30,000 soldiers a year come to practise their artillery skills. This has actually preserved the upper part of Coquetdale from modern development, and farming here has changed little over the years. The valley is rich in wildlife, and heron, sandpiper and grey wagtail are common. The exposed crags support rock-rose and thyme, and there are patches of ancient woodland.

The Kielder Forest covers 200 square miles, and is situated to the west of the National Park. It contains Europe's largest man-made lake, Kielder Water, opened by the Queen in 1982.

In the south of the National Park is by far the greater part of Hadrian's Wall, the best known Roman monument in Britain, and the best known Roman frontier in Europe. It stretches for 80 Roman miles (73 modern miles) across the country from Bowness-on-Solway in the west, to Wallsend in the east, and in 1987 was declared a UNESCO World Heritage Site. A national trail, the **Hadrian's Wall Path**, runs for 84 miles following the rolling, northern terrain along the entire length of the Wall, and from May to September, the Hadrian's Wall Bus Service

runs from Carlisle to Hexham (and Newcastle and Gateshead Metro Centre on a Sunday), stopping at the main attractions along the route. To see the Wall twisting across the moorland is an awe-inspiring site, and no visitor to Northumberland should miss it.

Hexham

| 🏯 Abbey | 🏯 Moot Hall | 🏯 St Mungo's Church |
| 🏛 Border History Library and Museum |
| 🎨 🖌 Queen's Hall Arts Centre |
| 🖌 Racecourse | 🟢 Tyne Green Country Park |

The picturesque market town of Hexham sits in the heart of Tynedale, and is its capital and administrative centre. It's rich in history and character and an ideal base from which

---

LOUGHBROW HOUSE

Hexham,
Northumberland NE46 1RS
Tel: 01434 603351
Fax: 01434 609774
website: www.loughbrowhouse.co.uk

Loughbrow House is a beautiful and comfortably furnished 18th-century house with five tasteful and welcoming guest bedrooms, situated in nine acres. It stands 600ft above the River Tyne looking over the market town of Hexham to the North Tyne Valley, yet only a mile form the centre of town.

Adjacent to Hadrian's Wall, in the heart of the Northumberland National Park, guests can access the newly opened Hadrian's Wall Trail and

enjoy the wonderful countryside and breathtaking views, the three adjacent golf courses and the many sights and attractions of the region.

Loughbrow House offers a total of 5 rooms on a B&B basis, all of which are en-suite or have private bathrooms. Dinner by prior arrangement for a minimum of 4 people.

🎭 stories and anecdotes 🦅 famous people 🎨 art and craft 🖌 entertainment and sport 🚶 walks

THE BOATSIDE INN

Warden, nr Hexham,
Northumberland NE46 4SQ
Tel: 01434 602233
e-mail: sales@theboatsideinn.com
website: www.theboatsideinn.com

The Boatside Inn nestles between the River South Tyne and the wooded slopes of Warden Hill, easy to find off the A69 Newcastle to Carlisle trunk road. Brian and Lorraine Dodd, very experienced in the licensed trade, have been in charge since 2005, enhancing the inn's reputation for quality, hospitality and service that extends far beyond the county.

The Boatside fills a variety of roles, from much-loved local to destination restaurant and comfortable Bed & Breakfast or self-catering holiday in one of our charming cottages. The bar is a convivial spot to enjoy a drink and a chat, with two real ales – such as Black Sheep Bitter and Wylam Gold Tankard - always on tap.

The menus offer excellent food that will satisfy all tastes, and three chefs are kept busy providing a fine range that covers bar snacks and light meals, traditional English dishes and more exotic options from the Continent or Asia. Crabmeat & crayfish fusilli, black pudding with a red wine and shallot sauce, roasted duck breast with a honey & soy sauce, steak & ale or steak & Guinness pie, salads for starters or mains, battered haddock, fillet of halibut with a pink grapefruit sauce, rocket & cherry tomato salad, tandoori marinated pork loin, steaks, Sunday roasts, cherry pie, ginger pudding with a

lemon & orange sauce... it's all fresh, delicious and very moreish, and it's complemented by a good wine list from both Old and New Worlds. There are 75 seats in the restaurant, 20 in the bar and a further 50 under parasols in the riverside garden.

The multi-award-winning Boatside is also a wonderful place for a break, either in the main building or in the cottages. The B&B rooms, 'Hadrian', 'Homer' and 'Quilter', are all spacious doubles, with access for disabled guests. The cottages, purpose-built and equipped with all the expected modern amenities, have abundant charm and rural character. 'North Tyne' has a double room, a twin room and a bathroom. 'South Tyne' has one en-suite double room.

This is superb walking country, with scenic woodland bridleways, glorious views and abundant wildlife. Warden Hill has been the site of an Iron Age fort, a Roman camp and a medieval village, and Warden has for many centuries been an important fording point on the River South Tyne. Hexham, Corbridge, the Northumberland National Park and Hadrian's Wall World Heritage Site and National Trail are all close by, and there are many opportunities for outdoor activities, including fishing, golf, riding, sailing, canoeing, mountain biking and shooting.

to explore the Tyne Valley and Hadrian's Wall.

Hexham Abbey, one of the most important churches in the north of England, was at one time known as 'the largest and most magnificent church this side of the Alps'. It was founded by St Wilfrid in 674 after Queen Etheldreda of Northumbria granted him some land. The crypt of this early church remains almost intact, access to it is via a stairway from the nave. The crypt was built using Roman stones, and on some of them you can still see inscriptions and carvings. Frith Stool, also known as St Wilfrid's chair, is a 1,300-year-old stone chair that is believed to have been used as a coronation throne for the ancient kings of Northumbria.

In 1130 a group of Augustinian canons set up an abbey on the site. The present church dates from the 13th century and contains some wonderful late-medieval architecture, which later restoration has not diminished. It has a rich heritage of carved stone-work, and the early 16th century rood screen has been described as the best in any monastic church in Britain.

The abbey was ransacked many times by the Scots armies, who at one time poured over the border into England. However, this was a two-way traffic, and the English did likewise to the abbeys at Melrose and Kelso.

The Abbey overlooks the Market Place, where a lively and colourful market is held each Tuesday. Nearby is the early 14th-century **Moot Hall**, built of Roman stone. In olden days it served as the courtroom of the Archbishop of York, who held the grand title of Lord of the Liberty and Regality of Hexham. Today, the hall houses the **Border History Library**, which contains material on

Border life, in particular the music and poetry of the region.

Nearby, the Manor Office was England's first purpose-built prison and was built by the Archbishop in 1332 as a gaol for his courthouse. The **Border History Museum** is located within the gaol and tells, in a vivid way, the story of the border struggles between Scotland and England. For centuries the borderlands were virtually without rule of law, ravaged by bands of men known as reivers – cattle rustlers and thieves who took advantage of the disputed border lands. Powerful wardens, or Lords of the Marches, themselves warlords of pitiless ferocity, were given almost complete authority by the king to control the reivers and anyone else who crossed their path. However, for all their power and ferocity they were singularly unsuccessful in controlling the bloodshed. This was the period of the great border ballads, violent and colourful tales of love, death, heroism and betrayal, which have found an enduring place in literature.

The award-winning **Queen's Hall Arts Centre** (see panel on page 40), with theatre, café, library and exhibitions, presents a full and varied programme throughout the year. The Centre, built in the 1860s, was originally used as Hexham's Town Hall and Corn Exchange, and now offers great opportunities for entertainment. Hexham Library can also be found here. A packed schedule of arts events is on offer throughout the year, and includes drama, opera, dance, films, comedy and live music. Much of the ground floor is given over to a spacious art gallery, with a second gallery on the first floor. At the Exchange café bar visitors can enjoy everything from cake and coffee to a substantial and tasty meal.

Queen's Hall Art Centre

Beaumont Street, Hexham, Northumberland NE46 3LS
Tel: 01434 652477   Fax: 01434 652478
e-mail: boxoffice@queenshall.co.uk
website: www.queenshall.co.uk

Found in the heart of Hexham, very close to the abbey, is the **Queen's Hall Art Centre**. This elegant 1860s building was originally used as Hexham's Town Hall and Corn Exchange, but now offers great opportunities for entertainment in its reincarnation as a lively arts centre. Hexham Library can also be found here.

A packed schedule of arts events is on offer throughout the year with visits from touring drama, opera and dance companies. Films, comedy nights and live music can also be enjoyed. Families are well catered for with child-friendly films, theatre and holiday workshops on offer. Recently, much of the ground floor of the Queen's Hall has been transformed into a spacious art gallery with a

second gallery located on the first floor. Artists of international stature regularly exhibit here.

The café bar at the Queen's Hall is a light and airy space with a great atmosphere. It was recently refurbished and renamed Exchange, and here visitors can sample everything from cake and coffee to a substantial meal.

Hexham has retained much of its character, with winding lanes and passageways, attractive 18th- and 19th-century houses, handsome terraces and some delightful shops and a market. There are some fine gardens around the abbey, and several attractive areas of open space. **Tyne Green Country Park** features lovely walks along the riverside and a picnic and barbecue site. Hexham National Hunt **Racecourse** is one of the most picturesque courses in the country. Call 01434 606881 for details of fixtures. At Simonburn, just ⌐rth of Hadrian's Wall, **St Mungo's ⌐hurch** is the Mother Church of the North ⌐ne Valley.

Around Hexham

CORBRIDGE
3 miles E of Hexham on the A69

🏛 St Andrew's Church   🏛 Parson's Pele

🏛 Corstorpitum

Corbridge is one of Northumberland's most attractive towns, a compact little place with venerable stone buildings at every turn. One of these is a good place to start exploring this lively market town. It was built around 1300, stands behind St Andrew's Church in the Market Place, and is considered one of the most authentic and least altered in the county. It's known as the **Parson's Pele,** or Vicar's

THE MARKET PLACE CAFÉ

6 Market Place, Corbridge, Northumberland NE46 5AN
Tel: 01434 634356
e-mail: jackie.webb@virgin.net

The attractive town of Corbridge is well worth taking time to explore, with its historic buildings that include the splendid Church of St Andrew. It's also a good place for exploring the sites and other reminders of the Romans, who built their important military base of Corstorpitum just outside present-day Corbridge. The town is also a good starting point for visiting the World Heritage Site of Hadrian's Wall, and there's no more pleasant a way to start a sightseeing trip or a day at Hexham races than a snack at **The Market Place Café**. Owned and run by Jackie and Roland Webb, this friendly family business in a handsome stone building offers a warm, genuine welcome to the many visitors to the town and to the loyal local clientele. The menu tempts with a good choice of snacks and light meals, from sandwiches and panini to salads, soups, jacket potatoes, all-day breakfasts, home-made scones (fruit or cheese), teacakes and assorted

tray bakes, ice creams and hot desserts like apple crumble and treacle sponge, all accompanied by a good selection of teas and coffees. Children can choose from their own list or tuck into a smaller portion of something from the main menu. The café also incorporates a gallery showing and selling paintings, prints and sculptures by local artists, along with a variety of gift ideas.

BROCKSBUSHES FARM SHOP & TEA ROOM

Corbridge, Northumberland NE43 7UB
Tel: 01434 633100   Fax: 01434 632965
e-mail: acd@brocksbushes.co.uk   website: www.brocksbushes.co.uk

Conveniently located alongside the main A69 Newcastle to Carlisle road, **Brocksbushes Farm Shop & Tea Room** opened some 20 years ago and just goes from strength to strength. To begin with, it was just a small shop that opened for the fruit season, selling produce from the surrounding farmland. Today, it is open every day of the year, including Bank Holidays, selling a huge variety of fresh fruit, vegetables and a range of dishes prepared in the farm's kitchen. Amongst these you will find cakes, pastries, cooked hams and a selection of frozen meals.

The shop also stocks jams, chutneys, sauces, cheeses, freshly baked bread and much, much more: ducks, seasonal game, smoked mussels, Italian Parma ham and salamis, chocolate Tiffin and drizzle cakes. During the season you can pick your own soft fruit or the asparagus for which the farm has become famous. Also on site is a coffee shop selling a wide range of delicious cakes, scones, quiches and savoury pies. All of these are made using fresh ingredients from the farm or from local suppliers. Light meals, sandwiches, jacket potatoes, afternoon teas and daily specials all add to the choice. In summer, you can enjoy your refreshments outside. Keep your eyes open for our amazing special events throughout the year, including The Strawberry Fayre and The Christmas Fayre.

JOYCE ANDERSON

42 Hill Street, Corbridge, Northumberland, NE45 5AA
Tel: 01434 632742
e-mail: sales@joyceanderson.co.uk   website: www.joyceanderson.co.uk

Joyce Anderson's shop in Corbridge is an Alladin's cave, where you will find a fabulous collection of jewellery, ladies' clothing and accessories. Quality, choice and great value are the three things that set this shop apart and make your visit a must.

There is something for every taste, outfit and budget in the wide choice of jewellery, which comprises; Pandora and Troll beads, pearls, semi-precious stones and silver, all delicate or chunky, and a growing selection of antique and second-hand jewellery. Additional pieces can usually be sourced on approval for customer requests and Joyce also sells antique and second-hand jewellery on behalf of customers.

The clothes include beautifully cut French separates from Antonelle and Weill, tops from a range including Dolores, Claire and Roberto Naldi, all a little bit different and very wearable. Joyce has Thai silk separates made to order for her in Bangkok, which can be made to order for customers, too.

The majority of the pearl and semi precious jewellery is made to Joyce's specifications in Asia where she does a lot of her buying. Buying direct from the Far East means there are no agents or wholesalers to pay and that Joyce's retail prices are often equivalent to UK wholesale prices.

For accessories there is a great range of scarves, handbags and purses, and in the winter, gloves and hats too. The choice of pashminas is one of the best in the area, and at £20 for a silk and fine wool mix, great value as well as beautiful.

Joyce's chocolate labrador, Lucy, goes to the shop with her most days where she has her own fan club!

Pele, a place of refuge for the priest on the many occasions when Corbridge was attacked by the Scots – they burnt the town to the ground three times in the 14th century.

The finest building in Corbridge is undoubtedly **St Andrew's Church**. It still retains many Saxon features, and the base of the tower was once the west porch of the Saxon nave. Within the tower wall is a complete Roman arch, no doubt removed from the Roman settlement of Corstorpitum at some time.

The original Roman town, **Corstorpitum**, lay half a mile to the northwest and was an important military installation guarding the river crossing. Visitors to the site can see the substantial remains of this strategic fort, which include a fine example of military granaries and two fortified medieval towers that provide evidence of more troubled times.

Running through the centre of the town is Dere Street, the Roman road built to link the important garrisons of York and Edinburgh. In medieval times the bridge was still bringing money into the town – tax returns of 1296 show that this little community was the second wealthiest town in Northumberland after Newcastle. The present bridge, with its seven graceful arches was built back in 1674 and very well built, too. It was the only Tyne bridge to survive the terrible floods of 1771 when the water was running so high that people could lean over the parapet and wash their hands.

In spring, Corbridge is the site of the

CORBRIDGE ANTIQUES CENTRE

Bishops Yard, Main Street, Corbridge, Northumberland, NE45 5LA
Tel: 01434 634936/07900 828493
e-mail: corbridgeantiques@tiscali.co.uk   website: www.corbridgeantiques.co.uk

The **Corbridge Antiques Centre** has been owned and run by Karen and Bill Hird since December 2007. The Centre specialises in quality items of furniture, especially that produced by the Arts and Crafts movement of the late 19th and early 20th century. Karen also has a fondness for quirky and unusual pieces, and her eclectic taste means that customers will always find items of exceptional interest dating from the 1700's through to the 1970's. There's also always a fine collection of clocks and mirrors, occasional tables, vases, decanters and much, much more. Vintage costume and jewellery, Moorcroft Pottery, dolls houses - the variety and choice is almost endless. Karen and Bill are highly knowledgeable and always happy to advise and they offer a worldwide delivery service. The Centre is open Sun, Mon 12.30pm to 4.30pm; and Tues - Sat from10.30pm to 5.30pm. There's a large free car park at the rear for the use of customers.

Northumberland County Show, held each year on the late May Bank Holiday Monday.

AYDON

4 miles E of Hexham off the B6321

🏰 Castle

Aydon Castle is a superb example of a fortified manor house, such protection being necessary in this region in times past to keep the reivers at bay. Built by Robert de Reymes in the late 13th century, it remains remarkably intact, and is often described as one of the best-preserved fortified manor houses in Britain, thanks to its early owners and now to English Heritage.

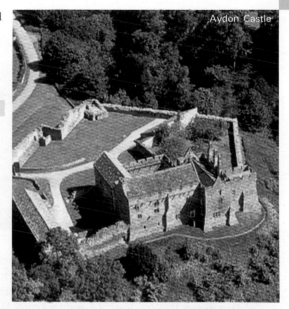
Aydon Castle

MATFEN HIGH HOUSE

Matfen, Corbridge, Northumberland NE20 0RG
Tel: 01661 886592 Fax: 01661 886847
e-mail: struan@struan.enterprise-plc.com
website: www.smoothhound.co.uk

Matfen High House is a spacious stone-built former farmhouse dating from 1735, set in a rural location just north of Hadrian's Wall, offering comfortable bed and breakfast accommodation. The rooms (two are en-suite) are furnished to a high standard and include tea/ coffee making facilities and colour TV. This makes an ideal base from which to explore the many attractions of the area and there is an 18 hole golf course two miles away. A range of pubs and restaurants can be found within a short drive. Children are welcome, and pets by prior arrangement. The house is non-smoking and has a Visit Britain four diamonds award.

📖 stories and anecdotes 🦅 famous people 🎨 art and craft 🎭 entertainment and sport 🚶 walks

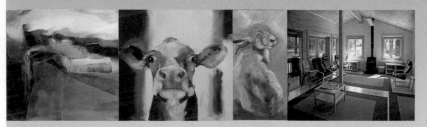

🏚 historic building 🏛 museum and heritage 🏛 historic site ⚜ scenic attraction 🌱 flora and fauna

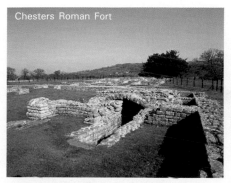
Chesters Roman Fort

Clayton Museum houses a remarkable collection of Roman antiquities. Remains of the Roman fort include a well-preserved bath house and barracks. Near to the bath house can be seen the foundations of a Roman bridge that carried a road across the Tyne.

CHOLLERTON
6 miles N of Hexham on the A6079

🏰 Chipchase Castle ⚔ Battle of Heavenfield

Chollerton, six miles north of Hexham, enjoys an exceptionally fine setting. Nearby is the site of the **Battle of Heavenfield**, where King (later St) Oswald defeated the army of Cadwalla, a Welsh king. Four miles NW of the village is **Chipchase Castle**, a combination of 14th-century tower, Jacobean mansion and Georgian interior. A walled nursery garden is open to the public throughout the summer months, but the castle itself is only open on June afternoons.

CHOLLERFORD
3 miles N of Hexham on the B6318

🏰 Chesters 🏛 Clayton Museum

The Roman fort of **Chesters**, or Cilurnum, to give it its Roman name, is situated in the parkland created by Nathaniel Clayton around the mansion he had built in 1771. The fort covers nearly six acres and was large enough to accommodate a full cavalry regiment. The

SIMONBURN TEA ROOMS

Guest House & Craft Shop, 1 The Mains, Simonburn, Hexham, Northumberland NE48 3AW
Tel: 01434 681321
e-mail: ann@simonburntearooms.com
website: www.simonburntearooms.com

Simonburn is a peaceful "Olde Worlde" village located just off the B6320, halfway between Hexham and Bellingham, in the beautiful North Tyne Valley. It's here you will find Ann Maddison's delightful **Simonburn Tea Rooms, Guest House & Craft Shop**. In the cosy dining room you can enjoy superb home-made cooking, with the typical fayre including quiches, soups, stews, hotpots and a range of hand-made cakes and scones. A vegetarian option is always available. During the summer months, you can also enjoy your refreshments in the terrace garden. A fine choice of

Organic teas and freshly brewed coffee is available all day. There is disabled access to both the Tearoom and the garden area. Before leaving do have a browse around the Craft Shop which stocks an enticing selection that includes hand-turned wooden ornaments made in Simonburn by the local wood-turner, knitted hat and scarf sets designed in Alston, Cumbria, greetings cards, jewellery, hand-made soaps and much more. The accommodation at Simonburn comprises three guest bedrooms with a choice of doubles, twins, and a family room. All are situated on the first floor, are very clean and comfortable and are equipped with colour TV and hospitality tray.

BARRASFORD

7 miles N of Hexham off the A6079

🏛 Haughton Castle

Barrasford sits on the North Tyne, across from **Haughton Castle**, of which there are fine views. The castle is one of the finest great houses in Northumberland, and dates originally from the 13th century. Over the succeeding years, additions and alterations have been made, with the west wing being designed by Anthony Salvin and built in 1876. The castle isn't open to the public.

LANGLEY

6 miles W of Hexham on the B6295

🏛 Castle

Langley Castle, now a hotel and restaurant,

was built around 1350. In 1450, Henry IV had it destroyed, but it was restored in the 1890s by a local historian, Cadwallader Bates. In the 17th and early 18th centuries, the castle was owned by the Earls of Derwentwater. In 1716 the third earl, James, was beheaded in London for his part in the 1715 Jacobite rebellion; his brother Charles was later beheaded for his part in the 1745 uprising. A memorial to them both sits beside the A686 not far from the castle.

BARDON MILL

10 miles W of Hexham on the A69

🏛 Hadrian's Wall   🏛 Roman Forts

Bardon Mill, a former mining village, stands on the north bank of the South Tyne. An important drovers' road crossed the river here

---

GIBBS HILL FARM

Bardon Hill, nr Hexham,
Northumberland NE47 7AP
Tel/Fax: 01434 344030
e-mail: val@gibbshillfarm.co.uk
website: www.gibbshillfarm.co.uk

A warm and genuine welcome awaits visitors to **Gibbs Hill Farm**, which stands in stunning countryside off the B6318 very close to Hadrian's Wall. The Gibson family offer a choice of accommodation on their traditional working hill farm, where they breed suckler cows, Swaledale-cross lambs and Highland cattle. In the farmhouse are five spacious, comfortable en-suite double or twin bedrooms for B&B guests, all with central heating, television, beverage tray and spring water, and views of the farm, the fells or Hadrian's Wall; a hearty breakfast starts the day, and packed lunches can be provided. The surrounding farmland includes a private stretch of water for trout fishing, and the farm can cater for guests who bring their own horse – stabling, grazing and a tack room are available. Three cottages sleeping from 2 to 6 offer self-catering accommodation, while the old hay barn has been converted to provide budget bunkhouse accommodation for up to 18 guests in three rooms with showers, toilets, a kitchen, sitting & dining areas and storage facilities.

🏛 historic building   🏛 museum and heritage   🏛 historic site   ⚜ scenic attraction   🌿 flora and fauna

and cattle were fitted with iron shoes at Bardon Mill to help them on their way to southern markets. The village is a convenient starting point for walks along **Hadrian's Wall** and the Roman forts of **Vindolanda** and **Housesteads** are nearby. At Vindolanda excavations reveal fascinating insights into Roman life. An

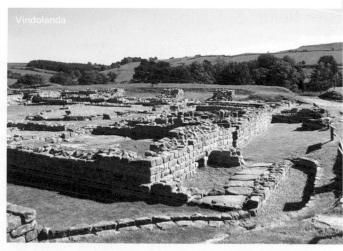
Vindolanda

open-air museum features a reconstructed temple, shop and house. Perched high on a ridge, with splendid views of the surrounding countryside, the remains of Housesteads Fort covers over five acres and is one of the finest sections of Hadrian's Wall. Nearby, **Once Brewed** is the main Visitor Centre for Hadrian's Wall and the Northumberland National Park.

Between Bardon Mill and Haydon Bridge lies the confluence of the South Tyne and the River Allen, which, like the Tyne, comes from two main tributaries – the East Allen and West Allen. The valleys of the East and West Allen really are hidden jewels. The 22,667 acres of Allen Banks, as the lower part of the valley near the Tyne is known, is a deep, wooded, limestone valley, rich in natural beauty, now owned by the National Trust.

Cawfields Crags from Quarry Pool

stories and anecdotes famous people art and craft entertainment and sport walks

Cawfields & Hallpeat Moss

Distance: *4.0 miles (6.4 kilometres)*

Typical time: *120 mins*

Height gain: *80 metres*

Map: *Explorer OL 43*

Walk: *www.walkingworld.com ID: 1857*

Contributor: *Julia Ewart*

ACCESS INFORMATION:

From Chollerford take the B6318, passing Once Brewed National Park centre. Continue on to the Milecastle Inn and turn right to Cawfields Quarry picnic site. Park in the main car park.

DESCRIPTION:

We leave the Cawfields Quarry picnic site to walk along part of Hadrian's Wall, passing Milecastle 42 on our way to Caw Gap with some magnificent views along the way. Leaving the wall at Turret 41a we cross pastures and the military road to Hallpeatmoss with its stone-flagged farmhouse roof, a rare sight now on old farmhouses in Northumberland. From here we cross the meadows to skirt the disused mineral workings and drift mine that once supplied the local limekilns. From Shield Hill we walk down past Milecastle Inn back to Milecastle 42 on the wall, then back to the car park.

ADDITIONAL INFORMATION:

A new bus service operates along the entire Hadrian's Wall length from Wallsend to Carlisle. The bus stops in the quarry car park. The timetable is available from tourist information centres. Toilets are available at the car park. Meals are available at the Milecastle Inn; check opening times.

FEATURES:

Lake/Loch, Pub, Toilets, National Trust/NTS, Birds, Great Views, Butterflies, Public Transport, Ancient Monument.

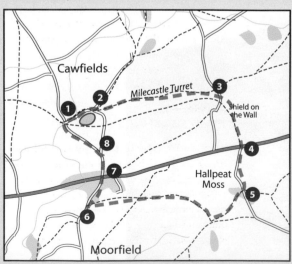

WALK DIRECTIONS:

1 | From the car park, follow the path that runs beside the small lake of the disused quarry, to a gate. Bear right to the gate in the wall.

2 | Turn left and walk alongside Hadrian's Wall to pass Milecastle 42, as the wall runs along the top of Cawfield Crags. Continue on along the wall as it climbs then dips, crossing stiles until reaching the road at Caw Gap.

3 | Cross the road to the fingerpost with two directions. Cross over the stile and bear right to walk around the mound and down over the burn, heading up to the corner of the wall. Keep straight ahead with the wall to your right to reach the road.

4 | Straight across the road (carefully!) and continue on to just past the entrance to Hallpeat Moss, where a fingerpost can be found to the right.

5 | Cross over the stile and head down to the opposite corner of the field, where a stile can be found in the wall. Cross this, then turn left to cross the next one. Bear right to walk just above the burn/crags to another stile. Cross over this stile and then follow a faint path straight ahead, with some trees on the horizon, to a ridge in the field. Once on the ridge, bear left to walk along a more visible track until reaching a stile onto the road.

6 | Cross over and turn right. Walk down the road to the crossroads and a small pub (limited opening hours).

7 | Straight across the road (carefully!), continue down to the corner and a fingerpost on the right.

8 | Turn right to follow the path across the field back to the wall and Milecastle 42. Turn left to retrace your footsteps back through the gates and along to the car park.

HALTWHISTLE
15 miles W of Hexham on the A69

🏛 Holy Cross Church 🚶 🕴 Walltown Quarry

The town lies close to the best-preserved stretch of Hadrian's Wall, which here follows the dramatic line of the Whin Sill ridge and provides some breathtaking views across five counties.

The origins of the name Haltwhistle are unknown, but two suggestions are the watch 'wessel' on the high 'alt' mound, or the high 'haut' fork of two streams 'twysell'. It is difficult to imagine that this pleasant little market town with its grey terraces was once a mining area, but evidence of the local industries remain. An old pele tower is incorporated into the Centre of Britain Hotel in the town centre. **Holy Cross Church**, behind the Market Place, dates back to the 13th century and is said to be on the site of an earlier church founded by William the Lion, King of Scotland, in 1178, when this area formed part of Scotland.

Three miles northwest of Haltwhistle, off the B6318, is **Walltown Quarry**, a recreation site built where an old quarry once stood. Today part of the Northumberland National Park, it contains laid-out trails and it is possible to spot oystercatchers, curlews, sandpipers and lapwings.

ALLENDALE
10 miles SW of Hexham on the B6295

Allendale Town lies on the River East Allen, set against a backdrop of heather clad moorland, and was once an important centre of the north Pennine lead-mining industry. It retains attractive houses from prosperous times and a surprisingly large number of existing or former inns around the Market

THE GOLDEN LION

The Market Place, Allendale, Hexham NE47 9BD
Tel: 01434 683 225

A fine old traditional hostelry, **The Golden Lion** has been dispensing hospitality since 1660. The interior is full of charm and character, especially when the open fires are blazing away. Mine hosts at this friendly and lively tavern are Gloria and Ian Armstrong who have been in the business for some 20 years.

Real ale lovers will be delighted to find no fewer than 5 different brews on tap including Black Sheep and local ales from Allendale and Wylam breweries. Other options include Bass draught and stout. The inn is well-known for its appetising home-cooked food with old favourites such as Steak & Ale Pie and Fisherman's Pie featuring on the menu along with dishes such as Chicken & Leek Pie and vegetarian choices.

The inn is very much the social centre of Allendale, regularly used by organisations such as the Allendale Lions and the Singers Club. It also has its own pool teams. The inn welcomes dogs and there's free parking outside the pub.

Square. A sundial in the churchyard records the fact that the village lies exactly at the midpoint between Beachy Head in Sussex and Cape Wrath in Scotland, making it the very centre of Britain.

ALLENHEADS

12 miles SW of Hexham on the B6295

Allenheads also has lead-mining connections, with its scatter of stone miners' cottages and an irregular village square with pub and chapel in a lovely setting. The village is a centre for fine, upland rambles through the surrounding hills, which still retain many signs of the former industrial activity. From here the main road climbs over Burtree Fell into Weardale, with wild moorland roads branching across to Rookhope to the east and Nenthead to the west.

BLANCHLAND

9 miles S of Hexham on the B6306

A small, serene estate village on the Northumberland and Durham border. This is another of the area's hidden places, and one well worth seeking out. The name 'Blanchland' (white land) comes from the white habits worn by the canons of the Premonstratensian Order who founded Blanchland Abbey in 1665. The abbey was dissolved by Henry VIII in 1537. In 1702, Lord Crewe, the Bishop of Durham, bought the Blanchland estate. On his death in 1721, the estates were left to the Lord Crewe Trustees who were responsible for building the picturesque village of Blanchland that you see today, using stone from the ruined Abbey buildings. Small cottages snuggle round a

Blanchland Priory

village square opposite the popular Lord Crewe Arms, housed in the west range of the priory next to the ancient abbey church of St Mary the Virgin.

SLALEY

4 miles SE of Hexham, off the B6306

Slaley is a quiet village consisting of one long street with some picturesque houses dating from the 17th, 18th and 19th centuries. One of the finest houses – Church View – stands opposite the 19th-century St Mary's Church. Two miles southwest, Slayley Hall has some interesting gardens and is now a first-class hotel with a famous 18-hole golf course, home to the De Vere Northumberland Seniors Classic, part of the PGA Seniors European Tour. Visitors welcome, with two-day golf breaks available.

Otterburn

Mill   Battle Site   Roman Sites

The village of Otterburn stands close to the centre of the National Park, in the broad valley of the River Rede. It makes an ideal base for exploring the surrounding countryside, an exhilarating area of open moorland and rounded hills. It was close to here, on a site marked by the 18th-century Percy Cross, that the **Battle of Otterburn** took place in 1388 between the English and the Scots. But it wasn't a full-scale battle as such and it might have remained relatively obscure if it were not for the number of ballads it spawned – from the English *Chevy Chase* to the Scottish *Battle of Otterbourne*. By all accounts it was a ferocious encounter, even by the standards of the day, and one commentator said that it 'was one of the sorest and best fought, without cowards or faint hearts'.

in 1388, under the command of Earl Douglas, a gathering of Scottish troops at Jedburgh had resolved to enter England in a two-pronged attack – one towards Carlisle and one down into Redesdale. In charge of the Redesdale contingent was the Earl of Douglas, who got as far as Durham before being forced back to the border by Henry Percy, better known as Hotspur, and his brother Ralph.

In August, the English caught up with the Scottish army at Otterburn, and went straight into attack. The battle continued for many hours, gradually descending into a series of hand to hand fights between individual soldiers. Gradually the Scots got the upper hand and captured both Percys. But it was a hollow victory, as the Earl of Douglas was killed. A second force under the Bishop of

OTTERBURN TOWER HOTEL

Otterburn, Northumberland NE19 1NS
Tel: 01830 520620
Fax: 01830 521504
e-mail: info@otterburntower.com
website: www.otterburntower.com

Otterburn Tower is a country house
hotel and restaurant of great distinction,
nestling among terraced lawns and
woodland on the edge of the Northumberland National Park
and Kielder Forest. It is an ideal base for exploring and
enjoying the great outdoors, and the many offerings are
superbly organised **Countryside Breaks**. These include
walking, with the Pennine Way close by and several walks
around the hotel to see Roman and Saxon settlements; golf
at a number of nearby courses; fishing, including their own
3-mile stretch of the River Rede; shooting – pheasant,
grouse, partridge, duck, rough shooting, stalking and clay
pigeon shooting with full instruction; and racing at Hexham,
Kelso and Newcastle and several point-to-point courses.

The building has been updated and tastefully added to
down the years without spoiling historic features such as
marble fireplaces, lofty ceilings, oak panelling and beautiful
décor. Each of the 18 bedrooms has its own special
features, but all are roomy and airy, with en suite bathroom,
satellite TV, direct-dial phone, trouser press, hairdryer,
hospitality and room service. The family suite has a
children's room full of toys, games and teddies, and

babysitting facilities are available. The cuisine at the Tower is also first-class, with lamb, beef
and game from the owner's farm – and the water on the tables comes from a natural spring on
the farm. The chefs set great store by local produce and use their skill and expertise to create
memorable dishes to enjoy in the 16th century oak-panelled dining room. Otterburn Tower is a
stunning venue for a wedding or other special occasions and is well set up for business
meetings, conferences and staff training.

KIRKHARLE COURTYARD

Tel: 01830 540362 Fax: 01830 540400
e-mail: enquiries@kirkharlecourtyard.net
website: www.kirkharlecourtyard.net

Kirkharle Courtyard, which stands just off the A696 a few miles
southeast of Otterburn, is home to a unique collection of galleries
and workshops in the midst of the stunning Northumberland
countryside. It has been developed in a series of converted barns, byres and other old farm
buildings at Kirkharle Hall, birthplace of the most famous of all landscape designers, Lancelot
'Capability' Brown. A wide diversity of specialities includes bespoke cabinet-makers and furniture
restorers; hand-cut silhouettes; designer jewellery in gold and silver; hand-knotted jewellery using
semi-precious stones; fabrics and garments in Northumberland tartan; papier maché; unusual
plants; ceramic and bronze sculpture; organic and traditional food; and walking guides and maps.
A coffee house on the site serves morning coffee, lunches and afternoon tea.

Durham hurried north when it heard the news, but it wisely decided not to engage in battle. A series of markers known as 'Golden Pots' are said to mark the journey of Douglas's body when it was taken back to Melrose.

Otterburn Mill dates from the 18th century, though a mill is thought to have stood on the site from at least the 15th century. Although production of woollens ceased in 1976, the mill is still open, and on display are Europe's only original working 'tenterhooks' where newly woven cloth was stretched and dried – hence the expression 'being on tenterhooks'.

There are some interesting walks round Otterburn, and some well preserved remains of an Iron Age fort can be seen on both Fawdon Hill and Camp Hill.

North of the village are the remains of **Bremenium** Roman fort. It was first built by Julius Agricola in the 1st century, though what the visitor sees now is mainly from the 3rd century. In its day the fort could hold up to 1,000 men, and was one of the defenses along the Roman road now known as Dere Street. Close by is the **Brigantium Archaeological Reconstruction Centre**, where you can see a stone circle of 4000 BC, Iron Age defences, cup-and-ring carvings and a section of Roman road.

Around Otterburn

ELSDON

3 miles E of Otterburn on the B6341

🏛 St Cuthbert's Church 🏴 Winter's Gibbet

The village of Elsdon is of great historical importance. Built around a wide green, with St **Cuthbert's Church** in the middle, it was the

Elsdon Tower

medieval capital of Redesdale – the most lawless place in Northumberland, and scene of some of the worst border fighting. In later years it became an important stopping point on the drovers' road.

In the late 19th century, when the church was being restored, over 1,000 skulls were uncovered. They are thought to be those of soldiers killed at the Battle of Otterburn.

Elsdon Tower, which in 1415 was referred to as the 'vicar's pele', dates from the 1300s, though it was largely rebuilt at a later date. Now a private residence, it remains one of the most important pele towers in the region.

Standing in the wild moorlands around Elsdon, above the tiny hamlet of Steng Cross, is the macabre sight of **Winter's Gibbet,** with a wooden replica of a severed head dangling from the gibbet arm. It provides a grisly reminder of the fate of

LORRAINE ARMSTRONG INTERIORS

Lambton House Shop, High Street, Rothbury,
Northumberland, NE65 7TA
Tel: 01669 621929   e-mail: lorraine41@talk21.com

Rothbury is filled with shops to suit most requirements, it has a wealth of specialist shops, plenty of quality tea rooms, cafés and pubs for the weary traveller.

In amongst these specialist shops is the much-loved **Lorraine Armstrong Interiors**, which has been open since May 2007. Lorraine originally worked from home but was forced to move into premises on High Street after her work became in such high demand. Known for her speciality in soft furnishings, Lorraine has created a library of fabric books, wallpaper books, trimming books etc to complement and furnish the home. Lorraine (who has a City and Guilds in upholstery and soft furnishings) welcomes you to share her enthusiasm for design and is more than happy to help with colour schemes and recommending items to accompany your furniture. Colour co-ordinated schemes are laid out to make choosing the perfect fabrics and wallpapers even easier.

The list of products is always expanding to keep up with her customers' demands and includes wallpaper, fabrics, poles, blinds, trimmings, carpets, curtains and much more! A visit to Lorraine Armstong Interiors will not dissapoint and whether you are looking to revamp a bedroom or your entire home, this is definitely the place to go.

ELM TREE COFFEE SHOP

High Street, Rothbury,
Northumberland NE65 7TE
Tel: 01669 621337

Helen Renton and her family have built up a fine reputation for quality and value for money in their ten years at the **Elm Tree Coffee Shop**. In this Victorian town house looking down the main street from its elevated site, two rooms create a delightful, unfussy ambience in which to enjoy good honest home cooking. Counter service provides excellent teas, coffees and other hot and cold drinks to accompany scones, cakes, filled rolls, toasted sandwiches, jacket potatoes and daily specials.

The Renton family and their staff are notably friendly, willing and helpful, ensuring that every visit here is a real pleasure. The Elm Tree is open from 10 to 5 (to 4 off season) seven days a week. The town of Rothbury needs plenty of time to explore, and one of the many attractions close to the Elm Tree is the National Trust's Cragside, a fine mock-Tudor Victorian mansion that was once the home of the industrialist Sir William Armstrong.

🏚 historic building   🏛 museum and heritage   🏚 historic site   ⚜ scenic attraction   🐦 flora and fauna

William Winter who, in 1791, was tried and found guilty of the murder of a local shopkeeper, Margaret Crozier. After his execution in Newcastle, Winter was brought to this spot, where his rotting corpse was left hanging for several months.

HEPPLE
8 miles E of Otterburn on the B6341

📖 Hepple Tower

Hepple has a reminder of the difficulty of life near the borders in the form of **Hepple Tower**, a 14th-century pele tower built so strongly that attempts to demolish it and use the stone for a new farmhouse had to be abandoned. West of the village, on the moors, are some fine examples of fortified houses and farms.

ROTHBURY
12 miles E of Otterburn on the B6341

📖 Cragside 📖 Simonside

📖 Lordenshaws 🔱 Rothbury Terraces

The attractive town of Rothbury is a natural focal point from which to explore the valley of the River Coquet. It is an excellent starting point for some delightful walks, either along the valley or through the nearby woodland. The most famous perhaps being the trail to the **Rothbury Terraces**, a series of parallel tracks along the hillside above the town.

Simonside, a hill offering a fine viewpoint, is steeped in history and the subject of several legends. Flint arrowheads have been recovered here, as well as bronze swords, shards of pottery, axe heads and ornaments.

COQUET WHISKY

The Haven, Back Crofts, Rothbury, Northumberland NE65 7YA
Tel: 01669 620577
e-mail: info@coquetwhisky.co.uk
website: www.coquetwhisky.co.uk

Spirit of the Coquet

Coquet Whisky is based in the beautiful market town of Rothbury in the Coquet Valley. Black Rory is a premium blend of whisky with a very high malt content, beautiful amber glow and a hint of peat. The whisky is named after the famous smuggler Black Rory, who roamed the hills and valley of Upper Coquetdale, in the early 19th-century.

The Coquet Valley's inaccessible nature made it ideal ground for smugglers to produce duty-free whisky at what were once some of Britain's most illicit stills. Gathering the necessary ingredients wasn't a problem for Black Rory, as local farmers were only too keen to help by supplying barley and peat

There is also a Gin in the range, which has been matured for ten years in oak barrels. A 20-year-old non-chill filtered single malt is being launched in 2008. Various gift packs are available, as well as a corporate and unique labelling service.

For information on stockists, phone 01669 620577.

📖 stories and anecdotes 🍃 famous people 🎨 art and craft 🖉 entertainment and sport 🔱 walks

Burial cairns abound, as do carved stones and ancient paths. The Northumberland National Park has prepared a leaflet, which guides you on a walk up and onto the hill.

To the north of Simonside is **Lordenshaws**, with a well-defined hill fort, Bronze Age burial mounds, rock carvings and cairns.

From the 18th century, the village developed into a natural marketplace for Upper Coquetdale, to which cattle and sheep were brought for sale, and the drovers were provided with numerous alehouses. Since the mid-1800s Rothbury has been a holiday resort for walkers and fishermen, and the railway, which opened in 1870, contributed further to its growth. The former Saxon parish church was almost entirely rebuilt in 1850 and it is worth visiting the interior to see the font that stands on part of the 9th-century Rothbury cross.

Just outside Rothbury is the house and estate of **Cragside** (See panel below), once the home of Sir William George Armstrong (1810-1900), arms manufacturer and industrialist. He bought 14,000 acres in the valley of the Debden Burn, and employed architect Norman Shaw to extend the existing house and make it suitable to entertain royalty and other wealthy guests. Work began in 1864, and what finally emerged in 1884 was a mock-Tudor Victorian mansion. A pioneer of the turbine, Armstrong designed various pieces of apparatus for the house, and devised his own hydroelectric systems, with man-made lakes, streams and miles of underground piping, making Cragside the first house in the world to be lit by hydroelectricity. The house, now owned by the National Trust, has been sympathetically restored to show how upper-

Cragside House, Gardens & Estate

Rothbury, Morpeth, Northumberland NE65 7PX
Tel: 01669 620333/620150
e-mail: cragside@nationaltrust.org.uk
website:www.nationaltrust.org.uk

The revolutionary home of Lord Armstrong, Victorian inventor and landscape genius, was a wonder of its age. Built on a rocky crag high above the Debdon Burn, **Cragside** is crammed with ingenious gadgets and was the first house in the world lit by hydroelectricity. Even the variety and scale of Cragside's gardens are incredible. Surrounding the house on all sides is one of the largest 'hand-made' rock gardens in Europe. In the Pinetum below, England's tallest Douglas Fir soars above other woodland giants. Across the valley, the Orchard House still produces many varieties of fresh fruit. Today, Armstrong's amazing creation can be explored on foot or by car and provides one of the last shelters for the endangered red squirrel. The lakeside walks, adventure play area and labyrinth all appeal, especially to families.

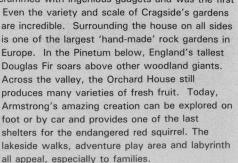

🏛 historic building 📷 museum and heritage 🏚 historic site ⚘ scenic attraction 🌿 flora and fauna

middle-class Victorians were beginning to combine comfort, opulence and all the latest technology in their homes.

WELDON BRIDGE
15 miles E of Otterburn on the A697

🏛 Brinkburn Priory

Weldon Bridge is an exceptionally elegant bridge across the River Coquet, dating from 1744. Although it no longer carries the main road it remains an impressive feature.

Nearby is **Brinkburn Priory**, standing in secluded woodland on the banks of the river. It was established in about 1135 by William de Bertram, 1st Baron Mitford, and is thought to have been built by the same masons who constructed nearby Longframlington church. It is in a beautiful setting surrounded by ancient trees and rhododendrons, and was once painted by Turner as a romantic ruin. Its church was restored in 1859 by Thomas Austin on behalf of the Cadogan family, and has many fine architectural features. It is also the setting for famous annual summer concerts.

BELLINGHAM AND WARK
7 miles SW of Otterburn on the B6320

🏛 St Cuthbert's Church

The North Tyne is fed by the Kielder Water which, on its way down to join the South Tyne above Hexham, passes by the interesting villages of Bellingham and Wark.

Bellingham (pronounced 'Bellin-jam') is a small market town in a moorland setting, with a broad main street, marketplace and the austere little **St Cuthbert's Church**, reflecting the constant troubles of the area in medieval times. To prevent marauding Scots from burning it down, a massive stone roof was added in the early 17th century.

In the churchyard an oddly-shaped tombstone, somewhat reminiscent of a peddler's pack, is associated with a foiled robbery attempt that took place in 1723. A peddler arrived at Lee Hall, a mansion once situated between Bellingham and Wark, and asked if he could be put up for the night. As her master was away at the time the maid refused, but said that he could leave his heavy pack at the Hall and collect it the next day.

Imagine her consternation when some time later the pack began to move.

Brinkburn Priory

🎬 stories and anecdotes   🐦 famous people   🎨 art and craft   ✒ entertainment and sport   🚶 walks

Hearing her screams for help, a servant rushed to the scene and fired his gun at the moving bundle. When blood poured out and the body of an armed man was discovered inside, the servants realised that this had been a clever attempt to burgle the Hall. They sounded a horn, which they found inside the pack next to the body, and when the robber's accomplices came running in response to the prearranged signal, they were speedily dealt with.

Wark, to the south of Bellingham, is an attractive estate village, once part of the lordship of Wark. The Scottish kings are said to have held court here in the 12th century.

On the slopes overlooking the North Tyne, are a large number of unusually named prehistoric settlements, such as Male Knock Camp, Good Wife Camp, Nigh Folds Camp, Carryhouse Camp and Shieldence Camp.

KIELDER
16 miles W of Otterburn off the B6320

🏰 Castle 🌲 Kielder Forest 🦋 🚶 Kielder Water

Kielder village was built in the 1950s to house workers employed in the man-made **Kielder Forest**, which covers 200 square miles to the west of the Northumberland National Park. Here at Kielder Forest you'll find one of the few areas in Britain that is home to more red squirrels than grey, thanks to careful forest planning that ensures a constant supply of conifer preferred by red squirrels. Otters too are resident in Kielder, and the area abounds with deer and rare birds and plants.

There's some excellent walking to be had, with several marked trails and routes to suit all abilities, from a leisurely stroll to an energetic climb, with maps and leaflets to guide you round. There are also cycle routes, including the 17-mile Kielder Water Cycle Route, and bicycles can be hired from the local visitors' centre.

Within the forest is **Kielder Water**. Opened by the Queen in 1982, it is the largest man-made lake in Northern Europe with over 27 miles of shoreline. The visitor can take a pleasure cruise aboard the *Osprey*, an 80-seat passenger cruiser that stops at several points of interest along the lake.

Located at sites around the lake and within the forest is an art and sculpture trail – art and architecture inspired by the surroundings. Don't miss the Kielder Skyspace – a chamber through which artist James Turrell manipulates interior and exterior light to spectacular effect.

To the northwest is **Kielder Castle**, at one time a hunting lodge for the Duke of Northumberland, and later offices for the Forestry Commission. It is now a fascinating visitor centre with exhibits describing the development of the forest and the birdlife that is found in Kielder.

Wooler

🏛 Humbledon Hill 🚶 Walks

Wooler is a small town standing on the A697 on the northern edge of the Cheviots, midway between Newcastle and Edinburgh, and is an excellent centre for exploring both the Cheviots and the border country. In the 18th and early 19th centuries it became an important halt on the main north-south coaching route and is now a small market town where many cattle fairs once took place.

There are no outstanding buildings in Wooler, though the town itself makes a pleasing whole. There are superb walking

JOHNSONS FAMILY BUTCHERS

61 High Street, Wooler, Northumberland NE71 6BD
Tel: 01668 281431

Alan Cowan and Derrick McDougal source the finest local meat and other produce for **Johnsons Family Butchers**, which has been serving the local community for 40 years. Some of the finest beef comes from the local aution mart. They also have all year round Belted Galloway and cross-bred Aberdeen Angus rumps and sirloins. All rare breed pork is sourced from Hunting Hall Farm. The local lamb is supplied from North Lyhtam and Infram Farms and free-range poultry from Blagdon Farm.

Gammon and bacon are cured on the premises, the sausages are homemade, and the shop sells a selection of cooked meats and its own pies and quiches, along with free-range eggs, chutneys and preserves. Holder of a Traditional Breeds Meat Marketing Award, Johnsons is located on the main street of Wooler; free parking for 45 minutes is available outside.

THE GOOD LIFE SHOP

50 High Street, Wooler,
Northumberland NE71 6BG
Tel: 01668 281700
e-mail: goodlife-wooler@hotmail.com
website: www.goodlifewooler.co.uk

'Wholesome food at reasonable prices' is the motto of **The Good Life Shop**, a specialist cheese shop and delicatessen on the main street of Wooler. Owner David Girdwood and his staff add friendly personal service to the pleasure of shopping for the very best foodstuffs. Local cheeses are among the stars of the show, including Admiral washed in Newcastle Brown Ale; Baltic; Berwick Edge made here in Wooler; Brinkburn goat's cheese, Cuddly's Cave and Swaledale. Among the many other fare on tempting display are local ice creams, chutneys and preserves, cooking sauces, Fenton Fine Foods, Loopy Lisa's fudge, chocolates, sticky toffee pudding and other goodies from Proof of the Pudding, daily baking, dried fruit, nuts, beans, herbs and spices, oils and vinegars, seeds, teas and coffees. Wheat-free and gluten-free products are always available. Shoppers who can't get to Wooler can order online.

opportunities in the surrounding area, for example, the Iron Age hill fort immediately west of the town, **Earle Whin** and **Wooler Common**, or via Harthope onto The Cheviot itself. Alternatively, the visitor can take a vehicle into the Harthope Valley with a choice of walks, easy or strenuous, up and through the magnificent hillsides of this part of the Northumberland National Park.

The visitor can also climb **Humbledon Hill**, on top of which are the remains of a hill fort, built about 300 BC. The Battle of Humbledon Hill was fought here in 1402 between the English and the Scots, who had been on a raiding mission as far south as Newcastle. Due to the firepower of Welsh bowmen in the English army, the Scottish army assembled within the fort was easily

defeated. Human and horse bones have been uncovered while ploughing the hill's northern slopes, and there is an area still known to this day as Red Riggs, from the blood that stained the ground during and after the battle.

Around Wooler

WOOPERTON
8 miles S of Wooler off the A697

🏚 Battle of Hedgeley Moor

Wooperton is close to the site of the **Battle of Hedgeley Moor**, which took place in 1464. In truth this was more of a skirmish, in which the Yorkist Lord Montague defeated the Lancastrian Sir Ralph Percy, who was killed. The site is marked by a

---

ROSEDEN FARM SHOP, TEA ROOM & BUTCHERY

Roseden, Wooperton, Alnwick, Northumberland NE66 4XU
Tel: 01668 217271
e-mail: enquiries@roseden.com
website: www.roseden.com

Roseden was one of the first farm shops in the region and has been serving and supporting the local community for more than 25 years. Trudi Walton sources top-quality produce for the superb home cooking that brings customers from all over the county. A wide range of dishes can be enjoyed in the tea room or to take away as ready meals for 2 to 8 people; popular choices include lasagne (meat or vegetable), fish pie, cottage pie, beef stroganoff and chicken & broccoli bake. Roseden also sells homemade meat pies and quiches, sausage rolls, fruit pies and crumbles, scones and buns, bread, dairy products (more than 30 cheeses), eggs, flour, fruit juices and cordials. From the on-site butchery come naturally reared beef, lamb and pork, honey-roast ham, sausages, burgers and home-cured bacon. Trudi also has available a self-catering holiday cottage sleeping up to 8. Just a mile from the A697 south of Wooler, this outstanding farm shop, tea room and butchery is open daily from 10 to 5.

🏚 historic building   🏛 museum and heritage   🏚 historic site   ♧ scenic attraction   ♈ flora and fauna

Cheviot Hills at Ramshope

now fields by the River Glen, lay the royal township of Gefrin or Ad-Gefrin, better known as **Yeavering**. Discovered in 1948 thanks to aerial photography, this was where, in the 7th century, King Edwin of Northumbria built a huge wooden palace that included a royal hall over 100 feet long, storehouses, stables, chapels and living quarters. A stone, and a board explaining the layout, now marks the place where this long-vanished royal establishment once stood.

If such historical associations were not enough, on the summit of a nearby hill known as **Yeavering Bell**, there is a magnificent Iron Age hill fort, the largest in Northumberland, enclosed by the remains of a thick wall and covering 13 acres. Over 130 hut circles and similar buildings have been traced on the summit, which commands impressive views for miles around.

carved stone called the Percy Cross and can be reached along a short footpath leading from the A697.

KIRKNEWTON
6 miles W of Wooler on the B6351

🏠 St Gregory's Church

🏛 Yeavering and Yeavering Bell

Kirknewton is a typical border village made up of cottages, a school and village church. **St Gregory's Church** dates mainly from the 19th century, though there are medieval fragments such as an unusual sculpture, which shows the Magi wearing kilts – a fascinating example of medieval artists presenting the Christian story in ways their audience could understand.

Josephine Butler, the great Victorian social reformer and fighter for women's rights, who retired to Northumberland and died here in 1906, is buried in the churchyard. Her father had been a wealthy landowner, and a cousin of British Prime Minister Earl Grey of Howick Hall near Craster.

Half a mile east of the village, in what are

BRANXTON
8 miles NW of Wooler off the A697

🏠 St Paul's Church 🏛 Battle of Flodden Field

The site of the famous **Battle of Flodden Field** can be found near Branxton, marked by a cross in a cornfield reached by a short path. It was here that the English army heavily defeated a Scottish army under the command of King James IV on 9th September 1513. The king was killed, and his body lay in **St Paul's Church** in Branxton, now rebuilt. An information board explains the background to the battle and how it was fought.

LOCATOR MAP

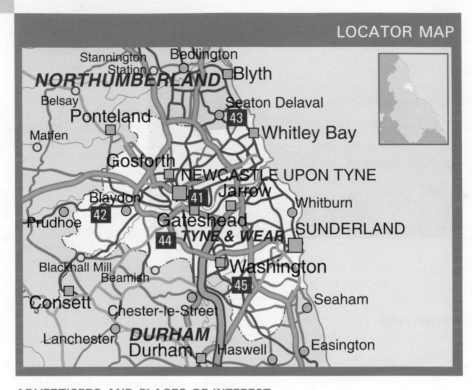

ADVERTISERS AND PLACES OF INTEREST

🏠 historic building   🏛 museum and heritage   🏛 historic site   🍃 scenic attraction   🌱 flora and fauna

2 | Tyne and Wear

The area inland from the north bank of the Tyne is mostly built-up, though there are still tracts of rural calm and beauty. Dominating this region is Newcastle-upon-Tyne, one of Britain's most important cities. It's metropolitan area stretches out as far as the small towns of Tynemouth and Whitley Bay to the east, Longbenton to the north, and Throckley to the west. Industry made this part of Britain. It is real Geordie country, steeped in hard work and refreshed by Newcastle Brown Ale. (Why Geordie? The most likely reason is that Newcastle was the only town in the region to take the side of King George I, keeping the Jacobite rebels outside the gates.) People found work in coalmines, great engineering works and shipbuilding, and never travelled far to spend their leisure times or holidays. They headed for Whitley Bay or Tynemouth, eight miles east of the city centre on the North Sea coast, but a lifetime away from their harsh living and working conditions. Alternatively, they could head north into rural Northumberland, one of the UK's most beautiful and unspoilt counties. The area south of the Tyne is largely industrial in character, encompassing large conurbations such as Gateshead, Sunderland and South Shields. But there is still plenty to see, as these places, just like Newcastle, are rediscovering themselves and their heritage. And open spaces and countryside, especially to the south, are still there to be explored.

Newcastle-upon-Tyne

🏛 Tyne Bridge	🏛 Quayside	🏛 Grainger Town
🏛 Castle Keep & Black Gate	🏛 West Walls
🏛 Cathedrals	🏛 Bessie Surtees House
🏛 Grey's Monument	🏛 🎨 Museums and Galleries

Newcastle, the region's capital, is rapidly becoming one of Britain's most exciting cities, and contains many magnificent public buildings and churches. Situated above the River Tyne, it is linked to its neighbour Gateshead by a series of road and rail bridges.

The **Tyne Bridge** has long been Newcastle's most famous symbol. Opened in 1928, it bears an uncanny resemblance to the Sydney Harbour Bridge, which isn't surprising as both were designed by the same civil engineering company. The city has several other well-known bridges. The Swing Bridge dates from 1876 and stands on the site of the original Roman bridge and its successors – it swings open to let ships through. The High Level Bridge was designed by Robert Stephenson and was opened in 1849; it carries both road and rail traffic high above the Tyne.

Newcastle has enjoyed a varied and colourful history and in its time has acted as a Roman frontier station, a medieval fortress town, an ecclesiastical centre, a great port, a mining, engineering and shipbuilding centre and a focal point of the Industrial Revolution that was to change the face of the world.

Thanks to the Metro Rapid Transport System, opened in 1980, the city and its surroundings are closely linked. It is the second largest underground rail network in Britain, linking South Shields and Gateshead,

---

🎭 stories and anecdotes   🦅 famous people   🎨 art and craft   🎟 entertainment and sport   🚶 walks

to the south of the city, with the northern coastal areas of Tynemouth and Whitley Bay. It also links up with Newcastle International Airport and takes just 20 minutes to get to the city centre. In 2002, the system was extended to Sunderland, 15 miles away, creating a regional network that can compete with some of the major underground and rapid transport systems in Europe.

The **Quayside** is the first view of Newcastle for visitors from the south, whether travelling by road or rail. The area is the symbolic and historic heart of this elegant city and boasts some 17th-century merchants' houses that mingle with Georgian architecture. It has been a focal point for activity since the first bridge was built across the river in Roman times and has been revitalised in recent years with some sensitive and imaginative restoration of the river front area. There are now a number of lively cafés and wine bars along with craft stalls, street entertainers and a regular Sunday market.

To the west of the Quayside is Central Station, designed by local architect John Dobson and officially opened by Queen Victoria in 1850. Behind the station, on South Street, are the former Stephenson railway workshops where the *Rocket* locomotive was built in 1829.

The city centre is compact, lying mostly within a square mile, so it is easy and rewarding to explore on foot. For the most part, the streets are wide and spacious, and like the later Quayside developments after the great fire of 1855, much of the architecture is in the Classical style. During the 17th and early 18th centuries Newcastle was a major coal port, with its core – still basically medieval in layout – near the riverside. But by the late 1700s the city began moving north,

and in the early 1800s architects like William Newton, John Stokoe and John Dobson began designing some elegant Georgian buildings and spacious squares.

Grainger Town, the historic centre of Newcastle, contains many fine examples of classical Victorian architecture. It was designed by Richard Grainger with architects John Dobson, John Wardle and George Walker. Up until recently the area was in a state of physical and economic decline but has been restored to its former splendour by the Grainger Town Project, just one of the examples that epitomises the renaissance that has transformed the city. Grainger, who died in 1828, is buried in the churchyard of St James in Benwell, on the western edge of the city.

Grey's Monument, a 19th-century landmark dedicated to the former Prime Minister Earl Grey to commemorate the Reform Act, stands at the head of **Grey Street** about which John Betjeman wrote that *'not even Regent Street in London, can compare with that subtle descending curve'*. The monument was designed by John Green and his son Benjamin, who also designed the nearby Theatre Royal. With over 40 per cent of its buildings officially listed, Grey Street was recently awarded the title of Britain's favourite street by listeners to the Radio 4 *Today* programme. A more recent addition to the city is the Blue Carpet, a pedestrianised public square outside the Laing Art gallery, constructed from purpose-made blue glass tiles that attracted considerable controversy when first unveiled. It is just one of over a hundred pieces of public art that can be found at locations across the city.

The **Castle Keep** at Castle Garth was built by Henry II in the 12th century on the site of the 'new castle', built in 1080 by Robert, eldest son of William I, on the site of the Roman fortifications of Pons Aelius. This earlier wooden castle, from which the city takes its name, is thought to have been the start of Hadrian's Wall before it was extended east. It was built after uprisings against the new Norman overlords that followed the killing of Bishop Walcher in Gateshead at a meeting to discuss local grievances.

Henry's impressive new structure was built entirely of stone, and reached 100 feet in height. Although the battlements and turrets were added in the 19th century, much of it is Norman. The only other remaining castle building is **Black Gate**, dating back to 1247. If at first glance the structure looks a little unusual, it is because of the house built on top of it in the 17th century. The castle was in use during the Civil War, when it was taken by the Scottish army after the Royalist defeat at the Battle of Newburn, five miles west of Newcastle, in 1640.

Many of the other medieval buildings were demolished in the mid-1800s to make way for the railway, and the Castle and Black Gate were fortunate not to have been destroyed as well. Today, the main East Coast rail line runs between the two en route to Scotland, the London branch passes to the west of the Castle Keep before crossing the King Edward VII Bridge.

At one time, Newcastle was surrounded by stout walls that were 20 to 30 feet high in places and seven feet thick. Parts of these survive and include a number of small towers that were built at regular intervals. Begun in 1265, the walls were eventually completed in the mid-1300s. They were described as having a *'strength and magnificence'* which *'far passeth all the walls of the cities of England and most of the cities of Europe'.* The

Castle Keep, Newcastle

best remaining sections are the **West Walls** behind Stowell Street, and the area between Forth Street and Hanover Street, south of Central Station, which leads you to spectacular views of the River Tyne from the 'Hanover Gardens' perched on the cliff side.

One unusual feature of the walls was that they passed right through the grounds of a 13th-century Dominican monastery, known as Blackfriars, causing the prior to protest loudly. To keep the peace, a door was cut through to allow the monks access to their orchards and gardens. Blackfriars was later converted and turned into almshouses for the destitute. Earmarked for demolition in the 1960s the building was eventually saved. The church is long gone, but the remaining buildings have been renovated and opened as a craft centre and restaurant grouped around a small square. It's another of the area's hidden places, and well worth a visit.

Life Science Centre

Times Square, Newcastle-upon-Tyne NE1 4EP
Tel: 0191 243 8210 Fax: 0191 243 8201
e-mail: info@life,org.uk
website: www.lifesciencecentre.org.uk

This spectacular visitor centre, which cost over £70 million and covers ten acres, has a unique purpose - it wants to study the secrets of life, and open them up to everyone. It takes you on a trip through four billion years, from when life started on earth to the present day. During the trip, you'll experience magical 3D shows, live theatre, film, sound, light and audience participation. Plus, you'll be learning about life

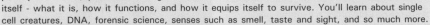

itself - what it is, how it functions, and how it equips itself to survive. You'll learn about single cell creatures, DNA, forensic science, senses such as smell, taste and sight, and so much more.

The **Life Science Centre** has many aspects. There's a Bioscience Centre, an Institute of Human Genetics (part of Newcastle University), a Life Lab, Times Square (the largest open square to be created in Newcastle for over 100 years), and the amazing Life Interactive World. This is divided into eight zones, each one highlighting an aspect of human development. Zone one, for instance, introduces you to evolution, zone two deals with DNA, which are the building blocks of life, zone three deals with cells, and so on until we reach zone nine, when we experience an amusement arcade of the future! Here visitors can test their co-ordination and reflexes - two of the basic skills that keep creatures alive in a hostile world! This is science presented in an imaginative and stimulating way. The most scary zone must surely be zone eight, where life is shown to be a rollercoaster, using the world's longest continual motion ride.

But all aspects of Life Interactive World are entertaining and fun, and visitor sometimes never realise that as they experience what's on offer, they're learning as well! Which brings us to the brain. Zone six deals with our most important organ, and we can actually step inside a huge one and follow a day in the life of a typical North East family. The Centre is the first time anywhere in the world that science, biotechnology, research, education, entertainment and ethics have been brought together on a single site. It's right in the centre of Newcastle, next to Central Station and a stop on the Metro. Within Times Square there are shops (including a souvenir shop), a restaurant and a café.

Opening times: 10-6 Monday to Saturday and 11-6 on Sunday.

🏠 historic building 🏛 museum and heritage 🏚 historic site ♧ scenic attraction 🌱 flora and fauna

St Nicholas's Cathedral, Newcastle

Newcastle has two cathedrals – the Anglican **St Nicholas's Cathedral** with its famous crown spire on St Nicholas Street, and the Roman Catholic **St Mary's Cathedral** on Clayton West Street. St Nicholas, dating from the 14th and 15th centuries, was formerly the city's parish church, and it still has the feel of an intimate parish church about it. Built in 1844, St Mary's was one of AWH Pugin's major works; the spire he originally designed was never built - the spire seen today dates from 1872.

This is a metropolitan city of great vibrancy and activity, and there's plenty to do, with a rich variety of entertainment on offer. There is a choice of theatres, cinemas, concert venues and an opera house. There are some excellent restaurants with every type of cuisine on offer, and menus to suit all budgets.

Newcastle is a city that is renowned for its shopping, attracting weekend trippers from as far afield as Scandinavia. The city boasts a wide range of museums and art galleries, including the Discovery Museum in Blandford Square, depicting Newcastle's social and industrial past; the **Laing Art Gallery**, New Bridge Street, with an impressive Pre-Raphaelite collection; the **Hancock Museum**, Barras Bridge – the region's premier natural history museum; the **Life Science Centre** (see panel opposite), Times Square – the science of genetics brought to life in a spectacular centre that cost £70 million and covers 10 acres; the Hatton Gallery, Newcastle University Art Dept – a permanent collection of West African sculpture; the **Museum of Antiquities,** King's Road; the **Shefton Museum,** Newcastle University – Greek Art and Archaeology; the **Side Gallery**, The Side – documentary photography exhibitions; **Military Vehicle Museum**, Exhibition Park; and the **Newburn Hall Motor Museum**, Townfield Gardens – a private collection of vintage vehicles.

Down near the quayside is a unique group of half-timbered houses known as **Bessie Surtees House**, owned by English Heritage. The rooms are richly decorated with elaborate plaster ceilings, and there is some beautiful 17th-century wall panelling.

To the west of the city, on the south bank of the Tyne, is **Blaydon,** famous for its races, which inspired one of Newcastle's anthems – *The Blaydon Races*. But horse racing hasn't been held here since 1916, and the racecourse is no more. Gosforth Park, to the north of the city, is where horse racing now takes place. Near Blaydon is the **Path Head Water Mill** (see panel above), a restored 18th-century mill.

🎞 stories and anecdotes 🐟 famous people 𝒫 art and craft ✍ entertainment and sport 𝕏 walks

Path Head Water Mill

Summerhill, Blaydon on Tyne NE21 4SP
Tel: 0191 414 6288
e-mail: enquiries@gatesheadmill.co.uk
website: www.gatesheadmill.co.uk

For many years, the 18th-century **Path Head Water Mill** lay abandoned and neglected. Then, in 1995, it was decided to restore it to its full working glory. In 1998 it opened to the public, though there is still a lot of work to be done. It is located in a picturesque, quiet dell, and here you can see how water was the main source of energy before the advent of the steam engine, and how a mill harnessed the power of water to turn its machinery. A small gallery of photographs shows you the stages in the mill's restoration, plus there's a tearoom. Opening Times: Tuesday-Sunday 11-3 in winter and 10-5 in summer. Closed Mondays, except for Bank Holidays. Admission charge.

Newcastle is a true northern capital – a proud city that doesn't look to the south for inspiration or guidance. There is an unmistakable air of confidence in the future. Along with neighbouring Gateshead, Newcastle staged a bid to become European City of Culture 2008. Narrowly missing out to Liverpool in the final stages, the city has none the less been designated as a Centre of Cultural Excellence with a wide range of events planned for the coming years.

Newcastle can claim several firsts. In 1859 it hosted the world's first serious dog show in the Town Hall. In 1881 Morley Street became the first street in the world to be lit by electric light. And in 1905 the world's first beauty contest was held at the Olympia Theatre. Notable sons of Newcastle include Admiral Collingwood, who took over the running of the Battle of Trafalgar after the death of Admiral Nelson; musicians Hank Marvin and Sting; the engineer Ove Arup; the actors Jimmy Nail, Rowan Atkinson and Kevin Whateley; and the footballer Alan Shearer.

Around Newcastle-upon-Tyne

WALLSEND
3 miles E of Newcastle on the A193

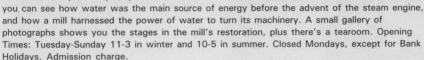

Segedunum Roman Fort & Museum

In Wallsend the mighty shipyards tower over **Segedunum Roman Fort and Museum** on Buddle Street. The fort was the last outpost on Hadrian's Wall. Segedunum (which means 'strong fort') stood at the eastern end of Hadrian's Wall. Originally the wall only went as far as Newcastle, but it was decided to extend it to deter sea attacks. There are only scant remains of the structure in the district nowadays. Segedunum is a reconstruction of what the Roman fort would have looked like. Over 600 Roman soldiers would have been garrisoned here at any one time, and the area must have been a bustling place. Now visitors can explore the reconstructed fort, get a stunning view from a 114-foot viewing tower, and watch archaeologists uncovering yet more foundations of the original wall.

NORTH SHIELDS

6m E of Newcastle

🏛 Railway Museum

Standing at the mouth of the River Tyne, the town is named after the 'shielings' (fishermen's huts) on the riverbank. The Fish Quay, dating back to 1225, grew up when fishermen where called upon to supply Tynemouth Priory. While the boats are smaller in number than in its heyday, the port is still a hive of activity. The best time to see fishing boats come into port and experience the hustle and bustle of the landing of catches is between 6pm and 7pm. Fabulous fresh fish can be bought from the numerous fishmongers. Many of the buildings on the Fish Quay are linked to the fishing industry. The 'High'and 'Low' lights are prominent landmarks on the upper and lower banks of the Fish Quay that were designed to guide vessels entering the Tyne, today they serve as residential properties.

Also worth a visit is the **Stephenson Railway Museum** in Middle Engine Lane. George Stephenson began his career as a humble engine-man at Willington Ballast Hill, before moving to Killingworth where he eventually became an engine-wright. He was the engineer on the world's first passenger rail line – the Stockton to Darlington railway, which opened in 1825. The museum remembers the man and his achievements, as well as explaining railway history in the area.

TYNEMOUTH, WHITLEY BAY AND CULLERCOATS

8 miles E of Newcastle on the A193

🏛 Collingwood Monument 🏛 Tynemouth Priory

🏛 St Mary's Lighthouse

These three towns form a linked resort. Nestling at the mouth of the River Tyne, Tynemouth boasts a proud maritime heritage. In 1864 the first Volunteer Life Brigade was created here and is still in operation today. Visitors can learn more about this vital service in the small museum attached to the lifeboat station. Overlooking the river is the notable **Collingwood Monument**, the grand statue of Admiral Lord Collingwood, Nelson's second in command at Trafalgar, who went on to win the battle after Nelson's death. The four guns below the statue are from his ship, the *Royal Sovereign*. **Tynemouth Priory** was built over the remains of a 7th-century monastery, which was the burial place of St Oswin, King of Deira (the part of Northumbria south of the Tees), who was murdered in 651. The priory was as much a fortress as a monastery, which explains the existence of the adjoining 13th-century castle ruins. Tynemouth station is the venue for a popular antique market held every weekend.

Long Sands is an award-winning and gloriously sandy beach that stretches from Tynemouth to Cullercoats, a small town renowned for its history of salt production. In

Tynemouth Priory

🎭 stories and anecdotes   🐦 famous people   🎨 art and craft   🎟 entertainment and sport   🚶 walks

the 1700s around 2,180 tons of salt were gathered here each year, abandoned caves were once the hiding place of smugglers who made their fortune illegally transporting it to Scotland. Much quieter than the neighbouring resorts of Tynemouth and North Shields, Cullercoats was a favourite retreat of the famous American artist Winslow Homer who painted some of his finest works here.

The seaside resort of Whitley Bay has a unique atmosphere at weekends and bank holidays when young people from all over the country come to sample its legendary nightlife. The town has some excellent safe beaches and in July hosts the Whitley Bay International Jazz Festival.

On a small island, easily reached on foot at low tide, is **St Mary's Lighthouse**. Visitors can climb the 137 steps to the top and get magnificent views of the Northumberland coast. Completed in 1898 the Lighthouse remained in operation until 1984, when it was superseded by modern navigational techniques. North Tyneside council now runs the Lighthouse and former keepers' cottages as a visitors' centre and bird sanctuary.

SEATON SLUICE
8 miles NE of Newcastle on the A193

🏛 Seaton Delaval Hall   🏛 St Mary's Chapel

Inland from Seaton Sluice is **Seaton Delaval Hall**. This superb Vanbrugh mansion, the ancestral home of the Delavals, was built in the Palladian style in the early 1700s for Admiral George Delaval and, although the building suffered from a series of damaging

---

JOHN J KERR

2 Hayward Avenue, Seaton Delaval, Whitley Bay, Tyne & Wear NE25 0AF
Tel: 01902 372360
e-mail: john@kerr7066.freeserve.co.uk
website: www.johnjkerr.co.uk

John J Kerr, a professional artist, and his daughter Dawn, a professional picture framer, run their successful joint enterprise in Seaton Delaval, close to Vanbrugh's magnificent Seaton Delaval Hall and just two miles from the coast. John started the business in a small shop further along Hayward Avenue in 1976. He moved to the present premises in 1981 and was later joined by his daughter, who runs the business on a day-to-day basis.

The showroom displays a selection of John's paintings and prints, whose subjects range from scenes of the North East and Lake District to portraits and animals. He accepts commissions for all the above, and almost anything else, in a variety of sizes and a choice of oil on canvas or watercolours on 250lbs paper. In the workrooms at the back of the premises Dawn provides a bespoke trade and contract framing service, along with embroidery and designs for sports shirts. Medals are another speciality, with a wide variety of mouldings to choose from. The brilliant website shows a selection of John's work arranged by category, along with ordering and commission details.

🏛 historic building   📷 museum and heritage   🏛 historic site   ⚘ scenic attraction   🌱 flora and fauna

fires, some restoration has been carried out. One wing contains Vanbrugh's magnificent stables. In the grounds of the house stands the Norman **St Mary's Chapel**.

Gateshead

🏛 Angel of the North 🏛 Millennium Bridge

🏠 Visitor Centre 🎨 Baltic Centre

🎨 Shipley Art Gallery

For generations Gateshead has lived very much in the shadow of neighbouring Newcastle, but no longer. Today, the city is at the heart of an impressive regeneration programme that has revitalised the area. In a bid hosted jointly with Newcastle, the city was shortlisted for Capital of Culture 2008, narrowly missing out to Liverpool in the final stages.

Visitors arriving in the city from the south are greeted by one of North East England's most important modern icons – **The Angel of the North**. Commissioned by Gateshead Council and created by renowned sculptor Antony Gormley, this vast and most impressive statue, made from 200 tonnes of steel, is 65 feet high and has a wingspan of 175 feet. Erected in February 1998, the statue has attracted worldwide attention.

Nowhere is the city's transformation more evident than on the Gateshead Quays, a major arts, leisure and cultural venue on the banks of the River Tyne. One of the most spectacular new attractions in Gateshead is the £21 million **Gateshead Millennium Bridge** (see panel below), erected across the Tyne in 2001 and designed to take both cyclists and pedestrians. Designed by

Gateshead Millenium Bridge

Gateshead, Tyne and Wear
Tel: 0191 433 3000 (Gateshead Council)
See one of the world's most stunning riverside landmarks - the **Gateshead Millenium Bridge**. The world's only tilting bridge opens to allow shipping to pass underneath its graceful arches. Don't forget to catch the bridge in the evening, when it is lit by a high-tech light display, able to create dazzling patterns in millions of colours.

It uses a tilting mechanism to open, turning on pivots on both sides of the river to form a spectacular gateway arch. Two concrete piers hide the massive hydraulic rams, pivots and motors that open the bridge. Each opening or closing

takes four minutes, powered by eight electric motors totalling 440 kilowatts or 589 horse power - more power than one of the fastest sports cars, a Ferrari F50. The main arch rises to 50 metres and is 126 metres wide - but precisely made to a tolerance of 3mm. The weight is over 850 tonnes - enough steel to make 64 double-decker buses.

The bridge was designed by Wilkinson Eyre Architects/Gifford & Partners, and built by Gateshead based construction company Harbour & General at a cost of £22 million - almost half of which was paid for by Lottery money through the Millenium Commission.

🎭 stories and anecdotes 🦅 famous people 🎨 art and craft 🎭 entertainment and sport 🚶 walks

Wilkinson Eyre Architects/Gifford & Partners, and built by Gateshead-based construction company Harbour & General, the main arch rises to 50 metres and is 126 metres wide, with enough steel to make 64 double-decker buses. A tilting mechanism enables the bridge to pivot at both ends, forming a gateway arch, underneath which ships can pass. This operation, which has been likened to a giant blinking eye, is an engineering world first for which the bridge has received many accolades. The bridge is particularly impressive at night when it is lit by a high-tech, multi-colour light display.

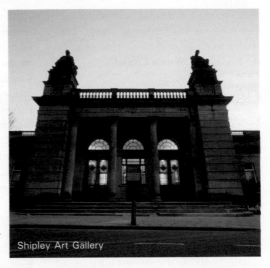
Shipley Art Gallery

The **Baltic Centre for Contemporary Arts** is a major new international centre for contemporary art, housed in a converted 1950s grain warehouse. It is one of the largest temporary art spaces in Europe and five galleries display an ever changing programme of work from resident artists. There is also a viewing platform with spectacular views of the Tyne Bridge. Admission is free. Next to the Baltic is the open-air performance square, Baltic Square, a venue for street artists and musical events.

Further along the Quayside and opened at the end of 2004 in a spectacular Norman Foster building, is The Sage Gateshead music centre. It boasts a 1,650-seat performance hall, 450-seat secondary hall and a school of music, and is also home to the Northern Sinfonia orchestra. It caters for all tastes – jazz, classical, folk and rock. Linking the Baltic with the Sage Gateshead is a £30 million leisure complex with an 18-screen cinema, bowling alley, nightclubs, fitness suites and restaurants.

The **Gateshead Quay Visitor Centre** is housed in the former St Mary's parish church,

a Grade I listed church with Norman origins. There is a display on Gateshead's history and future development plans and a tourist information centre.

Shipley Art Gallery first opened to the public in 1917 and houses a nationally renowned collection of contemporary crafts. Also on display is William C. Irving's painting of the Blaydon Races. The song, written by Geordie Ridley, a Victorian music hall singer, has become the folklore anthem of Tyneside. When the painting was first exhibited, in the window of an art dealer's shop in Newcastle, it drew such crowds that the police were forced to ask the dealer to draw the blinds.

Saltwell Park is an elegant Victorian park dating back to the 13th century that has impressive floral displays. Gateshead has achieved some notable successes in the Britain in Bloom competitions. In June, Gateshead Central Nursery hosts a major flower show.

The Metro Centre is an impressive shopping and leisure complex that is popular with locals and visitors to the area.

Sir Joseph Swan, pioneer of the electric light, was born in Sunderland but it was at his home in Gateshead that he demonstrated the world's first practical light bulb. The athlete Steve Cram and the footballer Paul Gascoigne were born in Gateshead, and Daniel Defoe wrote *Robinson Crusoe* while staying in the town in 1720. Gateshead was in the news recently as the home of Britain's first 'flat-pack' village, a development of 93 homes in St James's Village.

Around Gateshead

GIBSIDE CHAPEL
6 miles SW of Gateshead on the A694

🏠 Gibside Estate

The large mansion at **Gibside Estate** was owned by the Bowes family, and partially demolished in 1958. Now the place is chiefly visited for the Palladian Gibside Chapel, owned by the National Trust. Building work began in the 18th century but it wasn't until 1812 that the chapel was finally consecrated.

A stately building, looking more like a small mansion than a church, Gibside was built for

Sir George Bowes whose mausoleum lies beneath it. It is open from April to October, and once a month a church service is held.

JARROW
4 miles E of Gateshead on the A184/A194

🏠 St Paul's Church 🏛 Bede's World

Mixed memories surround the town of Jarrow. Once a thriving centre for the Tyneside shipbuilding industry, it gained fame during the famous **Jarrow Hunger March**, when some 200 unemployed men from the area walked the 270 miles to London to draw attention to their plight. Local shipyards had been hard hit by the Depression and other marches took place, but the Jarrow March of 1936 is by far the best known. A bas-relief at the Metro Station commemorates the event, as does a sculpture outside a local supermarket.

Jarrow also has a more propitious entry in history books. During the 7th century, Northumbria was a kingdom in its own right, and a shining beacon of learning and Christianity. **Bede's World** is a museum and outdoor interpretation centre were visitors can explore the extraordinary life of the Venerable Bede. The little herb garden at Bede's World is in four sections: culinary, Anglo-Saxon medicinal, aromatic and medicinal. It encompasses both a monastery and church, founded in the 7th century and dedicated to St Paul by Benedict Biscop. The original dedication stone of **St Paul's Church** can still be seen within its chancel, showing the date of 23rd April AD 685, together with

Bede's World

fragments of Anglo-Saxon stained glass, which scientific tests have established to be the oldest ecclesiastical stained glass in Europe, if not the world. More modern work includes carvings from 1973 by Fenwick Lawson and a stained-glass window by John Piper, unveiled by the Princess of Wales in 1985. It was here, at Jarrow monastery in the 7th and 8th centuries, that Bede wrote his famous *Ecclesiastical History of England*. He lived here from the age of 8 until his death in 736 at the age of 63. He was undoubtedly Britain's first genuine historian, employing methods of checking and double-checking his information that are still in use today. Jarrow Hall is a Georgian building that has been incorporated into the museum.

MARSDEN
9 miles E of Gateshead on the A183

🏛 Souter Lighthouse

The coast between South Shields and Roker is magnificent, with rocky cliffs projecting into the sea at Lizard Point and the impressive Marsden Bay. Marsden Rock was once a famous County Durham landmark – a rock formation shaped like the Arc de Triomphe, which stood in the bay. In 1996, however, it finally succumbed to the forces of nature and collapsed, leaving two tall stumps. The smaller stump proved so unstable that in 1997 it was demolished. The caves here, which were once home to smugglers, have been transformed into a bar and restaurant.

Souter Lighthouse (National Trust) at Lizard Point was built in 1871, and was the first reliable electric lighthouse in the world. It's a perfect example of Victorian technology, and features an engine room, fog horns and lighthouse keeper's living quarters.

SOUTH SHIELDS
8 miles E of Gateshead on the A184/A194

🏛 Museum 🏛 Arbeia 🦮 Catherine Cookson Trail

South Shields stretches out along the southern shore of the Tyne estuary. Though close to Newcastle and Gateshead, the North Sea coastline here is remarkably unspoiled, and can be walked along for many miles. King George V declared that the beach at South Shields was the finest he had seen. This is a stretch of fine firm sand, behind which a small but pleasant resort thrives. It was from this beach that the world's first purpose-built lifeboat was launched in 1790. It is the older part of South Shields that has given the town a new claim to fame, thanks to the work of one of the world's most popular novelists – Dame Catherine Cookson, who died in 1998. She was born Katie McMullen in 1906, in a house in Leam Lane, amid poverty and squalor, the illegitimate child of a woman called Kate Fawcett. The house is gone now, but a plaque was erected marking the spot.

Catherine Cookson wrote a series of best-selling novels that captured the world of her own childhood, and that of her parents and grandparents, with vivid clarity. It was a world that was shaped in the 19th century around the narrow streets and coal mines – a world of class warfare and conflict, passion and tragedy, violence and reconciliation.

A **Catherine Cookson Trail** has been laid out in the town, showing places associated with her and her books, and a leaflet is available to guide you round. The **South Shields Museum** has recently undergone a major redevelopment, which included an enhanced Catherine Cookson's gallery and an Arts Adventure Centre.

🏛 historic building 🏛 museum and heritage 🏛 historic site 🦮 scenic attraction 🌿 flora and fauna

In Baring Street you can see the extensive remains of the 2nd-century Roman fort, **Arbeia**. The West Gate has been faithfully reconstructed to match what experts believe to be its original appearance, with two three-storey towers, two gates and side walls. It is the biggest reconstruction of its kind in the country, and a truly magnificent achievement. It also incorporates the Commander's Accommodation and Barracks.

Much of the old harbour at South Shields has been restored, particularly around the Mill Dam, which is home to the Customs House offering a cinema, theatre, art galleries and an excellent Italian restaurant. Fine Georgian buildings and warehouses still survive in this area along the riverside.

Arbeia, South Shields

SPRINGWELL
3 miles S of Gateshead on the B1288

🏛 Bowes Railway

Springwell is home to the **Bowes Railway**, once a private rail system pulling coal-filled wagons from pit to port. The original wagonways were made of wood, with horses pulling the wagons. The line finally closed in 1974, but a section has since been reopened as an industrial heritage centre, jointly owned by Gateshead and Sunderland Councils.

Many of the buildings of the original Springwell Colliery have been retained, as well as the hauliers' houses at Blackham Hill. There are guided tours and train trips on selected days throughout the summer.

Sunderland

🏛 St Peter's Church Minster	🏛 Sunderland Minster
🏛 St Andrew's Church	🏛 Roker Pier
🏛 Winter Gardens and Museum & Art Gallery	
🏛 National Glass Centre	🏛 Monkwearmouth Station
🎨 Northern Gallery for Contemporary Art	
🎨 Vardy Art Gallery	🎨 Exchange Building
🎨 St Peter's Riverside Sculpture Trail	

Sunderland is one of Britain's newer cities and much of its history is told in an exhibition in the **Winter Gardens** and **Sunderland Museum and Art Gallery** on Burdon Road where examples of works by Lowry and JW Carmichael, along with the maritime paintings

Sunderland Museum and Winter Gardens at Night

The **Exchange Building**, the oldest public building in the city, is a venue for the whole community to enjoy. Exhibitions, meetings and functions take place there, plus there is a restaurant and café. The famous Empire Theatre – a Sunderland institution – attracts all the top productions.

St Michael and All Angels Church on High Street West is worth visiting. It was the first minster to be created in England since the Reformation, proclaimed **Sunderland Minster** in January 1998 to celebrate the town's elevation to city status.

On the north side of the Wear, in the suburb of Monkwearmouth, is **St Peter's Church**, one of the most important sites of early Christianity in the country. This tiny Saxon church was founded in AD 674 by

of Sunderland-born Royal Academician and theatre-set designer Clarkson Stanfield, are on display. The museum has been completely refurbished and the Winter Gardens, badly damaged in the Second World War, have been re-created – a green oasis in a glass rotunda, with exotic plants from all over the world and a water sculpture by William Pye. The museum and the Winter Gardens are contained within Mowbray Park, which has been fully restored with a rose arbour, shrub borders, formal bedding displays, a quarry garden, a limestone crag, themed walkways, poetry inscriptions, historical monuments, a lake and a bowling green. The award-winning **Northern Gallery for Contemporary Art** is on the top floor of the City Library and on Ryhope Road, south of the city centre, is the university-owned **Vardy Art Gallery**.

Benedict Biscop, a Northumbrian nobleman and thane of King Oswy, who had travelled to Rome and was inspired to found a monastery on his return. This was to become a great centre of culture and learning, rivalled only by Jarrow. The Venerable Bede, England's first great historian, worked here for a time and described the monastery's foundation in his *Ecclesiastical History of England*. The west tower and the wall of this most fascinating church have survived from Saxon times and the area around the church, where shipyards once stood, has been landscaped.

Close by, in Liberty Way, is the **National Glass Centre**. Glass was first made in Sunderland in the 7th century at St Peter's Church, so it's fitting that the centre was built here. Visitors can see how glass was made all those years ago, and watch modern glassblowing. There is a Glass Gallery, devoted to all forms of glass art, and in the Kaleidoscope Gallery there are several interactive exhibits showing glass's many amazing properties. Walking on the roof is not for the faint-hearted, as it's made of clear glass panels 30 feet above the riverside. However, some panels are opaque, so people who don't have a head for heights can still walk there and enjoy the view.

Art of another kind is to be found in the **St Peter's Riverside Sculpture Trail**. It was established in 1990, and comprises various works of outdoor sculpture – in metal, wood, glass and stone – placed along the banks of the Wear, mostly on the Monkwearmouth side.

Monkwearmouth Station is one of the most handsome small railway stations in the British Isles. Built in imposing neo-classical style, it looks more like a temple or a town hall. Trains no longer call here, and it has been converted into a small museum of the Victorian railway age.

Roker is one of Sunderland's suburbs, located to the north of the great breakwaters that form the city's harbour. The northern breakwater, known as **Roker Pier**, is 825 metres long and was opened in 1903. Roker Park has been carefully restored to its former Victorian splendour, and from Roker and Seaburn through to Sunderland there is a six-mile-long seaside promenade. Crowds of people gather here in July to witness front line jet fighters and vintage planes in action during the Sunderland International Air Show.

It is worth making your way to Roker to visit **St Andrew's Church** in Talbot Road, described as 'the Cathedral of the Arts and Crafts Movement'. Built in the early 1900s, it is crammed with treasures by the leading craftsmen of the period: silver lectern,

pulpit and altar furniture by Ernest Gimson, a font by A Randall Wells, stained glass in the east window by H A Payne, a painted chancel ceiling by Macdonald Gill, stone tablets engraved by Eric Gill, and Burne-Jones tapestry and carpets from the William Morris workshops.

Around Sunderland

PENSHAW
4 miles W of Sunderland off the A183

| 🏛 Penshaw Monument | 🏛 All Saints Church |
| 🏰 Lambton Castle | |

This mining village is famous for the **Penshaw Monument** – a fanciful Grecian temple modelled on the Temple of Theseus, and built in 1844 in memory of John George Lambton, 1st Earl of Durham and Governor of Canada. A waymarked circular walk of just over three miles links Penshaw Monument with the River Wear.

All Saints Church dates from 1745, and has one unusual feature. Inside it there is a monument to the Eliot family carved on a piece of stone from the Pyramid of Cheops in Egypt.

To the west is **Lambton Castle**, scene of an old tale about The Lambton Worm. Legend has it that many years go, the heir to the Lambton estate was fishing in the Wear one Sunday morning when he should have been at worship. Instead of a fish, he caught a huge worm, which he promptly threw into a well, where it grew to an enormous size. The worm became so big that it could coil itself around hillsides, and began to terrorise the neighbourhood. Meanwhile the heir, away in the Holy Land fighting in the Crusades, knew nothing of this. On his return he met a witch

who told him the secret
of how the worm could
be killed, on the
premise that having
done so he must then
kill the first living thing
he met on returning to
his village. If he failed
to do so the family
would be cursed and no
Lambton would die
peacefully in his or her
bed for nine

Washington Old Hall

generations. His father, hearing of this,
released an old dog close by. Unfortunately,
having successfully slain the worm, the young
heir didn't see the old dog, but saw his father
first. He refused to kill him and the witch's
prophesy about the next nine generations
came true.

WASHINGTON
6 miles W of Sunderland on the A1231

🐿 Washington Old Hall

🌿 Wildlife & Wetlands Centre

Present-day Washington is a new town with
modern districts scattered over a wide area
surrounding the town centre. Built to attract
industry into an area whose mining industry
was in decline, the town has achieved its aim.
The architecture is largely uninspiring,
though within the old village of Washington
to the east of the town centre, there is one
attraction well worth visiting – **Washington
Old Hall**, home of the Washington family,
ancestors of George Washington, the first
American president.

People tend to believe that Sulgrave Manor
in Northamptonshire was the Washingtons'
ancestral home, but the family only lived
there for about 100 years. Before that they

had been in Lancashire and Westmorland,
and prior to that they had lived at
Washington Hall for 430 years.

The Hall was originally a manor house built
in the 12th century for the de Wessington
family, whose descendants through a female
line finally quit the house in 1613, when it was
acquired by the Bishop of Durham.

The present house, in local sandstone, was
rebuilt on the medieval foundations in about
1623. In 1936 it was to be demolished, but a
hastily formed preservation committee
managed to save it, thanks to money from
across the Atlantic. In 1955 it was officially
re-opened by the American Ambassador, and
two years later it was acquired by the
National Trust. The interiors re-create a
typical manor house of the 17th century, and
there are some items on display that are
connected to George Washington himself,
though the man never visited or stayed here.
A peaceful stroll can also be enjoyed in the
formal Jacobean garden.

Washington is also the home to the
**Washington Wildfowl and Wetlands
Centre** (see panel opposite) – a conservation
area and bird-watchers' paradise covering
some 100 acres of ponds, lakes and woodland

Washington Wildfowl & Wetlands Centre

Washington, Tyne and Wear NE38 8LE
Tel: 0191 4165454 Fax: 0191 4165801
e-mail: info.washington@wwt.org.uk website: www.wwt.org.uk

Washington Wildfowl and Wetlands Centre is one of nine Centres run by the Wildfowl and Wetlands Trust, a registered charity. Here you can have a fantastic day out seeing, feeding and learning about wetland birds, whilst also helping WWT to conserve wetland habitats and their biodiversity.

At the Heron Hides, closed circuit cameras allow you to see individual nests during the breeding season of the largest colony of Grey Herons in the area. A variety of ducks, geese and swans can be seen in the reserve, including the Nene, state bird of Hawaii, saved from the brink of extinction by WWT. Having arrived at Washington in 1986, the Chilean Flamingo colony is now breeding well and often makes use of the Flamingo House, built with a donation from author Catherine Cookson. The James Steel Waterfowl Nursery, built in 1996, is the first home for most of the ducks and geese that hatch at Washington and

special tours take place during the breeding season.

You can take your time to stroll around the nature reserve, or explore Spring Gill Wood with its ponds, streams and woodland. The Hawthorn Wood Wild Bird Feeding Station attracts a variety of woodland birds such as woodpeckers and sparrowhawks that can be seen mostly during the winter. The centre also has an adventure play area for children, a waterside café and The Glaxo Wellcome Discovery Centre, with its displays and exhibits.

sloping down to the River Wear. One of nine centres run by the Wildfowl and Wetlands Trust, a registered charity, it provides a fantastic day out. More than 1,200 birds represent 105 different species, including mallard, widgeon, nene (the state bird of Hawaii), heron, Chilean flamingos, redshank and lapwing. At the Heron Hides, closed-circuit cameras allow visitors to see individual nests during the breeding season of the largest colony of grey herons in the area. The Glaxo Wellcome Wetland Discovery Centre has displays and interactive exhibits, a waterfowl nursery and a Waterside Café.

LOCATOR MAP

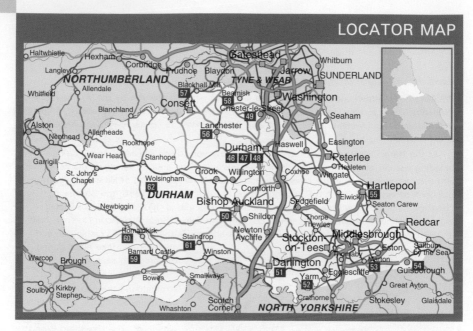

ADVERTISERS AND PLACES OF INTEREST

Accommodation, Food and Drink

Arts and Crafts

Fashions

Giftware

Home and Garden

Jewellery

Place of Interest

Specialist Food and Drink

🏛 historic building 🏛 museum and heritage 🏛 historic site 🦆 scenic attraction 🌿 flora and fauna

3 County Durham

County Durham's prosperity was founded on coalmining. Coal has been mined here for centuries, but it wasn't until the 18th century that the industry was established on a commercial basis. When the railways came along in the 1840s, the industry prospered creating great wealth for the landowners, and occasionally great misery for the miners. An explosion in Trimdon Grange Colliery in 1882 claimed the lives of 74 miners – some of them no more than boys. And in May 1951, an underground explosion in Easington Colliery killed 81 men.

Low Force Waterfall, Upper Teesdale

Now that the industry has all but disappeared, the scars it created are being swept away. Spoil heaps have been cleared or grassed over, pit heads demolished and old industrial sites tidied up. The colliery villages such as Pity Me, Shiney Row, Bearpark, Sunniside and Quebec still exist – tight-knit communities that retain an old-style sense of belonging and sharing, and even in the most unprepossessing of villages there are delightful surprises to be discovered, such as the near perfect Saxon church at Escomb.

Coal may have been king, but County Durham's countryside has always supported an important farming industry, and Central and South Durham still retains a gentle landscape of fields, woodland, streams and narrow country lanes. This area stretches from the east coast to the Pennines in the west, and from the old border with Yorkshire in the south to the edge of the Tyne and the Wear conurbations in the north. Within this area there are picturesque villages, cottages, grand houses, museums, snug pubs, old churches and castles aplenty.

The coastline, too, has been cleaned up. An 11-mile coastal footpath snakes through the district of Easington from Seaham Hall Beach in the north to Crimdon Park in the south. Much of it is along clifftops with spectacular views down onto the beaches. This coastal area has recently been designated a National Nature Reserve.

Travelling around the region, the visitor is constantly reminded of its rich social, industrial and Christian heritage. The Romans marched along Dere Street in County

Durham, and in the 9th and 10th centuries holy men carried the body of St Cuthbert with them as they sought a place of refuge from the marauding Vikings. More recently, the railways were born in the county in 1825, with the opening of the famous Stockton and Darlington Railway.

Dominating the whole area is the city of Durham – one of Europe's finest small cities. It was here, in 1832, that England's third great university was established.

Raby Castle, Staindrop

The towns of Darlington, Stockton-on-Tees, Hartlepool and Bishop Auckland are all worthy of exploration. At one time all falling within the borders of Durham County, local government reorganisation placed Hartlepool and Stockton-on-Tees in the county of Cleveland. Now that Cleveland itself is no more, they, along with Darlington, are unitary authorities and, strictly speaking, not part of County Durham at all, but old loyalties still exist.

To the west, County Durham sweeps up to the Northern Pennines – a hauntingly beautiful area of moorland, high fells and deep, green dales. Officially designated as an Area of Outstanding Natural Beauty in 1988, the North Pennines covers almost 2,000 square kilometres. It is one of the most remote and unspoiled places in the country and has been called 'England's last wilderness'.

The great northern rivers of the Wear, the Tees, the Tyne and the Derwent have their sources here. Tumbling mountain streams have cut deep into the rock, creating the impressive waterfalls of Low Force, High Force and Cauldron Snout. These are magical places and show just how water has shaped

the Durham Dales. The area is rich in wildlife. Hen harriers, merlins and other rare species breed here, and in spring and summer the plaintive call of the curlew can often be heard.

This is ideal country for walking and cycling, though in the winter months it can be wild and inhospitable. There are numerous rights-of-way to be explored, including the C2C (coast-to-coast) cycle path. The Pennine Way cuts through County Durham in the south, close to the towns of Barnard Castle and Middleton-in-Teesdale, continuing westward through Upper Teesdale until it enters Cumbria. Further north it enters Northumberland to the west of Haltwhistle and then the Northumberland National Park.

Man has left his mark here too, for this is working countryside. The lower reaches have been farmed for centuries, and the high fells are home to many flocks of sheep. At one time there were woollen mills in Barnard Castle, providing a ready market for local sheep farmers. Lead mining was a thriving industry, with mines located at Killhope, Ireshopeburn and St John's Chapel. Middleton-in-Teesdale was once the headquarters of the London Lead Company, a great Quaker business venture.

Durham City

- 🏛 Cathedral 🏛 Castle 🏛 Churches
- 🏛 The Old Fulling Mill 🏛 DLI Museum
- 🏛 University Museum 🏛 Battle of Neville's Cross
- 🌱 Botanic Gardens 🌱 Crook Hall

Arriving in Durham by train, the visitor is presented with what must be one of the most breathtaking urban views in Europe. Towering over the tumbling roofs of the city are the magnificent towers of **Durham Cathedral** and, close by, Durham Castle.

The Cathedral is third only to Canterbury and York in ecclesiastical significance, but excels them in architectural splendour, and is the finest and grandest example of Norman architecture in Europe. This was the power base of the inordinately wealthy Prince Bishops of Durham who once exercised king-like powers in an area known as the Palatinate of Durham. The powers vested in them by William I permitted them to administer civil and criminal law, issue pardons, hold their own parliament, mint their own money, create baronetcies and give market charters. They could even raise their own army. Though these powers were never used in later years, they continued in theory right up until 1836, when the last of the Prince Bishops, Bishop William Van Mildert, died. The Palatinate Courts, however, were only abolished in 1971. It is little wonder that the County Council now proudly presents the county to visitors as 'The Land of the Prince Bishops'.

The cathedral owes its origin to the monks of Lindisfarne who, in AD 875, fled from Viking attacks, taking with them the coffin of St Cuthbert, shepherd saint of Northumbria. In AD 883 they settled at Chester-le-Street. However, further Viking raids in AD 980

Durham Cathedral

caused them to move once more, and they eventually arrived at a more easily defended site about 10 miles to the south, where the River Wear makes a wide loop round a rocky outcrop. Here, in Durham, they built the White Church, where St Cuthbert's remains were finally laid to rest.

The present cathedral building was begun by William de St Carileph or St Calais, Bishop of Durham from 1081 to 1096. William arrived at the White Church bringing with him holy relics and a group of monks and scholars from Monkwearmouth and Jarrow. Forced to flee to Normandy in 1088, having been accused of plotting against William Rufus, William returned in 1091 after a pardon, determined to replace the little church with a building of the scale and style of the splendid new churches he saw being built in France at that time. In August 1093, the foundation stones were laid, witnessed by King Malcolm

III of Scotland, famed as the soldier who slew Macbeth in battle.

The main part of the great building was erected in a mere 40 years, but over ensuing centuries each generation has added magnificent work and detail, such as the 14th-century Episcopal Throne, said to be the highest in Christendom, and the Neville Screen made from creamy marble. On the North Door is a replica of the 12th-century Sanctuary knocker used by fugitives seeking a haven. They were allowed to remain within the church for 37 days, after which time, if they had failed to settle their affairs, they were given a safe passage to the coast carrying a cross and wearing a distinctive costume.

Nothing is more moving however, than the simple fragments of carved wood that survive from St Cuthbert's coffin, made for the saint's body in AD 698 and carried around the north of England by his devoted followers before being laid to rest in the mighty cathedral. The fragments are now kept in the **Treasures of St Cuthbert Exhibition**, within the cathedral, with examples of the Prince Bishops' own silver coins. The cathedral is also the resting place for the tomb of the Venerable Bede (AD 673-735), saint, scholar and Britain's first and pre-eminent historian.

Durham Castle (see panel below), sharing the same rocky peninsula and standing close to the cathedral, was founded in 1072 and belonged to the Prince Bishops. Such was the impregnability of the site that Durham was one of the few towns in Northumbria that was never captured by the Scots. Among the castle's most impressive features are the Chapel, dating from 1080, and the Great Hall, which was built in the middle of the 13th century. The 18th-century gatehouse has a Norman core, as does the massive keep, which was rebuilt in Victorian times.

Only open to the public at limited times, the Castle is now used as a hall of residence for the students of Durham University, and the Great Hall serves as the Dining Hall of University College. Students and visitors of a nervous disposition should beware – the castle is reputedly haunted by no less than three ghosts. One is supposed to be Jane, wife of Bishop Van Mildert, and takes the form of the top half of a woman in 19th century dress. She glides

Durham Castle

Palace Green, Durham,
Co Durham DH1 3RW
Tel: 01913 344106

In 1069, three years after landing in Britain, William the Conqueror finally subdued the North of England. William recognised the defensive potential of the rocky peninsula of Durham and a castle was founded there in 1072. Nine centuries later, Durham Castle remains one of England's largest and best-preserved Norman strongholds and one of the grandest Romanesque palaces. Since 1836 it has housed the Foundation College of Durham University, England's third oldest university after Oxford and Cambridge.

🏚 historic building   🏛 museum and heritage   🏛 historic site   🐾 scenic attraction   🌿 flora and fauna

CASTLEVIEW

4 Crossgate, Durham, Co Durham DH1 4PS
Tel: 01913 868852
e-mail: castle_view@hotmail.com

Castleview is a deservedly popular B&B located within easy walking distance of all the city's main sights. Built in 1731, this fine three-storey house in a fashionable part of town is immaculately maintained by current landlady Anne Williams, who has lived here for the past 20 odd years. All six rooms are tastefully furnished and each has its own TV, tea- and coffee-making facilities, hairdryer and a private en-suite. There are also ironing and telephone facilities available to all guests. All prices are per room per night and include a full English breakfast, which is served in the elegant dining room.

Outside in the summer, hanging baskets adorn the frontage, and round the back the walls are covered with climbing plants which you can appreciate while relaxing in the pretty courtyard. Castleview has WIFI and Internet access and is a non-smoking establishment. Children over the age of 5 are welcome.

along the Norman Gallery, leaving the scent of apple blossom in her wake. A second spirit is of university tutor Frederick Copeman who, in 1880, threw himself off the tower of the cathedral. His ghost is said to haunt his former room off the Norman Gallery. A further apparition, who has been seen at various locations within the castle, is a cowled monk of uncertain identity.

The university, England's third oldest after Oxford and Cambridge, was founded in 1832 by Bishop Van Mildert. In 1837 it moved into Durham Castle, though today its many buildings are scattered throughout the south of the city. The importance of the whole area surrounding the cathedral and castle was accorded international recognition in 1987 when it was designated a UNESCO World Heritage Site.

A favourite walk past the castle and cathedral follows the footpaths that run through the woodlands on each bank of the River Wear, around the great loop. You can begin at either Framwellgate Bridge or Elvet Bridge. The path along the inside of the loop goes past **The Old Fulling Mill**, situated below the cathedral, which now houses an archaeological museum containing material from excavations in and around the city. Prebends Bridge offers spectacular views of the Cathedral. If walking isn't to your taste you can take a cruise along the river from Elvet Bridge.

The rest of Durham reflects the long history of the castle and cathedral it served. There are winding streets, such as Saddler Street and Silver Street (whose names impart their medieval origin), the ancient Market Place, elegant Georgian houses - particularly around

South Bailey - and quiet courtyards and alleyways. Much of Durham's shopping area is closed to traffic. There are several churches worth visiting such as **St Nicholas's Church** in the Market Place, **St Mary le Bow Church** in North Bailey, which houses **The Durham Heritage Centre and Museum**, and **St Oswald's Church** in Church Street. Their presence highlights the fact that, in medieval times, this was a great place of pilgrimage.

Opened in 2002 the Durham Millennium Complex incorporates the Gala Theatre, a visitor centre with a large format cinema, craft workshops and a tourist information bureau.

The **DLI Museum and Durham Art Gallery** at Aykley Heads tells the story of the county's own regiment, the Durham Light Infantry, which was founded in 1758 and lasted right up until 1968. The horrors of the First World War are shown, as is a reconstruction of a Durham street during the Second World War. Individual acts of bravery are also remembered, such as the story of Adam Wakenshaw, the youngest of a family of 13, who refused to leave his comrades after his arm

was blown off. He died in action, and was awarded a Victoria Cross. The art gallery has a changing exhibition of paintings and sculpture.

The **Durham University Oriental Museum** houses a collection of oriental art of international importance with exhibits from Ancient Egypt, Tibet, India, China, Persia and Japan. Located in parkland off Elvet Hill Road to the south of the city, the museum entrance is guarded by two stately Chinese lion-dogs.

The university also manages the 18-acre **Botanic Gardens** on Hollingside Lane (off the A167) on the south side of the city. The gardens include a large collection of North American trees, including junior-sized giant redwoods, a series of small 'gardens-within-gardens' and walks through mature woodland. Two display greenhouses with trees and plants from all over the world feature cacti and a tropical 'jungle'.

Crook Hall and Gardens (see panel below) is on Frankland Lane, a 10-minute walk north of the Millburngate Shopping Centre. Centred on a lovely 14th-century medieval manor house, the gardens are quintessentially

Crook Hall and Gardens

Frankland Lane, Durham, Co Durham DH1 5SZ
Tel: 01913 848028
e-mail: info@kbacrookhall.co.uk
website: www.crookhallgardens.co.uk

Described by Alan Titchmarsh as 'a tapestry of colourful blooms', Crook Hall is a beautiful medieval manor house surrounded by romantic gardens, which include ancient fruit trees and climbing roses.

Visitors are invited to try out the maze, hunt down the ghosts, experience the peace and tranquillity of the walled gardens, or simply relax and enjoy a homemade cream tea in the pretty little courtyard café. The Hall is just a short walk from Durham's bustling market place yet the atmosphere is one of peace and tranquillity.

🏛 historic building 🏠 museum and heritage 🏛 historic site 🏵 scenic attraction 🌿 flora and fauna

English. The hall itself, with its haunted Jacobean Room, is also open to the public.

On the western outskirts of the city, and straddling the A167, is the site of the **Battle of Neville's Cross**, fought in 1346 between Scotland and England. The Scottish army was heavily defeated, and the Scottish king, David II, was taken prisoner.

Around Durham City

FINCHALE PRIORY
4 miles N of Durham off the A167

🚶 Cocken Wood

On a minor road off the A167 lies 13th-century Finchale (pronounced 'Finkle') Priory. It was built by the monks of Durham

Cathedral as a holiday retreat on the site of a hermitage founded by St Godric in about 1115. The ruins sit on a loop of the Wear in a beautiful location, across the river from **Cocken Wood Picnic Area**, which is linked to the priory by a bridge.

LANCHESTER
8 miles NW of Durham on the A691

🏛 All Saints Church

Lanchester owes its name to the Roman fort of *Longovicium* ('The Long Fort'), which stood on a hilltop half a mile to the southwest. The fort was built to guard Dere Street, the Roman road that linked York and the north. The scant remains sit on private land, however, and can't be visited. Stone from the fort was used in the mostly Norman **All Saints Church** and

---

PLAWSWORTH HALL FARM SELF-CATERING COTTAGES & APARTMENTS

Plawsworth Hall Farm, Chester-le-Street,
Co Durham DH2 3LD
Tel: 01913 710251 Fax: 01913 712101
e-mail: plawsworth@aol.com
website: www.plawsworth.com

Plawsworth is a peaceful village located between Durham and Chester-le-Street, with about 40 houses, a convivial pub and a working farm. On that farm, **Plawsworth Hall Farm Self-catering Cottages and Apartments** offer the perfect alternative to often impersonal, often expensive, hotels and make an ideal home from home for both business and leisure guests. Traditional stone and brick farm buildings have been skilfully converted and some new builds added to provide a choice of one- and two-bedroom apartments and two- and three-bedroom cottages. All are well furnished and comprehensively equipped, with gas-fired central heating, TV, telephone, fully fitted kitchen and comfortable living/dining areas. Letting periods are very flexible, and a weekly housekeeping service is available for longer stays. No pets.

Roman pillars can be seen supporting the north aisle. There is also a Roman altar in the south porch and some superb 12th-century carvings over the vestry door in the chancel.

One place worth visiting near Lanchester is Hall Hill Farm, on the B6296 four miles southwest of the village. It's a working sheep farm, which is open to the public all year.

The area to the south of Lanchester is a typical County Durham mining area, with several small former colliery villages such as Quebec, Esh Winning, Tow Law and Cornsay Colliery.

PITTINGTON
3 miles E of Durham off the B1283

🏛 St Laurence's Church

A small village, Pittington contains one of County Durham's hidden gems – the Saxon-Norman **St Laurence's Church** at Hallgarth. The present church dates from the 11th century, on the site of what is believed to be an even earlier Saxon church. The 12th-century paintings of St Cuthbert are well worth seeing.

BRANCEPETH
4 miles SW of Durham on the A690

🏛 Castle

Brancepeth is a small estate village built by Matthew Russell in the early 1800s, with picturesque Georgian-style cottages and an 18th-century rectory. To the south, in parkland, is the imposing **Brancepeth Castle**. The original 13th-century castle was owned by the Nevills, Earls of Westmorland, and for many years was the headquarters of the Durham Light Infantry. Constantly adapted, added to and evolving ever since, the castle has been the home of the Dobson family for over 25 years. Not routinely open to the

public, tours can be arranged for a modest charge, and some of the rooms can be seen during the Craft Fairs held on the last weekends in July and November. These three-day events provide a showcase for up to 100 exhibitors whose wares range from furniture to clothing, glass to painting, pottery and much more.

Close to the castle are the remains of St Brandon's Church. In 1998 a fire destroyed everything but the four walls and tower of what was once a beautiful and historic building. The church's magnificent woodwork, commissioned by its rector John Cosin in the early 1600s, was completely destroyed. Cosin went on to become Bishop of Durham, and restored many churches in the county. Thanks to an appeal, work has begun to restore the church.

Bishop Auckland

🏛 Castle 🏛 Town Hall 🏛 St Andrew's Church

Bishop Auckland is an ancient town, standing on the major Roman thoroughfare of Dere Street. Like many County Durham towns, it owed its later prosperity to coal mining. When the surrounding pits closed, the town went into decline, but it is now gradually rediscovering itself as new industries are established. As its name implies, up until the early 19th century, this was part of the territory of the Prince Bishops of Durham who controlled what was then a scattering of small villages. Rapid expansion occurred during the 19th century and Bishop Auckland became an important market town and administrative centre for the region.

Auckland Castle, at one time the principal country residence of the Prince Bishops, is now the official residence of the Bishop of Durham. The castle began as a small 12th century manor house.

Over the years, successive bishops added to it, and looking at it today, it appears largely 17th or 18th century. But the fabric is still basically medieval, although parts of it were destroyed during the Civil War when it was the headquarters of Sir Arthur Hazlerigg, Governor of the

Auckland Castle, Bishop Auckland

North. Bishop Cosin set about making it wind- and watertight after the Restoration, turning the Great Hall into a magnificent private chapel in 1665. Dedicated to St Peter, it is reputed to be the largest private chapel in Europe.

Cosin's successor, Nathaniel, Lord Crewe, made a gift of the beautifully toned 'Father Schmidt' organ with its unusual keyboard on which the black and white keys are reversed. And in the 1880s, Bishop Joseph Lightfoot presented the fine stained glass windows, which trace the growth of Christianity in the north east, vividly depicting incidents in the lives of St Oswald, St Aidan, St Cuthbert and St Bede.

The castle's greatest treasures however are the paintings now displayed in the Long Dining Room. Created by the 17th century Spanish artist Francesco Zurburán, these monumental works, seven feet high, depict Jacob and his 12 sons, the founders of the Tribes of Israel.

The palace grounds, within which there is an 18th century deer house, are open all year round; the palace itself is only open from May to September.

A market has been held in Bishop Auckland for centuries. Opposite the present marketplace is the imposing Franco-Flemish **Bishop Auckland Town Hall**, built in the early 1860s.

While the villages immediately surrounding Bishop Auckland are mainly industrial, there are still some attractions worth seeing. At South Church is the cathedralesque **St Andrew's Church**, 157 feet long and said to be the largest parish church in the county.

On display in a working men's club at West Auckland can be found the most unlikely of trophies – the World Cup, no less. In 1910 the village's football team headed off to Italy to represent England in the first ever World Cup. It competed against teams from Germany, Italy and Switzerland, and remarkably won the cup when it beat Juventus 2-0 in the final. The team returned the following year to defend its title, and again won the trophy, which earned them the right to retain it for all time. Sadly the trophy you see today is actually a replica, as the original was stolen.

stories and anecdotes · famous people · art and craft · entertainment and sport · walks

Bishop Auckland

Distance: *3.1 miles (5.0 kilometres)*
Typical time: *120 mins*
Height gain: *50 metres*
Map: *Explorer 305 or Landranger 93*
Walk: *www.walkingworld.com ID:324*
Contributor: *Jude Howat*

Bishop Auckland is accessible via both the A688
and the A689 from the A1(M) heading
westwards. Follow signs for the town centre,
then the marketplace. Take the small road
signposted to Binchester Fort. The car park is at
the foot of the hill, by the riverside.

DESCRIPTION:

Auckland Park was the deer park attached to
Auckland Castle, home of the Bishop of
Durham. This walk is round the outer perimeter
of the park, following paths alongside farmland
and part of the Auckland Walk (a reclaimed old
railway line from Bishop Auckland to
Spennymoor). Upon completing the walk it is
worth stopping at Auckland Castle or the park
before returning to the car park.

FFATURES:

Pub, Castle, Wildlife, Great Views.

WALK DIRECTIONS:

1 | Leave the car park and return to the
roadside. Turn left and walk along the
road out of town for ¾ of a km. After
the bridge, watch out for the footpath
sign heading up the hill.

2 | Follow the waymarked signs up the
hill, following the outer wall of the
park. There are quite a few stiles on
this section of the walk.

3 | As the path splits, with one going towards the
farm houses, keep to the right-hand path. This
continues up the hill close to the edge of the
fields. Basically the path continues in a straight
line uphill towards some trees, which is where
the railway line was.

4 | At the top of the hill you will reach a railway
bridge. Cross over the bridge and come down
the steps to reach the railway path.

5 | At the end of the golf course you will see a
stile into a field on the right. Take this path and
follow it until you reach the main road. Note, you
will cross a small road that leads into the golf
course, but continue on the path.

6 | On reaching the main road, turn right and
continue down the hill for around 200m. Take
next road signposted to the marketplace which
will lead you past the entrance to the castle.

7 | You can go either way round the marketplace,
although by going clockwise you will get the
nicest views of the architecture.

8 | On the far side of the marketplace you will
see the road down the hill to the car park, just in
front of the white pub.

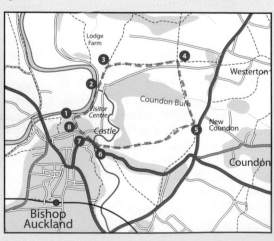

BROOM HILL FARM

West Auckland, Co Durham DL14 9PJ
Tel: 01388 834564 Fax: 01388 835299
e-mail: sales@broomhillfarm.co.uk
website: www.broomhillfarm.co.uk

After nearly 20 years of hard work, driven by their passion for fine food, developing the site and building up a potential customer base, Tracy and Matthew Betney opened **Broom Hill Farm** to the public in September 2007. Their aim is to provide customers with traditionally prepared cuts of meat and meat products, second to none in taste and quality. They breed and rear their own livestock, butcher it on site and produce all their own animal feed. The cures for the bacon and gammon are developed in-house and they make their own sausages. They also sell free-range eggs, farmhouse cheeses and other dairy produce, preserves, pickles and bread, as well as pies and quiches from their on-site bakery. Many of the superb foodstuffs for sale can be enjoyed in the tea room, which serves sandwiches, quiches, pies, all-day breakfasts, teas and coffees. Broom Hill has several attractions for

all the family, including animals to see on the farm, a waterwheel dating back more than 300 years, and a millpond reinstated to re-create the momentum for the wheel. The entrance to this splendid place is on the A688 west of Bishop Auckland towards the junction with the A68.

Around Bishop Auckland

SHILDON

2 miles SE of Bishop Auckland on the B6282

🏛 Locomotion

Timothy Hackworth served from 1825 as the resident engineer on the Stockton and Darlington Railway. In 1840 he resigned and left in order to develop the Soho Engine Works at Shildon and make his own locomotives. The first trains to run in Russia and Nova Scotia were built here. Today, the Engine Works, plus his house, can be seen at **Locomotion**, where the displays give a fascinating insight into the early days of rail and steam power in England, including a full size replica of the 'Sans Pareil' locomotive, built for the Liverpool-to-Manchester railway. This newly re-developed complex demonstrates vividly what made Shildon the first railway town in the world. It attracts thousands of tourists each year who want to find out about the transport revolution of the

Locomotion, Shildon

early 1800s. You don't need to be a railway buff to enjoy the museum. It has plenty of hands-on and interactive exhibits, and won the Pride of Northumberland award in 1999 for being the best visitor attraction of the year. It is open from Good Friday to the end of October, Wednesday to Saturday from 10 to 5.

BINCHESTER
1 mile N of Bishop Auckland off the A689

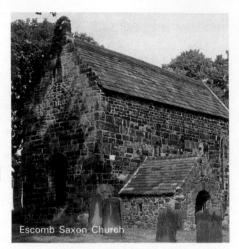

Escomb Saxon Church

🏛 Roman Fort

Binchester Roman Fort, known to the Romans as Vinovia, was built around AD 80. It was one of a chain of forts built along Dere Street, and has the best-preserved Roman military bath house in Britain, complete with a pillared hypocaust heating system. In addition to acting as a military centre controlling the local area, the fort also provided a stopping-off place for troops and supplies heading towards Hadrian's Wall. A portion of Dere Street has been preserved here.

CROOK
5 miles NW of Bishop Auckland on the A689

Crook is a small, spacious town with a wide square which, in summer, is full of flowers. At one time it was a centre of coal mining, and the quaintly named Billy Row to the north of the town centre is a typical coalfield hamlet of miners' cottages.

ESCOMB
2 miles NW of Bishop Auckland off the A688

🏛 Church of St John the Evangelist

In the small village of Escomb is one of the true hidden gems of County Durham – **St John the Evangelist Church**, built using stone from nearby Binchester Roman Fort. This is one of only three complete Saxon churches in Britain, and is typically Saxon in

layout, with its long, high nave and tiny chancel arch, which may have been taken from the Roman fort at Binchester. In the south wall of the nave is a curious sundial surrounded by serpents and surmounted by what may be a mythical beast.

WITTON-LE-WEAR
4 miles NW of Bishop Auckland off the A68

Overlooking the River Wear are the hillside terraces of the village of Witton-le-Wear, noted for its handsome green, its open views, attractive cottages and a pele tower attached to fragments of a medieval manor house in the High Street. The grounds of Witton Castle, a medieval fortified house just across the river, have been incorporated into a recreational area.

Darlington

🏛 St Cuthbert's Church   🏛 Railway Centre   🚂 Train

Darlington is an important regional centre serving the southern part of County Durham, Teesdale and much of North Yorkshire. It was founded in Saxon times, and has a bustling town centre with one of the largest marketplaces in England. On its west side is the Old Town Hall and indoor market, with an imposing Clock Tower designed by Alfred Waterhouse in 1864.

There are many fine buildings in Darlington, most notably **St Cuthbert's Church** with its tall spire on the east side of the marketplace. It is almost cathedral-like in its proportions, and was built by Bishop Pudsey between 1183 and 1230 as a collegiate church. Its slender lancet windows and steep roof enhance its beauty, which has earned it the name 'The Lady of the North'.

High Row, with its elevated street of shops, forms part of a compact but characterful shopping centre. The tall buildings evolved due to the narrowness of the plots of land in medieval times. The façades are pierced by tunnels, which at one time gave access to rear gardens. These have long since been built over and turned into yards that lend their name to this part of town. The 'Yards' now contain shops and small businesses and are public rights of way between High Row and Skinnergate.

Perhaps Darlington's greatest claim to fame lies in the role it played, with neighbouring Stockton, in the creation of the world's first commercially successful public railway, which opened in 1825. **Locomotion No 1** pulled a mixed train of coal wagons and wagons with seats on the journey to Stockton at an average speed of 12mph. It was the Darlington Quaker and banker, Edward Pease, who became the main driving force behind the scheme to link the Durham coalfields with the port of Stockton.

The original Darlington Station, built in 1842, was located at North Road Station. Today it serves as the **Darlington Railway Centre and Museum** (see panel below) – a museum of national importance, which houses relics of the pioneering Stockton and Darlington Railway. This includes a replica of Stephenson's Locomotion No 1, a Stockton and Darlington first-class coach carriage built in 1846, a Second World War newsstand, the **Derwent** (the earliest surviving Darlington-built locomotive) and even Victorian urinals. To the north of Bank Top station, on the main London-Edingburgh line, a notice indicates where the old Stockton-Darlington line crosses the main line

Darlington Railway Centre & Museum

North Road Station, Darlington DL3 6ST
Tel: 01325 460532 Fax: 01325 28/746
e-mail: museum@darlington.gov.uk
website: www.drcm.org.uk

Experience the atmosphere of the steam railway age as you step back in time to the North Road Passenger Station of 1842. See Stephenson's Locomotion, which hauled its first train on the Stockport and Darlington Railway in 1825. Explore the railway heritage of North East England through a collection of engines, carriages and wagons. Open daily 10-5pm, all year except 25th and 26th December and 1st January.

So much early railway history is to be seen in this part of County Durham that National Rail have named their local Bishop Auckland-Darlington-Middlesbrough line the Heritage Line.

Continuing with the railways theme, there's an unusual engine to be seen in Morton Retail Park, to the east of the town, off the A66. **Train** is a life-size brick sculpture, designed by sculptor David Mach, of the fastest-ever steam locomotive, *Mallard*. Bricks are not the first materials you associate with speed but Mach's replica of the streamlined record-holder is completely convincing and very impressive. It surges out from a tunnel of earth, its chimney belching smoke, which, incredibly, is also made of brick.

Around Darlington

GAINFORD
7 miles W of Darlington on the A67

🏛 St Mary's Church   🏛 Gainford Hall

Gainford village sits just north of the Tees. At its core is a jostling collection of quaint 18th- and 19th-century cottages and houses grouped around a village green.

At the southwest corner of the green is **St Mary's Church** – a large church, built mostly in the 12th century from stone that is believed to have come from Piercebridge Roman fort, three miles to the east. Certainly a Roman altar was found built into the tower during the restoration of 1864-65, and it can be seen in the museum of Durham Cathedral.

Gainford Hall is a large Jacobean mansion built by the Rev John Cradock in the early 1600s. Though not open to the public, it can be viewed from the road. It's hard to believe that in the 19th century this quiet village was a

spa, visited by people from all over the north of England. Some way away along the banks of the Tees to the west, a basin can be seen where the sulphurous waters were collected.

HEIGHINGTON
5 miles N of Darlington off the A6072

🏛 St Michael's Church

Heighington is an attractive village with neat cottages and a large green. **St Michael's Church** is predominantly Norman, and has a pre-Reformation oak pulpit with prayers inscribed on it for its donors, Alexander and Agnes Fletcher. About three miles west of the village, near Bolam, is the shaft of a 9th-century cross known as the Legs Cross.

LOW DINSDALE
4 miles SE of Darlington off the A67

🏛 Church of St John the Baptist

A visit on foot or by car to Low Dinsdale is well worthwhile, as the 12th-century red sandstone **St John the Baptist Church**, surrounded by copper beeches, is worthy of a postcard. Opposite stands a 16th-century manor house built on the site of a moated Norman manor owned by the Siward family. They later changed their name to Surtees, and became well-known throughout the north.

MIDDLETON ST GEORGE
3 miles E of Darlington off the A67

🏛 St George's Church

Middleton St George is a pleasant village on the banks of the River Tees to the east of Darlington, close to Teesside International Airport – once an airfield from which British and Canadian bombers flew during the Second World War. **St George's Church** dates from the 13th century with 18th- and 19th-century additions, and is detached from the village, standing among fields. Curiously, the stonework has been heavily patched with brick at some point. It is thought to have been built on the site of an old Saxon church and the Victorian pews are rather incongruous – more like old-fashioned waiting room seats than pews.

The nearby village of Middleton One Row is aptly named – consisting of a single row of Georgian cottages. The cottages have inevitably been altered over the years as the arrival of the railway inspired development in the region.

PIERCEBRIDGE
4½ miles W of Darlington on the A67

🏛 Roman Fort

Piercebridge Roman Fort

Driving past the picturesque village green of Piercebridge, most motorists will be unaware that they are passing through the centre of a once important **Roman Fort**. Piercebridge was one of a chain of forts on Dere Street, which linked the Roman headquarters at York with the north. Other forts in the chain were located at Catterick to the south and Binchester, just outside Bishop Auckland, to the north. The remains of the fort, which are still visible today, can be dated from coin evidence to around AD 270. The site is always open and admission is free. Finds from this site are housed in the Bowes Museum at Barnard Castle.

SEDGEFIELD
9 miles NE of Darlington on the A689

🏛 St Edmund's Church   🐾 Hardwick Hall Country Park

Sedgefield, famous nowadays for its race course, is a small town whose market charter was issued in 1315. The grand 15th-century tower of **St Edmund's Church** dominates the village green and the cluster of Georgian and early Victorian houses. It is famous for its intricately carved Cosin woodwork, which was on a par with the woodwork lost when Brancepeth church was destroyed by fire in 1998. Cosin's son-in-law, Denis Granville, was rector here in the late 17th century, and it was at this time that the woodwork was installed.

Hardwick Hall Country Park lies to the west of the town, beyond the A177. Developed as a pleasure garden between 1748 and 1792 the gardens were laid out and the ornamental buildings designed by the architect James Paine. The hall is now a luxury hotel, but the 50-acre park with its network of woodland walks and Gothic folly is open to the public.

Stockton-on-Tees

🏛 Parish Church 🏛 Green Dragon Museum

🏛 Preston Hall Museum

Stockton-on-Tees found fame with the opening of the Stockton and Darlington railway in 1825, constructed so that coal from the mines of South Durham could have access to the Tees, where it would be shipped south to London. The opening of the railways encouraged the growth of industry, and the subsequent discovery of ironstone in the Cleveland Hills in the 1850s, was to transform the fortunes of the town, providing great wealth for many of its citizens.

Nowadays it is a large, busy town, and no longer a part of County Durham after local government reorganisation created the county of Cleveland, and Stockton found itself on the wrong side of the border. When Cleveland itself was dissolved, the town became a unitary authority, taking in parts of former North Yorkshire.

In the centre of Stockton's High Street is the Old Town Hall and market cross dating from the mid-18th century, and in Theatre Yard off the High Street is the **Green Dragon Museum**, set in a former sweet factory

warehouse. Here the visitor can explore Stockton's heritage.

The red brick Parish Church was built between 1712 and 1713, and is one of only a handful of Anglican churches in England without a dedication. Its official title is **The Parish Church of Stockton-on-Tees**, though for many years it has been informally called St Thomas's. This unofficial dedication came from a chapel of ease that stood on the site when Stockton was part of the parish of Norton.

Captain James Cook is said to have served the early part of his apprenticeship in Stockton. A full-size replica of his ship, HM Bark *Endeavour*, is moored at Castlegate Quay on Stockton's riverside. Alongside is the *Teesside Princess*, a river cruiser that takes visitors on a pleasure trip as far inland as Yarm, stopping at Preston Hall. From the Quay visitors can walk across the stunning Millennium Footbridge linking Stockton with Thornaby on the opposite bank of the Tees.

Other famous characters connected with the town include John Walker, the inventor of the friction match, who was born in Stockton in 1781, and Thomas Sheraton, the furniture maker and designer, born here in 1751 and married in St Mary's Church, Norton. One of the town's citizens with a more unusual claim to fame was Ivy Close, who won Britain's first ever beauty contest held in Newcastle in 1908.

Preston Hall Museum, set in 110 acres of parkland to the south of the town on the banks of the Tees, is housed in the former home of local shipbuilder, Robert Ropner. Exhibits describe how life was lived in the area at the time the Hall was built in 1825. There is a re-created period street, a fully furnished drawing room of the 1820s and a collection of Arms and Armoury in the cellar. The museums most famous exhibit is

The Diceplayers, painted by Georges de la Tour in the 17th century.

Stockton may no longer be a busy port, but in recent years there has been a lot of development along the banks of the Tees. The spectacular £54 million Tees Barrage, built to stop the flow of pollution from the chemical plants being carried upstream by the tides, has transformed an 11-mile stretch of river. Features include Britain's finest purpose built White Water canoe slalom course, navigation lock, fish pass and recreation site with picnic area.

YARM
4 miles S of Stockton-on-Tees on the A67

Set within a loop of the River Tees, Yarm was a prosperous river port as far back as the 1300s, trading in wine, flax and sheepskins to tanneries set along the river banks. Its broad main street, one of the widest in England, is still lined with some fine Georgian houses and coaching inns but the bustling river traffic has gone, drawn away to the superior amenities of Stockton and Middlesbrough. Standing in the centre of the main street is an elegant Town Hall of 1710 with marks on its walls recording the levels of past river floods – the most damaging filling the whole marketplace to a depth of four feet. From this street, wynds – quaint passageways – lead down to the river where you can stroll along the banks and admire the handsome old bridge originally built around 1400. The most impressive structure, however, is the railway viaduct with its 40 arches soaring above the rooftops and extending for almost half a mile.

Captain Cook Museum

Stewart Park, Marton, Middlesbrough, TS7 6AS
Tel: 01642 311211
website: www.captcook-ne.co.uk

The **Captain Cook Birthplace Museum** opened on the 28th October 1978 - the 250th anniversary of Cook's birth. It is housed in a purpose-built building in Stewart Park, Marton, Middlesbrough, close to the granite urn marking the site of Cook's birthplace cottage. The museum tells the story of one of the world's greatest navigators and mariners through themed display galleries, temporary exhibitions, associated activities and events and a lively education programme. There is full disabled access throughout and additional facilities such as the Discovery Room (education and activities), the Endeavour Room (meetings and events), the Resolution Resources Room (archive and research), gift/book shop and a café. Entry is free.

Yarm has another important railway connection since it was at a meeting at the George and Dragon Hotel in 1820 that initial plans were drawn up for the construction of the Stockton and Darlington Railway, the first of all public railways.

Middlesbrough

🏛 Transporter Bridge   🏛 Ormesby Hall

🏛 Captain Cook Birthplace Museum

🏛 Dorman Museum

Dominating the skyline of this busy town is the **Transporter Bridge**. Opened in 1911, it is the only working bridge of its kind in Britain. It can carry nine cars or 200 pedestrians on each crossing. Captain Cook was born here in 1728 and his life story can be charted in the **Captain Cook Birthplace Museum** (see panel above). The **Dorman Museum** has themed displays on natural history, social history and world cultures. On the south edge of the town is the National Trust's **Ormesby Hall**, a beautiful 18th-century mansion.

Around Middlesbrough

KIRKLEATHAM
5 miles E of Middlesbrough on the A174

🏛 Museum   🍃 Owl Centre

Two good reasons for a visit here. **Kirkleatham Museum** is a 17th-century house with exhibitions on art, coast and country, and the region's ironstone mining and iron and steel heritage. **Kirkleatham Owl Centre** has one of the country's most important collections of owls, along with falcons, buzzards, vultures and caracaras. The Centre is open Tuesday to Sunday in summer, Thursday to Sunday out of season.

GUISBOROUGH
8 miles E of Middlesbrough on the A171

🏛 Priory

The stark remains of **Guisborough Priory** stand on an elevated site overlooked by the Cleveland Hills. Founded by the great landowner Robert de Bruis in 1119, the monastery became one of the most powerful

LEVEN CRAFTS

7-9 Chaloner Mews, Chaloner Street, Guisborough, North Yorkshire TS14 6SA
Tel: 01287 610207
e-mail: info@levencrafts.co.uk
website: www.levencrafts.co.uk

Stan and Beryl Frank who have owned and run the award winning **Leven Crafts** for 10 years, provide everything for cross-stitch, embroidery, patchwork and knitting, and are the region's leading stockists of many brands.

Shoppers will find the friendly and knowledgeable staff ready to help with advice on the huge range of products including – cross-stitch from Lanarte, Rico, Dimensions; embroidery threads and tapestry wools from DMC, Anchor, Appleton's, Caron, Kreinik, Paterna; knitting yarns from Sirdar, Designer Yarns, Rowan, Patons; patchwork fabrics from Moda, Stof, Hoffman, Makower; lighting and accessories from Daylight Company, BWH frames and stands, Lowery.

Leven Crafts hosts a variety of courses and group activities, including day workshops, knit and chat sessions, sewing retreat weekends and comprehensive 10-week courses on all aspects of embroidery, patchwork, quilting, knitting and crochet work.

Opening Hours 9.30–4.30 Monday–Saturday.

in Yorkshire. Much extended in 1200, and rebuilt after a fire destroyed the whole site, the estate was sold in 1540 to a Thomas Chaloner, who cannibalised much of the fabric to grace ornamental gardens at his grand mansion nearby. Nothing remains of that mansion, and of the Priory itself the great arch at the east end is the most striking survival. The grounds are a popular venue for picnics.

Redcar

🚣 Zetland Lifeboat Museum

This popular town and holiday resort is home to the oldest lifeboat in the world, on display at the **Zetland Lifeboat Museum**. It was built in 1802 by H Greathead and stands among exhibitions on fishing history, models,

photographs, paintings and cards in a handsome listed building in King Street.

Around Redcar

SALTBURN-BY-THE-SEA
5 miles SE of Redcar on the A174

🏛 Inclined Tramway   🏛 Smugglers Heritage Centre

🌿 Italian Gardens

This charming seaside town (complete with a pier) at the northern end of the 36-mile Heritage Coast, is largely the work of the Victorians. It stands on a cliff high above a long, sandy beach, and to transport visitors from the town to the promenade and beach, the ingenious **Inclined Tramway** was built. It is still in use, the oldest such tramway to survive in Britain. A miniature railway runs from the seafront to the **Italian Gardens** and the Woodland Centre, set between the formal pleasure gardens and the wild natural woodland beyond. The pre-Victorian Saltburn was a notorious haunt of smugglers, and those days are brought to life in the **Smugglers Heritage Centre**, set in old fishermen's cottages next to the Ship Inn in Old Saltburn.

Hartlepool

🏛 Sandwellgate	🏛 St Hilda's Church
🏛 Historic Quay	🏛 HMS Trincomalee
🏛 Museum	🎨 Art Gallery

There are really two Hartlepools – the old town on the headland, and the newer part with the marina and town centre, formerly known as West Hartlepool. Up until 1968 they were separate boroughs, but have now been combined under the one name. The town, like Stockton-on-Tees and Darlington, is a unitary authority.

A proud maritime town, the old part of Hartlepool dates back centuries. In the Middle

Ages it was the only port within County Durham that was allowed to trade outside the Palatinate, thus confirming its importance. After the Norman Conquest, the Bruce family, whose most notable member was Robert the Bruce, King of Scotland, acquired the town. In 1201 King John bestowed a market charter on Hartlepool and ordered that walls be built to defend it against the marauding Scots. Today, parts of the wall remain and continue to stand guard over the headland. There is a particularly fine gatehouse, called **Sandwellgate**, with solid turrets on either side. Go through the pointed archway and you find yourself on the beach.

Built by the Bruces as a burial place, the ornate 13th-century **St Hilda's Church** stands on the site of a monastery founded by St Aidan in AD 647. The church is dedicated to St Hilda – its most famous abbess, celebrated for her teachings and her mentoring of a poor cowherd Caedmon, now regarded as the creator of religious verse. Hilda subsequently went on to found the great monastery at Whitby, where the Synod of Whitby was held in AD 664. The church houses a collection of religious artefacts, Saxon wall carvings and a tomb, made of Frosterley marble, believed to be that of Robert the Bruce. Parts of the cemetery were excavated in the 19th century, and some of the finds are on display in Durham and Newcastle.

Hartlepool's harbour gradually went into decline, and by the early 1700s the place was no more than a fishing village. In 1835 work started on opening up the harbour once more, and rail

Hartlepool Marina

Hartlepool Historic Quay & Museum

Jackson Dock, Maritime Avenue,
Hartlepool, TS24 0XZ
Tel: 01429 860006 Fax: 01429 867332
e-mail: historic.quay@hartlepool.gov.uk
website: www.thisishartlepool.com

Open every day all year round and voted one of the top six Heritage and History attractions in the UK, **Hartlepool Historic Quay and Museum** is a fun day out for all the family. Here you will find a re-creation of an 18th-century seaport, which tells the story of life at sea at the time of Captain Cook and Nelson and the Battle of Trafalgar. As well as the coffee shop and gift shop, authentic reconstructions of harbour-

side shops surround the Quay, including gunsmiths, tailors and instrument makers. A film presentation shows how two brothers were pressganged into serving aboard ship and 'Fighting Ships' lets you experience the noise and drama of a naval sea battle.

Guided tours are available of HMS Trincomalee, launched in Bombay in 1817. The oldest floating warship in Britain, it has been lovingly restored at Hartlepool Historic Quay.

The Museum tells the story of Hartlepool from prehistoric times to the present day and includes exhibits such as sea monsters, a Celtic 'Roundhouse', the first 'gas illuminated lighthouse', models, computer interactive displays and PSS *Wingfield* - a fully restored Paddle Steamer.

links were established with the coalfields. But the project faced stiff competition. In 1847 work started on the West Harbour and Coal Dock, and by 1860 it was thriving with timber and shipyards. Other docks were opened and Ralph Ward Jackson, a local entrepreneur, instigated the building of a new town with streets of terraced houses to accommodate the workers. So West Hartlepool was born.

On December 16th 1914 Hartlepool was the first town in Britain to suffer from enemy action during the First World War when it was shelled by German warships lying off the coast.

Nowadays, the town is a thriving shopping centre, with some interesting tourist attractions, including the **Hartlepool Historic Quay and Museum** (see panel above). A small seaport has been constructed around one of the old docks, showing what life was like in the early part of the 19th century when Britain was at war with France. Grouped around the small dock are various businesses and shops, such as a printer, gunsmith, naval tailor, swordsmith and instrument maker. Visitors can also go aboard **HMS Trincomalee**, a British warship originally launched in 1817. Open every day all

📖 stories and anecdotes 🦆 famous people ✂ art and craft 🖉 entertainment and sport 𓂃 walks

year round, the site was voted one of the top six Heritage and History attractions in the UK.

Next door is the **Hartlepool Museum**, with exhibits depicting life in the town through the ages. It features tales of 'sea monsters' and the legend of the Hartlepool monkey. Washed ashore on a piece of wreckage during the Napoleonic Wars, local fishermen, unable to understand the monkey's gibberings, presumed it to be a French spy and hung it from a gibbet on Fish Sands. Visitors to the museum can have coffee aboard the PSS *Wingfield Castle*, an old paddle steamer.

Hartlepool Art Gallery is housed within a beautifully-restored Victorian church on Church Square. It features a collection of contemporary art and photographic exhibitions. A 100-feet-high viewing tower affords the visitor great views of the town. The local tourist information office is located here, too.

Around Hartlepool

BILLINGHAM
5 miles SW of Hartlepool off the A19

🏛 St Cuthbert's Church

Modern Billingham grew up as a result of the great chemical plants that surrounded the River Tees. Although the town looks modern, it is in fact an ancient place, possibly founded by Bishop Ecgred of Lindisfarne in the 9th century. **St Cuthbert's Church** has a 10th-century Saxon tower, and Saxon walls survive in the nave. The chancel was rebuilt and widened in 1939 to provide for the town's growing population due to the influx of workers to the chemical plants. In August, Billingham hosts the week-long Billingham

International Folklore Festival. Close by is the attractive village of Wolviston.

ELWICK
4 miles W of Hartlepool off the A19

🏛 St Peter's Church

Elwick is a small, pretty village with patches of village green running up each side of a main street lined with neat, unassuming cottages. **St Peter's Church** has a nave dating from the 13th century. The chancel was rebuilt in the 17th century using materials from the previous chancel, and its tower was added on in 1813. On either side of the chancel arch are two small Saxon carvings – possibly fragments of grave markers.

HART
2 miles NW of Hartlepool on the A179

🏛 Church of St Mary Magdalene

In this quiet village stands the mother church of Hartlepool – **Church of St Mary Magdalene** with its varied examples of architecture. The nave is Saxon, the tower and font are Norman, and the chancel is early 19th century.

On the outer wall of the White Hart Inn is a figurehead, said to have been a relic from the *Rising Sun*, which was shipwrecked off Hartlepool in 1861.

PETERLEE
6 miles N of Hartlepool off the A19

🏛 St Mary's Church

🐑 Castle Eden Dene Nature Reserve

Peterlee is a new town, established in 1948 to rehouse the mining families from the colliery villages around Easington and Shotton. The town has a modern shopping centre, a tourist information office and a market. Close by is the village of **Easington** whose fine old **St Mary's Church** sits on a low hill. The church tower is Norman, and the interior contains some examples of Cosin-style woodwork.

Castle Eden Dene National Nature Reserve, on the south side of the town, is of national importance, being one of the largest woodlands in the North East that has not been planted or extensively altered by man. It covers 500 acres and lies in a steep-sided valley on magnesian limestone, with a wide variety of native trees and shrubs, wild flowers, bird life and butterflies, including the Castle Eden Argus, which is found only in eastern County Durham. There is a network of footpaths, some steep and narrow. Visitors are requested to keep to paths at all times to avoid damage.

SEAL SANDS
3 miles S of Hartlepool off the A689

Standing in the shadows of Hartlepool Nuclear Power Station is Seal Sands and the Teesmouth Field Centre. Local organisations have come together to protect and enhance the marshes, tidal flats and dunes here on the north shore of the Tees estuary. The area is protected as a Nature Reserve and popular with people who come to view its large Common and Grey seal population and thousands of migratory birds.

TRIMDON
9 miles W of Hartlepool on the B1278

🏚 St Mary Magdalene Church

There are a trio of villages with the word 'Trimdon' in their name – Trimdon Grange, Trimdon Colliery and Trimdon itself. It's a quiet village with a wide main street and the unpretentious medieval **St Mary Magdalene Church**.

Trimdon Colliery is two miles to the northeast, and it was here, in 1882, that the Trimdon Colliery pit disaster took place. A great underground explosion claimed the lives of 74 miners.

Consett

🏛 Shotley Bridge 🌊 Hownsgill Viaduct
🌲 Derwent Walk Country Park 🌲 Allensford
🌲 Deneburn Wood

Steel-making first started in this area of County Durham at **Shotley Bridge**, when craftsmen from Germany set up their furnaces in the 1600s and began making swords and cutlery. When the railway came here to serve the local iron works and surrounding collieries in the 19th century, Shotley Bridge began to develop something of a reputation as a spa town, and its popularity as such is evident from the many fine houses to be seen here, such as Dial House.

Steel-making on a grand scale began in Consett in 1840, when the Derwent Iron Company built two blast furnaces. By 1890 over 7,500 people were employed in the industry, and over one million tonnes of steel were being produced. In the late 1960s, 6,000 people were still employed in the steelworks, though this wasn't to last. The demand for steel dropped, and in 1980 the works closed forever.

Consett is now cleaning itself up. Land reclamation schemes have smartened up the area where the steelworks once stood, and its attendant spoil heaps have made way for green hillocks dotted with young trees. The countryside outside the town has some interesting places to visit.

A redundant railway line north of the town is linked to the **Derwent Walk Country**

COUNTRY HOMES AND GIFTS & GALLERY COFFEE SHOP

22 Front Street, Lanchester, Co. Durham DH7 0ER
Tel: 01207 520383
e-mail: info@countryhomesandgifts.co.uk
website: www.countryhomesandgifts.co.uk

Centrally located in the picturesque, historic village of Lanchester, **Country Homes and Gifts** offers an eclectic range of quality giftware and home furnishings, all personally sourced for quality and price by the owners . You'll find silver and costume jewellery sourced from companies in the UK and Europe, Thailand, Australia and China; distinctive fashion handbags and leather ware by leading manufacturers such as Gigi, Smith & Canova, Fabio Derrici, Visconti, Rich Bags and Leathersmith of London. Home accessories on offer include cushions and soft furnishings by Evans Lichfield and RV Astley, table lamps and table ware, decorative glassware, and small pieces of occasional decorative furniture.

There's more: quality greeting cards and stationery; Lanchester souvenir linen ware, prints and mugs; Collectable Bears and door stops by Trendle from America; scented candles, pot pourri, room fragrances and oils, and aromatics, perfume, bath salts, gels and soaps by Arran Aromatics from Scotland. And when you've browsed and bought, enjoy a relaxing coffee, espresso or latte in the Gallery Coffee Shop which also serves snacks and light lunches, all home-made to order. Open Mon-Sat 9:30am to 5pm.

THE FAT QUARTERS

No. 5 Chopwell Road, Blackhall Mill,
Newcastle-upon-Tyne NE17 7TN
Tel: 01207 565 728
e-mail: sales@thefatquarters.co.uk
website: www.thefatquarters.co.uk

The Fat Quarters is a patchwork and quilting supplies shop based in Blackhall Mill, about 5 miles outside Newcastle. Originally established by Kim Suleman in August 2005, it provides a wide range of quilting and patchwork related goods and services. You'll find just about everything necessary for these crafts in The Fat Quarters colourful showroom or on its website - anything from mother-of-pearl buttons to pattern books; from waddings and interfacings to needles and threads. In addition the shop sells speciality books, patterns and magazines. The shop is also the only retail outlet in the north selling Husquarvana Viking sewing machines. As well as selling supplies of fabrics, thread and accessories, The Fat Quarters also offer lessons, help and advice. A wide range of classes, from beginners level up to the advanced quilter, is available and the shop hosts regular clubs from Monday to Saturday. The shop has been attracting enthusiastic quilters from most parts of the North East Region where this craft has a long history. For example, Beamish Museum has a very famous collection.

Park. The park covers 425 acres of woodland and riverside meadow, and the Derwent Walk itself is the track bed of the old Derwent Valley Railway between Consett and Swalwell. The main walk is 11 miles long, and suitable for cycles, horses and wheelchairs. It gives access to a number of paths, which include nature trails, the South Tyne Cycleway and the Heritage Way. Swalwell Visitor Centre, situated at the northern end of the Derwent Walk, is the starting point for a history trail and has a large pond and butterfly garden. There is another visitors' centre at Thornley Woodlands.

The local council has produced a small guidebook outlining various walks, none more than six-and-a-half miles long, near the town. To the southwest of Consett, almost in the North Pennines, is **Allensford Park**. It sits off the A68, on the County Durham and Northumberland border, and on the banks of the Derwent. It has a picnic park, caravan site and woodland walks. **Deneburn Wood**, a 10-acre plot of woodland with some delightful walks, also contains wood carvings by well-known sculptor David Gross.

To the south of the town is **Hownsgill**

Viaduct, constructed in 1857 to take the track of the Stanhope and Tyne Railway. Visitors can now walk across it, and there are some spectacular views.

Around Consett

EBCHESTER
10 miles SW of Gateshead on the A694

> St Ebba's Church

Ebchester is the site of a Roman fort called Vindomora, and some scant remains can be seen in the churchyard of **St Ebba's Church**. It was one of a string of forts on Dere Street, the Roman road that linked York with the north. Inside the church are a number of inscribed Roman stones, including an altar to the god Jupiter, 'the greatest and the best'.

Chester-le-Street

> Church of St Mary & St Cuthbert   Lumley Castle
> Ankers House Museum
> Waldridge Fell Country Park

Chester-le-Street is a busy market town built around the confluence of Cong Burn and the River Wear. There was a Roman fort here at one time, and the street on which the town once stood was a Roman road, later replaced by the Great North Road.

The medieval **St Mary's and St Cuthbert's Church** is built on the site of a cathedral established in AD 883 by the monks of Lindisfarne carrying the body of St Cuthbert. His

Lumley Castle, Chester-le-Street

stories and anecdotes   famous people   art and craft   entertainment and sport   walks

coffin rested here for 113 years until the monks took it to its final resting place at Durham. There are no less than 14 effigies (not all of them genuine) of members of the Lumley family within the church, though they don't mark the sites of their graves. Next to the church is the **Ankers House Museum**, situated in the medieval anchorite. Between 1383 and 1547, various anchorites, or Christian hermits, lived here.

Lumley Castle, to the east across the River Wear, was built in 1389 by Sir Ralph Lumley, whose descendant, Sir Richard Lumley, became the 1st Earl of Scarborough in the 1690s. In the early 18th century it was refashioned by the architect Vanbrugh for the 2nd Earl, and turned into a magnificent stately home. But gradually the castle fell out of favour with the Lumley family, and they chose to stay in their estates in Yorkshire instead. For a while it was owned by Durham University before being turned into the luxurious hotel that it is today.

Waldridge Fell Country Park, two miles southwest of Chester-le-Street and close to Waldridge village, is County Durham's last surviving area of lowland heathland. A car park and signed footpaths give access to over 300 acres of open countryside, rich in natural history.

Beamish Museum

Beamish, County Durham DH9 0RG
Tel: 01913 704000 Fax: 01913 704001
e-mail: museum@beamish.org.uk
website: www.beamish.org.uk

No trip to County Durham is complete without a trip to the award-winning **North of England Open Air Museum at Beamish**. Set in 300 acres of countryside, it illustrates life in the North of England in the early 1800s and 1900s. There is so much to see. Stroll down a cobbled street full of shops, banks and offices, visit an old Methodist chapel, find out how life was lived on a farm in the late 19th century, take a trip on a tram or steam train, visit an old dentist's surgery (and be grateful you didn't live in those days and needed a filling!), walk through a colliery village, and go down a drift mine.

You can also see the world's third oldest surviving railway engine, which dates from 1822, housed in a specially created Great Engine Shed. There's also Pockerley Manor and Horse Yard, based on a small fortified manor house. Here you experience life as it was lived 200 years ago. Stroll the terraced gardens, walk through the fine horse yard, and see the costumes from that time.

Beamish is justly famous as a great day out for all the family. Reasonably priced meals and snacks are available, and there's a friendly shop where you can buy souvenirs.

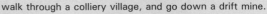
🏛 historic building　🏛 museum and heritage　🏛 historic site　🝆 scenic attraction　🌿 flora and fauna

Around Chester-le-Street

BEAMISH
4 miles N of Chester-le-Street on the A693

🏠 North of England Open Air Museum

🏛 Causey Arch 🏠 Tanfield Railway

The award-winning **Beamish, The North of England Open Air Museum** (see panel opposite) is situated in 300 acres of beautiful County Durham countryside and vividly illustrates life in the North of England in the early 1800s and 1900s. This is one of the North East's leading tourist attractions. Buildings from throughout the region have been brought to Beamish, rebuilt and furnished as they once were, so that visitors can stroll down a cobbled street full of shops, banks and offices, visit an old Methodist chapel, find out how life was lived on a farm in the late 19th century, take a trip on a tram or steam train, visit an old dentist's surgery (and be grateful you weren't alive to have to visit one back then!), walk through a colliery village and go down a drift mine. You can also see the world's third-oldest surviving railway engine, which dates from 1822 and is housed in a specially created Great Engine Shed. Costumed staff welcome visitors and demonstrate the past way of life. The museum is open April to October 10am to 5pm (last admission 3pm), November to March 10am to 4pm; closed Mondays and Fridays.

Two miles to the northwest is **Causey Arch**, reputed to be the world's first single-arch railway bridge. It was designed by Ralph Wood, a local stonemason, and carried the **Tanfield Railway**, opened in 1725, between Sunniside and Causey. In those days the wagons were pulled by horses, though steam power eventually took over. Trains now run along three miles of line between Sunniside and East Tanfield. There is a car park and picnic area close by, and rights of way link them to Beamish.

SEAHAM
4 miles S of Sunderland on the B1287

🏛 St Mary the Virgin Church 🏛 Seaham Hall

🚶 Durham Coastal Footpath

Seaham was developed by the Marquises of Londonderry. In 1821, the family bought what was then the old village of Seaham in order to build a harbour from which to transport coal from the family's collieries to London and the Continent. The present town grew up around the harbour, and although most of the collieries have now closed, Seaham is still very much a working town.

All that now remains of the original village is **St Mary the Virgin Church** (some parts of which date from Saxon times), its vicarage, and **Seaham Hall** on the northern outskirts of the town. This was once the home of the Milbanke family, where in 1815 Lord Byron met and married Anne Isabella Milbanke – a marriage that was to last for only one year. There is a fine sandy beach in Seaham and a new sculpture trail running between the harbour and Seaham Hall celebrating the town's heritage. A major feature of the coast is the **Durham Coastal Footpath**, an 11-mile route that runs from Seaham to Crimdon Park. It passes through dramatic clifftop scenery and deep ravines carved into the Magnesian limestone rock.

The Durham Dales

There are two great County Durham dales – Teesdale to the south and Weardale to the north. Of the two, Teesdale is the softer,

River Wear, Durham

neighbouring Teesdale. The scars on the landscape expose the regions past as one of the most heavily industrialised upland landscapes in England. Farming developed hand-in-hand with mining, as the miners supported their variable income with produce from their smallholdings. Methodism was very strong within the communities and many former Methodist chapels can still be seen in the area. There are plenty of attractions to see here, such as the lead mining museum at Killhope, the curious fossilised tree stump at Stanhope, and the village of Blanchland, a few miles to the north in Derwentdale.

particularly in its lower reaches, which share an affinity with the Yorkshire Dales. This isn't surprising, for at one time part of the River Tees formed the boundary between County Durham and Yorkshire. The lower dale is dotted with charming villages that nestle along the bank of the River Tees, as it winds its way between the historic towns of Barnard Castle and Middleton-in-Teesdale. Small farms, whitewashed in the local tradition, are surrounded by dry stone wall enclosures. Travelling up the dale the vista opens out into miles of open moorland, home to a multitude of wildlife and unique flora. Beyond Middleton-in-Teesdale the B6277 winds up and over some bleak but beautiful scenery until it finally arrives at Alston in Cumbria, England's highest market town.

The A689, which winds its way through Weardale further north, follows an alternative route to Alston, passing through a dale that was once the hunting ground of Durham's Prince Bishops. Life, at one time, must have been harsh here and the houses and villages seem grittier somehow than those of

Barnard Castle

🏠 Castle   🏠 Market Cross   🏛 Bowes Museum

This historic market town is a natural centre for exploring Teesdale and the Northern Pennines. Set beside the River Tees, 'Barney' is recognised nationally as one of the 51 most historically and architecturally important towns in Great Britain. The town gets its name from **Barnard Castle**, founded in the 12th century by Bernard, son of Guy de Baliol, one of the knights who fought alongside William I. The castle played an important role in the defeat of the Northern Earls who rose against Elizabeth I in 1569. Besieged by rebel forces for 11 days, the castle was ultimately forced to surrender, but not before its resistance had provided time for Queen Elizabeth's army, under the Earl of

Sussex, to speed to York and force the rebels to flee. Many were executed and those leading families who had supported the plans to overthrow Elizabeth I lost their lands.

The castle ruins, with the imposing round keep overlooking the River Tees, have a gaunt beauty. There are picturesque riverside walks through the woods that once formed part of the castle's hunting grounds. A narrow arched bridge, built in 1569, traverses the fast flowing River Tees. Formerly spanning the boundaries of two counties, and the lands of two bishops, illicit weddings were regularly conducted in the centre of the bridge, where neither bishop could object.

The town has an especially rich architectural heritage, with handsome houses, cottages, shops and inns dating from the 17th to the 19th centuries. The octagonal **Market Cross** is a most impressive building, which dates back to 1747 and has served numerous purposes such as courthouse, town hall and jail. Underneath the veranda (a later addition) a lively butter market took place. You can still see the bullet holes in the weather-vane, resulting from a wager by two local men in 1804, shooting from outside the Turk's Head, 100 yards away, to determine who was the best shot. The building was fully restored in 1999.

The Bank was once the town's main commercial street and you can still see several Victorian shop windows. Blagraves House is the oldest inhabited building and it is here that Oliver Cromwell is reputed to have sojourned in 1648. The locality is now an excellent centre for antiques collectors. At the bottom of the Bank glimpses of the town's industrial roots can still be found in Thorngate and Bridgegate. Weavers' cottages have been converted into modern dwellings and grassy slopes cover the remains of the riverside woollen mills.

A walk along Newgate will bring you to the **Bowes Museum** (see panel on page 112), surely one of the most spectacular buildings in England and one of County Durham's great surprises. Housed in a magnificent French-style chateau, the museum was the inspiration of John Bowes, an English aristocrat, and Josephine, his French actress wife. The architect was the Frenchman Jules Pellechet. The owners' love of the arts and a desire that people from all walks of life should be able to partake in such riches resulted in this superb legacy. Sadly both died

Castle Ruins, Barnard Castle

Bowes Museum

Barnard Castle, County Durham DL12 8NP
Tel: 01833 690606   Fax: 01833 637163
e-mail: info@bowesmuseum.org.uk
website: www.bowesmuseum.org.uk

The **Bowes Museum** is one of County Durham's great surprises - a beautiful and grand French chateau-style museum on the outskirts of the historic town of Barnard Castle. It was built by John Bowes, illegitimate son of the 10th Earl of Strathmore, and his Parisian actress wife, Josephine, Countess of Montalbo, between 1862 and 1875. They wanted to house the vast collection of works of art they had amassed from all corners of Europe so that people from all walks of life could see and enjoy them, but unfortunately they died before their dream was realised.

But realised it eventually was, and today it has an outstanding collection that will take your breath away. County Durham is lucky to have a such a museum and gallery - one that is undoubtedly of international importance. Here the visitor can admire a vast range objets d'arts and paintings, including what is acknowledged to be the most important collection of Spanish paintings in Britain. There are works by Goya and El Greco as well as by painters of the calibre of Canaletto, Boudin and Tiepola. Tapestries, ceramics, woodwork, fine furniture and clocks can also be seen - a feast of the finest craftsmanship that could be found in Europe at the time. But John and Josephine Bowes didn't just restrict themselves to the grand and the prestigious, there is also a wonderful display of toys, including the world's first toy train set.

The Museum's most famous exhibit is undoubtedly the Silver Swan. The life-sized bird, with its exquisite silver plumage, is an automaton and musical box, set in a stream made from twisted glass rods with small fish "swimming" among them. When it is wound up, the glass rods rotate, a tinkling tune is played, and the swan preens itself before lowering its head towards the water and seemingly picking up a fish. It then raises its head once more and appears to swallow the fish.

The museum is under the care of Durham County Council, and runs a regular programme of temporary exhibitions and displays. There are also occasional craft fairs and musical events (programme available from the Museum), plus special free guided tours. The licensed café sells snacks and light meals, and there's a shop where you can buy a souvenir or gift. Parking is free, and, apart from one or two areas, the museum is disabled-friendly. There are also 23 acres of gardens and parkland to enjoy

Opening Times: 11-5 daily, except Christmas Day, Boxing Day and New Year's Day.

before their dream could be realised. However, the museum was completed and opened to the public in 1892. Today, the museum houses one of England's finest art collections, which has received Designated status from the Government and is unrivalled in the North. Artists displayed include El Greco, Tiepolo, Canaletto, Boucher, Goya and Courbet. The most famous and best-loved exhibit is undoubtedly the Silver Swan, a 230-year-old life-sized beautifully crafted mechanical bird that appears to pick up and swallow a fish from a silver stream to the backdrop of a tinkly music box. The museum boasts 23 acres of beautiful parkland, including a splendid parterre garden.

Mortham Tower, Greta Bridge

Around Barnard Castle

GRETA BRIDGE
4 miles SE of Barnard Castle on the A66

🏠 Mortham Tower 🌿 Thorpe Farm Centre

🚶 Rokeby Park

Lovers of romantic landscape should make their way south of Barnard Castle to Greta Bridge on the A66 – the graceful old bridge immortalised in paintings by great English water-colourists such as Cotman and Turner. Footpaths run by the riverside, through the edge of **Rokeby Park**. Close by are the ruins of medieval **Mortham Tower**, subject of Sir Walter Scott's narrative poem of colourful chivalry and courtly love, *Rokeby*. The elegant Palladian house, where Scott stayed to write his poem, is open to the public during the summer months.

Just to the south east of Greta Bridge lies **Thorpe Farm Centre**, a 17th-century farm complex which has been transformed into one of the area's main tourist attractions.

EGGLESTONE ABBEY
2 miles S of Barnard Castle, near the A66

Southeast of Barnard Castle the road leads over an old packhorse bridge to Egglestone Abbey. It is made up of the ruins of a Premonstratensian abbey of which most of the nave and chancel, built in the 13th and 14th centuries, survives. Close by is the Meeting of the Waters where the river Greta joins the River Tees, creating splendid views.

BOWES
4 miles SW of Barnard Castle off the A66

📖 Nicholas Nickleby 🌿 Otter Trust Reserve

The ruined Norman castle of Bowes was built on the site of a Roman fort, guarding the approach to Stainmore Pass. In 1838 Charles Dickens visited the village to collect material for his third novel **Nicholas Nickleby**, and noticed an academy for boys run by William Shaw in the main street. The school became the model for *Dotheboys Hall* and Shaw was immortalised as Wackford Squeers. Shaw is buried in the churchyard of St Giles' church along with George Taylor, Dickens' inspiration for Smike. 'I think,' Dickens later said, 'his ghost put Smike into my head upon the spot.'

Three miles west of Bowes on the A66 is the **Otter Trust's North Pennines Reserve**, a 230-acre wildlife reserve with British and Asian otters and bird hides overlooking wetland areas.

COTHERSTONE
3 miles NW of Barnard Castle on the B6277

Cotherstone is one of the most attractive of the Teesside villages. The River Balder flows into the Tees here and the foaming 'meeting of the waters' is an impressive sight after a rainy spell. A delightful riverside walk leads westwards to

Hury, Blackton and Balderhead reservoirs. Cotherstone Castle, licensed by King John in 1200, is now just a steep mound to the north of the village, but the village has a fine Victorian church, several greens and a charming mix of houses of various ages and styles.

ROMALDKIRK
4 miles NW of Barnard Castle on the B6277

Between Middleton and Barnard Castle, the B6277 follows the south bank of the River Tees passing through a series of pretty, unspoiled villages to Romaldkirk whose impressive church is known as the Cathedral of the Dales. It is dedicated to the little-known St Romald or Rumwald, son of a Northumbrian king who could miraculously speak at birth. Beautiful stone houses are set around spacious greens and there are

---

THE ROSE & CROWN
Romaldkirk, nr Barnard Castle, Co Durham DL12 9EB
Tel: 01833 650213
e-mail: hotel@rose-and-crown.co.uk
website: www.rose-and-crown.co.uk

The Rose & Crown is a place of enormous and varied appeal, equally popular as somewhere to meet for a drink, to enjoy a quick snack, to settle down to an excellent meal, or to take a break to discover the many scenic and historic delights of Teesdale. Visitors who step inside the front door enter a traditional backdrop of polished panelling, old beams, gleaming brass and fresh flowers. The bar, with its oak settles, daily newspapers, old prints, carriage lamps and a crackling fire in the grate is the perfect spot to relax with a drink, and the lounge is a quiet retreat with books, magazines and comfortable wing chairs. The heart of the very best inns is the kitchen, and the Rose & Crown is no exception. Lunches and suppers are served daily in the Crown Brasserie, and in the elegant restaurant an excellent fixed-price menu keeps the patrons happy every evening and Sunday lunchtime. The Rose & Crown's outstanding accommodation comprises 12 en-suite bedrooms, seven in the main house and five in the courtyard. All feature delightful furnishings and fabrics, extra-comfortable beds and superb bathrooms, and two have a private sitting room. The surrounding countryside provides wonderful walks, glorious scenery and an abundance of wild flowers and birdlife, and the inn has a supply of maps and walking guides.

🏛 historic building 🏛 museum and heritage 🏚 historic site 🍃 scenic attraction 🐦 flora and fauna

delightful walks close to the river.

EGGLESTON
6 miles NW of Barnard Castle on the B6281

🌿 Eggleston Hall Gardens

Within the grounds of Eggleston Hall are the **Eggleston Hall Gardens**, which are open to the public all year. There are four acres of garden here within the high wall that once enclosed the kitchen garden. The ornamental gardens are laid out informally, with many rare herbaceous plants and shrubs to be seen. Vegetables are cultivated using the traditional organic methods. Close by, the ruins of an old church can be explored.

MIDDLETON-IN-TEESDALE
10 miles NW of Barnard Castle on the B6277

💧 High Force 💧 Low Force 💧 Cauldron Snout

🚶 The Pennine Way

Middleton-in-Teesdale, the capital of Upper Teesdale, is a small working town in a dramatically beautiful setting with the River Tees running below, while all around is a great backcloth of green hills within the North Pennines Area of Outstanding Natural Beauty. The town's links with the lead-mining industry can be seen in the Market Square, where there is a handsome cast-iron fountain, which was purchased and placed there in 1877 by the employees of the Quaker owned London Lead Mining Company. The expense was covered from subscriptions raised for the retirement of the company's local superintendent, Robert Bainbridge. At the west end of Hude is Middleton House, the company's former headquarters.

Although the lead-mining industry disappeared at the beginning of the 19th century, Middleton still retains the strong feeling of being a busy working town. The surrounding hills still bear the scars, with the remains of old workings, spoil-heaps and deep, and often dangerous, shafts. The town's agricultural links remain strong, too, with streets bearing names such as Market Place, Horsemarket and Seed Hill.

Like Barnard Castle, it is increasing in popularity as a base from which to explore Teesdale and the Northern Pennines. Middleton is the centre for some magnificent walks in Upper Teesdale. The most famous of these is **The Pennine Way**, which passes through the town on its 250-mile route from Derbyshire to Kirk Yetholm in Scotland. Turning west along Teesdale the track passes through flower-rich meadows, traditional, whitewashed farmsteads and spectacular, riverside scenery, including the thrilling waterfalls at Low Force, High Force and Cauldron Snout.

High Force Waterfall

Bowlees Picnic Area & Low Force

Distance: *2.5 miles (4.0 kilometres)*
Typical time: *60 mins*
Height gain: *15 metres*
Map: *Explorer OL 31*
Walk: *www.walkingworld.com ID:1174*
Contributor: *Jude Howat*

ACCESS INFORMATION:

There is a good car park at the Bowlees Picnic Area. From Middleton-on-Teesdale continue north, following tourist signs for High Force. Bowlees is signposted to the right before you reach High Force.

DESCRIPTION:

A short circular walk to the falls of Low Force on the River Tees. Low Force is the smaller neighbour to nearby High Force, the well-known waterfall. The walk returns to Bowlees and has an optional add-on to Gibson's Cave and waterfall.

FEATURES:

River, Great Views, Café, Gift Shop, Good for Kids, Mostly Flat, Waterfall.

WALK DIRECTIONS:

1 | From the car park cross the small bridge and climb the stairs towards the visitors centre. The centre itself is worth a visit and is full of displays and information about the area. To continue the walk, keep to the path along the left hand side of the visitors centre to reach a minor road.

Carry on straight ahead, to the right of the buildings. This will bring you to a junction with the main road.

2 | Turn right at this junction for a few metres, to cross the road and follow the footpath sign into the field opposite. Pass through two fields to reach the trees at the far side. Pass through the squeeze-stile to enter the woods. The path leads down to Wynch Bridge, an old suspension bridge over the River Tees just below the falls of Low Force. Having crossed the bridge, Low Force can be seen from the view point on the right - or alternatively follow the footpath to the right for about 50m to stand close to the top of the falls.

3 | Having crossed Wynch Bridge turn sharp left and take the rocky path slightly uphill, close to the riverbank. Do not be tempted to take the clear path through the wooden gate into the fields. Follow the riverside path along the banks of the Tees until the next bridge is reached.

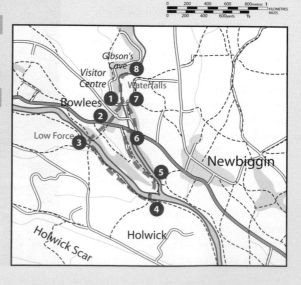

4 | At the lifebelt, follow the path down to the bridge and cross to the far side. Cross the field, which normally has cattle in it, heading towards the old farm buildings. Pass to the right of the shed to enter the next field via a gate. Continue straight ahead towards the gate in the far left corner of the field.

5 | Pass through the gate to enter a wide grassy area with trees on either side. Follow the track towards the white farm building, which will be seen in the distance. Keep to the right of the farm building to pass through the farmyard. Follow the farm track on the far side to reach the road.

6 | Turn right at the road and walk a short distance to reach the entrance road to the picnic area. Turn left and follow the road back to the picnic area. The walk can be finished here, or alternatively continue to view the falls at Gibson's Cave, which are worth the extra distance.

7 | At the far end of the car park, pass the barrier to join the nature trail to Gibson's Cave (there is an information board just on the left, close to the bridge crossed in Waymark 1). Follow the wide path past the toilet block and continue. At the first split in the path, keep to the right. The path is clear from this point until Gibson's Cave is reached.

8 | The falls at Gibson's Cave. The path ends at this point. Retrace your steps to the car park.

The majestic **High Force** is England's largest waterfall in terms of water flow, with a dramatic 21-metre drop over Great Whin Sill at the end of a wooded gorge. After heavy rainfall its rumble can be heard over a mile away. Visitors can enjoy the pretty woodland walk, which twists and turns with a different view every few metres. Then the distant rumble turns into a roar, you peer through the trees and there it is. The sight will astound you. **Low Force** isn't so much a waterfall as a series of cascades, and while less spectacular than its up-stream neighbour, it is arguably more beautiful. Further up the Dale is Cow Green Reservoir and below it **Cauldron Snout**, a 61-metre cascade down dolerite steps. Look out for the Blue Gentian, a rare flower dating back to the last Ice Age.

About three miles west of Middleton-in-Teesdale, near the village of Newbiggin, is the Bowlees Visitor Centre, where information on the natural history and geology of the area can be obtained. A picnic area and car park have been provided.

STAINDROP
5 miles NE of Barnard Castle on the A688

Raby Castle   St Mary's Church

Set in a magnificent 200-acre deer park on the outskirts of the village, **Raby Castle** (see panel on page 118) is one of the country's finest medieval castles, a romantic, fairy-tale building that was once the home of the powerful Nevill family. Described as 'the most perfect of all our northern castles', most of the present castle was built in the 1300s and is miraculously well preserved. There's a sturdy Gatehouse, complete with portcullis and conduits for pouring boiling oil on attackers; a series of mighty towers, including Bulmer's Tower, which is unique in England in having five sides. It also has an extraordinary,

art and craft   entertainment and sport   walks

Raby Castle

Staindrop, County Durham DL2 3AH
Tel: 01833 660202 Fax: 01833 660835
e-mail:rabyestate@rabycastle.com
website: www.rabycastle.com

Raby Castle is not merely a medieval fortress but the home of Lord Barnard. Built in the 14th century by the Nevills, most of the interior now dates from the 18th and 19th centuries, although its medieval heart remains. Every room, from the grand Entrance Hall to the Servant's Bedroom, gives an insight to life through the ages.

Throughout the Castle, the many rooms display fine furniture and furnishings, impressive paintings and elaborate architecture for all to see. The kitchen, built in 1360, remains almost untouched, showing its original medieval form. The cooking equipment has been updated and was in use until 1954. Wander across the terrace in front of the Castle and look out over the lake to the deer park where 200 Red and 200 Fallow deer graze, or take time to enjoy a stroll through the historic gardens. See the formal lawns, ornamental pond and rose garden that are bound by grand yew hedges and towering conifer trees.

cavernous kitchen dating back to 1360, and a Garrison Room with walls between 10 and 20 feet thick. In rich contrast is the sumptuously furnished and decorated Octagon Drawing Room, added in the 1840s. The most breathtaking room, however, is the medieval Baron's Hall where, in 1569, 700 dissident nobles gathered to plot the doomed Rising of the North in support of Mary, Queen of Scots. The failed insurrection caused the downfall of the Nevills, and since 1626 Raby Castle has been the seat of the Vane family. Other attractions at Raby include its beautiful walled gardens, a deer park and a collection of wonderful old coaches. The Stable Tearooms serve tasty and fortifying refreshments.

Staindrop itself is a delightful, very typical, Durham village, with a long village green lined with Georgian houses. **St Mary's Church,** with its Saxon core, houses tombs of the Nevill and Vane families.

HAMSTERLEY FOREST
9 miles N of Barnard Castle off the A68

🏃 Hamsterley Forest

Hamsterley Forest is one of the Forestry Commission's most attractive forest parks. This huge area encompassing over 5,500 acres of mature woodland is managed for timber production, and has 1,100 acres available for recreation. A wide range of activities are on offer for visitors including informal or guided walks, orienteering, horse-riding and cycling (bikes can be hired). There is a visitors centre with displays on forestry, wildlife and timber usage, and large, grassy areas make splendid picnic spots.

Surprisingly, the forest is relatively recent in origin, having been planted only 40 to 50 years ago. Much of it covers areas once worked by the lead-mining industry. This is a good spot to discover a range of wild flowers and, in the damper places, funghi. Red squirrels can still be seen along with roe deer, badgers, adders and up to 40 species of birds including heron, woodcock, sparrow hawk, woodpeckers, fieldfare and goldfinch.

WYCLIFFE
6 miles E of Barnard Castle off the A66

Wycliffe is a picturesque hamlet nestling beside the River Tees, and was once the crossing point from Yorkshire into Co Durham. It is believed to be the birthplace of John Wycliffe, the English theologian and proponent of the reformation of the Roman Catholic Church, who made the first translation of the Bible into English. The imposing stone church of St Mary's is an ancient building, rebuilt by Edward III in the 14th century.

Stanhope

🏛 Castle 🏛 Stanhope Old Hall 🏛 Heathery Burn

Stanhope, the capital of Upper Weardale, is a small town of great character and individuality, which marks the boundary between the softer scenery of lower Weardale and the wilder scenery to the west. The stone cross in the Market Place is the only reminder of a weekly market held in the town by virtue of a 1421 charter. The market continued until Victorian times. Today the town continues to serve the surrounding villages as an important local centre for shops and supplies.

Enjoying an attractive rural setting in the centre of the dale, with a choice of local walks, Stanhope, in its quiet way, is becoming a small tourist centre with pleasant shops and cafés. The town itself is well worth exploring on foot and a useful 'walkabout' town trail is available locally or from information centres.

Stanhope enjoyed its greatest period of prosperity in the 18th and 19th centuries when the lead and iron-stone industries were at their height, as reflected in the town's buildings and architecture

The most dominant building in the Market Square is **Stanhope Castle**, a rambling structure complete with mock-Gothic crenellated towers, galleries and battlements. The building is, in fact, an elaborate folly built by the MP for Gateshead, Cuthbert Rippon, in 1798.

In 1875 it was enlarged to hold a private collection of mineral displays and stuffed birds for the entertainment of Victorian grouse-shooting parties. In the gardens is the Durham Dales Tourist Information Centre.

St Thomas's Church, by the Market Square, has a tower whose base is Norman, and some medieval glass in the west window. In the churchyard you'll find a remarkable **fossil tree stump** which was discovered in 1962 in a local quarry.

Stanhope Old Hall, above Stanhope Burn Bridge, is generally accepted to be one of the most impressive buildings in Weardale. This huge, fortified manor house was designed to repel Scottish raiders. The hall itself is part medieval, part Elizabethan and part Jacobean. The outbuildings included a cornmill, a brew house and cattle yards. It is now a hotel.

One of the most important Bronze Age archaeological finds ever made in Britain was at **Heathery Burn**, a side valley off Stanhope Burn. In 1850, quarrymen cut through the floor of a cave to find a huge hoard of bronze and gold ornaments, amber necklaces, pottery, spearheads, animal bones and parts of chariots. The treasures are now kept in the British Museum.

Around Stanhope

COWSHILL
8 miles W of Stanhope on the A689

🏛 Lead Mining Museum

In a hollow between Cowshill and Nenthead lies Killhope Mine. The Pennines have been worked for their mineral riches, lead in particular, since Roman times, but until the 18th century the industry remained relatively primitive and small scale. Mechanisation, in the late 1700s and early 1800s, allowed the industry to grow until it was second only to coal as a major extractive industry in the region. Now the country's best-preserved lead-mining site, Killhope Mine is the focal point of what is now the **North of England Lead Mining Museum**, dominated by the massive 34-foot high water wheel. It used moorland streams, feeding a small reservoir, to provide power for the lead-ore crushing mills, where the lead-ore from the hillside mines was washed and crushed ready for smelting into lead pigs. Much of the machinery has been carefully restored by Durham County Council over recent years, together with part of the smelting mill, workshops, a smithy, tools and miner's sleeping quarters.

FROSTERLEY
3 miles E of Stanhope on the A689

The village is famous for Frosterley marble, a black, heavily fossilised limestone that in former times was used extensively for rich decorative work and ornamentation on great public and private buildings throughout the north. The Chapel of the Nine Altars in Durham Cathedral makes extensive use of this stone, sometimes called Durham Marble.

IRESHOPEBURN
8 miles W of Stanhope on the A689

🏛 Weardale Museum

At Ireshopeburn, between Cowshill and St John's Chapel, is the delightful little **Weardale Museum**, situated in the former minister's house next to an 18th-century Methodist chapel. High House Chapel, built in 1760, is thought to be the world's oldest Methodist chapel still in use. The displays include a carefully re-created room in a typical Weardale lead-miner's cottage kitchen, with period furnishings and costumes. There is a room dedicated to John Wesley, who visited the area on several occasions. The museum is open during the summer months only.

POW HILL COUNTRY PARK
7 miles N of Stanhope on the B6306

🏞 Pow Hill

Set in moorland overlooking the Derwent Reservoir, **Pow Hill** lies on the south shore and has great views of the lake. Conserved for its special wildlife interest, this valley bog habitat is home to goldcrests, coal tits, roe deer and red squirrels. The western end of the lake is protected as a nature reserve. In winter large flocks of migrant waders and wildfowl gather here.

ROOKHOPE
3 miles NW of Stanhope off the A689

Rookhope (pronounced 'Rook-up'), in lonely Rookhope Dale, is on the C2C (sea to sea) cycle route, and has a history lost in antiquity, dating back to Roman times.

Another old-fashioned Dales village, Rookhope is set in a hidden North Pennine valley. The remains of lead and iron mine activity now blend into quiet rural beauty. At one point the road climbs past Rookhope Chimney, part of a lead-smelting mill where poisonous and metallic-rich fumes were refined in long flues.

ST JOHN'S CHAPEL
7 miles W of Stanhope on the A689

St John's Chapel is named after its parish church, dedicated to St John the Baptist. Like many of the surrounding villages, it was once a lead-mining centre and is still the home of an annual Pennine sheep auction in September, which attracts farmers from all over the North Pennines. This is the only village in Durham to boast a town hall, a small building dating from 1868 overlooking the village green.

The road from St John's Chapel to Langdon Beck in Teesdale rises to 2,056 feet as it passes over Harthope Fell, making it the highest classified road in England.

WESTGATE AND EASTGATE
4 miles W of Stanhope on the A689

The area between the lovely stone-built villages of Westgate and Eastgate was once the Bishop of Durham's deer park, kept to provide him with an abundant supply of venison. The villages are so called because they were the east and west gates to the park. The foundations of the Bishop's castle can still be seen at Westgate along with an old mill and water wheel. In 1327 the troops of Edward III camped at Eastgate en route to Scotland to face the Scottish army.

WOLSINGHAM
5 miles E of Stanhope on the A689

📖 🐾 Tunstall Reservoir

Wolsingham is one of the oldest market towns in County Durham and has its origins in Saxon times. The town has strong links with the iron and steel industries; Charles Attwood, who was one of the great pioneers in the manufacture of steel, founded the town steelworks, which once cast a variety of anchors and propellers for ships.

Tunstall Reservoir, north of Wolsingham, and reached by a narrow lane, lies in a valley of ancient oak woods alongside Waskerley Beck. The reservoir was built in the mid-19th century, originally to provide lime-free water for the locomotives of the Stockton and Darlington Railway to prevent their boilers from scaling like a domestic kettle. It now forms part of a delightful area to stroll, picnic or go fishing.

THE BAY HORSE HOTEL

59 Uppertown, Wolsingham, Weardale,
Co Durham DL13 3EX
Tel: 01388 527220

The **Bay Horse Hotel** is one of the best-known landmarks in one of the oldest towns in County Durham. It's an excellent choice for a drink, a meal or an overnight or longer stay, proving equally popular with local residents and visitors to the region. The restaurant boasts a fine, sophisticated menu of high-quality dishes complemented by a superb wine list. The contemporary lounge mixes café style with old-world comfort, and the restaurant provides relaxed, comfortable seating for 50. The accommodation also combines style and comfort, with a family room, a suite, three doubles and two twins, all with bath and shower en-suite.

4 North Yorkshire: Coast, Moors and Dales

Some 40 miles across and about 20 miles deep, the North York Moors National Park encompasses a remarkable diversity of scenery. There are great rolling swathes of moorland rising to 1,400 feet above sea level, stark and inhospitable in winter, still wild and romantic in summer, and softened only in early autumn when they are mantled by a purple haze of flowering heather. Almost one-fifth of the area is woodland, most of it managed by Forest Enterprise, which has established many picnic sites and forest drives. Settlements are few and far between: indeed, there may have been more people living here in the Bronze Age (1500-500 BC) than there are now to judge by the more than 3,000 'howes', or burial mounds, that have been discovered.

Also scattered across these uplands is a remarkable collection of medieval stone crosses. There are more than 30 of them and

Helmsley

one, the Lilla Cross, is reckoned to be the oldest Christian monument in northern England. It commemorates the warrior Lilla who in AD 626 died protecting his King, Edwin, from an assassin's dagger. Most of them have names – like Fat Betty, which has a stumpy base surmounted by the top of a wheelhead cross. Perhaps the finest example is Ralph Cross, high on Westerdale Moor. It stands nine feet tall at almost precisely the geographical centre of the moors and has been adopted by the North York Moors National Park as its emblem.

Wild as they look, the moors are actually cultivated land, or perhaps 'managed by fire' is the better term. Each year, gamekeepers burn off patches of the old heather in carefully limited areas called swiddens or swizzens. The new growth that soon appears is a crucial resource for the red grouse, which live only in heather moorland, eat little else but heather and find the young green shoots particularly appetising. The older heather that remains provides the birds with protective cover during their nesting season.

Just as the Yorkshire Dales have large areas of moorland, so the North York Moors have many dales - Eskdale, Ryedale, Farndale for example - more than 100 of them in all. They cut deep into the great upland tracts and are as picturesque, soft and pastoral as anywhere in Yorkshire. To the west lies the mighty bulk of the Cleveland Hills; to the east the rugged cliffs of the Heritage Coast. This is marvellously unspoilt countryside, a happy state of affairs that has come about as a result

Canal, nr Kildwick

of the waymarked walks that range from easy trails to treks for the more adventurous. Alternatively, the Forestry Commission's Newtondale Forest Drive takes motorists through some splendidly rugged scenery.

Between Saltburn and Filey lies some of the most striking coastal scenery in the country. Along this stretch of the Heritage Coast you'll find the highest cliffs in the

of the Moors being designated a National Park in 1952, a status that severely restricts any development that would adversely affect either its natural or man-made beauty.

Two spectacularly scenic railways wind their way through this enchanting landscape. Both of them provide a satisfying and environmentally friendly way of exploring this comparatively undiscovered area, anciently known as Blackamor. The Middlesbrough to Whitby route, called the Esk Valley Line, runs from west to east following the course of the River Esk and passes through a succession of delightful villages. The vintage steam locomotives of the North York Moors Railway start at Pickering and run northwards for 18 miles through Newtondale to join the Esk Valley Line at Grosmont. The dramatic route through this glacial channel was originally engineered by George Stephenson himself. During the season, the Moors Railway runs special Pullman Dining Coaches for either dinner or Sunday lunch – a memorable experience. A popular excursion is to take the train to Newtondale Halt and then follow one

country, a shoreline fretted with rocky coves, with miles of golden sandy beaches, a scattering of picture postcard fishing villages and, at its heart, the historic port of Whitby dramatically set around the mouth of the River Esk.

This glorious seaboard was designated as a Heritage Coast in 1979 in recognition of its beauty and its long history. From its small ports, fishermen have for centuries sailed out in their distinctive cobles to harvest the sea; from Whitby, sturdy whaling ships set off on their dangerous and now, thankfully, abandoned trade. It was at Whitby that one of England's greatest mariners, Captain Cook, learnt his seafaring skills and it was from here that he departed in the tiny bark, *Endeavour*, a mere 370 tons, on his astonishing journeys of exploration.

Further down the coast are the popular resorts of Scarborough (where visitors were frolicking naked in the sea as early as 1735), and Filey, both of them offering long stretches of sandy beach and a huge variety of holiday entertainments.

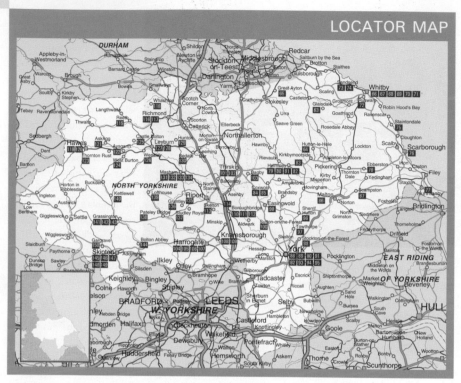

LOCATOR MAP

ADVERTISERS AND PLACES OF INTEREST

🏛 historic building   🏛 museum and heritage   🏛 historic site   🌿 scenic attraction   🐾 flora and fauna

NORTH YORKSHIRE: COAST, MOORS AND DALES

Eskdale

River Esk, Eskdale

Eskdale is the largest, and one of the loveliest, of the dales within the National Park. It is unusual in that it runs east-west, the Esk being the only moorland river that doesn't find its way to the Humber. Instead, the river winds tortuously through the dale to join the sea beneath the picturesque cliffs at Whitby. Along the way, many smaller dales branch off to the north and south – Fryup, Danby, Glaisdale – while even narrower ones can only be explored on foot. The Esk is famed for its salmon fishing, but permits are required. These can be obtained from the local branches of the National Rivers Authority. Walkers will appreciate the Esk Valley walk, a group of 10 linking walks that traverse the length of the valley.

DANBY

12 miles W of Whitby off the A174

🏛 Duck Bridge ⚘ 🎿 Moors Centre

A visit to **The Moors Centre** at Danby Lodge provides an excellent introduction to the North York Moors National Park. The Centre is housed in a former shooting lodge and set in 13 acres of riverside, meadow, woodland, formal gardens and picnic areas. Visitors can either wander on their own along the waymarked woodland walks and nature trails, or join one of the frequent guided walks. Inside the Lodge various exhibits interpret the natural and local history of the moors, there's a bookshop stocked with a wide range of books, maps and guides, and a tea room serving refreshments. The centre is open all year round except for January.

Downstream from The Moors Centre is a superb 14th century packhorse bridge, one of three to be found in Eskdale. This one is known as **Duck Bridge** but the name has nothing to do with aquatic birds. It was originally called Castle Bridge but re-named after an 18th-century benefactor, George Duck, a wealthy mason who paid for the bridge to be repaired. To the south of Duck Bridge are the remains of Danby Castle, now a private farmhouse and not open to the public. Built in the 14th century, and originally much larger, it was once the home of Catherine Parr, the sixth wife of Henry VIII. In Elizabethan times, the justices met here and the Danby Court Leet and Baron, which administers the common land and rights of way over the 11,000 acres of the Danby Estate, still meets here every year in the throne room. One of the court's

Duck Bridge, Danby

War; inside there is some fine work by Robert Thompson, the famous 'Mouseman of Kilburn'. The benches, organ screen and panelling at each side of the altar all bear his distinctive 'signature' of a crouching mouse.

LEALHOLM
9 miles W of Whitby off the A171

From The Moors Centre at Danby a scenic minor road winds along the Esk Valley and brings you to the attractive village of Lealholm, its houses clustering around a 250-year-old bridge over the Esk. A short walk leads to some picturesque stepping stones across the river. The village was one of Canon Atkinson's favourite places – 'Elsewhere , you have to go in search of beautiful views,' he wrote, 'here, they come and offer themselves to be looked at.'

On one of the stone houses, now a tea room and restaurant, a carved inscription reads, 'Loyal Order of Ancient Shepherds' together with the date 1873 in Roman numerals. The Loyal Order ran their lodge on the lines of a men-only London club, but their annual procession through the village and the subsequent festivities were one of the highlights of the autumn. In recent years, Lealholm has become very popular with naturalists who come to study the wealth of trees, ferns, flowers and rare plants in the deep, dramatic ravine known as Crunkley Gill. The ravine is privately owned and not open to the public.

responsibilities is issuing licences for the gathering of sphagnum moss, a material once used for stuffing mattresses but now more commonly required for flower arranging.

For most of the latter half of the 19th century, Danby's vicar was Canon J C Atkinson, who married three times, fathered 13 children and was the authore of one of the most fascinating books ever written about rural England in Victorian times. His *Forty Years in a Moorland Parish* is still in print and well worth seeking out.

CASTLETON
14 miles W of Whitby off the A171

Spread across the hillside above the River Esk, Castleton is a charming village which at one time was the largest settlement in Eskdale. It still has a station on the scenic Esk Valley railway that runs between Whitby and Middlesbrough, and a well-used cricket field in a lovely setting on the valley floor. The village's amber-coloured Church of St Michael and St George was built in memory of the men who fell during the First World

Rosedale Railway

Distance: *6.1 miles (9.9 kilometres)*
Typical time: *180 mins*
Height gain: *30 metres*
Map: *Explorer OL 26*
Walk: *www.walkingworld.com ID:1813*
Contributor: *Jude Howat*

ACCESS INFORMATION:

From the A171 Guisborough to Whitby road, initially take the Danby junction. Pass through Danby to follow signs towards Castleton. Having passed through Castleton keep left along Blakey Ridge (signposted towards Hutton-le-Hole).

DESCRIPTION:

A gentle circular walk that follows part of the route of the old Rosedale Railway. Walking close to the upper edge of the dale, this walk provides an abundance of views. There is free parking past the Lion Inn on the left, opposite the junction to Church Houses.

FEATURES:

Pub, Great Views, Good for Kids, Mostly Flat.

WALK DIRECTIONS:

1 | Having walked a short distance from the car park to the main track, turn left and begin to follow the old railway route around the dale.

2 | Continue straight ahead at the first crossing path, following the railway path to the northern edge of the dale. Once around the peak of the dale, continue along the railway route down the far side of the valley.

3 | Again continue past the path joining from the right (this would be a shortcut back to the starting point if required). The path leads you towards a disused mine, then continues into a farmyard. Pass through the farmyard to exit onto the road.

4 | Turn right and follow the road. Follow the road for around 1.5 kms to turn left at the farm road.

5 | Turn left at the farm junction, and follow the road towards Hollin Bush Farm.

6 | Upon reaching Hollin Bush Farm, turn left to pass through the gate and follow the track up the far side of the dale. Follow the track until you reach a footpath sign branching off to the left.

7 | Leave the farm track at this point and continue up the side of the dale to rejoin the old railway track.

8 | Joining the railway route, turn right for a short distance, then return to the start point and car park.

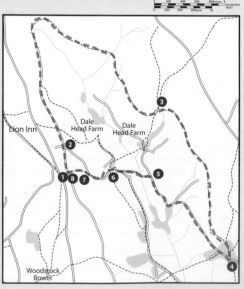

GLAISDALE
8 miles W of Whitby off the A171

From Lealholm a country lane leads to Glaisdale, another picturesque village set at the foot of a narrow dale beside the River Esk with Arncliffe Woods a short walk away. The ancient stone bridge here was built around 1620 by Thomas Ferris, Mayor of Hull. As an impoverished young man he had lived in Glaisdale and fell in love with Agnes Richardson, the squire's daughter. To see Agnes, he had to wade or swim across the river and he swore that if he prospered in life he would build a bridge here. Fortunately, he joined a ship that sailed against the Spanish Armada and captured a galleon laden with gold. Tom returned to Glaisdale a rich man, married Agnes and later honoured his promise by building what has always been called The Beggar's Bridge.

EGTON BRIDGE
7 miles W of Whitby off the A171

🏛 Church of St Hedda 🏆 Gooseberry Show

This little village tucked around a bend in the River Esk plays host each year to the famous **Gooseberry Show**. Established in 1800, the show is held on the first Tuesday in August. It attracts entrants from all over the world who bring prize specimens in an attempt to beat the current record of 2.18oz for a single berry. The village is dominated by the massive **Church of St Hedda** built in 1866. It has a dazzling roof painted blue with gold stars and the altar incorporates some distinguished Belgian terracotta work. Appropriately, St

---

RED HOUSE FARM COTTAGES AND B&B

Glaisdale, nr Whitby, North Yorkshire YO21 2PZ.
Tel: 01947 897242
e-mail: spashettredhouse@aol.com   website: www.redhousefarm.com

Tom and Sandra Spashett bought **Red House Farm** in 1987 and converted the 18th-century traditional barn buildings into supremely comfortable and charming cottages alongside excellent Bed & Breakfast accommodation in the farmhouse itself. There's an air of timeless peace about the place, and the grounds are home to Longhorn cattle, hens, ducks on their own big duck pond and a pony or two. There are no noisy tractors to break the peace, and no obtrusive modern buildings. Guests can bring horses by arrangement and there's stabling for up to 4 horses. Guests have the use of a games room with a billiards table.

Glaisdale is a picturesque village set in the North York Moors National Park at the foot of a narrow valley by the River Esk. This is wonderful walking country, and Wainwright's coast-to-coast footpath passes close by. A short drive brings visitors to many attractions, including The Moors Centre at Danby, the splendid Church of St Hedda at Egton Bridge and the North Yorkshire Moors Railway at Grosmont. The coast at Whitby is just eight miles away.

🎬 stories and anecdotes 🦅 famous people ✍ art and craft 🎭 entertainment and sport 🚶 walks

Hedda's is a Roman Catholic church since it was at Egton Bridge that the martyr Nicholas Postgate was born in 1596. He was ordained as a priest in France but returned to the moors to minister to those still loyal to the outlawed Catholic faith. He travelled disguised as a jobbing gardener and eluded capture for many years, but was finally betrayed for a reward of £20. He was 81 years old when he was hung, drawn and quartered at York. A sad story to be associated with such a delightful village.

GROSMONT
6 miles SW of Whitby off the A169 or A171

🏠 North Yorkshire Moors Railway

Grosmont is the northern terminus of the **North Yorkshire Moors Railway**, the nation's most popular heritage railway, and houses the vintage steam locomotives that ply the 18-mile-long route. The station itself has been restored to the British Railways style of the 1960s and contains a tea room and two shops with a wide variety of rail-related and other items on sale. In high season as many as eight trains a day in each direction are in service and there are many special events throughout the year. And if you have ever harboured the dream of driving a train, the NYMR offers a range of courses, from one day to a full week, enabling you to realise the fantasy.

Central Moors

The area around Goathland provides some of the wildest scenery in the National Park. Murk Mire Moor, Black Rigg, Howl Moor – the very names conjure up the rigours of these upland tracts where heather reigns supreme. Even those who know the moors well treat its sudden mists and savage storms with respect. The historian of the area, Joseph Ford,

recollected hearing as a child of an itinerant trader who travelled the moorland paths selling bottle corks to farmers' wives. During one particularly severe winter it was remarked that he had not paid his usual calls. The following autumn, a skeleton was found on Wintergill Moor: the unfortunate victim was only 'identified by the scattered bottle corks lying nearby'. As Ford noted, 'the story was not unusual'.

It's a very different picture in the narrow dales that cleave their way down to the rivers. The sheltered villages here are as pretty as any in the better known western dales.

GOATHLAND
7 miles SW of Whitby off the A169

🏠 Station   🏠 Exhibition Centre   🝔 Mallyan Spout
🝐 Wade's Way   🝐 Rail Trail

Goathland today is perhaps best known as 'Aidensfield' – the main location for the

Mallyan Spout, nr Goathland

television series *Heartbeat*. Mostyn's Garage & Funeral Services (actually the Goathland Garage); The Aidensfield Arms (The Goathland Hotel) and the Aidensfield Stores all attract thousands of visitors each year, as does **Goathland Station** on the North Yorkshire Moors Railway whose vintage steam locomotives have often featured in the series. The station also served as Hogsmeade Station in the film *Harry Potter and the Philosopher's Stone*.

This attractive village 500 feet up on the moors, where old stone houses are scattered randomly around spacious sheep-groomed greens, was popular long before television. Earlier visitors mostly came in order to see **Mallyan Spout**, a 70-foot-high waterfall locked into a crescent of rocks and trees. They were also interested in Goathland's rugged church and the odd memorial in its graveyard to William Jefferson and his wife. The couple died in 1923 within a few days of each other, at the ages of 80 and 79, and chose to have their final resting place marked by an enormous anchor.

In the award-winning **Goathland Exhibition Centre** you'll find a full explanation of the curious tradition of the Plough Stots Service, performed at Goathland every January. It's an ancient ritual for greeting the new year that originated with the Norsemen who settled here more than a thousand years ago. 'Stots' is the Scandinavian word for the bullocks that were used to drag a plough through the village, followed by dancers brandishing 30-inch swords. This pagan rite is still faithfully observed but with the difference that nowadays Goathland's young men have replaced the 'stots' in the plough harness.

The Exhibition Centre can also provide you with information about the many walks in the

Wade's Way, nr Goathland

area and guide you to one of the oldest thoroughfares in the country, **Wade's Way**. If you believe the legend, it was built by a giant of that name, but it is actually a remarkably well-preserved stretch of Roman road. A popular walk is the **Rail Trail**, a three-and-a-half mile route along the track bed of the original railway line between Goathland and Grosmont, and a return by steam train.

BECK HOLE
8 miles SW of Whitby off the A169

📌 World Quoits Championship

A mile or so up the dale from Goathland is the pretty little hamlet of Beck Hole. When the North Yorkshire Moors Railway was constructed in the 1830s (designed by no less an engineer than George Stephenson himself), the trains were made up of stage coaches placed on top of simple bogies and pulled by horses. At Beck Hole, however, there was a 1 in 15 incline up to Goathland so the carriages had to be hauled by a complicated system of ropes and water-filled tanks. (Charles Dickens was an early passenger on this route and wrote a hair-raising description of his journey.) The precipitous incline caused many accidents so, in 1865, a 'Deviation Line' was blasted through solid rock. The gradient is still one of the steepest in the country at 1 in 49, but it opened up this route to steam trains. The original 1 in 15 incline is now a footpath, so modern walkers will understand

the effort needed to get themselves to the summit, let alone a fully laden carriage.

Every year, this little village plays host to the **World Quoits Championship**. The game, which appears to have originated in Eskdale, involves throwing a small iron hoop over an iron pin set about 25 feet away. Appropriately enough, one of the houses on the green has a quoit serving as a door knocker.

On the hillside, a mile or so to the west of Beck Hole, is the curiously-named **Randy Mere**, the last place in England where leeches were gathered commercially. An elderly resident of Goathland in 1945 recalled how as

Ryedale Folk Museum

Hutton-le-Hole, York YO62 6UA
Tel: 01751 417367
e-mail: info@ryedalefolkmuseum.co.uk

Ryedale Folk Museum is a wonderful working museum offering an insight into bygone eras. Here you will find the finest collection of thatched buildings in Yorkshire - the rescued and restored houses chart the changes in rural life, from the simplicity of the early Tudor crofter's cottage to the cosy Victorian clutter of the White Cottage.

There were mines and railways in nearby Rosedale, bringing a completely different way of life to the moors - explore the story behind these and the Elizabethan glass furnace and other moorland industries. Rural workers, such as tinsmith, wheelwright, blacksmith, saddler, shoemaker and joiner, each have a workshop with

the tools of their trade on display, and regular demonstrations - including weaving, spinning, woodwork and cane and rushwork - take place. An outstanding collection of tools, from wooden pitchforks onwards, also records the extraordinary changes in agriculture over the last 300 years.

In the growing gardens, there are the medicinal herbs of the crofter's garth alongside the more recent cottage garden flowers, while the Victorian vegetable garden contains old varieties of vegetables as they used to be. The working landscape explores the way it was once used and how the way of life has altered it over the years. Farm animals, rare wild flowers and historic crops are sights to be seen here and a project is underway to help conserve the vanishing cornfield flowers. Over 40 varieties are growing here.

A gift shop sells a selection of books, maps and souvenirs. Open March to November - ring for details.

🏠 historic building 🏛 museum and heritage 🏚 historic site 🌳 scenic attraction 🌱 flora and fauna

a young man he had waded into the lake and emerged in minutes with the slug-like creatures firmly attached to his skin. For those interested in repeating his exploit, the leeches are still there.

LOCKTON
15 miles SW of Whitby off the A169

About three miles north of Lockton, the Hole of Horcum is a huge natural amphitheatre, which, so the story goes, was scooped out of Levisham Moor by the giant Wade. It is now a popular centre for hang-gliders. Lockton village itself is set high above a deep ravine, boasts one of the few duck ponds to have survived in the National Park, and offers some fine walks.

LEVISHAM
15 miles SW of Whitby off the A169

Just to the west of the village, in the scenic valley of Newton Dale, lies Levisham Station, one of several that lie on the route of the North Yorkshire Moors Railway. This stop is the ideal location for walking with a wide variety of wildlife and flowers within a short distance of the station.

APPLETON-LE-MOORS
5 miles NW of Pickering off the A170

Located just inside the southern boundary of the Moors National Park, Appleton-le-Moors is noted for its fine church whose tower and spire provide a landmark for miles around. It was built in Victorian times to a design by J L Pearson, the architect of Truro Cathedral, and it reflects the same Gothic style as the Cornish cathedral.

CROPTON
4 miles NW of Pickering off the A170

This tiny village, records hold, has been brewing ales from as far back as 1613 even though home-brewing was illegal in the 17th century. Despite a lapse in the intervening decades, brewing returned to the village when, in 1984, the cellars of the village pub were converted to accommodate Cropton Brewery, a micro-brewery with visitors' centre, guided tours and regional dishes.

HUTTON-LE-HOLE
10 miles NW of Pickering off the A170

🏫 St Mary's Church at Lastingham

🏛 Ryedale Folk Museum

Long regarded as one of Yorkshire's prettiest villages, Hutton-le-Hole has a character all of its own. 'It is all up and down,' wrote Arthur Mee, visiting half a century ago, 'with a hurrying stream winding among houses scattered here and there, standing at all angles.' Fifty years on, little has changed.

Facing the green is the **Ryedale Folk Museum** (see panel opposite), an imaginative celebration of 4,000 years of life in North

Hutton-le-Hole village

🎬 stories and anecdotes 🐦 famous people 🎨 art and craft 🎭 entertainment and sport 🚶 walks

Yorkshire. Among the 13 historic buildings is a complete Elizabethan Manor House rescued from nearby Harome and reconstructed here; a medieval crofter's cottage with a thatched, hipped roof, peat fire and garth; and the old village shop and post office fitted out as it would have looked just after Elizabeth II's coronation in 1953. Other exhibits include workshops of traditional crafts such as tinsmiths, coopers and wheelwrights, and an Edwardian photographic studio. The National Park has an Information Centre here and throughout the year there are special events such as a Rare Breeds Day and re-enactments of Civil War battles by the Sealed Knot.

Anyone interested in unusual churches should make the short trip from Hutton-le-Hole to **St Mary's Church** at Lastingham, about three miles to the east. The building of a monastery here in the 7th century was recorded by no less an authority than the Venerable Bede who visited Lastingham not long after it was completed. That monastery was rebuilt in 1078 with a massively impressive crypt that is still in place – a claustrophobic space with heavy Norman arches rising from squat round pillars. The church above is equally atmospheric, lit only by a small window at one end.

GILLAMOOR
10 miles NW of Pickering off the A170

🐾 Surprise View

This pleasant little village is well worth a visit to see its very rare, and very elegant four-faced sundial erected in 1800, and to enjoy the famous **Surprise View**. This is a ravishing panoramic vista of Farndale with the River Dove flowing through the valley far below and white dusty roads climbing the hillside to the heather-covered moors beyond.

Also of interest is the nearby village church, which was once the church at Bransdale about six miles away. In the late 1700s, Bransdale Church was in good repair but little used; Gillamoor's was dilapidated but the villagers wanted a place of worship. This was achieved by commissioning a single stonemason, James Smith, to remove Bransdale church stone by stone and re-erect it at Gillamoor.

ROSEDALE ABBEY
11 miles NW of Pickering off the A170

🏛 Old Ralph Cross

To the east of Farndale is another lovely dale, Rosedale, a nine-mile-long steep-sided valley through which runs the River Seven. The largest settlement in the dale is Rosedale Abbey, which takes its name from the small nunnery founded here in 1158. Nothing of the old Abbey has survived although some of its stones were recycled to build the village houses. A peaceful village now, Rosedale was once crowded with workers employed in iron-ore mines on the moors. It was said that, such was the shortage of lodgings during the 1870s, 'the beds were never cold' as workers from different shifts took turns to sleep in them. The great chimney of the smelting furnace was once a striking landmark on the summit of the moor, but in 1972 it was found to be unsafe and demolished. Its former presence is still recalled at Chimney Bank where a steep and twisting road, with gradients of 1 in 3, leads up to the moor. High on these moors stands **Old Ralph Cross**, nine feet tall and one of more than 30 such stone crosses dotted across the moors. It was erected in medieval times as a waymark for travellers and when the North York Moors National Park was established in 1952, the Park authorities adopted Old Ralph Cross as its emblem.

🏛 historic building   🏛 museum and heritage   🏛 historic site   🐾 scenic attraction   🐪 flora and fauna

Old Ralph Cross

smothered in thousands of wild daffodils, a short-stemmed variety whose colours shade from a pale buttercup yellow to a rich orange-gold. According to local tradition, the bulbs were cultivated by monks who used the petals in their medical concoctions. Yorkshire folk often refer to daffodils as Lenten Lilies because of the time of year in which they bloom. The flowers, once mercilessly plundered by visitors, are now protected by law with 2,000 acres of Farndale designated as a local nature reserve.

Great Ayton

Captain Cook Schoolroom Museum

This appealing village, set around the River Leven, is an essential stopping point for anyone following the Captain Cook Country Tour, a 70-mile circular trip taking in all the major locations associated with the great seafarer. Cook's family moved to Great Ayton when he was eight years old, and he attended the little school that is now the **Captain Cook Schoolroom Museum**, open daily from April to October. The building dates bck to 1785 and was built as a school and poorhouse on the site of the original charity school that was built in 1704 by

CHURCH HOUSES
17 miles NW of Pickering off the A170

Farndale

A few miles north of Hutton-le-Hole, the moorland road comes to Lowna, set beside the River Dove in one of the Moors most famous beauty spots, **Farndale**. In spring, some six miles of the river banks are

STOKESLEY BUTCHERS

75 High Street, Great Ayton, nr Middlesbrough, North Yorkshire TS9 6NF
Tel: 01642 722245

With its cheerful red awning, **Stokesley Butchers** is easy to spot on the main street of Great Ayton, a pleasant village on the River Leven. Paul Barnes, who has been in the trade all his working life, sources his meat from local farms, and a board announces which farms have supplied the current week's beef, lamb and pork. The chickens are all reared and slaughtered in Yorkshire. The shop also sells its own excellent pies and sausages, along with preserves and sauces.

stories and anecdotes 🐦 famous people 🎨 art and craft 🎭 entertainment and sport 🚶 walks

Michael Postgate, a wealthy local landowner. It was at the Postgate School that James received his early education, paid for by Thomas Skottowe his father's employer. The museum first opened in the 1920s and the exhibits here relate to Cook's life and to the 18th-century village in which he lived. The family had moved to Great Ayton in 1736, but in 1745 Cook moved to Staithes before finally becoming an apprentice seaman in Whitby. James Cook joined the Royal Navy in 1755 and first surveyed the coast of Canada before being appointed First Lieutenant in 1768 and given command of his most famous ship, *Endeavour*. After locating Tahiti and New Zealand in 1769, Cook went on to Australia in 1770 and, following further voyages in the Pacific, was killed by native Hawaiians in 1779.

On High Green, a statue commissioned by Hambleton District Council and sculpted by Nicholas Dimbleby portrays Cook at the age of 18 when he left the village for Staithes.

The house in Easby Lane where the Cook family lived is sadly no longer here. In 1934 it was transported to Australia brick by brick, together with the climbing plants that covered them, and re-erected in Fitzroy Park, Melbourne. A cairn of stones is all that remains to mark the site. A much more impressive monument is the 60-foot obelisk to Cook's memory erected on Easby Moor above the village by Robert Campion, a Whitby banker, in 1827. It can only be reached by a steepish climb on foot but it is well worth making the effort: from the base of the monument there are stupendous views over the Moors, the Vale of Mowbray and across to the oddly shaped hill called Roseberry Topping. The loftiest of the Cleveland Hills and sometimes called the

Matterhorn of Yorkshire, Roseberry's summit towers 1,000 feet above Great Ayton.

The Great Ayton of today is very different from the village that Cook would have known. Now a pleasant place with two spacious greens, with the River Leven flowing through it, this conservation area was, in the 18th and 19th centuries, home to much industrial activity including weaving, tanning, brewing and tile-making. Situated in a secluded position on Low Green is the 12th-century Church of All Saints, still medieval in structure though the original tower and western portion of the nave were demolished in the late 19th century to make room for burials.

Around Great Ayton

INGLEBY GREENHOW
2 miles S of Great Ayton off the B1257

Located on the very edge of the National Park, Ingleby Greenhow enjoys a favoured position, protected from east winds by the great mass of Ingleby Moor. The beckside church looks small and unimposing from the outside, but inside there is a wealth of rugged Norman arches and pillars, the stonework carved with fanciful figures of grotesque men and animals.

STOKESLEY
3 miles SE of Great Ayton on the A172

This pleasing market town lies beneath the northern edge of the moors, its peace only troubled on market day, which has taken place here every Friday since its charter was granted in 1223. Nikolaus Pevsner called Stokesley 'one of the most attractive small towns in the county'. There are rows of elegant Georgian and Regency houses reached by little bridges over the River Leven, which flows through the town, and an old water wheel that marks the entrance to the town.

In the Middle Ages, Stokesley was owned by the Balliol family, one of whose scions is remembered as the founder of the Oxford college of that name.

CARLTON IN CLEVELAND
5 miles SE of Great Ayton off the A172

A pleasing little village just inside the National Park, Carlton has a haunted Manor House and a church that was destroyed by fire in 1881, just weeks after its rector had spent years rebuilding it with his own hands. An later incumbent, Canon John Kyle, fervently maintained the 18th century traditions of the 'squarson' – a parson who was also the village squire. Canon Kyle took the latter of these two roles much more seriously, riding to hounds, running three farms, boxing with the local lads, and also running the village pub, the Fox and Hounds. The Archbishop of York was not pleased that one of his ministers owned a drinking house, but the canon pointed out that his proprietorship allowed him to close the pub on Sundays.

Whitby and the Heritage Coast

From Sandsend, the A174 skirts the shore and then passes between open fields and a breezy cliff-top golf course before entering one of North Yorkshire's most historic and attractive towns.

Whitby

- Dracula Experience · Abbey
- St Mary's Church · Victorian Jet Works
- Captain Cook Memorial Museum
- Whitby Museum & Pennett Art Gallery
- Archives Heritage Centre · Sutcliffe Gallery
- Museum of Victorian Whitby

Whitby is famed as one of the earliest and most important centres of Christianity in England; as Captain James Cook's home port, and as the place where, according to Bram Stoker's famous novel, Count Dracula in the form of a large dog loped ashore from a crewless ship that had drifted into the harbour. The classic 1931 film version of the story, starring Bela Lugosi, was filmed at the

Whitby Abbey

Whitby, Yorkshire YO22 4JT
Tel: 01947 603568
website: www.english-heritage.org.uk

The stark and magnificent ruins of Whitby Abbey are much more than a spectacular cliff-top landmark. Since prehistory, successive generations have been drawn to this dramatic headland as a site of settlement, religious devotion and even literary inspiration.

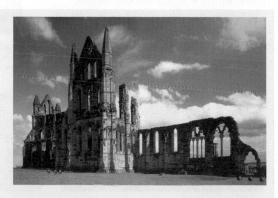

stories and anecdotes · famous people · art and craft · entertainment and sport · walks

THE SHEPHERD'S PURSE

95 Church Street, Whitby,
North Yorkshire YO22 4BH
Tel: 01947 820228
e-mail: shepherds.purse@virgin.net

The **Shepherd's Purse** is one of the most interesting enterprises in the region. It's a family run business comprising of three separate activities.

THE WHOLEFOOD DELI

The Wholefood Deli tempts with an array of top-quality delicatessen products, all vegetarian, including cheeses, olives, prepared vegetables and ready-to-eat snacks. Also on the shelves are herbs and spices and a wide range of teas and coffees from around the world.

THE BOUTIQUE

The Boutique is stocked with a very elegant and very feminine range of ladies' clothes, sourced from leading brands such as Noa Noa, Nougat, Pink Soda and Amano Bolivian knitwear. Shoppers will also find a selection of shoes and jewellery perfect to accesorize the beautiful outfits. The boutique also stocks candles, baskets, dried flowers, soaps and bath oils sold in lovely old-style dispensing chemists' bottles. A perfect treat for someone special.

ACCOMMODATION

Accommodation at the Shepherd's Purse provides a very cosy and welcoming place to spend the night. There are 5 en-suite rooms, 2 shared bathroom rooms and a top floor family room altogether, some with four-poster beds. Each room is equipped with TV and beverage tray with coffee and organic tea and sugar. For a special occasion, flowers, champagne, chocolates and luxury toiletries can be organised.

 historic building 🖾 museum and heritage 🏛 historic site 𝒬 scenic attraction 🦋 flora and fauna

original locations in Whitby and there were several reports of holidaymakers being startled by coming across the Count, cloaked and fanged, as he rested between takes. The **Dracula Experience** on Marine Parade gives a lively rendition of the enduring tale with the help of live actors and electronic special effects.

High on the cliff that towers above the old town stand the imposing and romantic ruins of **Whitby Abbey** (see panel on page 137 - English Heritage). In AD 664, many of the most eminent prelates of the Christian Church were summoned here to attend the Synod of Whitby. They were charged with settling once and for all a festering dispute that had riven Christendom for generations: the precise date on which Easter should be celebrated. The complicated formula they devised to solve this problem is still in use today. Just across from the Abbey, a recently opened Visitor Centre combines the best of modern technology with displays of artefacts in tracing the long history of the site.

A short walk from the Abbey is **St Mary's Church**, a unique building 'not unlike a house outside and very much like a ship inside.' Indeed, the fascinating interior with its clutter of box-pews, iron pillars and long galleries was reputedly fashioned by Whitby seamen during the course of the 18th century. The three-decker pulpit is from the same period; the huge ear trumpets for a rector's deaf wife were put in place about 50 years later. Outside, a carved sandstone cross commemorates Brother Caedmon whose 7th-century poem, *The Song of Creation*, is the earliest known poem in English.

LA MAISON

6 Flowergate, Whitby,
North Yorkshire YO21 3BA
Tel: 01947 825444
e-mail: janebooth@tiscali.co.uk

Jane Booth took over **La Maison** in 2007 and has completely revitalised the shop, which stands among other attractive retail outlets in a street just above the harbour. Jane fills her shop with an ever-changing selection of lovely things for the home and gift ideas, all personally chosen with an eye to style and quality. Shoppers will discover ranges of fragrances and toiletries, tablecloths and tea towels, fabrics from Cath Kidston, chinaware and glassware, Roger Lascelles clocks, light holders from Grand Illusions and designer accessories by Posh Graffiti and Gisella Graham (specialising in boats and seagulls for the bathroom). Among the larger items are French antiques – tables, chairs, settees and chaises longues. If you love to give your home a festive look at Christmas, the vast range of stock also includes very tasteful Christmas decorations. La Maison is open from 10 to 5 Monday to Saturday, 12 to 4 Sunday.

St Mary's stands atop the cliff: the old town clusters around the harbour mouth far below. Linking them are the famous 199 steps that wind up the hillside: many a churchgoer or visitor has been grateful for the frequent seats thoughtfully provided along the way.

The old port of Whitby developed on the slim shelf of land that runs along the east bank of the River Esk, an intricate muddle of narrow, cobbled streets and shoulder-width alleys. **Grape Lane** is typical, a cramped little street where ancient houses lean wearily against each other. Young James Cook lived here during his apprenticeship: the handsome house in Grape Lane where he lodged is now the **Captain Cook Memorial Museum.** The rich collection includes period rooms, models, maps and manuscripts, ships' plans, furniture, artefacts from Cook's voyages, and many original drawings, prints and paintings, including one of Cook's notorious contemporary, Captain Bligh of the *Bounty*.

By the early 19th century, old Whitby was full to bursting and a new town began to burgeon on the west bank of the River Esk. The new Whitby, or 'West Cliff', was carefully planned with the nascent industry of tourism in mind. There was a quayside walk or 'promenade', a bandstand, luxury hotels, and a Royal Crescent of upmarket dwellings reminiscent of Buxton or Cheltenham, but with the added advantage of enjoying a sea air universally acknowledged as 'invariably beneficial to the health of the most injured constitution'.

In a dominating position on West Cliff, a bronze statue of Captain Cook gazes out over the harbour he knew so well. Nearby,

THE LEEWAY

1 Havelock Place, Whitby,
North Yorkshire YO21 3ER
Tel: 01947 602604
e-mail: enquiries@theleeway.co.uk
website: www.theleeway.co.uk

A warm Yorkshire welcome from Karen and Garry Walker awaits guests at **The Leeway**, a large Victorian town house that they have refurbished, modernised and turned into Whitby's best B&B. It's ideally situated on the West Cliff, a few minutes' walk from the seafront and harbour, shops, restaurants and railway station. The bedrooms, all smartly furnished and stylishly decorated, have television with DVD and CD player, radio-alarm clock, hairdryer, complimentary toiletries and hospitality tray – even wine glasses and corkscrew/bottle-opener. There's also a DVD library for guests to choose from, and free Wi-Fi. Superior rooms also have memory foam mattresses, leather seating areas and rain-effect shower heads. All rooms are en-suite except the single, which has a private bathroom. An excellent breakfast is served in the

spacious modern dining room. Whitby has much to interest the visitor, and the hospitality extended at The Leeway adds to the pleasure of a stay in this historic town.

THE MOON & SIXPENCE

Marine Parade, Whitby, North Yorkshire YO21 3PR
Tel: 01947 604416
website: www.moon-and-sixpence.co.uk

On Marine Parade, overlooking the harbour, the **Moon & Sixpence** is a relaxed and stylish bar and brasserie serving an outstanding variety of food and drink. It's a great place for lovers of seafood, with a fine selection that includes mussels, scallops and several ways with oysters rushed up daily from Mersea Island. Other choices on a very tempting menu might be fillet of black bream served on French peas, and bouillabaisse with an aïoli-glazed fillet of red mullet. Seafood may be king, but there's also a fine choice for meat-eaters and vegetarians. The bar serves a range of exciting cocktails, champagnes, fine wines, spirits, beers from around the world and fruit juices. Above the restaurant is a beautifully appointed guest suite with a double shower, Jacuzzi, king-size bed and 40 inch wall-mounted satellite TV.

THE MARINE

website: www.the-marine-hotel.com

In the same delightful setting the Moon & Sixpence's team has renovated and converted an old cafe to create a stylish set of four luxurious suites with up-to-the-minute appointments and accessories; the two at the front have balconies overlooking the harbour. This splendid new amenity, called **The Marine**, comes on stream in May 2008. There is also a bar and restaurant in The Marine.

the huge jawbone of a whale, raised as an arch, recalls those other great Whitby seafarers, the whalers. Between 1753 and 1833, Whitby was the capital of the whaling industry, bringing home 2,761 whales in 80 years. Much of that success was due to the skills of the great whaling captains William Scoresby and his son, also named William. The elder William was celebrated for his great daring and navigational skills, as well as for the invention of the crow's nest, or masthead lookout. His son was driven by a restless, enquiring mind and occupied himself with various experiments during the long days at sea in the icy Arctic waters. He is most noted for his discoveries of the forms of snow crystals and the invention of the 'Greenland' magnet, which made ships'

compasses more reliable. The whaling industry is now, thankfully, long dead, but fortunately the fishing industry is not, as many of Whitby's restaurants bear witness, being famous for their seafood menus.

One of Whitby's unique attractions is **The Sutcliffe Gallery** in Flowergate. The Gallery celebrates the great photographer Frank Meadow Sutcliffe who was born in Whitby in 1853. His studies of local people, places and events powerfully evoke the Whitby of late-Victorian and Edwardian times in photographs that are both beautifully composed and technically immaculate. Few visitors to the Gallery can resist the temptation to purchase at least one of the nostalgic prints on sale.

Another popular souvenir of the town is jet

stone, a lustrous black stone that enjoyed an enormous vogue in Victorian times. After the death of Prince Albert, jewellery in jet was the only ornament the Queen would allow herself to wear. The Court and the middle classes naturally followed her example and for several decades Whitby prospered greatly from the trade in jet. By 1914, workable deposits of the stone were virtually exhausted and a new generation shunned its gloomy association with death. Recent years have seen a revival of interest in the glossy stone and several shops have extensive displays of jet ornaments and jewellery. The original **Victorian Jet Works**, established in 1867, are open daily and visitors can see the craftspeople at work as well as purchase jet from a wide range of interesting and contemporary jewellery designs. Whitby often features in the TV series, *Heartbeat*.

On the southeastern edge of the town the **Whitby Museum and Pannett Art Gallery** stands in the attractive setting of Pannett Park. The museum contains a nationally-important collection of Whitby jet jewellery, relics of Captain Cook and the lands he visited, displays on whaling and many other items from Whitby's past.

The **Whitby Archives Heritage Centre**, which is open all year, holds an exhibition of local photographs and, along with its local history research facilities, has a shop and heritage gallery. The **Museum of Victorian Whitby** has a re-creation of a 19th century lane in the town complete with interiors and shop windows, along with miniature rooms and settings.

Around Whitby

STAITHES
9 miles NW of Whitby off the A174

Visitors to this much-photographed fishing port leave their cars in the car park in the modern village at the top of the cliff and then walk down the steep road to the old wharf. Take care – one of these narrow stepped alleys is called Slippery Hill, for reasons that can become painfully clear. The old stone chapels and rather austere houses testify to the days when Staithes was a stronghold of Methodism.

The little port is proud of its associations with Captain James Cook. He came here, not as a famous mariner, but as a 17-year-old assistant in Mr William Sanderson's haberdashery shop. Cook didn't stay long, leaving in 1746 to begin his naval apprenticeship in Whitby with Thomas Scottowe, a friend of Sanderson.

Staithes remains a working port with one of the few fleets in England still catching crabs and lobsters. Moored in the harbour and along the river are the fishermen's distinctive boats. Known as cobles, they have an ancestry that goes back to Viking times. Nearby is a small sandy beach, popular with families (and artists), and a rocky shoreline

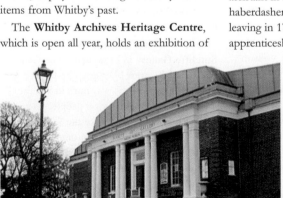
Whitby Museum and Pannett Art Gallery

🏛 historic building   🏛 museum and heritage   🏛 historic site   🍃 scenic attraction   🐾 flora and fauna

Staithes Harbour

and almost everyone would avert their gaze or cross the road to avoid someone afflicted with the 'Evil Eye'. In the late 1800s, the Revd Cooper, Vicar of Filey, visited the village and came across a 'perfectly horrible superstition'. Apparently, it was considered unlucky to save a drowning man. The Vicar was told of 'men nearly dragged ashore, and then, by the advice of the elders, abandoned to their fate lest ill-fortune should result from saving them'.

extending north and south pitted with thousands of rock pools hiding starfish and anemones. The rocks here are also rich in fossils and you may even find ingots of 'fools gold' – actually iron pyrites and virtually worthless.

A little further up the coast rises Boulby Cliff, at 666 feet (202m) the highest point on the east coast of England.

RUNSWICK BAY
6 miles NW of Whitby, off the A174

A little further down the coast, Runswick Bay is another picturesque fishing village with attractive cottages clinging to the steep sides of the cliff. This perilous position proved disastrous in 1682 when the cliff face collapsed during a violent storm and the whole of Runswick, with the exception of a single cottage, tumbled into the sea. A disaster fund was set up and a new village established.

At Runswick, as in most of Yorkshire's remote communities, superstition was once widespread. Even at the beginning of the 20th century, many still believed in witches

GOLDSBOROUGH
5 miles NW of Whitby off the A174

Just outside this small village are the remains of one of five signal stations built by the Romans in the 4th century when Saxon pirates were continually raiding the coastal towns. The stations were all built to a similar design with a timber or stone watchtower surrounded by a wide ditch.

LYTHE
4 miles NW of Whitby off the A174

🏛 Mulgrave Castle

Perched on a hill top, Lythe is a small cluster of houses with a sturdy little church that is well worth a visit. Just south of the village is **Mulgrave Castle**, hereditary home of the Marquis of Normanby. The Castle grounds, which are open to the public, contain the ruins of Foss Castle built shortly after the Norman Conquest. Charles Dickens once spent a

Runswick Bay

Distance: *3.1 miles (5.0 kilometres)*
Typical time: *120 mins*
Height gain: *30 metres*
Map: *Explorer OL 27*
Walk: *www.walkingworld.com ID:1398*
Contributor: *Jude Howat*

ACCESS INFORMATION:

Runswick Bay is off the A174 north of Whitby.
From the A174, follow signs from Hinderwell (if
travelling from the north), or Ellerby (if travelling
from the south). There is parking at the village cross,
however in summer this can get busy.

DESCRIPTION:

A pleasant cliff walk from the picturesque seaside
village of Runswick, north along the cliff tops to
Port Mulgrave. The walk then heads inland - to the
pub - before returning to Runswick. A nice walk for
children, although do take care near the cliff edge. It
is worth extending the walk by following the steep
road down to the actual bay itself - perhaps for an
ice cream if it's a nice hot day!

FEATURES:

Sea, Pub, Birds, Flowers, Great Views, Butterflies,
Café, Good for Kids, Mostly Flat.

WALK DIRECTIONS:

1 | Having parked at the upper car park in Runswick
(do not take the steep road down to the coast), the
walk starts by passing through the pub car park ,
where you will find a footpath continuing in the
direction of the hedge. The path takes you through
a hedge-lined section to follow along the right-hand
edge of a field, aiming towards the headland.

2 | As you approach the headland, there is a split in
the path. A small path leads off to the right (it
looked rather disused when we were there). Cross
the stile and turn left, following the clifftop path. At
this point there are nice views to the south, over

Runswick Bay itself. Follow the cliff path as it
undulates along the coastline.

3 | Eventually you will reach a gate with a path
leading off to the left at 90 degrees, with another
continuing north, dropping down through a field.
Take the wide left-hand path and follow it inland.
This path follows the outer edge of the field, so you
will walk inland, then head north again towards
some cottages in the distance. (Alternatively, you
could follow the path through the field, aiming for
the cottages.)

4 | Upon reaching the cottages (at Port Mulgrave),
turn left and join the country lane heading inland
away from the coast. Follow it, past one junction,
until you reach a T-junction facing you.

5 | Turn left at the T-junction, passing the church
(on your right), to reach the main road a short
distance further on.

6 | Turn left at this T-junction to walk along the
pavement by the 'main' road, through Hinderwell.
(There is a nice stop-off point along here for a beer
should you wish - having sat at the front beer-
garden, we discovered that there was actually a
children's play area round the back.) Continue along
the main road, to reach the Y-junction signposted
towards Runswick.

7 | Branch left to follow the road back towards
Runswick Bay and your starting point.

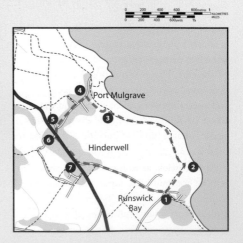

holiday at Mulgrave Castle and 'danced on its lawns in ecstasy at its beauty'. It's not known whether the great author witnessed the ancient custom of 'Firing the Stiddy'. This celebrates notable events in the Normanby family and begins with dragging the anvil from the blacksmith's shop, upturning it, and placing a charge of gunpowder on its base. A fearless villager then approaches with a 20-foot long metal bar, its tip red hot, and detonates the powder.

In the 1850s, Mulgrave Castle was leased by an exiled Indian Maharajah, Duleep Singh. He enjoyed going hawking on the moors in full oriental dress and the story is often told of how he had the first road between Sandsend and Whitby constructed because his elephants disliked walking along the beach. Much as one would like to believe this tale, no one has yet proved it to be true.

SANDSEND
2 miles NW of Whitby on the A174

From Runswick Bay, the A174 drops down the notoriously steep Lythe Bank to Sandsend, a pretty village that grew up alongside the Mulgrave Beck as it runs into the sea at 'sands' end' – the northern tip of the long sandy beach that stretches some two-and-a-half miles from here to Whitby.

The Romans had a cement works nearby, later generations mined the surrounding hills for the elusive jet stone and for alum, and the Victorians built a scenic railway along the coast. The railway track was dismantled in the 1950s but sections of the route now form part

RAITHWAITE HALL LUXURY COTTAGES

Sandsend, Whitby, North Yorkshire YO21 3ST
Tel: 01947 893284
e-mail: admin@raithwaite.co.uk
website: www.raithwaite.co.uk

In a secluded valley just off the coast road north of Whitby, **Raithwaite Hall Luxury Cottages** offer some of the best self-catering holiday accommodation in the region. Recently converted stone-built cottages provide an excellent base for tourists, families, walkers and cyclists. The smallest of the cottages sleeps 2 people, with the largest sleeping up to 9. All of the cottages are fully equipped to ensure a relaxed, comfortable, go-as-you-please holiday. The 60 acres of grounds around the cottages are perfect for an afternoon stroll. The grounds have a wealth of mature woodland, rare plants, wonderful rhododendrons, tumbling streams, trout fishing on the lake and a variety of wildlife. One of the finest stretches of sand on the Yorkshire coast is a short walk away and the North York Moors National Park, that provides wonderful walking almost on the doorstep.

TURNSTONE GALLERY

Sandsend, nr Whitby, North Yorkshire YO21 3SU
Tel: 01947 893289
e-mail: info@turnstonegallery.net
website: www.turnstonegallery.net

Turnstone Gallery overlooks the fine sandy bay at Sandsend, a village three miles up the coast from Whitby. Harry and Bridget Casson opened the gallery in 2002 with the aim of showing the best in fine art and ceramics, specialising in work from the region. At the Turnstone visitors will always find a broad range of contemporary work – original paintings, etchings, ceramics, sculpture, photographs and enamels.

The aim is to make high quality artwork accessible to all, and the gallery has an open and friendly atmosphere where everyone is welcome. The light and airy space, with large windows looking out to the headland and sea, provides an ideal setting for viewing the work.

With regularly changing displays of work, and exhibitions twice a year, there is always something new to find and enjoy. The gallery participates in the 'Own Art' scheme, supported by the Arts Council, which provides interest-free loans for customers purchasing artwork. An area for children to sit and draw allows parents time to look around the gallery.

🏛 historic building   🏛 museum and heritage   🏛 historic site   🍃 scenic attraction   🌿 flora and fauna

of the Sandsend Trail, a pleasant and leisurely two-and-a-half hour walk around the village, which is made particularly interesting if you follow it with the National Park's booklet describing the route.

ROBIN HOOD'S BAY
5 miles S of Whitby off the A171

🏠 Fyling Hall Pigsty 🏛 Old Coastguard Station

🏛 Museum 🏛 Music in Miniature

Artists never tire of painting this 'Clovelly of the North', a picturesque huddle of red-roofed houses clinging to the steep face of the cliff. Bay Town, as locals call the village, was a thriving fishing port throughout the 18th and 19th centuries. By 1920, however, there were only two fishing families left in the Bay, mainly because the harbour was so dilapidated, and the industry died out. Today, small boats are once again harvesting the prolific crab grounds that lie along this stretch of the coast.

Because of the natural isolation of the bay, smuggling was just as important as fishing to the local economy. The houses and inns in the Bay were said to have connecting cellars and cupboards, and it was claimed that 'a bale of silk could pass from the bottom of the village to the top without seeing daylight'. Those were the days when press gangs from the Royal Navy were active in the area since recruits with a knowledge of the sea were highly prized. Apparently, these mariners were also highly prized by local women: they smartly despatched the press gangs by means of pans and rolling pins.

Shipwrecks in the Bay were frequent, with many a mighty vessel tossed onto its reefs by North Sea storms. On one memorable occasion in the winter of 1881, a large brig called *The Visitor* was driven onto the rocks. The seas were too rough for the lifeboat at Whitby to be launched there so it was dragged eight miles through the snow and let down the cliffside by ropes. Six men were rescued. The same wild seas threatened the village itself, every storm eroding a little more of the chalk cliff to which it clings. Fortunately, Robin Hood's Bay is now protected by a sturdy sea wall.

The most extraordinary building in Robin Hood's Bay is undoubtedly **Fyling Hall Pigsty**. It was built in the 1880s by Squire

Robin Hood's Bay

🎭 stories and anecdotes 🐦 famous people ✏ art and craft 🖋 entertainment and sport 🚶 walks

Barry of Fyling Hall in the classical style, although the pillars supporting the portico are of wood rather than marble. Here the Squire's two favourite pigs could enjoy plenty of space and a superb view over the Bay. The building is now managed by the Landmark Trust who rent it out to holidaymakers.

Detailed information about the village and the Bay is on display at the **Old Coastguard Station** on The Dock. This National Trust property also houses the National Park Visitor and Education Centre. Also worth a visit are the **Robin Hood's Bay Museum**, and **Music in Miniature**, a unique exhibition of 50 dioramas at a scale of 1:12 created by a local craftswoman.

RAVENSCAR
10 miles N of Scarborough off the A171

🐾 Lyke Wake Walk   🐾 Staintondale Shire Horse Farm

🐾 Wellington Lodge Llama Trekking

The coastline around Ravenscar is particularly dramatic and, fortunately, most of it is under the protection of the National Trust. There are some splendid cliff-top walks and outstanding views across Robin Hood's Bay. Ravenscar is the eastern terminus of the 42-mile hike across the moors to Osmotherley known as the **Lyke Wake Walk**.

During the late 19th century there was an unsuccesful attempt to turn this scattered village, then known as Peak, into a small town and, although the roads were built, little of the land that was made available to potential buyers was ever developed. Thus, it retains a tranquil air, along with a small church and a couple of village shops - the only building of any size here is the Raven Hall Hotel. Local legend has it that King George III visited the Hall when it was a private house, while recovering from one of his recurring bouts of mental illness.

About three miles south of Ravenscar, at Staintondale, are two very different animal centres. At the **Staintondale Shire Horse Farm** (see panel below) visitors can enjoy a 'hands-on' experience with these noble

Staintondale Shire Horse Farm

Staintondale, Scarborough,
North Yorkshire YO13 0EY
Tel: 01723 870458
website: www.shirehorsefarm.co.uk

If you are a smitten horse and pony lover, enjoy the countryside and a happy relaxing environment, this is the place for you. In total, there are 18 horses and ponies, from tiny Shetlands to massive Shire Horses. In between, a variety of all shapes and sizes. It really is about family fun and you can enjoy watching various live shows with both the Shires and the ponies.

The farm is idyllicly set in 40 acres of North Yorks National Park coastline and offers excellent facilities for a truly relaxing day out. There are picnic and play areas in safe amenity enclosures and some pretty farm walks to elevated fields where you can enjoy the magnificent coastal and sea views. A timeless flagged floor café and gift shop complete the picture, with tea made from the farm's own fresh spring water. Open Sunday, Tuesday, Wednesday, Friday and Bank Holiday Mondays from mid-May to mid-September.

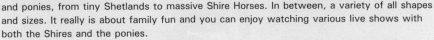

🏠 historic building 🏛 museum and heritage 🏚 historic site 🗻 scenic attraction 🐾 flora and fauna

creatures, watch a video of the horses working and follow a scenic route around the area. Cart rides are also usually available. There's also a café, souvenir shop, picnic area and a play area with a variety of small farm animals to entertain the children.

At nearby **Wellington Lodge Llama Trekking**, a variety of treks with llamas is on offer, ranging from a three- or four-hour journey to a whole day with a three-course meal included in the price. The llamas have many years of trekking experience and are sure-footed and friendly. They carry heavy loads of food, drink, stools and extra clothing, leaving you free to admire the splendid surroundings. Handlers and specialist guides accompany walkers.

HACKNESS
5 miles NW of Scarborough off the A170 or A171

For generations the Forge Valley has attracted sightseers – especially in autumn when the steep wooded banks of the ravine present a dazzling display of colours. There are several splendid walks along this lovely two-mile stretch of the River Derwent, a valley that takes its name from the ancient iron workings of which today not a trace remains. Nothing has survived, either, of the monastery established at Hackness in AD 681 by the first Abbess of Whitby, although some of its stones were used in the building of St Peter's Church, founded in 1060. Inside the church is a fragment of an Anglo-Saxon cross with inscriptions in English, Latin and runic characters. The grandest building in the village is Hackness Hall (private), a Georgian mansion that is the home of Lord Derwent.

CLOUGHTON
4 miles N of Scarborough on the A171

Cloughton village lies less than a mile from the coast and the rocky inlet of Cloughton Wyke. Here, in 1932, a huge whale was cast, or threw itself, ashore. Press photographers and postcard publishers rushed to the scene and paid the smallest local children they could find to pose beside the stranded Leviathan. For a while, Cloughton village was busy with a steady stream of sightseers. Their numbers quickly diminished as the six tons of blubber began to rot. In Cloughton itself, residents came to dread an east wind: it reached them only after washing over the vast hulk lying on the rocks. It's surely the worst thing that has ever happened to this pleasant little village, set around a sharp kink in the A171, where the breezes now – depending on the direction of the wind – either bring a fresh tang of ozone from the sea or the soft perfume of heather from the moors.

Scarborough

| 🏰 Castle | 🌳 Peasholm Park | 🎨 Art Gallery |
| 🏛 Rotunda Museum | 🐟 Sea Life Marine Sanctuary |
| 🎭 Stephen Joseph Theatre in the Round |

With its two splendid bays and dramatic cliff-top castle, Scarborough was targeted by the early railway tycoons as the natural candidate for Yorkshire's first seaside resort. The railway arrived in 1846, followed by the construction of luxury hotels, elegant promenades and spacious gardens, all of which confirmed the town's claim to the title 'Queen of Watering Places'. The 'quality', people like the eccentric Earls of Londesborough, established palatial summer residences here, and an excellent train

Scarborough

remote little town to sample the spring water discovered by Mrs Tomyzin Farrer in 1626 and popularised in a book published by a certain Dr Wittie who named the site Scarborough Spaw. Anne Brontë came here in the hope that the spa town's invigorating air would improve her health, a hope that was not fulfilled. She died at the age of 29 and her grave lies in St Mary's churchyard at the foot of the castle.

Scarborough Castle itself can be precisely dated to the decade between 1158 and 1168 and surviving records show that construction costs totalled £650. The castle was built on the site of a Roman fort and signal station and its gaunt remains stand high on Castle Rock Headland,

service brought thousands of excursionists from the industrial cities of the West Riding.

Even before the advent of the railway, Scarborough had been well-known to a select few. They travelled to what was then a

Central Tramway Company Ltd

1 Marine Parade, St Nicholas Cliff, Scarborough, North Yorkshire YO11 2ER
Tel: 01723 501754

The Central Tramway Company Scarborough Limited was created and registered in 1880. The lift was designed for steam operation and first opened to the public in August 1881. It was located in the real centre of the South Bay to link the city to the shore just beside the Grand Hotel.

Below the track and about 60 feet from the top station the steam operated winch gear was housed. The driver of the lift had no view of the cars and relied on an indicator with other visual airs such as string tied on to the haulage rope, and chalk marks on the winch drums to indicate the arrival of the cars at the top and bottom stations. In 1910, the steam was abandoned and the gear converted to electric drive. In 1932, the cars were replaced and the motor placed under the top station. Control was from a driving position at the top of the station with full view of the cars. For emergency use each car is fitted with a screw on and wedge safety brake that operates on a safety rail down the centre of each track and the rail also carries the rollers for the support of the cables.

🏛 historic building   🏛 museum and heritage   🏛 historic site   🍂 scenic attraction   🌱 flora and fauna

dominating the two sweeping bays. The spectacular ruins often provide a splendid backdrop for staged battles commemorating the invasions of the Danes, Saxons and the later incursions of Napoleon's troops. The surrounding cliffs are also well worth exploring – just follow the final part of the famous Cleveland Way.

If you happen to be visiting the resort on Shrove Tuesday, be prepared for the unusual sight of respectable citizens exercising their ancient right to skip along the highways. This unexpected traffic hazard is now mostly confined to the area around Foreshore Road. Another tradition maintained by local people around this time is the sounding of the Pancake Bell, a custom started by the wives of the town to alert their menfolk in the fields and in the harbour that they were about to begin cooking the pancakes.

As befits such a long-established resort, Scarborough offers a vast variety of entertainment. If you tire of the two sandy beaches, there's **Peasholm Park** to explore, with its glorious gardens and regular events, among them the unique sea battle in miniature on the lake. Or you could seek out the intellectual attractions of the **Rotunda Museum** (due to re-open in 2008) on Vernon Road, 'the finest Georgian museum in Britain', which includes among its exhibits a genuine ducking stool for 'witches'; the art collections at the **Scarborough Art Gallery**; or the futuristic world of holograms at Corrigans Arcade on Foreshore Road. **The Stephen Joseph Theatre in the Round** is well known for staging the premiere performances of comedies written by its resident director, the prolific playwright Sir Alan Ayckbourn. And at Scalby Mills, on the northern edge of the town, **Sea Life Marine Sanctuary** offers the chance of close encounters with a huge variety of marine creatures from shrimps to sharks, octopuses to eels.

Around Scarborough

CAYTON
3 miles S of Scarborough on the B1261

🖈 Stained Glass Centre

Cayton is one of only 31 'Thankful Villages' in England. They were so named after the First World War because all of their men came back safely from that horrific conflict. Cayton had all the more reason to be grateful since 43 of its men returned – more than to any other of the Thankful Villages. The term was first used by Arthur Mee in the 1930s. Other Thankful Villages in Yorkshire are Catwick, north of Beverley, Cundall east of Ripon and its neighbour Norton-le-Clay.

An unusual attraction here is the **Stained Glass Centre** where Valerie Green and her team produce stained glass and leaded lights for churches, hotels, restaurants, public houses and homes throughout the country. Visitors can watch the craftspeople at work, browse in the showroom and examine the exhibition of stained glass.

FILEY
7 miles S of Scarborough on the A1039

🏛 Folk Museum 🏛 Edwardian Festival
🚶 Cleveland Way

With its six-mile crescent of safe, sandy beach, Filey was one of the first Yorkshire resorts to benefit from the early 19th century craze for sea bathing. Filey's popularity continued throughout Victorian times but the little town always prided itself on being rather more select than its brasher neighbour just up the coast, Scarborough. Inevitably, modern

Filey Parish Church

times have brought the usual scattering of amusement arcades, fast food outlets and, from 1939 to 1983, a Butlin's Holiday Camp capable of accommodating 10,000 visitors. But Filey has suffered less than most seaside towns and with its many public parks and gardens still retains a winning, rather genteel atmosphere.

Until the Local Government reforms of 1974, the boundary between the East and North Ridings cut right through Filey. The town lay in the East Riding, the parish church and graveyard in the North. This curious arrangement gave rise to some typically pawky Yorkshire humour. If, as a resident of Filey town, you admitted that you were feeling poorly, the response might well be, 'Aye, then tha'll straightly be off t'North Riding' – in other words, the graveyard.

Filey's parish church, the oldest parts of which date back to the 12th century, is appropriately dedicated to St Oswald, patron saint of fishermen, and the Fishermen's Window here commemorates men from the town who died at sea. At the **Filey Folk Museum**, housed in a lovely old building dating back to 1696, you can explore the town's long history, while the **Edwardian Festival**, held every June, re-creates the pleasures of an earlier, more innocent age.

Just to the north of the town, the rocky promontory known as Filey Brigg strikes out into the sea, a massive mile-long breakwater protecting the town from the worst of the North Sea's winter storms. From the Brigg, there are grand views southwards along the six-mile-long bay to the cliffs that rise up to Flamborough Head and Scarborough Castle. Despite the fact that there is no harbour at Filey, it was once quite a busy fishing port and one can still occasionally see a few cobles – direct descendants of the Viking longships that arrived here more than a millennium ago – beached on the slipways.

Filey Brigg is the southern starting point for the oddly-named **Cleveland Way**, odd because only a few miles of the 110-mile footpath actually pass through Cleveland. The path follows the coast as far north as Saltburn-by-the-Sea, then turns south to Roseberry Topping and the Cleveland Hills, finally ending up at Helmsley.

HUNMANBY
3 miles SW of Filey between the A165 and A1039

Here's a question worthy of Trivial Pursuit: 'On which vehicle was the wing mirror first used?' Your answer is almost certainly wrong unless you know about the grave of a

WRANGHAM HOUSE HOTEL & RESTAURANT

Stonegate, Hunmanby, nr Filey, North Yorkshire YO14 0NS
Tel: 01723 891333 Fax: 01723 892973
e-mail: staciedevos@aol.com
website: www.wranghamhouse.co.uk

Wrangham House Hotel & Restaurant began life as the village vicarage. The building dates back in parts to 1675, with Georgian additions, and is set in three acres of lovely mature gardens. Owners Stacie and Peter Devos have refurbished much of the hotel including the dining room and restaurant. There are 12 individually styled bedrooms all en-suite, 8 of which have also been refurbished. Four rooms have four-poster beds, most have king-sized beds, and two rooms are on the ground floor. There are two stylish yet traditional lounges and bars with cosy fires, lovely paintings on the walls, comfortable seating and room enough to host family celebrations – within the past year the hotel has been granted a licence to conduct civil wedding ceremonies – while the restaurant has earned a growing reputation for the finest food and drink in the area. Peter is a serious wine buff with an excellent wine list to match. He is also an accomplished chef, trained in European hotels, and creates a menu of tempting dishes such as roast rack of lamb, fillet steak, spinach and ricotta cheese tortellini and more, all expertly prepared using the freshest ingredients. Specialising in short stays and golfing breaks, the hotel caters for both the business and leisure traveller.

1st-century British charioteer uncovered at Hunmanby in 1907. Along with his bones, those of his horses, and fragments of the chariot wheels was a rectangular strip of shiny metal: archaeologists are convinced that this was fixed to the side of the chariot as a mirror so that the driver could see the competitors behind him.

Another curiosity in Hunmanby is the village lock-up with two cells and tiny windows designed for human miscreants, and next to it a circular stone pinfold intended for straying cattle.

The Vale of Pickering

Not all that long ago, the Vale of Pickering was the Lake of Pickering, an immense stretch of water far larger than any English lake today, about 32 miles long and four to eight miles wide. As the Ice Age retreated, the waters gradually drained away leaving a low-lying plain of good arable soil based on Kimmeridge clay. Much of it remained marshy however and at Star Carr, near Seamer, archaeologists have uncovered a late Stone Age lake community, dating back some 7,500 years, where the houses were built on stilts above the water. Sadly, the remains of this fascinating excavation lie on private land and are not open to the public. It is only in comparatively recent times that the Vale has been properly drained, which explains why most of the towns and villages lie around its edge in a rough kind of horseshoe formation.

For much of its length, the Vale is watered by the River Derwent, which was also powerfully affected by the changes that occurred during the Ice Age. Originally it entered the sea near Scarborough but an Ice Age glacier blocked that outlet. The Derwent still flows to within a mile-and-a-half of Scarborough, but now turns abruptly and makes a 90-mile detour through the vale and then southwards to join the River Ouse near Howden.

Pickering Castle

The main traffic artery through the vale is the Thirsk to Scarborough road, the A170, which in summer peak periods can become very congested. But you only have to turn off this busy thoroughfare to find yourself in quiet country lanes leading to sleepy market towns and unspoilt villages. To the north rise the intricate folds of the North York Moors; to the south, the Yorkshire Wolds roll gently away towards Beverley, Hull and the River Humber. Our exploration of the vale begins at the eastern end of this broad, low-lying corridor, at East Ayton near Scarborough, and follows it westwards to the lower slopes of the Hambleton Hills.

Pickering

🏠 Church of St Peter & St Paul 🏛 Beck Isle Museum
🏛 North Yorkshire Moors Railway 🌿 Trout Lake

This busy little town developed around the important crossroads where the Malton to Whitby and the Thirsk to Scarborough roads intersect. It's the largest of the four market towns in Ryedale and possibly the oldest, claiming to date from 270 BC when (so it's said) it was founded by a King of the Brigantes called Peredurus. William the Conqueror's attempts to dominate the area are

recalled by Pickering's ruined **Castle** (English Heritage), and the many inns and posting houses reflect the town's prosperity during the stage coach era. Lying at the heart of the fertile Vale of Pickering, the town's reputation was originally based on its famous pigs and horses. Vast quantities of pork were transported across the moors to Whitby, salted and used as shipboard rations. The famous Cleveland Bay horses, with their jet-black manes and tails, were extensively bred in the area. (In Eskdale, a little further north, they still are.) These sweet-natured, sturdy and tireless animals have always been in great demand. During the 19th century, their equable temperament made them ideal for pulling Hansom cabs and street-cars, and nowadays they are often seen in more dignified events such as State Processions.

The parish church of **St Peter and St Paul** is well worth visiting for its remarkable 15th-century murals. During the glum days of Puritanism, these lively paintings were denounced as idolatrous and plastered over. They stayed forgotten for some 200 years but were rediscovered when the church was being restored in 1851. Unfortunately, the vicar at that time shared the Puritans' sentiments and, despite opposition from his parishioners and

🏠 historic building 🏛 museum and heritage 🏛 historic site 🌿 scenic attraction 🐦 flora and fauna

even from his bishop, had them smothered again under whitewash. A more liberal successor to that vicar had the murals restored once again in 1878 and they now give one a vivid idea of how cheerful, colourful and entertaining many English churches were before the unforgivable vandalism of the Puritan years. These superb paintings, sharp, vigorous and well-observed, happily embrace scenes from the Bible, old legends and actual history: a real insight into the medieval mind that had no difficulty in accepting both the story of St George slaying the dragon and the martyrdom of St Thomas à Becket as equally real, and inspiring, events.

Also not to be missed in Pickering is the **Beck Isle Museum** housed in a gracious Regency mansion. Its 27 display areas are crammed with a 'magnificent assortment of items curious, mysterious, marvellous and commonplace from the last 200 years'. There are intriguing re-creations of typical Victorian domestic rooms, shops, workshops and even a pub. The comprehensive collection of photographs by Sydney Smith presents a remarkable picture of the Ryedale area as it was between 1909 and the 1950s. The exhibition is made even more interesting by its acquisition of the very cameras and other photographic equipment used by Sydney Smith.

Collectors of antiques can really indulge themselves at the Pickering Antique Centre where 32 dealers display their wares in 3,500 square feet of showrooms.

If you catch a whiff of sulphurous smoke, then you must be close to the station. Pickering is the southern terminus of the **North Yorkshire Moors Railway** and here you can board a steam-drawn train for an 18-mile journey along one of the oldest and most dramatically scenic railways in the country. Thanks to a grant from the Heritage Lottery Fund, the Booking and Parcels Office has been restored to how it was in 1937. The station's refreshment room is now a tea room and there's a shop with a wide range of gifts, books and videos.

Just up the road, at the **Pickering Trout Lake,** you can hire a rod and tackle and attempt to beat the record for the largest fish ever caught here – it currently stands at a mighty 25lb 4oz (11.45 kg).

Around Pickering

EAST AYTON
13 miles E of Pickering on the A170

🏛 Castle

Victorian visitors to Scarborough, occasionally tiring of its urban attractions, welcomed excursions to beauty spots such as the Forge Valley near East Ayton. Aeons ago, a sharp-edged glacier excavated the valley; then centuries of natural growth softened its hills, clothed them with over-arching trees and, quite by chance, created one of the loveliest woodland walks in England. For a steady walker, going say four miles an hour, the round trip walk from East Ayton to the old forge from which the valley derives its name – along one side of the river returning on the other, takes about 2.5 hours. A short diversion will lead you to the ruins of **Ayton Castle** at the edge of the road near the junction of the A170 and B1261. Dating from around 1400, this is one of the most southerly of the hundreds of pele towers built in those turbulent times as a protection against invading Scottish marauders. In more peaceful days, many of these towers had a more comfortable mansion added but their defensive origins are still clearly recognisable.

BROMPTON-BY-SAWDON
10 miles E of Pickering on the A170

It was in the medieval church of this small village, on an autumn day in 1802, that William Wordsworth was married to Mary Hutchinson whose family lived at nearby Gallows Hill Farm. *'A perfect woman,'* he wrote of Mary,
'nobly planned,
To warn, to comfort, and command,
And yet a spirit still, and bright,
With something of an angelic light'.

Mary's home, now the Wordsworth Gallery, plays host to an exhibition on the poets Wordsworth and Coleridge, while the medieval barn is now filled with designer gifts, ladies clothes and licensed tea rooms. The gallery is open Tuesday to Saturday all year round.

Wydale Hall (private) was the home of the Squire of Brompton, Sir George Cayley (1773-1857), a pioneer aviator who achieved successful flights with small gliders although it was his coachman who was actually dragooned into being the pilot. Sir George is also credited with inventing the caterpillar tractor.

EBBERSTON
7 miles E of Pickering on the A170

🏛 Ebberston Hall

About a mile to the west of Ebberston, in 1718, Mr William Thompson, MP for Scarborough, built for himself what is possibly the smallest stately home in England, **Ebberston Hall.** From the front, the house appears to be just one storey high, with a pillared doorway approached by a

STUDLEY HOUSE FARM

67 Main Street, Ebberston, Scarborough,
North Yorkshire YO13 9NR
Tel: 01723 859285
e-mail: brenda@yorkshireancestors.com
website: www.studleyhousefarm.co.uk or
www.yorkshireancestors.com

Brenda and David Green and their daughter Katie welcome visitors to **Studley House Farm** with a choice of award-winning holiday accommodation on the edge of the North York Moors National Park. B&B rooms in the lovely Victorian farmhouse are superbly appointed, with en-suite facilities and lots of little extras, and the day starts with an excellent English breakfast. Self-catering accommodation is available in Cow Pasture and Swallowtail Cottages, and there are spaces for up to eight caravans or motor homes in the old apple orchard, with hardstandings, hook-ups and water to all pitches. All guests at the farm have the use of laundry facilities. The setting is peaceful and attractive, with

extensive gardens, scenic walks and an abundance of wildlife. The farm has another, possibly unique attraction in the shape of a family history research library, a well-equipped library with genealogical books, local history books, Yorkshire indexes and computer access. Guests staying at the farm are welcome to use this amenity, and day visitors also access it by prior appointment. The owners hold tutored 2-hour beginners' classes twice a month.

🏛 historic building 🏛 museum and heritage 🏛 historic site ♧ scenic attraction 🍃 flora and fauna

157

grand flight of stone steps flanked by a moderately sized room on each side. In fact, behind this modest front, there's also an extensive basement – 'deceptively spacious' as the estate agents say. Ebberston Hall can only be viewed from the road or churchyard as it is now a private house.

THORNTON-LE-DALE
2 miles E of Pickering on the A170

🐦 ⋀ Dalby Forest Drive

As long ago as 1907, a *Yorkshire Post* poll of its readers acclaimed Thornton-le-Dale as the most beautiful village in Yorkshire. Despite stiff competition for that title, most visitors still find themselves in agreement.

If further proof were needed, just off the A170, near the parish church of All Saints, you'll find one of the most photographed houses in Britain. The thatched cottage, set beside a sparkling beck, appears regularly on chocolate boxes, jigsaws and calendars. On the nearby village green there's an ancient cross and a set of wooden stocks and, across the road, are Lady Lumley's Almshouses, 12 dwellings built in 1670 and still serving their original purpose. The North York Moors National Park actually creates a special loop in its boundary to include this picture-postcard village which, somewhat confusingly, is also frequently shown on maps as 'Thornton Dale'.

About three miles north of Thornton-le-Dale, the Dalby Visitor Centre is the starting point for the **Dalby Forest Drive**, a nine-mile circuit through what was once the royal hunting Forest of Pickering. The Visitor Centre can provide plentiful details of the various facilities available – waymarked walks, cycle routes, picnic/barbecue sites, children's play areas, an orienteering course and wildlife observation hide, and much more.

KIRBY MISPERTON
3 miles S of Pickering, off the A169

🐦 Flamingo Land

The 375 acres of wooded parkland surrounding Kirby Misperton Hall provide the setting for **Flamingo Land,** a zoo and fun park that is home to more than 1,000 birds, animals and reptiles. Red-necked wallabies, meerkats, Bactrian camels, lynx, tigers, rheas, scimitar-horned oryx, bison, sea lions, baboons and guanacos (a South American relative of the camel) are just some of the many exotic creatures in residence. Beyond doubt, the most spectacular sight is that of the flock of pink flamingos gathered around the lake fringed with willow trees. With more than 100 different attractions, including a fun fair with some truly scary rides, an adventure playground and a real working farm, it's no surprise to learn that Flamingo Land is the fourth most visited theme park in the country.

SINNINGTON
4 miles W of Pickering off the A170

At Sinnington the River Seven drops down from the moors and the valley of Rosedale into the more open country of the Vale of Pickering. Now a stream, it passes through this tiny village, running alongside a broad green in the centre of which stands a graceful old packhorse bridge. At one time this medieval bridge must have served a useful purpose but whatever old watercourse that once flowed beneath it has long since disappeared - thus the bridge is known as the 'dry' bridge.

An excellent walk begins and ends at Sinnington. Covering some 7½ miles (12.1km), though it can also be done in parts, it starts at the village's fascinating Saxon and

NORTH YORKSHIRE: COAST, MOORS AND DALES

🎬 stories and anecdotes 🦜 famous people 🎨 art and craft 🎭 entertainment and sport ⋀ walks

PENNITA FASHIONS

1 Castlegate, Helmsley, North Yorkshire YO62 5AB
Tel: 01439 770567

PENNITA PLUS

Meeting House Court, Helmsley,
North Yorkshire YO62 5DW
Tel: 01439 771567

'Wear the Wow Factor!'

Pennita Fashions is the brainchild of Penny Brudenell, who invites her customers to come in, look around and share her passion for fashion.

She offers a wide range of designer and occasion wear in a relaxed atmosphere where customers are assured of the very best service.

Everything on display is personally selected by Penny, who has created an individual and unique experience that has changed the face of fashion in North Yorkshire.

Specialising in Mother of the Bride/Groom, the extensive range of clothing also includes everyday, formal, party and racing wear, complemented by a fabulous selection of quality handbags, shoes, exotic hats/fascinators, amazing jewellery and other wonderful accessories.

The first Pennita, established in 2000, occupies the recently refurbished and expanded Castlegate premises and offers luxurious fitting rooms in glamorous surroundings for a relaxing shopping experience offering sizes from 8 to 16.

In 2007 Penny opened a sister shop, Pennita Plus, for sizes 16 to 26 in nearby Meeting House Court, offering a similar range and equally high standards of service.

Over 30 continental designer labels are always available including:

Michel Ambers	Marina Rinaldi
Ann Balon	Joseph Ribkoff
John Charles	Claudia Stevens
Maria Coca	Tina Taylor
Marcelane	Frank Usher
Renato Nucci	Paule Vasseur

Pennita is the One Stop Shop for Head to Toe style and elegance.

Norman church and leads along woodland paths and farm tracks towards Cropton, Rosedale and Lastingham to Lower Askew, then back through Appleton-le-Moors to the starting point. Details available from North York Moors National Park (tel. 01439 770173).

Helmsley

🏯 Duncombe Park 🏯 Castle 🏯 Rievaulx Abbey

🌱 Rievaulx Terrace 🌱 Walled Garden

One of North Yorkshire's most popular and attractive towns, with lots of speciality shops and a market every Friday, Helmsley lies on the banks of the River Rye on the edge of the North York Moors National Park. The spacious cobbled market square is typical of the area but the Gothic memorial to the 2nd Earl of

Feversham that stands there is definitely not. This astonishingly ornate construction was designed by Sir Giles Gilbert Scott and looks like a smaller version of his famous memorial to Sir Walter Scott in Edinburgh.

The Earls of Feversham lived at **Duncombe Park** whose extensive grounds sweep up to within a few yards of the Market Place. Most of the original mansion, designed by Vanbrugh, was gutted by a disastrous fire in 1879; only the north wing remained habitable and that in its turn was ruined by a second fire in 1895. The Fevershams lavished a fortune on rebuilding the grand old house, largely to the original design, but the financial burden eventually forced them to lease the house and grounds as a preparatory school for girls. Happily, the Fevershams were able to return

DAZZLE GALLERY

4 Bridge Street, Helmsley, North Yorkshire YO62 5BG
Tel: 01439 771010

A passion for her work as a teacher of art, sculpture and ceramics led Annie Wright to an ambition to open her own gallery. She turned that ambition into reality in 2000 when she established **Dazzle Gallery**. A collector at heart, she has filled the gallery with a colourful, ever-changing display of British work – jewellery, glass, ceramics, quirky clocks, sculptures, paintings and limited edition prints – that really does dazzle. She exhibits the work of some 130 artists/designers, all of whom she has met and many of whom have become friends. Jewellers include Diana Porter, Anthony Blakeney, Scarlett and Melanie Tomlinson; glassmakers Stuart Ackroyd, Bob Crookes and Martin Andrews display a collection of perfume bottles, baubles, bowls and vases. There are wonderful handbuilt sculptures in stoneware by Simon Griffiths; lustreware by Mark Haillay and Jessica Ball; raku by Tony White; hares by Shrimpboat; Joanne Cooke's lovely dogs; decorated tableware by Vivienne Ross and much much more. All the artists who display their work at Dazzle welcome commissions.

🎭 stories and anecdotes 🐦 famous people 🎨 art and craft 🎭 entertainment and sport 🚶 walks

to their ancestral home in 1985 and the beautifully restored house with its 35 acres of lovely gardens and a further 400 acres of superbly landscaped grounds are now open to the public.

Before they were ennobled, the Fevershams' family name was Duncombe and it was Sir Thomas Duncombe, a wealthy London goldsmith, who established the family seat here when he bought **Helmsley Castle** (English Heritage) and its estate in 1687. Founded in the early 1100s, seriously knocked about during the Civil War, the castle was in a dilapidated state but its previous owner, the Duke of Buckingham, had continued to live there in some squalor and discomfort. Sir Thomas quickly decided to build a more suitable residence nearby, abandoning the ruins to lovers of the romantic and picturesque.

Helmsley Village

With the castle as its backdrop, **Helmsley Walled Garden** (see panel below) comprises five acres of lovely gardens containing many unusual varieties of flowers, vegetables and herbs. Originally established in the 1700s, the

Helmsley Walled Garden

Cleveland Way, Helmsley, York,
North Yorkshire YO62 5AT
Tel: 01439 771427

Helmsley Walled Garden is a 5-acre walled garden built in 1758 and set beneath Helmsley Castle. The garden produced fruit and vegetables for Duncombe park until it fell into ruin. The garden lay derelict until 1994 when a charity was established to restore it and provide horticultural therapy. A plantsman's garden it includes 350 varities of Clematis, 52 Yorkshire apples, 34 Victorian vines, Victorian glasshouses, a Paeonia garden, Dipping Well, Rainbow border and much more. You'll also find craft workshops, an unusual plant nursery, vegetarian café and ethical shop. Open daily from 1st April to 31st October, 10.30am - 5pm. Dogs welcome on leads. Full wheelchair access.

🏛 historic building   🏛 museum and heritage   🏛 historic site   ✤ scenic attraction   🌢 flora and fauna

garden had become a wilderness by the late 1900s, but has now been completely restored and work is currently underway to bring the Victorian glasshouses back into service. Plants, cut and dried flowers, vegetables and herbs are on sale; there's a café, shop and picnic area.

Just to the west of Helmsley rise the indescribably beautiful remains of **Rievaulx Abbey**

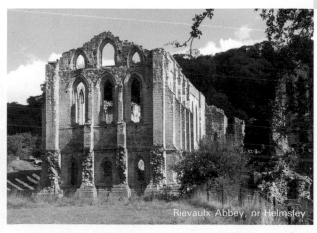

Rievaulx Abbey, nr Helmsley

(English Heritage), standing among wooded hills beside the River Rye – 'the most beautiful monastic site in Europe'. JMW Turner was enchanted by this idyllic landscape; Dorothy Wordsworth, 'spellbound'. Founded in 1131, Rievaulx was the first Cistercian abbey in Yorkshire and, with some 700 people – monks, lay brothers, servants – eventually living within its walls, became one of the largest. Like Kirkham Abbey a few years earlier, Rievaulx was endowed by Walter l'Espec, Lord of Helmsley, still mourning the loss of his only son in a riding accident. The Abbey was soon a major landowner in the county, earning a healthy income from farming and at one time owning more than 14,000 sheep. The Abbey also had its own fishery at Teesmouth, and iron-ore mines at Bilsdale and near Wakefield.

Looking down on the extensive remains of the Abbey is **Rievaulx Terrace** (National Trust), a breathtaking example of landscape gardening completed in 1758. The cunningly contrived avenues draw your eyes to incomparable views of the Abbey itself, to vistas along the Rye Valley and to the rolling contours of the hills beyond. At each end of the terrace is a classical temple, one of which is elaborately furnished and decorated as a dining room.

Around Helmsley

KIRKBYMOORSIDE
4 miles E of Helmsley on the A170

Set off the main road, this agreeable market town (markets are on Wednesdays) of fine Georgian houses, narrow twisting lanes, family-owned shops and a cobbled marketplace, straggles up the hillside. After you pass the last house on the hill, you enter the great open spaces of the North York Moors National Park, 553 square miles of outstanding natural beauty, which, since they were accorded the status of a National Park in 1952, have been protected from insensitive encroachments. Within the park you don't have to worry about traffic lights – there aren't any. But you may well have to step down firmly on your brakes to avoid sheep crossing the road at their own leisurely and disdainful pace.

BEADLAM GRANGE FARM SHOP & TEA ROOM

Main Road (A170), nr Helmsley, North Yorkshire YO62 7TD
Tel: 01439 770303
e-mail: mark.rooke@farming.co.uk
website: www.beadlamgrange.co.uk

Newly converted traditional farm buildings on the A170, 2 miles east of Helmsley, house an outstanding Farmshop and Tearoom. Mark and Jenny Rooke set up their business at **Beadlam Grange** in June 2007 and have created a 'unique farm shopping experience' in lovely surroundings where customers can purchase home produced meat from a fresh meat counter, as well as fresh fruit and vegetables, local cheeses, dairy produce, bread, home-made cakes and so much more! In the delightful Granary Tearoom the menu makes good use of the produce in the farmshop and everything is cooked fresh to order, including farmhouse breakfasts, light lunches, home-make cakes and scones, roast Sunday lunches, Yorkshire farm teas and daily

specials. Beadlam Grange is open from 9.30 to 5 (Sunday 10 to 4; closed Mondays in winter). It has ample free parking and full disabled access. The owners also have a self-catering holiday cottage on the farm together with a small 5-van caravan site.

Of the several old coaching inns in Kirkbymoorside, the timbered Black Swan is believed to be the most venerable – the intricately carved entrance porch bears the date 1692.

It was in another ancient inn, the King Head's Hotel, that one of the 17th century's most reviled politicians expired. In what is now Buckingham House, but was then part of the adjoining hotel, George Villiers, 2nd Duke of Buckingham died. The duke had been a favourite of Charles II and a member of the notorious 'Cabal' of the king's five most powerful ministers who colluded with him in trying to frustrate the democratic instincts of the elected Parliament. Each letter of the word 'Cabal' represented the initial of one of its five members – Buckingham being the 'B'.

The Duke had come to Kirkbymoorside to take part in a hunt through the nearby Forest of Pickering. In the heat of the chase he was thrown from his horse and mortally wounded. The duke's retainers carried him to the King's Head Inn where he died later that day. In the parish register for 1687 the passing of a once-mighty politician merited only a laconic, phonetic entry: *Died: April 17th George Viluas: Lord Dooke of Bookingham.*

NUNNINGTON
5 miles SE of Helmsley off the B1257

🏠 Nunnington Hall

Nunnington Hall (National Trust) is a late-17th-century manor house in a beautiful setting beside the River Rye with a picturesque packhorse bridge within its grounds. Inside, there is a magnificent panelled hall, fine tapestries and china, and the famous Carlisle collection of miniature rooms exquisitely furnished in different period styles to one-eighth life size.

COXWOLD

8 miles S of Helmsley off the A19 or A170

🏛 Shandy Hall 🏛 Church of St Michael

🏛 Newburgh Priory 🏛 Byland Abbey

Coxwold enjoys a particularly lovely setting in the narrow valley that runs between the Hambleton and Howardian Hills. At the western end of the village stands the 500-year-old **Shandy Hall,** home of Laurence Sterne, vicar of Coxwold in the 1760s. Sterne was the author of *Tristram Shandy,* that wonderfully bizarre novel that opened a vein of English surreal comedy leading directly to The Goons and the Monty Python team. The architecture of the Hall, Tudor in origin,

includes some appropriately eccentric features – strangely-shaped balustrades on the wooden staircases, a Heath Robinson kind of contraption in the bedroom powder-closet by which Sterne could draw up pails of water for his ablutions, and a tiny, eye-shaped window in the huge chimney stack opening from the study to the right of the entrance. A more conventional attraction is the priceless collection of Sterne's books and manuscripts.

The Revd Sterne much preferred the cosmopolitan diversions of London to the rustic pleasures of his Yorkshire parish and rarely officiated at the imposing **Church of St Michael** nearby with its striking octagonal tower, three-decker pulpit and Fauconberg family tombs. A curiosity here is a floor brass in the nave recording the death of Sir John Manston in 1464. A space was left for his wife Elizabeth's name to be added at a later date. The space is still blank. Outside, against the

Newburgh Priory

Coxwold, York, Yorkshire HG4 5AE
Tel: 01347 868435
website: www.newburghpriory.co.uk

Newburgh Priory is a large and imposing house near Coxwold, North Yorkshire. Standing on the site of an old priory, it is a fine stately home in a superb setting with breathtaking views to the Kilburn White Horse in the distance. The extensive grounds contain a water garden, walled garden, topiary yews and woodland walks.

Originally an Augustinian monastery, founded in 1145, it provided priests for the surrounding churches in return for gifts of land and money from the rich landowners. The house was the country seat for the Belassis family in the 16th and 17th century. It is reputed to be the burial place of Oliver Cromwell whose remains were said to have been brought to Newburgh Priory by his daughter Mary when she married the 2nd viscount.

Newburgh belonged formerly to the Earls of Fauconberg and is presently the home of Sir George and Lady Wombwell, who open the Priory to visitors for guided tours from April to June.

NORTH YORKSHIRE: COAST, MOORS AND DALES

THE FAUCONBERG ARMS

Coxwold, nr Thirsk,
North Yorkshire YO61 4AD
Tel: 01347 868214
e-mail: simon@fauconbergarms.co.uk
website: www.fauconbergarms.com

Having been empty for the past 2 years, local family Simon, Helen, Harriet and Jonathan have breathed new life into the **Fauconberg Arms**, an attractive old hostelry in a charming village setting. Behind the handsome stone exterior huge beams and joists, flagstones and log fires preserve an inviting traditional atmosphere, and in the summer the scene shifts to the garden with its distant views of Byland Abbey. The bar stocks real ales including varieties from Theakston and Thwaites breweries, and menus ranging from sandwiches and snacks to a full dinner menu conplemented by seasonal daily specials that offer excellent value for money, complemented by a well-chosen selection of wines.

If you're looking for somewhere to stay overnight, The Fauconberg Arms offers four cosy bedrooms all equipped with generously sized beds and en-suite facilities – and the breakfasts that start the day are a real treat.

There's plenty to attract the visitor to Coxwold and the surrounding area, including the 500-year-old Shandy Hall, the imposing Church of St Michael, Byland Abbey and Newburgh Priory. The last-named was once the home of the Fauconberg family from whom the Fauconberg Arms takes its name. Simon and family will do their upmost to make sure that you have a pleasant visit whether it be for some of their fine food or a comfortable night in one of the bedrooms. The Fauconberg Arms is a real treat and well worth a visit if your are in the area.

wall of the nave, is Sterne's original tombstone, moved here from London's Bayswater when the churchyard there was deconsecrated in 1969.

Just to the south of Coxwold is **Newburgh Priory** (see panel on page 163), founded in 1145 as an Augustinian monastery and now a mostly Georgian country house with fine interiors and a beautiful water garden. Until recently the Priory had been the home of the Fauconberg family. An old tradition asserts that Oliver Cromwell's body is interred here.

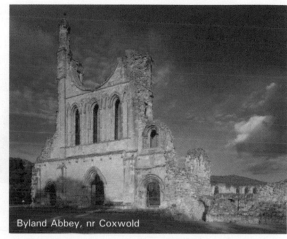
Byland Abbey, nr Coxwold

Cromwell's daughter, Mary, was married to Lord Fauconberg and when Charles II had her father's corpse hanged at Tyburn and his head struck off, Lady Fauconberg claimed the decapitated body, brought it to Newburgh and, it is said, buried the remains under the floorboards of an attic room. The supposed tomb has never been opened, the Fauconbergs even resisting a royal appeal from Edward VII when, as Prince of Wales, he was a guest at the Priory. The house and its extensive grounds are open to the public for guided tours from April to June.

From Coxwold, follow the minor road northeastwards towards Ampleforth. After about two miles, you will see the lovely, cream-coloured ruins of **Byland Abbey** (English Heritage). The Cistercians began building their vast compound in 1177 and it grew to become the largest Cistercian church in Britain. Much of the damage to its fabric was caused by Scottish soldiers after the Battle of Byland in 1322. The English king, Edward II had been staying at the Abbey but fled after his defeat, abandoning vital stores and priceless treasures. In a frenzy of looting, the Scots made off with everything the king had left and ransacked the Abbey for good measure. The ruined west front of the Abbey, although only the lower arc of its great rose window is still in place, gives a vivid impression of how glorious this building must once have been.

AMPLEFORTH
5 miles S of Helmsley off the A170

College

Set on the southern slopes of the Hambleton Hills, Ampleforth is perhaps best known for its Roman Catholic public school, Ampleforth College, established by the Benedictine community that came here in 1809, fleeing from persecution in post-revolutionary France. The monks built an austere-looking Abbey in the Romanesque style among whose treasures are an altar stone rescued from Byland Abbey and finely crafted woodwork by the 'Mouseman of Kilburn', Robert Thompson.

NORTH YORKSHIRE: COAST, MOORS AND DALES

stories and anecdotes   famous people   art and craft   entertainment and sport   walks

KILBURN

8 miles S of Helmsley off the A170

⛪ White Horse

🐿 'Mouseman of Kilburn'

Kilburn was the home of one of the most famous of modern Yorkshire craftsmen, Robert Thompson – the **'Mouseman of Kilburn'**. Robert's father was a carpenter but he apprenticed his son to an engineer. At the age of 20 however, inspired by seeing the medieval wood carvings in Ripon Cathedral, Robert returned to Kilburn and begged his father to train him as a carpenter. An early commission from Ampleforth Abbey to carve a cross settled his destiny: from then until his death in 1955 Robert's beautifully crafted ecclesiastical and domestic furniture was in constant demand. His work can be seen in more than 700 churches, including Westminster Abbey and York Minster. Each piece bears his 'signature' – a tiny carved mouse placed in some inconspicuous corner of the work. According to a family story, Robert adopted this symbol when one of his assistants happened to use the phrase 'as poor as a church mouse'. (Signing one's work wasn't an entirely new tradition: the 17th-century woodcarver Grinling Gibbons' personal stamp was a pod of peas.) Robert Thompson's two grandsons have continued his work and their grandfather's former home is now both a memorial to his genius and a showroom for their own creations.

You can see several of the Mouseman's creations in Kilburn village church – there's one perched on the traceried pulpit, another clinging to a desk in the sanctuary, and a third sitting cheekily on the lectern.

From the northern end of the village a winding lane leads to the famous **White**

The Mouseman Visitor Centre, Kilburn

Horse, inspired by the prehistoric White Horse hill-carving at Uffingham in Berkshire. John Hodgson, Kilburn's village schoolmaster, enthused his pupils and villagers into creating this splendid folly in 1857. It is 314 feet long and 228 feet high and visible from as far away as Harrogate and Otley. Unlike its prehistoric predecessor in Berkshire, where the chalk hillside keeps it naturally white, Kilburn's 'white' horse is scraped from grey limestone which needs to be regularly groomed with lime-washing and a liberal spreading of chalk chippings.

Malton

🏛 St Mary's Priory   🏚 Eden Camp

🌿 Scrampton Hall

Malton has been the historic centre of Ryedale ever since the Romans came. They built a large fort and called it Derventio after the river Derwent beside which it stands. For many years, archaeologists were puzzled by the large scale of the fort, a mystery solved in 1970 when a building dedication was uncovered which revealed that the fort housed a cavalry regiment, the Ala Picentiana – the extra space was needed to accommodate their horses. Many fine relics from the site showing the sophisticated lifestyles of the Roman centurions and civilians can be seen in the Malton Museum, along with items from the Iron Age settlement that preceded the Roman garrison.

The River Derwent was vitally important to Malton. The river rises in the moors near Scarborough, then runs inland through the Vale of Pickering bringing an essential element for what was once a major industry in Malton – brewing. In the 19th century, there were nine breweries here, now only the Malton Brewery Company survives. It operates in a converted stable block behind Suddabys Crown Hotel in Wheelgate and welcomes visitors, but call them first on 01653 697580.

Charles Dickens stayed in the area with his friend, Charles Smithson, a solicitor. He is believed to have modelled Scrooge's Counting House in *A Christmas Carol* on Smithson's office in Chancery Lane.

Old Malton is located just to the north of the Roman Fort, an interesting and historic area on the edge of open countryside. Nearby villages such as Settrington and their secluded country lanes are home to many famous racehorse stables: if you are up and about

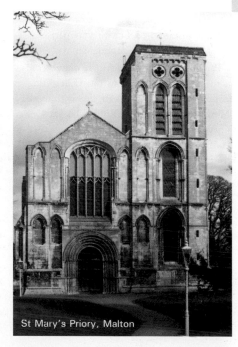

St Mary's Priory, Malton

early enough you will see the horses out on their daily exercises. In the centre of Old Malton stands the beautiful remains of **St Mary's Priory**, incorporating a particularly fine Norman doorway. The Priory was built around 1155 by the only monastic order in Christendom to have originated entirely in

---

J R LEEFE & SON STATIONERY & ART

57 Market Place, Malton, North Yorkshire YO17 7LX
Tel/Fax: 01653 692366
e-mail: aleefe06@aol.com

Alistair Leefe is the fifth generation of his family to run **JR Leefe & Son**, an outstanding specialist art and stationery specialist shop situated on Malton's market place. On the art side there are painting materials – paints, oils, easels – from Windsor & Newton, Pro Arte brushes, sketch pads and books and Derwent pencils. Stationery includes the top names in pens and pencils, games and puzzles, craft sets, calligraphy sets, painting by numbers and greetings cards.

🎞 stories and anecdotes   🐦 famous people   🎨 art and craft   🎭 entertainment and sport   🚶 walks

England – the Gilbertines. The order was founded in 1148 by a Lincolnshire parish priest, St Gilbert of Sempringham.

Parts of the parish church are quite as old as the Priory but one of its most interesting features is relatively modern, the work of the 'Mouseman of Kilburn', Robert Thompson. A gifted woodcarver and furniture maker, Thompson 'signed' all his pieces with a discreetly placed carving of a mouse. There's one on the stout oak door of the church and, inside, the stalls are carved elaborately with all manner of wondrous beasts along with historical and mythical scenes.

A mile or so north of Old Malton is **Eden Camp**, a theme museum dedicated to re-creating the dramatic experiences of ordinary people living through the Second World War. This unique museum is housed in some 30 huts of a genuine prisoner-of-war camp, built in 1942. Sound, lighting effects, smells, even smoke generators are deployed to make you feel that you are actually there. Visitors can find out what it was like to live through an air raid, to be a prisoner of war or a sailor in a U-boat under attack. Among the many other exhibits are displays on Fashion in the 1940s, Children at War, and even one on Rationing. In 1941, one discovers, the cheese ration was down to 1oz (28 grams) a week!

New this year is the walled garden at **Scampston Hall** (see panel below) a few miles northeast of Malton off the A64. Designed by Piet Oudolf, who was awarded a Gold Veitch Memorial Medal by the RHS in 2002 in recognition of services given in the advancement of the science and practice of horticulture, the 4.5-acre garden is a series of hedged enclosures with a dazzling display of modern and colourful planting. A grass

Scampston Hall

Malton, North Yorkshire YO17 8NG
Tel: 01944 759111
e-mail: info@scampston.co.uk   website: www.scampston.co.uk

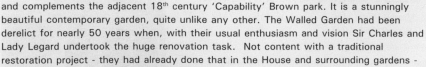

Open for just one month a year, and sitting in its own traditional gardens, Scampston Hall is one of the finest country houses in Yorkshire.

Set within the 18th century walls of the original kitchen garden for the Hall, you'll find the Walled Garden, which today has an exciting and unashamedly modern feel to it and complements the adjacent 18th century 'Capability' Brown park. It is a stunningly beautiful contemporary garden, quite unlike any other. The Walled Garden had been derelict for nearly 50 years when, with their usual enthusiasm and vision Sir Charles and Lady Legard undertook the huge renovation task. Not content with a traditional restoration project - they had already done that in the House and surrounding gardens -

they set about producing a stunning garden with a contemporary feel.

Having enlisted the help of leading garden designer, Piet Oudolf, and a dedicated team of gardeners led by Tim Marshall, they are delighted with the result.

🏚 historic building 🏛 museum and heritage 🏛 historic site ⚲ scenic attraction 🌿 flora and fauna

pyramid makes for an observation mount from where you can see this marvellous creation in all its glory. The site also offers a selection of plants for sale as well as an excellent restaurant.

Around Malton

THIXENDALE
12 miles SE of Malton off the A166

The site of a glacial dry valley with up to four others merging with it. There are wonderful walks along the chalk slopes and valleys, listed on notice boards in the centre of the village.

EAST HESLERTON
7 miles NE of Malton on the A64

This little village is distinguished by one of the many churches gifted by Sir Tatton Sykes of Sledmere House in the mid-1800s. Designed in 13th-century style the church has a fine west portico, a vaulted chancel and an iron screen of very fine workmanship. The north tower has an octagonal belfry and spire, and statues of the four Latin Doctors (Ambrose, Augustine, Gregory and Jerome) originally sculpted for Bristol Cathedral.

HOVINGHAM
8 miles W of Malton on the B1257

'Hall, church and village gather round like a happy family,' wrote Arthur Mee describing Hovingham some 60 years ago. Today, the idyllic scene remains unspoilt, a lovely place with no fewer than three village greens. Overlooking one of them is a Victorian school, still in use and boasting an elegant oriel window.

Nearby Hovingham Hall, an imposing Georgian mansion, was built in 1760 for Sir

Thomas Worsley, Surveyor General to George III, and almost exactly 200 years later, on June 8th 1961, his descendant Katherine Worsley returned here for a royal reception following her marriage to the Duke of Kent. The Worsley family still live at the Hall so it is only open to visitors for a short time in summer, but you can see its unusual entrance that leads directly off the village green. The huge archway opens, not as you would expect, into a drive leading to the Hall, but to a vast riding school and stables through which visitors have to pass. Within the Hall's grounds is the village's cricket pitch, enjoying what is surely the most picturesque setting for the game.

CASTLE HOWARD
5 miles W of Malton off the A64

🏛 Castle Howard

Lying in the folds of the Howardian Hills about five miles southwest of Malton stands one of the most glorious stately homes in Britain, **Castle Howard**. Well known to TV viewers as the Brideshead of *Brideshead Revisited*, Castle Howard has astonished visitors ever since it was completed in the early 1700s.

Even that world-weary 18th-century socialite Horace Walpole was stirred to enthusiasm: 'Nobody had informed me,' he wrote, 'that at one view I should see a palace, a town, a fortified city, temples on high places ... the noblest lawn in the world fenced by half the horizon and a mausoleum that would tempt one to be buried alive: in short, I have seen gigantic places before, but never a sublime one.'

Winner of York Tourism Bureau's 'Out of Town Attraction of the Year' award, this magnificent 18th-century house with its extensive collections and breathtaking

Castle Howard

to found another great abbey at Rievaulx.) Visitors to Kirkham pass through a noble, exquisitely decorated gatehouse but one of the most memorable sights at the Priory, perhaps because it is so unexpected, is the sumptuous lavatorium in the ruined cloister. Here the monks washed their hands at two bays with lavishly moulded arches supported by slender pillars, each bay adorned with tracery.

grounds, featuring temples, lakes and fountains, includes various refreshment stops and a plant centre and tree nursey. A varied programme of events takes place throughout the year, including the Proms Spectacular and Archaeology Weekends.

Perhaps the most astonishing fact of all concerns the architect of Castle Howard, Sir John Vanbrugh. Vanbrugh had been a soldier and a playwright but until he began this sublime building had never before overseen the placing of one block of masonry on another.

Castle Howard is open daily between February and November. A land-train is available to transport visitors from the car park to the house, and there is disabled access to many parts.

KIRKHAM
5 miles SW of Malton off the A64

🏛 Priory

In a lovely, peaceful setting beside the River Derwent, stand the remains of **Kirkham Priory**. According to legend, the priory was founded in 1125 by Walter l'Espec after his only son was thrown from his horse and killed at this very spot. (A few years later, Walter was

York and the Surrounding Area

This region of North Yorkshire, between the North York Moors and the East Riding, between West Yorkshire and the Heritage Coast, is dominated by the city of York. The first settlement of any note here was created by the Romans, who named their garrison town 'Eboracum', and, from then on, York has been an important and influential force not only in Yorkshire but also in the rest of the country. Known to the Saxons as 'Eoferwic' and the Vikings as 'Jorvik', it was the creation of the magnificent Minster, started in the early 13th century that saw the city truly begin to develop. A major trading centre and, at one time, the second largest city in the country, York is also remembered as the heart of the railway network in the north of England. Not surprisingly, there is plenty to see here and, along with the numerous imaginative museums and galleries, visitors will want to walk around its medieval streets and soak up the atmosphere that encompasses architectural styles from the past 700 years.

The Vale of York or Plain is rich agricultural land that stretches some 60 miles northwards from York almost to the Tees. Although flat itself, there are almost always hills in view: the Hambleton and Cleveland Hills to the east, the Dales and the Pennines to the west. In between lies this fertile corridor of rich farmland and low-lying meadows, a vast plain bisected by the Great North Road linking London and Edinburgh. For most of its life, the Great North Road has been a rocky, pot-holed and swampy obstacle course. The best stretches, by far, were those where it ran along the meticulously engineered course the Romans had built centuries earlier. It took more than 1,800 years for the English to realise for themselves the importance of constructing viable, all-weather roads. Throughout this area the skyline is dotted with the spires and towers of churches that were built in those relatively prosperous times. The two towns of Harrogate and Knaresborough dominate the lower section of Nidderdale and though, today, Harrogate is the larger, Knaresborough, for centuries, was the more important of the two. Older than its neighbour, Knaresborough was inhabited long before the days of the Romans and, along with its Norman castle, it is now best known as being the home of England's most famous prophetess, Mother Shipton, and the Petrifying Well that stands beside her birthplace.

A small village until the 17th century, Harrogate developed into one of the country's foremost spa towns following the discovery of a chalybeate well in the late 16th century. As the fame of its healing waters spread, along with the fashion for seeking cures for any number of ailments increased, so Harrogate grew into the elegant and genteel town that remains today. The key features here are the Georgian and Victorian architecture along with the wide tree-lined boulevards and the numerous gardens.

York

- Minster Multangular Tower
- Roman Bath Inn Barley Hall
- Merchant Adventurers Hall Fairfax House
- Jorvik Viking Centre National Railway Museum
- Museum of Automata York Castle Museum
- Yorkshire Museum & Gardens Mystery Plays
- Archaeological Research Centre
- The Shambles Original Ghostwalk

'The history of York is the history of England,' said the Duke of York, later to become George VI. A bold claim but well justified. For almost 2,000 years the city has

THE INDEPENDENT

Haxby Road/Lowther Road, York YO31 7ND
Tel: 01904 624549

Experienced publicans Katherine and Richard extend a warm welcome to patrons of **The Independent**, which stands just north of the city centre a short walk from the glorious Minster. Quality beers and lagers and a good choice of wines are served in the roomy, comfortable bar, and the kitchen produces good food at exceptionally reasonable prices, from ciabatta sandwiches to fish and hand-cut chips, lasagne, steaks and steak pies, all-day breakfast, red wine lamb stew, honey-roast ham, the Sunday roasts and an amazing range of beef and chicken burgers.

 stories and anecdotes famous people art and craft entertainment and sport walks

WOODCARVERS OF THE SHAMBLES

39 The Shambles, York, North Yorkshire YO1 7LX
Tel: 01904 621242
e-mail: sales@woodcarversyork.co.uk
website: www.woodcarversyork.co.uk

Superb craftsmanship catches the eye at every turn at Woodcarvers of the Shambles, which Mike and Evelyne Robertson acquired in 2001. Located in the most famous of the city's ancient streets, Woodcarvers is stocked with a wide variety of masterpieces in wood, each of which would make a marvellous gift for the right occasion. The ever-changing stock includes lovespoons, egg-timers, pens, carved birds, photo frames, jewellery boxes, puzzles and chess sets. In addition, the Woodcarvers also caries the very popular ranges of Willow Tree, Jim Shore and Lilliput Lane. A full range of the products can be seen on the excellent Woodcarvers website.

PANDORA GIFT SHOPS

74 Low Petergate, York,
North Yorkshire YO1 7HZ
Tel: 01904 647002

39 Stonegate, York,
North Yorkshire YO1 8AW
Tel: 01904 624046
website: www.pandorayork.co.uk

In two prestigious premises, one in Lower Petergate, the other in Stonegate, **Pandora Gift Shops** are predominantly souvenir shops selling both York and UK souvenirs. They are filled with an outstanding array of gifts large and small for all occasions and to suit all pockets. Their range includes thimbles, Russian dolls, branded Guinness memorabilia, Souvenir T-shirts, Willow Tree and Betty Boop, as well as the naughty collectable Bad Taste Bears. Pandora are well known for their large range of Yorkshire-made coal pieces, which includes superb models of classic, steam locomotives.

CHRISTMAS ANGELS

47 Low Petergate, York, North Yorkshire YO1 7HT
Tel: 01904 639908
e-mail: enquiries@christmasangels.co.uk
website: www.christmasangels.co.uk

Just a short stroll from York Minster is the magical **Christmas Angels** shop. The all-year Christmas section is laid out as a village market with stalls full of fascinating and unusual Christmas accessories, many of them are hand-crafted in the Erzebirge region of Germany. The remainder of this charming shop is given over to a splendid array of traditional wooden toys, games and puzzles. Upstairs is the extensive Teddy Bear gallery - home to bears, gollies and soft toys in all shapes and sizes!

🏚 historic building 🏛 museum and heritage 🏛 historic site ⚘ scenic attraction 🌱 flora and fauna

been at the centre of great events and, better than any other city in England, it has preserved the evidence of each era of its glorious past.

One of the grandest cityscapes in the country opens up as you walk along the old city walls towards **York Minster** (see panel below), a sublime expression of medieval faith. The Minster stands on the site of an even older building, the headquarters of the Roman legions. The Imperial troops arrived here in AD 71 when the governor, Quintus Petilius Cerealis, chose this strategic position astride the Rivers Ouse and Foss as his base for a campaign against the pesky tribe of the Brigantes. The settlement was named Eboracum. From this garrison, Hadrian directed the construction of his great wall and a later general, Constantine, was proclaimed

Emperor here. The legions finally left the city around AD 410, but the evidence of their three-and-a-half centuries of occupation is manifest all around York in buildings like the **Multangular Tower,** in rich artefacts treasured in the city's museums and even in a pub: at the **Roman Bath Inn** you can see the remains of steam baths used by the garrison residents.

Little is known of York during the Dark Ages but by the 8th century the city had been colonised by the Anglo-Saxons, who named it Eoferwic, and it was already an important Christian and academic centre. The Vikings put an end to that when they invaded in the 9th century and changed the name once again, this time to Jorvik. The story of York during those years of Danish rule is imaginatively told in the many displays at the **Jorvik Viking**

York Minster

Deangate, York, Yorkshire YO1 7JA
Tel: 01904 557226/557200
website: www.yorkminster.org.uk

York Minster acts as a beacon welcoming all visitors to the City of York. Built over 250 years, and renowned worldwide as an artistic and architectural masterpiece, it offers a wealth of things to see for people of all ages, and thrilling memories for all who visit.

The Minster is much more than a superb building. It is a site where history has been made over the centuries. The Emperor Constantine began his progress to greatness here, and the Roman buildings in which he lived still stand beneath the central tower. St Paulinus baptised the local Saxon King here, and here are buried many of the Archbishops of York, including St William of York.

York Minster provides a wealth of history for you to discover. The Minster itself is an architectural masterpiece and a treasure house of stained glass. It is a living community of Christian worship where the sound of choral music has lifted the spirits of visitors and pilgrims for centuries.

Centre in Coppergate, celebrating a 1,000-year-old story. This world-famous centre transports visitors back in time to experience the sights, sounds and – perhaps most famously – the smells of 10th century York. Visitors are shown that, in AD 975, York was a bustling commercial centre where 10,000 people lived and worked. Travelling in state-of-the-art 'time capsules', visitors are carried past and through two-storey dwellings, enjoying views over back gardens and rooftops, and even glimpsing the Viking Age equivalent of today's Minster. Journeying through representations of real-life Viking Age York, you pass through a bustling market thronged with Danes bartering for chickens, corn and other provisions and wares, penetrate dark smoky houses, cross a busy wharf where goods transported along the rivers Ouse and Foss are being off-loaded.

Both fun and educational, 20 years after it first opened, Jorvik still retains its status as one of the world's iconic attractions, and its many superb features make it an enduring favourite with children and adults alike.

After the Norman Conquest, the city suffered badly during the Harrowing of the North when William the Conqueror mounted a brutal campaign against his rebellious northern subjects. Vast tracts of Yorkshire and Northumberland were laid waste and some historians reckon that it took more than 100 years for the area to recover from this wholesale devastation.

In later Norman times, however, York entered one of its most glorious periods. The Minster, the largest Gothic cathedral in Northern Europe, was begun around 1230 and the work was on such a scale that it would not be completed until two-and-a-half

centuries later. Its stained glass windows – there are more than 100 of them – cast a celestial light over the many treasures within. A guided tour of the Great Tower gives dizzying views across the city; a visit to the crypt reveals some of the relics from the Roman fortress that stood here nearly 2,000 years ago.

This superb building has survived three major fires. The first occurred in 1829 and was started by a madman, Jonathan Martin. Believing that God wanted him to destroy the church, he started a fire using prayer and hymn books. The fire was not discovered until the following morning by which time the east end of the Minster had been severely damaged. A second blaze, in 1840, was caused by a workman leaving a candle burning. As a result of his carelessness, the central part of the nave was destroyed. The most recent conflagration was in July 1984, shortly after a controversial Bishop of Durham had been installed. Some attributed the fire to God's wrath at the Bishop's appointment; the more prosaic view was that it had been caused by lightning. The subsequent restoration has allowed modern masons and craftsmen to demonstrate that they possess skills just as impressive as those of their medieval forebears.

The network of medieval streets around the Minster is one of the city's major delights. Narrow lanes are criss-crossed by even narrower footpaths - ginnels, snickets or 'snickelways' - which have survived as public rights of way despite being built over, above and around. Narrowest of all the snickelways is Pope's Head Alley, more than 100 feet long but only 31 inches wide. The alley became known as Introduction Lane – if you wanted

The Shambles, York

to know someone better, you simply timed your walk along the lane so as to meet the other party half-way. Whip-ma-Whop-ma-Gate is the shortest street at 35 yds with the longest name and is, allegedly, where felons used to be 'whipped and whopped'. Probably most famous of these ancient streets is **The Shambles**. Its name comes from 'Fleshammels', the street of butchers and slaughter houses. The houses here were deliberately built to keep the street out of direct sunlight, thus protecting the carcasses, which were hung outside the houses on hooks. Many of the hooks are still in place.

During these years, York was the second largest city in England and it was then that the town walls and their 'bars', or gates, were built.

🏠 stories and anecdotes 🦜 famous people 🎨 art and craft 🎭 entertainment and sport 🚶 walks

The trade guilds were also at their most powerful and in Fossgate one of them built the lovely black and white timbered **Merchant Adventurers Hall.** The Merchant Adventurers controlled the lucrative trade in 'all goods bought and sold foreign' and they spared no expense in building the Great Hall where they conducted their affairs beneath a complex timbered roof displaying many colourful banners of York's medieval guilds. To this period, too, belong the **York Mystery Plays**, first performed in 1397 and subsequently every four years.

During Tudor times, York's importance steadily declined but re-emerged in the 18th century as a fashionable social centre. Many elegant Georgian houses, of which **Fairfax House** in Castlegate is perhaps the most

splendid, were built at this time and they add another attractive architectural dimension to the city. Fairfax House was built in the early 1700s and elegantly remodelled by John Carr half a century later. The gracious old house has had an unfortunate history. It passed through a succession of private owners and by 1909 was divided between three building societies and the York City Club. The final indignity came in 1919 when the city council permitted a cinema to be built alongside and its superb first floor rooms to be converted into a dance hall. The York Civic Trust was able to purchase the house in 1981 and has restored this splendid old mansion to its former state of grace. The original furnishings have long since been dispersed but in their place are the marvellous pieces from the Noel

OLD FIZZYWIGS

21 Stonegate, York,
North Yorkshire YO1 8AW
Tel: 01904 638885

Old Fizzywigs is a splendid little shop located on one of York's most renowned streets, just a minute's walk from the wonderful Minster, which brings visitors in their millions to this marvellous city.

Behind the merry jumble in the window, owner Mark Gayson has filled the shop with things to delight the eye and the palate, to satisfy the collector and the gourmet, and to provide the answer for anyone looking for a special gift or a well-deserved treat.

For the food-lover there's an excellent selection of goodies, including own-brand preserves and chutneys, old-fashioned boiled sweets and fudge, fruit wines and the local St Peter's beer.

Among the ever-changing display of gift ideas are wooden birds, branded key rings, retro clocks, plaques, telephones and radios, Simon Drew cards and super models of cars, planes, motorbikes and tractors.

Yorkshire Museum and Gardens, York

Terry collection of fine furniture and clocks, which includes many rare and unusual pieces.

The 19th century saw York take on a completely different role as the hub of the railway system in the north. At the heart of this transformation was the charismatic entrepreneur George Hudson, founder of what became the Great Northern Railway. Part visionary, part crook, Hudson's wheeler-dealing eventually led to his disgrace but even then the citizens of York twice elected him as Lord Mayor and he has a street named after him. It was thanks to Hudson that York's magnificent railway station, with its great curving roof of glass, was built, a tourist attraction in its own right.

Nearby, in Leeman Road, is the **National Railway Museum** (free of charge), the largest of its kind in the world. This fascinating museum covers some 200 years of railway history, from Stephenson's *Rocket* to the Channel Tunnel. Among the thousands of exhibits demonstrating the technical and social impact of the Iron Horse are Gresley's record-breaking locomotive, *Mallard,* Queen Victoria's royal carriage, and displays demonstrating the workings of the railway system. The museum also now houses *The Flying Scotsman*. There's an extensive library and

reading room (booking advised), and the Brief Encounter restaurant is themed on the classic movie.

Another aspect of railway history is on view at the York Model Railway, next door to the station, which has almost one third of a mile of track and up to 14 trains running at any one time.

A city with such a long and colourful history naturally boasts some fine museums. Set in botanical gardens close to the Minster and beside the River Ouse, the **Yorkshire Museum and Gardens** has an outstanding collection of Roman, Viking and medieval artefacts, including the exquisite Middleham Jewel, which was uncovered close to Middleham Castle. Made of finely engraved gold and adorned with a brilliant sapphire it is one of the most dazzling pieces to have been discovered from that period.

At the **York Castle Museum** visitors can venture into the prison cell of notorious highwayman Dick Turpin; stroll along Victorian and Edwardian streets complete with fully equipped shops, hostelries and houses; or browse among the more than 100,000 items on display. One of the country's most popular museums of everyday life, its exhibits range from crafts and costumes to automobiles and machine guns, from mod cons and medicines to toys and technology.

Insights into medieval daily life are provided at **Barley Hall,** a superbly restored late medieval townhouse, which, in Tudor times, was the home of William Snawsell, a goldsmith who became Lord Mayor of York. Visitors can try out the furniture, handle all the pottery, glass and metal wares, and even try on some medieval costumes.

In a beautifully restored church close to the Shambles is the **Archaeological Research Centre**, an award-winning hands-on exploration of archaeology for visitors of all ages. Here you can meet practising archaeologists who will demonstrate how to sort and identify genuine finds or to try out ancient crafts. For the more technically minded, there's a series of interactive computer displays that illustrate how modern technology helps to discover and interpret the past.

Very popular with those who have an interest in the more macabre aspects of York's long history is the **Original Ghostwalk of York**, which starts at the

Archaeological Research Centre, York

King's Arms pub on Ouse Bridge and sets off at 8pm every evening. At the last count, York was reckoned to have some 140 resident ghosts within its walls – on this guided walk you visit some of their haunts and hear dark tales, grim accounts of murder, torture and intrigue. Prepare to have your blood chilled.

It's impossible here to list all York's museums, galleries and fine buildings, but you will find a wealth of additional information at the Tourist Information Centre close to one of the historic old gateways to the city, Bootham Bar.

North and East of York

STAMFORD BRIDGE
7 miles NE of York on the A166

🏛 Battle Site

Everyone knows that 1066 was the year of the Battle of Hastings but, just a few days before that battle, King Harold had clashed at the **Battle of Stamford Bridge** with his half-brother Tostig and Hardrada, King of Norway, who between them had mustered some 60,000 men. On a rise near the corn mill is a stone commemorating the event with an inscription in English and Danish. Up until 1878, a Sunday in September was designated 'Spear Day Feast' in commemoration of the battle. On this day, boat-shaped pies were made bearing the impression of the fatal spear, in memory of the Saxon soldier in his boat who slew the single Norseman defending the wooden bridge. Harold's troops were triumphant but immediately after this victory they marched southwards to Hastings and a much more famous defeat.

SHERIFF HUTTON

10 miles N of York off the A64

🏰 Castle

The first **Castle** was built in 1140 by Sir Bertram de Bulmer, Sheriff of Yorkshire, near the Church of St Helen & the Holy Cross. The present Plantagenet Castle was built by Ralph Neville, 1st Earl of Westmorland, and a later Neville, Richard, Warwick the Kingmaker, used it as a power base during the Wars of the Roses. In 1484 Richard III established it as a residence for his new Council of the North, a role it fulfilled for over a century. By 1618 the Castle had become a ruin and was soon dismantled to build Sheriff Hutton Hall, houses and farm buildings. The Castle has had many royal owners: Richard III, Henry VII, Henry VIII, Edward VI, Jane, Mary I, Elizabeth I and James I. All that remains of what was once one of the grandest castles in the land are the four corners and part of the tower.

MURTON

3 miles E of York off the A64

🏛 Yorkshire Museum of Farming

Although a small village, Murton is an important, modern livestock centre and also home to the **Yorkshire Museum of Farming**, found at Murton Park. As well as wandering around the fields and pens, visitors can also see reconstructions of a Roman fort, a Danelaw village from the Dark Ages and Celtic Roundhouses, along with bumping into Romans, Viking and Saxons. Other attractions at the park include the Derwent Valley Light

🎭 stories and anecdotes   🦜 famous people   🎨 art and craft   🎵 entertainment and sport   🚶 walks

THE FARMERS CART

Towthorpe Grange, Towthorpe Moor Lane, York YO32 9ST
Tel: 01904 499183   Fax: 01904 491918
e-mail: info@thefarmerscart.co.uk
website: www.thefarmerscart.co.uk

The Sykes family have farmed here for many generations, and Geoff, Margaret and their son Edward, along with a team of hardworking, passionate helpers, are dedicated to bringing customers fresh seasonal food, much of it produced on their 152-acre farm and fully traceable. In their shop, the **Farmers Cart**, which opened in 1997, they sell a vast selection of home-grown fruit and vegetables, dairy products, preserves and superb home-reared meat prepared by butchers who are always ready with advice and cooking tips. The farmhouse kitchen bakes bread, pies, quiches, cakes and pastries daily, and the farmhouse café/restaurant uses much of the home produce in super Yorkshire breakfasts, delicious lunches, snacks and specials. A fine array of ready-meals, all made on the farm, can be bought in the farm shop. The award-winning delicatessen counter sells a wide variety of regionally sourced artisan foods, including prime British cheeses, pies and pâtés, cooked and cured meats, fishcakes, salads, soups, dressings and preserves, along with olives and marinated vegetables. Tours of the farm are both educational and hugely enjoyable, and attractions at various times of the year include PYO strawberries, sheep shearing and shire horse displays. The Farmers Cart lies west of Towthorpe, 2 miles off the A64 or A1237, and 5 miles north of York.

MERRICOTE COTTAGES AT VERTIGROW PLANT NURSERY

Malton Road, North Yorkshire YO32 9TL
Tel: 01904 400256   Fax: 01904 400846
e-mail: merricote@hotmail.com
website: www.merricote-holiday-cottages.co.uk

Situated in eight acres of rural Yorkshire three miles from the centre of York, **Merricote Cottages** are a perfect place to relax and an ideal base for exploring the region. Buildings at the heart of what was once a traditional working farm have been sympathetically converted to create seven superb self-catering cottages, each with its own character, along with a detached four-bedroom bungalow. All the accommodation is centrally heated, with modern bathrooms, well-equipped kitchen and comfortable seating areas with TV and Broadband. Other facilities include ample safe parking and a laundry service. Children are very welcome, and in addition to a secure play area they will find plenty to keep them busy and happy in the vicinity.

Cots and high chairs can be provided for toddlers. The warm, welcoming atmosphere generated by the owner and the high standard of accommodation bring guests back to the cottages, which are located off the A64 York to Scarborough road. They are open throughout the year.

🏚 historic building 🏛 museum and heritage 🏛 historic site 🞯 scenic attraction 🌱 flora and fauna

Railway, a children's play area and a café fashioned on a farmhouse kitchen.

NEWTON-ON-OUSE
7 miles NW of York off the A19

🏛 Beningbrough Hall

About a mile to the south of Newton on Ouse is **Beningbrough Hall** (National Trust), a baroque masterpiece from the early 18th century with seven acres of gardens, wilderness play area, pike ponds and scenic walks. There's also a fully-operational Victorian laundry, which demonstrates the painstaking drudgery of a 19th-century washing day. A major attraction here is the permanent exhibition of more than 100 portraits on loan from the National Portrait Gallery. Other exhibitions are often held at the Hall – for these there is usually an additional charge.

Easingwold

🏛 Market Cross   🏛 Sutton Park

This agreeable market town was once surrounded by the Forest of Galtres, a vast hunting preserve of Norman kings. It lies at the foot of the Howardian Hills, an Area of Outstanding Natural Beauty covering 77 acres of woods, farmland and historic parkland. Easingwold's prosperity dates back to the 18th century when it flourished as a major stage coach post – at that period the town could offer a choice of some 26 public houses and inns. Until the recent construction of a bypass the old town was clogged with traffic, but it is

TEA HEE! ESPRESSO BAR & CHEESEMONGER

Market Place, Easingwold, Yorkshire YO61 3AB
Tel: 01347 823533
e-mail: mail@teahee.co.uk
website: www.teahee.co.uk

On the charming Georgian market square in Easingwold, **Tea Hee!** Is an award-winning espresso bar and cheesemonger. The aroma of freshly ground coffee, the finest leaf tea and baking straight from the oven is hard to resist, and the friendly welcome from owner Sophie Smith and her team adds to the pleasure of a visit. A tempting menu of soups, salads and panini highlight fresh local ingredients, and all the home-baked tarts, cakes and pastries are available to enjoy on the premises or to take away by the slice or whole. The shelves are stocked with a variety of delights, including olives, handmade Italian pasta, jams, chutneys and relishes. Superb chocolates and beautifully wrapped fudge cater for the sweeter tooth. The cheese is a well-cared for selection of British and Irish artisan farmhouse varieties supplied by the top-class Neal's Yard Dairy in London. Shop hours are Monday to Friday from 7am to 6pm, Saturday 7am to 5pm; closed Sunday.

📖 stories and anecdotes   🐦 famous people   🎨 art and craft   🎭 entertainment and sport   🚶 walks

now a pleasure again to wander around the marketplace with its impressive **Market Cross** and, nearby, the outline of the old bull-baiting ring set in the cobbles. Easingwold used to enjoy the distinction of having its own private railway, a two-and-a-half mile stretch of track along which it took all of 10 minutes to reach the main east coast line at Alne. Older residents fondly remember the ancient, tall-chimneyed steam locomotive that plied this route until its deeply regretted closure to passenger traffic in 1948.

A little to the south of Easingwold, on the B1363, is **Sutton Park,** a noble early 18th-century mansion, built in 1730 by Thomas Atkinson and containing some fine examples of Sheraton and Chippendale furniture, and much admired decorative plasterwork by the Italian maestro in this craft, Cortese. The ubiquitous Capability Brown designed the lovely gardens and parkland in which you'll find a Georgian ice-house, well-signposted woodland walks and a nature trail. There's also a gift shop and a café.

Sutton Park, nr Easingwold

Around Easingwold

STILLINGTON
4 miles E of Easingwold on the B1363

▥ Hall

In 1758, one of the great works of English

THE BUSY FARMER FARM SHOP & TEA ROOM

Sutton Grange, Sutton-on-the-Forest, North Yorkshire YO61 1EN
Tel: 01347 811977   Fax: 01347 810881
website: www.thebusyfarmer.co.uk

The owners and staff at the **Busy Farmer** are dedicated to growing, harvesting, sourcing and cooking the finest and freshest-tasting food. The range includes local traditionally reared meats, home-grown seasonal vegetables, fresh farm eggs, pick-your-own fruit, and home-made bread, cakes and jams. The tea room serves freshly made sandwiches and home-cooked meals, including farmhouse breakfasts. This outstanding outlet, which stands on the B1363 6 miles north of York, is open throughout the day every day except Tuesday. It's a place for all the family, and children can romp in safely in the gardens and feed the hens and ponies.

▥ historic building   ▦ museum and heritage   ▥ historic site   ⚘ scenic attraction   ❦ flora and fauna

literature almost perished in the fireplace of **Stillington Hall**. The parson of Coxwold had been invited to dinner and when the meal ended was asked to read from a book he had just completed. The guests had all wined and dined well and were soon dozing off. Incensed by their inattention the parson threw the pages of his manuscript onto the fire. Fortunately his host, the Squire of Stillington, rescued them from the flames and Laurence Sterne's immortal *Tristram Shandy* was saved for posterity.

HUSTHWAITE
4 miles N of Easingwold off the A19

Old stone houses mingle with mellow Victorian and Edwardian brick, and overlooking the village green, where three lanes meet, the Church of St Nicholas still retains its original Norman doorway. Just outside the village, on the road to Coxwold, there's a stunning view across to the Hambleton Hills and the White Horse of Kilburn.

Thirsk

🏛 St Mary's Church 🏛 Sion Hill Hall 📷 Museum

🕊 Bird of Prey Centre 🐾 World of James Herriott

Thirsk has become famous as the home of veterinary surgeon Alf Wight, better known as James Herriot, author of *All Creatures Great and Small*, who died in 1995. In his immensely popular books, Thirsk is clearly recognisable as 'Darrowby'. The Easter of 1999 saw the opening in Thirsk of a £1.4m tribute to the celebrated vet. **The World of James Herriot** (see panel on page 184) is housed in the original surgery in Kirkgate and offers visitors a trip back in time to the 1940s, exploring the

life and times of the world's most famous country vet. There's also the opportunity to take part in a TV production, and a Visible Farm exhibit where you can explore farm animals inside and out!

Just across the road from the surgery is the birthplace of another famous son of Thirsk. The building is now the town's **Museum** and a plaque outside records that Thomas Lord was born here in 1755: 30 years later he was to create the famous cricket ground in Marylebone that took his name. A more recent celebrity whose home was in Thirsk was Bill Foggitt (died September 2004, aged 91). He was renowned for his weather forecasts based on precise observations of nature.

This pleasant small town of mellow brick houses has a sprawling Market Place and the magnificent 15th-century **St Mary's Church**, which is generally regarded as the finest parish church in North Yorkshire. It was here that the real life 'James Herriot' married his wife, Helen. Cod Beck, a tributary of the River Swale, wanders through the town, providing some delightful - and well-signposted - riverside walks.

Thirsk appeared in the *Domesday Book* not long after William the Conqueror had granted the Manor of Thirsk to one of his barons, Robert de Mowbray. The Mowbrays became a powerful family in the area, a fact reflected in the naming of the area to the north and west of Thirsk as the Vale of Mowbray. In the early 1100s the family received permission to hold a market at Thirsk, but then blotted their copybook by rebelling against Henry II in 1173. The rebellion failed and their castle at Thirsk was burnt to the ground. Not a trace of it remains. The market, however, is still thriving, held twice-weekly on Mondays and

Saturdays. An old market by-law used to stipulate that no butcher be allowed to kill a bull for sale in the market until the beast had been baited by the town dogs. That by-law was abandoned in the early 1800s and the bull-ring to which the animal was tethered has also disappeared.

On the edge of town, housed in a mid-Victorian maltings, Treske specialises in producing bespoke furniture made from solid hardwoods and designer upholstery fabrics. Among Treske's most notable commissions are some 400 chairs for the OBE chapel in St Paul's Cathedral, bedroom furniture for the College of St George's, Windsor Castle, and period replica furniture for the monks' cells at Mount Grace Priory. The showrooms are open daily and group tours of the workshop

are available by prior arrangement. Nearby is Thirsk Racecourse, known to devotees of the turf as the 'Country Racecourse'. There are around 12 race meetings each year, all well attended by visitors keen to experience this intrinsic feature of Yorkshire life. Travelling through the areas between the Dales and the North York Moors, one is constantly reminded of the great tradition of horse-breeding that the county is famous for. The tradition runs deep: even the long flat straight stretch of main railway line between York and Darlington is known as the 'racecourse'.

Sion Hill Hall, about four miles northwest of Thirsk, is celebrated as the 'last of the great country houses'. Its light, airy and well-proportioned rooms, all facing south, are typical of the work of the celebrated Yorkshire

🏛 historic building 🏛 museum and heritage 🏛 historic site ⌖ scenic attraction 🌱 flora and fauna

architect, Walter Brierley – the 'Lutyens of the North'. He completed the building in 1913 for Percy Stancliffe and his wife Ethel, the wealthy daughter of a whisky distiller. The rooms haven't altered one bit since they were built, but the furniture and furnishings certainly have. In 1962, the Hall was bought by Herbert Mawer, a compulsive but highly discerning collector of antiques. During the 20 years he lived at Sion Hill, Mawer continued to add to what was already probably the best collection of Georgian, Victorian and Edwardian artefacts in the north of England. Furniture, paintings, porcelain, clocks (all working) and ephemera crowd the 20 richly-furnished rooms and make Sion Hill a delight to visit. A recent addition to the many sumptuous displays is a charming exhibition of dolls from the early 1900s.

In the Hall's Victorian Walled Garden is another major visitor attraction – **Falconry UK's Bird of Prey and Conservation Centre**. More than 80 birds from 34 different species have their home here: owls, hawks, falcons, buzzards, vultures and eagles from all around the world. At regular intervals throughout the day these fierce-eyed, sharp-beaked predators behave in a remarkably docile and co-operative way as they take part in fascinating flying demonstrations.

Thirsk Falconry Centre

Around Thirsk

SOWERBY
1 mile S of Thirsk on the B1448

Georgian houses stand beneath a majestic avenue of lime trees, an old packhorse bridge crosses Cod Beck, footpaths lead across fields and the quiet stream provides a peaceful refuge. An undeniably attractive village.

SPITAL HILL

York Road, Thirsk, North Yorkshire YO7 3AE
Tel: 01845 522273   Fax: 01845 524970
e-mail: spitalhill@spitalhill.entadsl.com
website: www.spitalhill.co.uk

At **Spital Hill**, a handsome, substantial house located a short drive south of Thirsk, Ann and Robin Clough offer top-quality Bed & Breakfast accommodation in three elegantly furnished and luxuriously appointed bedrooms, 2 with en-suite and 1 with private bath. A superb breakfast, with fresh garden produce and home-baked bread, starts the day, and an evening meal is available by arrangement. Guests can enjoy a stroll in the lovely garden or plan their days in the comfortable lounge. A few steps away from the main house, Groom's Cottage provides an equally outstanding self-catering base for up to 4 guests.

🎬 stories and anecdotes 🦐 famous people 🎨 art and craft ✏ entertainment and sport ⚲ walks

SUTTON-UNDER-WHITESTONECLIFF

3 miles E of Thirsk on the A170

🔱 Sutton Bank   🌿 Lake Gormire

Boasting the longest place-name in England, Sutton is more famous for the precipitous cliff that towers above it, **Sutton Bank**. For one of the grandest landscape views in England, go to the top of Sutton Bank and look across the vast expanse of the Vale of York to the Pennine hills far away to the west. The real-life James Herriot called it the 'finest view in England'. He knew this area well since his large veterinary practice covered the farms from here right over to the Dales. A continuation of the Cleveland Hills, the Hambleton Hills themselves lead into the Howardian Hills: together they form the mighty southwest flank of the North York Moors.

There's a National Park Information Centre at the summit of Sutton Bank and a well-marked Nature Trail leads steeply down to, and around, **Lake Gormire,** an Ice Age lake trapped here by a landslip. Gormire is one of Yorkshire's only two natural lakes, the other being Semerwater in Wensleydale. Gormire is set in a large basin with no river running from it: any overflow disappears down a 'swallow hole' and emerges beneath White Mare Cliffs.

Sutton Bank used to be a graveyard for caravans because of its steep (1 in 3) climb and sharp bends. On one Saturday in July 1977, some 30 vehicles broke down on the ascent and five breakdown vehicles spent all day retrieving them. Caravans are now banned

---

MONK PARK FARM

Bagby, nr Thirsk, North Yorkshire YO7 2AG
Tel: 01845 597730
Website: www.monkpark.co.uk

Once a haven for monks who lived here off the land, **Monk Park** is now a paradise for children – and families. The Hebden family started developing the site as a visitor farm in 1994, opening for visits in May 1999. In the following years they had to overcome many problems, including foot and mouth disease, and the Farm now attracts upwards of 60,000 visitors a year. It is home to a wide variety of animals, from guinea pigs and rabbits to be cuddled to ponies to ride, several breeds of sheep and cattle, pigs, llamas, wallabies (brown, grey and albino), rheas, chicken, ducks and swans. Also on site are picnic areas, an adventure playground, a tea room and gift shop. The staff are justly as friendly as the animals at the Farm, which is set in beautiful rural surroundings off the A170 east of Thirsk; it is open from 11 to 5.30 between March and October and also during the February school half-term holiday.

🏛 historic building   🖼 museum and heritage   🏚 historic site   🔱 scenic attraction   🌿 flora and fauna

from this route. Sutton Bank may be tough on cars, but its sheer-sided cliffs create powerful thermals making this a favoured spot for gliders and bright-winged hang-gliders.

BOLTBY
5 miles NE of Thirsk, off the A170

Boltby is an engaging village tucked away at the foot of the Hambleton Hills, close to where the oddly-named Gurt of Beck tumbles down the hillside and, depending on how much rain has fallen on the moors, passes either under or over a little humpback bridge. On the plain below is Nevison House, reputed to be the home of the 17th-century highwayman, William Nevison, 'Swift Nick' as Charles II dubbed him. Some historians claim that it was Swift Nick, not Dick Turpin, who made the legendary ride on Black Bess from London to York to establish an alibi.

Northallerton

🏛 Battle of the Standard

The county town of North Yorkshire, Northallerton has the broad High Street, almost half a mile long, typical of the county's market towns. (Wednesday and Saturday are the market days here.) In stagecoach days the town was an important stop on the route from Newcastle to London and several old coaching inns still stand along the High Street. The most ancient is The Old Fleece, a favoured drinking haunt of Charles Dickens during his several visits to the town. It's a truly Dickensian place with great oak beams and a charming olde-worlde atmosphere. The Old Fleece recalls the great days of the stage coach, which came to an abrupt end with the arrival of the railway. One day in 1847, a coach called the Wellington made the whole

of the 290-mile journey from Newcastle to London, via Northallerton, completely empty. The era of this romantic – if uncomfortable and extremely expensive – mode of transport was over.

Northallerton has many old buildings of interest, including an ancient Grammar School whose history goes back to at least 1322. The school was rebuilt in 1776 at the northern end of the High Street – a building that is now a solicitors' office. By the end of the 19th century the school had 'no great reputation' and by 1902 only 13 pupils were registered. Things went from bad to worse the next year when the headmaster was convicted of being drunk and disorderly. Fortunately, the school, now Northallerton College and in new buildings, has recovered its reputation for academic excellence.

The town also boasts a grand medieval church, a 15th-century almshouse and, of more recent provenance, a majestic County Hall built in 1906 and designed by the famous Yorkshire architect Walter Brierley. The oldest private house in Northallerton is Porch House, which bears a carved inscription with the date 1584. According to tradition, Charles I came here as a guest in 1640 and returned seven years later as a prisoner.

Two miles north of the town, a stone obelisk beside the A167 commemorates the **Battle of the Standard**, fought here in 1138. It was one of the countless conflicts fought between the English and the Scots, and also one of the bloodiest with more than 12,000 of the Scots, led by King David, perishing under a rain of English arrows. The battle took its name from the unusual standard raised by the English: the mast of a ship mounted on a wagon and, crowning its top, a pyx containing the consecrated Host.

Around Northallerton

Mount Grace Priory, Osmotherley

DANBY WISKE
4 miles NW of Northallerton off the A167 or B6271

This pleasant little village takes its name from the Danby family, once great landowners with huge properties across North Yorkshire, and the little River Wiske. It has a moated former rectory and a village green overlooked by a traditional hostelry.

OSMOTHERLEY
5 miles NE of Northallerton off the A19

🏛 Mount Grace Priory

Long-distance walkers will be familiar with this attractive moorland village since it is the western starting point for the Lyke Wake Walk, which winds for more than 40 miles over the moors to Ravenscar on the coast. At the centre of the village is a heavily carved cross and, next to it, a low stone table thatwas probably once a market stall and also served John Wesley as a pulpit.

About a mile northeast of the village, **Mount Grace Priory** (English Heritage & National Trust) is quite unique among Yorkshire's ecclesiastical treasures. The 14th-century building set in tranquil surroundings was bought in 1904 by Sir Lothian Bell who decided to rebuild one of the well-preserved cells, a violation of the building's 'integrity' that would provoke howls of outrage from purists if it were proposed today. When English Heritage inherited the Carthusian Priory, however, it decided to go still further by reconstructing other outbuildings and filling them with replica furniture and artefacts to create a vivid impression of what life was like in a 14th-century monastic house. The Carthusians were an upper-class order whose members dedicated themselves to solitude – even their meals were served through an angled hatch so they would not see the servant who brought them. Most visitors find themselves fascinated by Mount Grace's sanitary arrangements which were ingeniously designed to take full advantage of a nearby spring and the sloping site on which the Priory is built. Along with discovering what life was like for a monk in this almost hermit-like order, visitors can also wander around the remains of the Great Cloister and outer court, and see the new monks' herb garden designed specifically to aid contemplation and spiritual renewal. Mount Grace Priory is open all year though times are limited in the winter months.

🏛 historic building 📷 museum and heritage 🏛 historic site ♧ scenic attraction 🌱 flora and fauna

South and West of York

ELVINGTON
7 miles SE of York off the B1228

🏛 Yorkshire Air Museum

During the Second World War RAF Elvington was the base for British, Canadian and French bomber crews flying missions to occupied Europe. With virtually all its original buildings still intact, the base now provides an authentic setting for the **Yorkshire Air Museum** and is the largest Second World War Bomber Command Station open to the public in the UK. In addition to examining the many exhibits tracing the history of aviation, including a unique Halifax bomber, visitors can visit the control tower, browse among the historic military vehicle collection, watch engineers restoring vintage planes – and enjoy home-cooked food in the NAAFI restaurant. The museum hosts many special events throughout the year and offers conference and corporate event facilities.

LONG MARSTON
7 miles W of York off the B1224

🏛 Battle of Marston Moor

Lying on the edge of the Vale of York and sheltered by a hill, this village is an ancient agricultural community. However, in July 1644, its tranquillity was shattered by the **Battle of Marston Moor**, one of the most important encounters of the Civil War and one which the Royalists lost. The night before the battle, Oliver Cromwell and his chief officers stayed at Long Marston Hall and the bedroom they used is still called The Cromwell Room.

Each year the anniversary of the battle is commemorated by the members of the Sealed Knot and, it is said, that the ghosts of those who fell in battle haunt the site. Certainly, local farmers still occasionally unearth cannonballs used in the battle when they are out ploughing the fields.

Less than 100 years later, Long Marston Hall saw the birth, in 1707, of the mother of General James Wolfe, the famous English soldier who scaled the Heights of Abraham to relieve the siege of Quebec.

TADCASTER
9 miles SW of York off the A64

🏛 The Ark 🏛 Hazelwood Castle

The lovely magnesian limestone used in so many fine Yorkshire churches came from the quarries established here in Roman times. Their name for Tadcaster was simply 'Calcaria'

Monument to the Battle of Marston Moor

NORTH YORKSHIRE: COAST, MOORS AND DALES

🎬 stories and anecdotes 🐾 famous people 🎨 art and craft 🎭 entertainment and sport 🚶 walks

- limestone. By 1341 however, brewing had become the town's major industry, using water from River Wharfe. Three major breweries are still based in Tadcaster: Samuel Smiths, established in 1758 and the oldest in Yorkshire; John Smith's, whose bitter is the best selling ale in Britain; and Coors Tower Brewery. The distinctive brewery buildings dominate the town's skyline and provide the basis of its prosperity. Guided tours of the breweries are available by prior booking.

Also worth visiting is **The Ark**, the oldest building in Tadcaster dating back to the 1490s. During its long history, The Ark has served as a meeting place, a post office, an inn, a butcher's shop, and a museum. It now houses the Town Council offices and is open to the public in office hours. This appealing half-timbered building takes its name from the two carved heads on the first floor beams. They are thought to represent Noah and his wife, hence the name. Tadcaster also offers some attractive riverside walks, one of which takes you across the 'Virgin Viaduct' over the River Wharfe. Built in 1849 by the great railway entrepreneur George Hudson, the viaduct was intended to be part of a direct line from Leeds to York. Before the tracks were laid however Hudson was convicted of fraud on a stupendous scale and this route was never completed.

About four miles southwest of Tadcaster is **Hazelwood Castle,** now a superb hotel and conference centre. But for more than eight centuries it was the home of the Vavasour family who built it with the lovely white limestone from their quarry at Thevesdale – the same quarry that provided the stone for York Minster and King's College Chapel, Cambridge. The well-maintained gardens and nature trail are open every afternoon (tea room and shop open on Sundays only), and guided tours of the Castle with its superb Great Hall and 13th century Chapel, can be arranged by telephoning 01937 832738.

HEALAUGH
5 miles N of Tadcaster off the A64

In the 12th century an Augustinian Priory was founded here but none of the remaining fragments date from earlier than the 15th century. However, the village Church of St Helen and St John, which dates from around 1150, not only has outstanding views over the dale to the Pennines, but also has a bullet hole which, it is alleged, was made by a Cromwellian trooper on his way to Marsden Moor.

SPOFFORTH
13m W of York on the A661

🏛 Stockeld Park 🏛 Castle

This ancient village, situated on the tiny River Crimple, is home to the splendid Palladian mansion, **Stockeld Park**, built between 1758 and 1763 by Paine. Containing some excellent furniture and a fine picture collection, the house is surrounded by extensive parkland that offers garden walks. Though privately owned, the house is open by appointment.

Spofforth Castle (English Heritage) is another place of note, an historic building whose sight stirs the imagination, despite its ruined state. The powerful Percy family originally built the castle here in the 16th century to replace the manor house that had been repeatedly laid to waste. The castle itself is now a crumbling ruin after it was destroyed during the Civil War. According to some accounts, the castle was the birthplace of Harry Hotspur.

NORTH YORKSHIRE: COAST, MOORS AND DALES

GOLDSBOROUGH
11 miles W of York off the A59

🏛 Church of St Mary

This rather special village was an estate village from the time of the Norman Conquest until the 1950s when it was sold by the Earl of Harewood to pay enormous death duties. The charming 12th-century **Church of St Mary** has some interesting features including a Norman doorhead and an effigy of a knight. It is also a 'green man church' and the image of the Celtic god of fertility, with his oak-leafed head, is well hidden on one of the many Goldsborough family tombs. In 1859, while the church was being restored, a lead casket was discovered containing Viking jewellery and coins. In the 1920s, Mary, the daughter of George V and Queen Mary, lived in the village after her marriage and her eldest son, George, was christened in the church.

Valley Gardens, Harrogate

Harrogate

🏛 Royal Baths Assembly Rooms ☙ Agatha Christie
🖼 Royal Pump Room Museum ⚲ Mercer Art Gallery
🖼 🌱 Museum of Gardening ⚘ Valley Gardens
🌱 Great Yorkshire Show ⚘ The Stray

One of England's most attractive towns and a frequent winner of Britain in Bloom, Harrogate features acres of gardens that offer an array of colour throughout the year, open spaces, and broad tree-lined boulevards. However, until the 17th century Harrogate - or 'Haregate' as it was then called - was just a collection of cottages close to the thriving market town of Knaresborough. It was William Slingsby, of Bilton Hall near Knaresborough, who, while out walking his dog, discovered a spring bubbling up out of the rock that was to found the fortunes of the town. Tasting the waters, Slingsby found them to be similar to those he had tasted at the fashionable wells of Spaw, in Belgium. Expert opinion was sought and, in 1596, Dr Timothy Bright confirmed the spring to be a chalybeate well and the waters to have medicinal powers – curing a wide variety of illness and ailments from gout to vertigo.

Slingsby's well became known as Tewit Well, after the local name for peewits, and it can still be seen today, covered by a dome on pillars. Other wells were also found in the area, St John's Well in 1631 and the Old Sulphur Well, which went on to become the most famous of Harrogate's springs. Though this spring had been known locally for years, it

RAMUS SEAFOOD EMPORIUM

136 Kings Road, Harrogate, North Yorkshire HG1 5HY
Tel: 01423 563271
e-mail: info@ramus.co.uk   website: www.ramus.co.uk

"Nobody's pickier about seafood"

Based in the historic spa town of Harrogate, Ramus Seafoods has for 35 years been bringing the best of seafood from all over the world to the people of North Yorkshire and beyond. The business started in 1973 and has been developed with quality and service in mind and the customer as the number one priority. These watchwords still apply and Ramus is firmly established as one of the premier seafood specialists in the country.

The superb Ramus Seafood Emporium opened in October 2000 is like no fish shop you have ever seen. It was described by one journalist as "Knightsbridge comes to Harrogate" and by another as a "temple to piscine pleasure". This new concept in seafood retailing immediately began to attract country wide attention with the emporium being voted Independent Seafood Retailer two years running. The shop is open from Monday to Saturday 9 till 5 with an amazing variety of 60 different fish and shellfish, along with many other superb fine foods. A speciality is their famous seafood platters crammed with mouth – watering shellfish such as lobsters, crab, king prawns and smoked salmon. They can be bought from the counter or if required can be designed for your specific requirements to suit any occasion or any number.

Another highlight is the famous Ramus Seafoods Lobster Festival held throughout June with hundreds of fresh lobsters sold every week both in the Emporium and also in conjunction with many of Ramus's finest restaurant customers.

If you are not fortunate to be able to visit the Ramus Seafood Emporium in person then you can check out their most interesting and informative website. You can order online from an excellent range of fresh fish and shellfish along with the famous seafood platters all delivered via overnight courier. Along with online ordering you can download from a vast library of recipes and see tips on how to get the most from your seafood.

Simply visit www.ramus.co.uk for the best fish on the net!

🏤 historic building   🏛 museum and heritage   🏛 historic site   ⚜ scenic attraction   🌿 flora and fauna

was not until 1656 that the sulphurous, vile-smelling waters, nicknamed 'the Stinking Spaw', began to attract attention.

During the mid-17th century bathing in the heated sulphurous waters became fashionable as well as a cure for various ailments and lodging houses were built around the sulphur well in Low Harrogate. Bathing took place in the evening and, each morning, the patients would drink a glass of the water with their breakfast. The cupola seen over the well was erected in 1804.

In order to serve the growing number of people arriving at Harrogate seeking a cure for their ailments, the Queen's Head Hotel was built and it is probably the oldest inn here as it dates from before 1687. When stagecoaches began to arrive in the 18th century the inn moved with the times and became the first at the spa to serve the needs of the coaches.

By the late 1700s it was one of the largest hotels in the fast growing town and, though the hotel changed its name to the Queen's Hotel in 1828 and underwent extensive renovation and remodelling in the mid-19th century, it did not survive the decline of the spa and, in 1951, it became the offices for the Regional Hospital Board. Many other hotels were built including the Crown Inn, next to the Old Sulphur Well, which became a coaching inn in 1772 and hosted a visit by Lord Byron in 1806. However, one of the town's most famous hotels, The Majestic, a turn of the century red brick building, does survive and it was the place where Elgar stayed while visiting Harrogate.

The **Royal Pump Room Museum** was

THE CHEESEBOARD OF HARROGATE

1 Commercial Street, Harrogate,
North Yorkshire HG1 1UB
Tel: 01423 508837
e-mail: info@thecheeseboard.net
website: www.thecheeseboard.net

The **Cheeseboard of Harrogate** is an independently run shop specialising for the past 25 years in the finest cheese from the UK and the Continent. Behind the glossy black frontage of Gemma Aykroyd's little shop hidden down a side street, artisan cheeses – up to 200 at any one time – are displayed on marble or wooden shelves. Customers will also find a variety of other delectable edibles, including pâtés, olives, baked fig balls, chutneys, pickles and crackers. This excellent shop is at the forefront of a splendid innovation – the cheese wedding cake, made up of layers of several different cheeses. Gemma and her friendly, knowledgeable team are on hand to dispense expert advice and help - and samples! They can also provide gift ideas and make up bespoke hampers. Shoppers who can't visit the shop in person can browse and order online.

built in 1842 to enclose the Old Sulphur Well and this major watering place for spa visitors has been painstakingly restored to illustrate all the aspects of Harrogate's history. Beneath the building the sulphur water still rises to the surface and can be sampled by visitors.

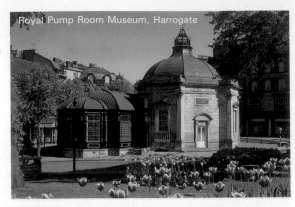

Royal Pump Room Museum, Harrogate

There will be few Harrogate residents who have not heard of Betty Lupton, the almost legendary 'Queen of the Wells' who, for over 50 years, dispensed the spa waters, dishing out cupfuls to paying visitors, who were then encouraged to walk off the dubious effects of the medicine by taking a trip around the Bogs Fields, known today as **Valley Gardens**. She conducted her business in the ostentatiously named **Royal Baths Assembly Rooms** which, in their heyday, were full of rich visitors sampling the waters. Today, the buildings have been restored to house the Turkish Baths where visitors can enjoy a sauna, beauty treatment and massage.

ALAMAH GUEST HOUSE

88 Kings Road, Harrogate,
North Yorkshire HG1 5JX
Tel: 01423 502187
e-mail: alamahguesthouse@btconnect.com
website: www.alamah.co.uk

Alamah is a comfortable, friendly and very civilised guest house close to Harrogate's International Conference Centre and a short walk from most of the town's many attractions. Built of Yorkshire stone in the 1880s as a private residence, it retains much of its original character after sympathetic modernisation and has been a guest house since the mid-1970s. The seven B&B guest rooms – two singles, two twins, two doubles and a family room – all have en-suite shower, television, wireless internet access, tea/coffee tray, hairdryer and ironing facilities. Private parking is available at the rear. Conference delegates are frequent users of this well-maintained guest house, which is also a good base for exploring the town and discovering the many places of interest in the region, including market towns and picturesque villages, castles and churches, as well as the countryside with several Areas of Outstanding Natural Beauty.

Mercer Art Gallery, Harrogate

fashionable place, a sought after conference location, home of the annual Northern Antiques Fair, and a town with much to offer the visitor.

As well as a spa, Harrogate developed into a centre for shopping for the well-to-do and the many old-fashioned shops are typified by Montpellier Parade, a crescent of shops surrounded by trees and flowerbeds. Another attractive aspect of the town is **The Stray**, which is unique to Harrogate and virtually encircles the town centre. The 215 acres of open space are protected by ancient law to ensure that the residents of, and visitors to, the town always have access for sports, events, and walking. The spacious lawns are at their most picturesque during the spring when edged with crocus and daffodils. Originally part of the Forest of Knaresborough the land was, fortunately, not enclosed under the 1770 Act of Parliament. The large gritstone pillar beside The Stray marks the boundary of the Leeds and Ripon turnpike. On The Stray stands the Commemorative Oak Tree, planted in 1902 by Samson Fox to commemorate the ox roasting that took place here as part of the celebrations for Queen Victoria's Jubilee in 1887 and the end of the Boer War in 1902.

A well-known tale associated with Harrogate is the disappearance of **Agatha Christie** in 1926. In a set of circumstances reminiscent of one of her novels, Agatha went missing in the December of that year, possibly as a result of marital difficulties. Her crashed car was discovered near a chalk pit close to her home but the novelist was nowhere to be found and one of the largest police manhunts was put into operation. Agatha had, in fact, travelled to Harrogate after abandoning her car, and booked into the Old Swan Hotel under the name of her

The baths are open to the public daily. The **Mercer Art Gallery** is housed in the oldest of the town's surviving spa buildings, originally built in 1806. The Promenade Room has been restored to its former glory and displays a superb collection of fine art along with the Kent Bequest – an archaeological collection that includes finds from both ancient Greece and Egypt.

By the late 18th century Harrogate had become one of Europe's most fashionable spa towns and it was not only serving the needs of those with acute and chronic ailments but also members of 'good society'. Fuelled by competition from spa towns abroad, Harrogate sought to provide not only medical care for the sick, but also to appeal to the needs of the fashionable. In 1858, Charles Dickens visited the town and described it as 'the queerest place, with the strangest people in it leading the oddest lives of dancing, newspaper reading, and table d'hôte.' Though its status as a spa town has declined, it is still a

husband's mistress, Theresa Neele. After 10 days she was spotted and her husband came to collect her, putting her disappearance down to loss of memory. However, this did not dispel rumours that the marriage was in trouble or that the surprising event was nothing more than a publicity stunt. Whatever the truth, two years later the couple divorced and Colonel Christie married his long-time mistress Theresa.

One of Harrogate's major visitor attractions is the **RHS Harlow Carr Botanical Gardens**, just over a mile from the town centre. Established in 1948 by the Northern Horticultural Society and now covering some 58 acres, the gardens feature all manner of plants in a wide variety of landscapes, which allows members of the public to see how they perform in the unsympathetic conditions of northern England. The society, as well as

having their study centre here, has also opened a fascinating **Museum of Gardening**.

A major summer event is the **Great Yorkshire Show,** a three day event that includes top class show-jumping, displays and demonstrations of various kinds, some 10,000 animals, miles of shopping, a flower show and much, much more.

Around Harrogate

HAMPSTHWAITE
4 miles NW of Harrogate off the A59

This picturesque Nidderdale village lies on an ancient Roman way between Ilkley and Aldborough and traces of Roman tin mining have been found in the area. The village Church of St Thomas has remnants of a Saxon building in the tower and, in the churchyard, is

---

CENTRAL HOUSE FARM

Haverah Park, Harrogate,
North Yorkshire HG3 1SQ
Tel: 01423 566050
Fax: 01423 709152
e-mail: jayne@centralhousefarm.freeserve.co.uk

Central House offers homely hospitality on a working dairy and sheep farm in a tranquil setting off the A59 and B6161, three miles from the centre of Harrogate. In her historic Yorkshire farmhouse Jayne Ryder provides high-quality Bed & Breakfast accommodation in tastefully decorated and well-furnished bedrooms, each with en-suite shower room, TV, beverage tray, clock-radio and central heating. A full Aga-cooked breakfast gets the day off to a fine start, and guests can relax or plan their days in the warm, comfortable sitting room.

The farm stands in a beautiful valley with footpaths leading to Norwood and Beckwithshaw, making it easy for guests to enjoy the bracing air and the lovely views. The area is rich in scenic and historic interest, and a wide variety of outdoor pursuits is catered for in the locality.

The house cannot board pets, but kennelling can be arranged locally.

🏠 historic building 🏛 museum and heritage 🏚 historic site ♙ scenic attraction 🍃 flora and fauna

buried Peter Barker. Known as 'Blind Peter', Barker was a local character very much in the tradition of Jack Metcalfe (see page 201) and he did not let his disability hinder him: he was a skilled cabinet-maker, glazier and musician. The mysterious portrait of the bearded man hanging in the church, painted by the local vicar's daughter, may well be of Blind Peter.

BECKWITHSHAW
3 miles SW of Harrogate on the B6161

This village, as its name suggests, was once bounded by a stream and woodland though, sadly, most of the trees are now gone. It was once part of the great Forest of Knaresborough and a local legend tells how John O'Gaunt promised John Havcrah, a cripple, as much land as he could hop around between sunrise and sunset. By throwing his crutch the last few yards, just as the sun was setting, John Haverah managed to secure himself seven square miles, the remainder of which is today called Haverah Park.

KNARESBOROUGH
3 miles NE of Harrogate on the A59

🏛 Castle 🏛 House in the Rock 🏛 St Robert's Cave
🏛 Conyngham Hall 🏛 🎭 Mother Shipton's Cave
🎭 Blind Jack 🎨 Knaresborough Festival
🚶 Plumpton Rocks

This ancient town of pantiled cottages and Georgian houses is precariously balanced on a hillside by the River Nidd. A stately railway viaduct, 90 feet high and 338 feet long, completed in 1851, spans the gorge. There are many unusual and attractive features in the town, among them a maze of steep stepped narrow streets leading down to the river and numerous alleyways. In addition to boating on the river, there are many enjoyable riverside walks.

The town is dominated by the ruins of **Knaresborough Castle**, built high on a crag overlooking the River Nidd by Serlo de Burgh, who had fought alongside William the Conqueror at Hastings. Throughout the Middle Ages, the castle was a favourite with the court and it was to Knaresborough that the murderers of Thomas à Becket fled in 1170. Queen Philippa, wife of Edward III, also enjoyed staying at Knaresborough and she and her family spent many summers here. However, following the Civil War, during which the town and its castle had remained loyal to the king, Cromwell ordered the castle's destruction.

Also in the town is the Old Courthouse Museum, which tells the history of the town and houses a rare Tudor Courtroom. The nearby Bebra Gardens are named

River Nidd, Knaresborough

🎭 stories and anecdotes 🐦 famous people 🎨 art and craft 🎨 entertainment and sport 🚶 walks

Knaresborough

Distance: *6.5 miles (10.4 kilometres)*

Typical time: *180 mins*

Height gain: *100 metres*

Map: *Explorer 289*

Walk: *www.walkingworld.com ID:1915*

Contributor: *Sam Roebuck*

ACCESS INFORMATION:

The walk starts from Conyngham Hall Car Park, which is on the A59 Harrogate Road out of Knaresborough. It is just over the bridge from Mother Shipton's Cave and so can be easily found simply by following the brown signs to that attraction. There are good bus and rail links to Knaresborough, with the start of the walk being easily reached from the town (follow the tourist signs down hill to 'Mother Shipton's Cave').

DESCRIPTION:

The often overlooked little town of Knaresborough has many attractions over and above the famous Mother Shipton's Cave and it's worth taking plenty of time to explore it. But when you're done, why not try this walk along the beautiful Nidd Gorge, which runs into the town from the north-west. The Woodland Trust-owned broadleaved woodland is well geared up for walkers and though popular with locals, is yet to be discovered by a wider visitor base. Once the walk leaves the gorge, the return is via the higher pasture and meadowland between Harrogate and Knaresborough. On a sunny June day, the chocolate-box views can take your breath away. The walk itself is mostly circular, but the first and last 1.5 kilometres are along almost the same route.

FEATURES:

Hills or Fells, River, Pub, Wildlife, Birds, Flowers, Great Views, Public Transport, Nature Trail, Woodland.

WALK DIRECTIONS:

1 | Leave the car park, go back onto the A59 and turn right to cross the bridge.

2 | Opposite Mother Shipton's Cave entrance, turn right just before The Yorkshire Lass pub and pass through the gate. Within 100m, pass the memorial plaque dedicating the cycleway to Beryl Burton OBE (seven times world cycling champion). After another 150m, as the cycleway bears left and uphill, look for a fingerpost for the 'Ringway Footpath' on the right-hand side of the main cycle path. Follow this footpath half-left and up hill, initially paralleling the cycleway. At the top of the hill, the path meets once more with the cycleway opposite a small cattle grid and gate. Cross this and continue ahead on the cycleway.

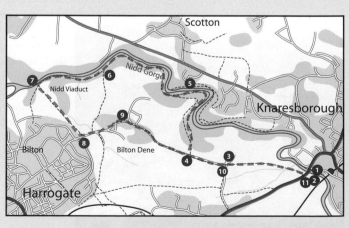

3 | Within half a kilometre, the cycleway emerges onto a lane at a T-junction. Continue ahead and follow the lane for around half a kilometre.

4 | After 600m, look for a field gate on the right. Go through, and follow the footpath as it enters the woods and then drops very gradually, before reaching the valley floor in around a kilometre. Follow the obvious path as it parallels the river.

5 | Soon, you will see a large footbridge leading over the river. Ignore this and continue on the path along the gorge for around two-and-a-half kilometres.

6 | Look for a set of steps on the left. Climb these steps until another path merges from the left. Within a few metres, there is another flight of steps going up and a route going down and to the right. Take the steps/boardwalk down and to the right and continue on this path back to the valley floor, passing a large weir. Soon you cross a small footbridge and ascend slightly to meet a fence. Keep the fence on your right and follow the path as it ascends out of the valley and into the open. Follow the right-hand side of the meadow, looking for a disused viaduct on your right.

7 | At the viaduct, turn left and follow the track bed of the disused railway for just over a kilometre.

8 | The railway path emerges onto a minor road. Turn left and follow the road as it passes the Gardeners Arms and soon deteriorates into a track.

9 | A barrier blocks the way for vehicular access. Continue ahead.

10 | Around two kilometres after you left the railway path, the lane turns sharp right. Continue ahead onto the cycleway. Within half a kilometre, the cycleway crosses a small cattle grid and bears right. Follow the cycleway downhill until meeting the river and emerging onto the A59.

11 | Mother Shipton's Cave should be directly in front of you. Turn left and cross the bridge. In 100m, turn left into the car park.

after Knaresborough's twin town in Germany and its attractive flower beds are complemented by luxurious lawns and a paddling pool. In the Market Square, visitors should also keep an eye out for Ye Oldest Chemists' Shoppe in England, which was first recorded in 1720 although the building is probably a hundred years older. The old chemist's drawers, each marked with the scientific name of its contents, are still in place but the pungent potions have been replaced by a wide selection of quality confectionery.

Knaresborough boasts not only the oldest chemist's shop, but also the oldest tourist attraction in the UK, **Mother Shipton's Cave**, which opened in 1630. It was the birthplace of the famous prophetess and its Petrifying Well has fascinated visitors for generations. The effects that the well's lime-rich water has on objects are truly amazing and an array of paraphernalia, from old boots to bunches of grapes, are on view – seemingly turned to stone. It is little wonder that these were considered magical properties by the superstitious over the centuries or that the well was associated with witchcraft and various other interesting tales.

The foremost tale concerns Mother Shipton, who was said to have been born in the cavern situated by the well on 6th July 1488 and who has the reputation of being England's most famous fortune-teller. The story says that she was born in the midst of a terrible storm and was soon found to have a strange ability to see the future. As she grew older her prophetic visions became more widely known and feared throughout England. However, the most singular feature about Mother Shipton has to be that she died peacefully in her bed, as opposed to being burnt at the stake as most witches were at that time.

Mother Shipton's Cave, Knaresborough

was arrested on a charge of treason at Cawood. Among her many other prophesies she reputedly foretold the invasion and defeat of the Spanish Armada in 1588 and Samuel Pepys recorded that it was Mother Shipton who prophesied the disastrous Great Fire of London in 1666.

While in Knaresborough, it is well worth taking the opportunity to visit the **House in the Rock** hewn out of solid rock by Thomas Hill, an eccentric weaver, between 1770 and 1786. It was Hill's son who renamed the house Fort Montagu and flew a flag and fired a gun salute on special occasions. On the banks of the River Nidd there is also **St Robert's Cave**, which is an ancient hermitage. St

She had been threatened with burning by, among others, Cardinal Wolsey, when she had warned him on a visit to York that he might see the city again but never enter. True to her prediction Wolsey never did enter York, for he

---

MUNGO DELI

11 Castlegate, Knaresborough,
North Yorkshire HG5 8AR
Tel: 01423 862351
e-mail: info@mungodeli.co.uk
website: www.mungodeli.co.uk

Mungo Deli Organic Grocery is stocked with products that are kind to people, animals and the planet, in a way that promotes justice and fair shares for all. It's packed to the rafters with ethically sourced and traded goods and lines that you won't find in a supermarket. Prime produce includes seasonal fruit and vegetables (the organic box scheme is very popular); hand-baked breads in many varieties (malts, 100% rye, wholewheat, spelt, olive, herbs, sun-dried tomato); chutneys, sauces, preserves, oils and vinegars, herbs and spices; bottled olives and artichokes, pesto and passata; rice, polenta and pulses; and organic beers and wines. Shoppers will also find a selection of environmentally-friendly household products and animal-friendly cosmetics and toiletries. Another definite bonus for shoppers is owner Jonathan Smith's product knowledge: he and his staff are always happy to dispense sourcing details as well as tips on cookery and entertaining.

Robert was the son of a mayor of York who, at the time of his death in 1218, was so beloved that the people of Knaresborough would not allow the monks of Fountains Abbey to bury him. Instead they kept his bones and finally interred him in a place near the altar in the Chapel of Our Lady of the Crag. It is guarded by the statue of a larger than life-size figure of a knight in the act of drawing his sword.

In the tradition of this town's reputation for exceptional and odd characters is '**Blind Jack of Knaresborough'**. Jack Metcalfe was born in 1717 and lost his sight at the age of six, but went on to achieve fame as a roadmaker. He was a remarkable person who never allowed his blindness to bar him from any normal activities – he rode, climbed trees, swam, and was often employed to guide travellers through the wild Forest of Knaresborough. He was a talented fiddle player and one of his more roguish exploits was his elopement with Dolly Benson, the daughter of the innkeeper of the Royal Oak in Harrogate, on the night before she was due to marry another man. His most memorable achievement however, was the laying of roads over the surrounding bogs and marshes, which he achieved by laying a foundation of bundles of heather, a technique that had never been used before.

Another of Knaresborough's attractive amenities is **Conyngham Hall,** a majestic old house enclosed within a loop of the River Nidd. Once the home of Lord Macintosh, the Halifax toffee magnate, the Hall itself is not open to the public but its landscaped grounds, stretching down to the river, are, and provide

---

ART IN THE MILL

Green Dragon Yard Off Castlegate, Knaresborough, North Yorkshire HG5 8AU
Tel: 01423 862963
e-mail: mail@artinthemill.co.uk website: www.artinthemill.co.uk

Art in the Mill is a showcase for original contemporary artwork in beautiful, inspiring surroundings close to the ruins of Knaresborough castle.

The Mill is the perfect setting to display paintings, sculpture, glassworks, ceramics, metalworks and much more by acclaimed artists from Yorkshire and further afield. Displays can be found across three floors and the building which retains much of the charm of the original mill, delights visitors and locals alike. From the rustic charm of the ground floor where brick and stone floors create an atmosphere of their own, up to the light bright space of the top floor gallery with original beams and whitewashed walls, visitors can browse at leisure in this informal and homely setting.

This old flax mill built in 1808 stands in a beautiful cobbled courtyard right in the heart of this picturesque Yorkshire market town and was recently awarded a blue plaque by the Civic Society in recognition of its contribution to Knaresborough's pre-eminence in the linen trade. Nowadays, the Mill continues to play a significant role in the local community by featuring exhibitions and workshops throughout the year with exciting themes (see website for details). During the annual FEVA event the Mill features on Knaresborough's Visual Arts Trail and guest artists can be found painting alfresco in the courtyard.

📖 stories and anecdotes   🐦 famous people   🎨 art and craft   🎭 entertainment and sport   🚶 walks

tennis, putting and other activities. The annual **Knaresborough Festival of Entertainment and Visual Arts** (FEVA) runs for ten days in early August. The market place hosts daily performances by street entertainers and a varied selection of music, theatre and the spoken word takes place at various venues. Town Criers from far and wide compete in a competiton.

A mile or so to the south of Knaresborough, **Plumpton Rocks** provide an ideal picnic spot. There's an idyllic lake surrounded by dramatic millstone grit rocks and woodland paths that were laid out in the 18th century. It has been declared a garden of special historic interest by English Heritage and is open every weekend, on public holidays as well as daily from March to October.

RIPLEY
3 miles N of Harrogate off the A61

🏛 Castle

In the outer walls of the parish church, built around 1400, are holes said to have been caused by musket balls from Cromwell's firing squad who executed Royalist prisoners here after the battle of Marston Moor. Inside, there is a fine rood screen dating from the reign of King Stephen, a mid-14th century tomb chest, and the stone base of an old weeping cross (where one was expected to kneel in the stone grooves and weep for penance) survives in the churchyard.

Ripley, still very much an estate village, is a quiet and pretty place, with cobbled streets, a castle, a wonderful hotel, and an interesting history. A knighthood was granted to Thomas Ingilby in the 1300s for killing a wild boar in Knaresborough Forest that was charging at King Edward III.

Visitors strolling around Ripley cannot fail to notice the Hotel de Ville – the Town Hall. Sir William Amcotts Ingilby was responsible for this curiosity when, in 1827, he began to remodel the entire village on one that he had seen in Alsace-Lorraine. The original thatched cottages were replaced with those seen today and now Ripley is a conservation area with every pre-1980 dwelling being a Grade II listed building.

Magnificent **Ripley Castle** has been home to the Ingilby family for nearly 700 years. The castle is open to the public and is set in an outstanding Capability Brown landscape, with lakes, a deer park, and an avenue of tall beeches over which the attractive towers only just seem to peek. Its tranquillity belies the events that took place here after the battle at Marston Moor, when Cromwell, exhausted after his day's slaughter, camped his Roundheads here and chose to rest in the castle.

The Ingilbys, however, were Royalists and his intrusion was met with as much ill-will as possible; they offered neither food nor a bed. Jane Ingilby, aptly named 'Trooper Jane' due to her fighting skills, was the house's occupant and, having forced the self-styled Lord Protector of England to sleep on a sofa with two pistols pointing at his head, declared the next morning, 'It was well that he behaved in so peaceable a manner; had it been otherwise, he would not have left the house alive.' Cromwell, his pride severely damaged by a woman, ordered the immediate execution of his Royalist prisoners and left Trooper Jane regretting staying her hand during the previous night.

BURNT YATES
2 miles W of Ripley on the B6165

Located at one of the highest points in Nidderdale, Burnt Yates enjoys some fine views of the surrounding hills and moors. Its tiny village school of 1750 still stands. Its original endowment provided for 30 poor boys to be taught the three Rs and for an equivalent number of poor girls to learns the skills of needlework and spinning.

BOROUGHBRIDGE

7 miles SE of Ripon on the B6265

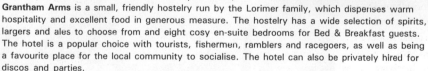 Devil's Arrows

This attractive and historic town dates from the reign of William the Conqueror though it was once on a main thoroughfare used by both the Celts of Brigantia and, later, the Romans. The bridge over the River Ure, from which the village takes its name, was built in 1562 and formed part of an important road link between Edinburgh and London. Busy throughout the coaching days with traffic passing from the West Riding of Yorkshire to the North, Boroughbridge has returned to its former unassuming role of a small wayside town now bypassed by the A1(M), which takes most of the 21st-century traffic from its streets.

The great **Devil's Arrows**, three massive Bronze Age monoliths, stand like guardians close to the new road and form Yorkshire's most famous ancient monument: thought to date from around 2000 BC, the tallest is 30 feet high. The monoliths stand in a line running north-south and are fashioned from

---

THE GRANTHAM ARMS HOTEL

Milby Roundabout, Boroughbridge, North Yorkshire YO51 9BW
Tel: 01423 322261
e-mail: simon@lorimer.eclipse.co.uk
website: www.granthamarms.com

On the edge of Boroughbridge, five minutes from the A1(M) and very close to the River Ure and the Ripon Canal, the **Grantham Arms** is a small, friendly hostelry run by the Lorimer family, which dispenses warm hospitality and excellent food in generous measure. The hostelry has a wide selection of spirits, largers and ales to choose from and eight cosy en-suite bedrooms for Bed & Breakfast guests. The hotel is a popular choice with tourists, fishermen, ramblers and racegoers, as well as being a favourite place for the local community to socialise. The hotel can also be privately hired for discos and parties.

THE FRUIT BASKET & DELICATESSEN

14 High Street, Boroughbridge, North Yorkshire YO51 9AW
Tel: 01123 324188

On the main street of Boroughbridge, the **Fruit Basket & Delicatessen** is a high-quality food emporium, an Aladdin's Cave for gourmets. Owner Julie and Chris source much of the stock from small independent firms. The shop stocks a wide range of fruit and vegetables, along with dried fruit, salads, nuts and pulses, herbs and spices (including Indian and Oriental cooking ingredients), dairy products, oils and vinegars and speciality flours for bread-making. Fresh fish comes from Ramus Seafoods, smoked products from Mackenzies, soups from the Yorkshire Soup Company and local speciality sausages. Flowers and plants are also available with tailor-made sprays and arrangements.

ISSIMA

6 High Street, Boroughbridge,
North Yorkshire YO51 9AW
Tel: 01423 325979

'Beautiful Gifts for Beautiful Homes'

Since 1999, Sarah Lamb has owned and run **Issima**, one of the loveliest lifestyle shops in Yorkshire. The constantly changing stock covers a wide range of goods and gifts for the home and garden, along with jewellery and fashion accessories, new baby and wedding presents, cards and wrap (a gift wrap service is available). Quality, style and variety are watchwords, and among the brands on display are Jan Constantine – hand-embroidered cushions and hearts; Little Dye House – ladies' clothes; Blondie mania – leather handbags; Ginny D – jewellery; Cath Kidston – homeware; English Country Pottery; Maxwell & Williams – crockery; Culinary Concepts – specialist tableware including cheese knives and olive spoons; DWCD – doorstops and scented hearts; Arran Aromatics; and Thomas Kent, clockmaker. Opening hours are 10 to 5 Monday to Saturday.

millstone grit, which has been seriously fluted by weathering. A local legend, however, attributes the great stones to the Devil, suggesting that they were actually crossbow bolts that he fired at nearby Aldborough which, at the time, was a Christian settlement.

Devil's Arrows, Boroughbridge

SKELTON

3 miles W of Boroughbridge off the B6265

This charming little village has some surviving cottages, dating from 1540, which are built from small handmade bricks with pantiled roofs. A ferry used to cross the River Ure at this point to Bishop Monkton and, in 1869, it was the scene of a notorious hunting accident. Members of the York and Ainsty Hunt boarded the ferry in order to follow a fox that

NEWBY HALL AND GARDEN

Skelton, nr Ripon,
North Yorkshire HG4 5AE
Tel: 01423 322583   Fax: 01423 324452
website: www.newbyhall.com

Newby Hall, the family home of Mr and Mrs Richard Compton, is one of England's finest houses, an exceptional example of 18th-century interior decoration. Built in the 1690s in the style of Sir Christopher Wren, the house was later enlarged and adapted by John Carr and subsequently Robert Adam. The superb contents of the house, collected on the Grand Tour by Weddell, ancestor of the Compton family, include a rare set of Gobelins tapestries, a gallery of classical statuary and some of Chippendale's finest furniture. From June 1st each year, Newby hosts a contemporary sculpture exhibition with around 60 sculptures sited in the woodland walk and gardens.

Newby Hall's 25 acres of award-winning **Gardens**, created in the early 1920s, have evolved (and are still evolving) over the years and have made a major contribution to 20th-century gardening. The gardens are a haven for both specialist and amateur gardeners. Alongside one of Europe's longest double herbaceous borders you'll find numerous formal 'compartmented' gardens such as the Rose Garden, Autumn Garden and Sylvia's Garden. With a water garden and tropical garden this truly is a garden for all seasons. Newby also holds the National Collection of Cornus (dogwood). Opening times for 2008 are Tuesday to Sunday 21st March to 28th September, plus Bank Holidays and Mondays in July and August.

NEWBY HALL FARM SHOP

Leeming Lane, Langthorpe, nr Boroughbridge,
North Yorkshire YO51 9DE
Tel: 01423 326452

Newby Hall Farm Shop, which opened in September 2006, is a joint venture between Richard Compton, owner of the Newby Hall estate, and local farmers David and Richard Lister of JC Farms. The brothers have a large local pig enterprise and manage 2,000 acres of Newby Hall. The shop specialises in meat and game traditionally raised on the estate and surrounding farms. Over 90% of the produce sold comes from within 40 miles of the farm, including seasonal lamb, matured beef, dry-cured pork and award-winning cheese, ice creams and baked goods, as well as fruit and vegetables. In its first year the farm shop was a national finalist in the awards of the National Farmers Retail & Markets Association (FARMA).

had swum across the river. Half way across the horses panicked, capsizing the boat, and the boatman, along with five hunt members, were drowned. Also here is **Newby Hall** (see panel on page 205), a beautiful Adams style house with award-winning gardens.

ALDBOROUGH

1 mile E of Boroughbridge off the B6265

🏛 Church of St Andrew   🏛 Roman Museum

The ancient Roman town of Isurium Brigantum, or Aldborough, as it is known today, was once the home of the 9th Legion, who wrested it from the Celtic Brigantian tribe. The modern-day focal point of the village is the tall maypole on the village green, around which traditional dances take place each May. At one end of the green is a raised platform, which is all that remains of the Old Court House and it bears an inscription recalling that up to 150 years ago the election of members of Parliament was announced here. Below are some well-preserved stocks that are, in fact, only replicas of the originals. The **Aldborough Roman Museum** houses relics of the town's past. This was once a thriving Roman city of vital strategic importance and near the museum are some of the original walls and tessellated pavements of that city.

The **Church of St Andrew** was built in 1330 on the site of a Norman church that was burnt down by the Scots in 1318. This in turn had been built on the site of an ancient Temple of Mercury. Modern archaeologists no doubt reel in horror at the thought that parts of the present church were built with stones from the Temple's walls. One ancient relic that is still preserved in the church's grounds is an Anglo-Saxon sundial known as the Ulph Stone.

The Yorkshire Dales

The Yorkshire Dales, one of England and Wales's 11 National Parks, is an area rich in farmland, high moorland and deep valleys. The predominant limestone found here gives rise to many of the area's interesting geological features, such as those found around Malham, the waterfalls at Aysgarth and Hardraw and White Scar Cave, while there is also an abundance of potholes and disappearing rivers that characterise the area. Considered by many to be the most appealing and beautiful region in the country, the Yorkshire Dales have been receiving

Langstrothdale

increasing numbers of visitors since the arrival of the railways in the 19th century, though many of the settlements date back to the Bronze and Iron Ages. With the large industrial areas of Yorkshire and nearby Lancashire close to hand, the Dales are easily accessible but, with so much open countryside, visitors are able to avoid the more popular attractions and enjoy the beauty of the region in solitude.

The largest of the northern Dales, Swaledale is also one of the grandest and it has a rugged beauty that is in contrast to the pretty and busier Wensleydale to the south. It is this dale's sheep, the Swaledale, with their characteristic black faces, white muzzles and grey speckled legs, which have been adopted as the symbol for the National Park. The valley of the River Ure, Wensleydale, is, perhaps, the one that most people associate with the Yorkshire Dales. One of the longer dales, it is a place of green pastureland grazed by flocks of Wensleydale sheep, lines of drystone walls and, of course, this is where the famous cheese is made. Further south again, is Wharfedale, a spectacular valley that is home to one of the National Park's most famous features, the Strid, where the River Wharfe charges through a narrow gorge just to the north of Bolton Abbey. To the east lies Nidderdale, a charming valley that was dubbed 'Little Switzerland' by the Victorians as its upper reaches are steep and wooded with the River Nidd flowing through narrow gorges. To the west is Ribblesdale that is overlooked by the famous Three Peaks of Whernside, Ingleborough and Pen-ghent, and that is also home to a spectacular stretch of the famous Settle to Carlisle Railway. Finally, there is Airedale, the valley of the River Aire, where, near the river's source, can be found the extraordinary limestone landscape around

Malham Tarn. Further downstream lies Skipton, an ancient market town and 'Gateway to the Dales' that is often many people's first experience of this glorious region of Britain.

The Yorkshire Dales provide the perfect setting for walking with at least 1,000 miles of public footpaths and ancient trackways, along with miles of bridleways. The **Pennine Way**, Britain's first long-distance footpath, is some 270 miles in length and particularly inviting for ramblers in part or as a whole. Meanwhile, the much shorter **Dales Way**, from Leeds to Lake Windermere in Cumbria, takes in old textile villages and the towns of West Yorkshire before heading through the western section of the Dales and on into Lancashire. There is also the **Trans Pennine Trail** that not only runs right across the country from east to west but also has a variety of extra, small diversions for those wishing to undertake shorter walks.

Swaledale

For many, Swaledale is the loveliest of the Yorkshire Dales. From historic Richmond it runs westwards through countryside that ranges from the dramatic lower dale with its steep-sided wooded hills to austere upper reaches – a terrain where your nearest neighbour could be several miles away. Its rugged beauty makes quite a contrast to pretty and busier Wensleydale just to the south. There are several other noticeable differences: the villages in Swaledale all have harsher, Nordic sounding names, the dale is much less populated, and the rivers and becks are more fast-flowing mountain streams.

At one time Swaledale was a hive of activity and enjoyed a prosperous century and more when the lead-mining industry flourished

📖 stories and anecdotes 🦢 famous people 🎨 art and craft 🖋 entertainment and sport 🚶 walks

Swaledale Folk Museum

The Green, Reeth,
North Yorkshire DL11 6QT
Tel: 01748 884118

The Museum was opened in 1974, and is based in the old Methodist School, which took in its first pupils in 1836. It is a fascinating repository of over 1,000 objects connected with living and working in the Dale. If you want to learn about lead mining this is the place for you, where lead and its associated rocks, minerals and fossils were yielded up by the hard labour of the 19th-century maps, and imagine what it must have been like to work underground with only candlelight for a guide. Sheep farming has been the mainstay of Swaledale agriculture since Tudor Times.

here. The valley of the River Swale still bears many of the scars left behind since the mining declined and the dale once again became a remote and under-populated place. The attractive market town of Richmond, first settled by the Romans, has for many years been the major focal point of this northerly region of Yorkshire. With several interesting museums, a fine Norman castle and excellent shopping facilities, Richmond is still the key town in the northern dales.

Swaledale sheep will be a familiar sight to anyone who spends time in the Dales. Recognised by their black faces, white muzzle and grey speckled legs, the Swaledale sheep were introduced to the area in the 1920s. Each flock knows its own territory – they are said to be *'heafed'* to the moor. The sheep have to cope with extremely wild weather and their hardiness is typified by the warmth and durability of their wool. No surprise to find that the ram has been adopted as the emblem of the Yorkshire Dales National Park.

There are several side dales to Swaledale: the small, thriving market town of Reeth lies

at the junction of Arkengarthdale and the valley of the River Swale. First settled by Norsemen who preferred wild and remote countryside, the valley of Arkle Beck was not considered important enough to gain an entry in the *Domesday Book*. There is much evidence of the old lead-mining days although the dale is now chiefly populated by hardy Swaledale sheep. At the head of this rather bleak and barren dale lies England's highest inn, Tan Hill. Though only a short section of the River Tees flows through Yorkshire, the section of Teesdale around Piercebridge is particularly charming and well worth a visit.

We begin at the northern end of the dale and follow the Swale downstream.

Reeth

Swaledale Folk Museum   Craft Workshops

Considered the capital of Upper Swaledale, this small town is poised at the junction of the River Swale and its main tributary, Arkle Beck. The local lead-mining industry, which was begun by the Romans, served the town well for many years, until competition from abroad gradually caused its decline and Reeth became chiefly an agricultural centre. Noted in the *Domesday Book*, while everything else in the area was written off as untaxable wasteland, Reeth prospered and it is still today a much-visited place.

Until the end of the 19th century, a total of four fairs were held here annually, as well as a weekly market. Today, the annual agricultural show in September is a magnet for farmers from the entire length of the dale and beyond. Along the top of the green is High Row, with its inns and shops and outstanding Georgian architecture, reflecting the affluence of the town in the 18th century when the trade in wool and lead was booming.

The newly refurbished **Swaledale Folk Museum** (see panel opposite), housed in what was once the old Methodist Sunday School, is the home for exhibits of local farming methods, crafts and mining skills, as well as displays on local pastimes, the impact of Wesleyan Methodism, and the exodus of the population to the industrial areas of the south Pennines and America when the lead mines closed.

This little town is noted for its variety of craft shops. There's a cluster of them at the **Reeth Craft Workshops** near the green. Here you'll find a cabinet maker, a furniture maker, a guitar maker, a pottery shop, a clock maker and restorer, a sculptor, a silversmith, a photographer and Stef's Models where visitors can see the production of beautifully crafted animal models. Paintings are also on sale here.

Running northwestwards from Reeth, Arkengarthdale is a small and remote valley, mostly treeless moorland with scarcely a human habitation in sight. It was first settled by Norsemen and their presence is still reflected in the dale's place names – Booze, Eskeleth, and Whaw. Overlooked completely during the Domesday survey, when it was considered of no value, the dale experienced a period of prosperity in the 18th and 19th centuries from lead-mining. Ruins of the old industrial buildings are scattered around the valley, as yet overlooked by the heritage industry.

Around Reeth

KELD
10 miles W of Reeth on the B6270

The little cluster of stone buildings that make up this village stand beside the early stages of the River Swale. The place is alive with the sound of rushing water and it comes as no surprise that the word *keld* is Nordic for spring. For lovers of green woodlands and breathtaking waterfalls, this village is definitely well worth a visit and it has also managed to retain an impression of being untouched by modern life.

Wain Wath Force, with rugged Cotterby Scar providing a fine backdrop, can be found alongside the Birkdale road. Catrake Force, with its stepped formation, can be reached from the cottages on the left at the bottom of the street in the village. Though on private land the falls and, beside them, the entrance to an old lead mine can still be seen. For less adventurous pedestrians Kisdon Force, the most impressive waterfall in Swaledale, can be reached by a gentle stroll of less than a mile from the village along a well-trodden path.

For really serious walkers, Keld is the most important crossroads in northern England. Here the south-to-north Pennine Way and the east-to-west Coast-to-Coast long-distance walks intersect.

THWAITE
10 miles W of Reeth on the B6270

🏃 Buttertubs Pass

Surrounded by dramatic countryside, which includes Kisdon Hill, Great Shunnor, High Seat and Lovely Seat, this is a tiny village of ancient origins. Like so many places in the area the name comes from the Nordic language, in this case *thveit*, meaning a clearing in the wood. The woodlands that once provided shelter and fuel for the Viking settlers have long since gone.

To the southwest of the village lies **Buttertubs Pass**, one of the highest and most forbidding mountain passes in the

The Buttertubs, Thwaite

country. The Buttertubs themselves are a curious natural feature of closely packed vertical stone stacks rising from some unseen, underground base to the level of the road. A local Victorian guide to the Buttertubs, perhaps aware that the view from above was not all that impressive, solemnly assured his client that 'some of the Buttertubs had no bottom, and some were deeper than that'. No one is quite sure where the Buttertubs name came from. The most plausible explanation is that farmers used its deep-chilled shelves as a convenient refrigerator for the butter they couldn't sell immediately.

Unusually, these potholes are not linked by a series of passages as most are, but are free-standing and bear only a slight resemblance to the objects after which they are named. The narrow road from Thwaite across the Buttertubs Pass is not for the faint-hearted driver. Only a flimsy post and wire fence separates the road from a sheer drop of Alpine proportions. In any case, it's much more satisfying to cross the pass from the other direction, from Hawes: from the south, as you crest the summit you will be rewarded with a stupendous view of Swaledale stretching for miles.

MUKER
8 miles W of Reeth on the B6270

🏚 Church of St Mary

An old stone bridge leads into this engaging village, which consists of a collection of beige-coloured stone cottages overlooked by the **Church of St Mary**, which dates back to the time of Elizabeth I - one of the very few to be built in England during her reign. Most church builders until that time had spared no expense in glorifying the house of God. At Muker they were more economical: the church roof was covered in thatch, its floor in rushes. No seating was provided. Despite such penny-pinching measures, the new church of 1580 was warmly welcomed since it brought to an end the tedious journey for bereaved relatives along the Corpse Way to the dale's mother church at Grinton, some eight miles further to the east.

The good people of Muker devised means of making further savings. For many years, the thrifty mourners of the parish shared a communal coffin. Year after year the same coffin would bear the departed to the churchyard where the shrouded body was removed, placed in the grave and the coffin retrieved for use at the next funeral. It wasn't until 1735 that the vicar decreed that everyone buried in his parish deserved the dignity of a personal coffin.

On the gravestones in the churchyard local family names, such as Harker, Alderson and Fawcett, feature prominently as they do among the villagers still living here.

Close by the church is a quaint little building identified as the Literary Institute from whence you may hear the strains of a brass band rehearsing. In Victorian times, most of the Dales villages had their own brass band – Muker's is one of the few survivors and is in great demand at various events throughout the year.

Swaledale cuisine is equally durable: specialities on offer in the local tearooms include Swaledale Curd Tart, Yorkshire Rarebit, and Deep Apple Pie with Wensleydale cheese. And the main crafts still revolve around the wool provided by the hardy Swaledale sheep, popular with carpet manufacturers and for jumpers worn by fell walkers, climbers, and anyone else trying to defeat the British weather.

IVELET
7 miles W of Reeth off the B6270

🌉 Packhorse Bridge

Just a few hundreds yard off the B6270, the 14th-century **Packhorse Bridge** at Ivelet is regarded as one of the finest in Yorkshire. It's a very picturesque spot and you can also join a delightful riverside walk here.

GUNNERSIDE
6 miles W of Reeth on the B6270

🌉 Methodist Chapel

🏛 Old Working Smithy & Museum

This charming Dales village in the heart of Swaledale was, until the late 19th century, a thriving lead-mining village. Gunnerside became known as the Klondyke of Swaledale and, although the boom centred around lead rather than gold, the Old Gang Mines are the most famous in Yorkshire. The paths and trackways here are mainly those trodden by the many successions of miners travelling to their work, and the valley's sides still show the signs of the mine workings. In the village, one can visit tearooms that offer such delights as Lead Miners' Bait and the delicious Gunnerside Cheese Cake made from a recipe handed down from mining days.

After the closure of the mines, many families left the village to find work elsewhere in northern England while others emigrated to America and even as far afield as Australia. For many years afterwards, one of the village's most important days was Midsummer Sunday when those who had left would, if able, return and catch up with their families and friends.

Gunnerside's most impressive building is its **Methodist Chapel**, a classically elegant building, wonderfully light and airy. The indefatigable John Wesley visited Gunnerside in 1761 and found the local congregation 'earnest, loving and simple people'.

What makes **The Old Working Smithy & Museum** rather special is the fact that nothing has been bought in – all the artefacts on show are from the smithy itself, indeed many of them were actually made here. The smithy was established in 1795 and over the years little has been thrown away. Cartwheels, cobblers' tools, horseshoes, fireside implements and a miner's 'tub' (railway wagon) from a lead mine are just some of the vintage articles on show. This is still a working smithy. Stephen Calvert is the 6th generation of his family to pursue the trade of blacksmith and he still uses the original forge and hand bellows to create a wide range of wrought ironwork.

Gunnerside's picturesque hump-backed bridge over the Swale is reputed to be haunted by a headless ghost. Oddly, no gruesome tale has grown up around this unfortunate spirit.

LOW ROW
4 miles W of Reeth on the B6270

🐦 Hazel Brow Organic Farm & Visitor Centre

In medieval times the track along the hillside above Low Row formed part of the Corpse Way along which relays of bearers would carry the deceased in a large wicker basket on a journey that could take two days to complete. Along their route, you can still see the large stone slabs where they rested their burden. Even more convenient was the 'Dead Barn' above Low Row where the carriers could deposit the body and scramble downhill for a convivial evening at the Punch Bowl Inn.

Located on the edge of the village, **Hazel Brow Organic Farm and Visitor Centre** provides a popular family day out. Set in glorious Swaledale scenery the 200-acre

traditional family-run farm offers children the opportunity of bottle-feeding lambs, riding a pony or helping to feed the calves, sheep and pigs. The farm also has a tea room, children's play area and gift shop, and hosts various demonstrations of farming activities throughout the year.

Just west of Low Row, a road to the left attracts many visitors with its signpost pointing to 'Crackpot'. All you will find is a perfectly sensible-looking cluster of working farmhouses. Crackpot simply means a place where crows (crack) congregate around a deep hole in the hills (a pot).

LANGTHWAITE
3 miles NW of Reeth off the B6270

Langthwaite, the main village of Arkengarthdale, will seem familiar to many who have never been here before as its bridge featured in the title sequence of the popular television series *All Creatures Great and Small*. Just outside this beautiful place stands the cryptically named CB Hotel – named after Charles Bathurst, an 18th-century lord of the manor who was responsible for the development of the lead-mining industry in the dale. His grandfather, Dr John Bathurst, physician to Oliver Cromwell, had purchased the land here in 1659 with the exploitation of its mineral wealth in mind.

TAN HILL
10 miles NW of Reeth off the B6270

🐦 Sheep Fair

Standing at the head of Arkengarthdale on the border with County Durham, 1,732 feet above sea level, is England's highest pub, the Tan Hill Inn. Why on earth should there be a pub here, in one of the most remote and barren stretches of the north Pennines, frequently cut off and in total isolation during the winter? A century ago, the inn's patrons didn't need to ask. Most of them were workers from the Tan Hill coal mines; others were drivers waiting for their horse-drawn carts to be filled with coal. The coal mines have long since closed, but an open coal fire still burns in the inn 365 days a year and some 50,000 visitors a year still find their way to Tan Hill. Many of them are walkers who stagger in from one of the most gruelling stretches of the Pennine Way Walk and, clutching a pint of Theakston's Old Peculier, collapse on the nearest settle.

During the long winters, when the moorland roads have disappeared under 12-feet deep snowdrifts and, despite cellar walls three feet thick, the pub's beer-pumps have frozen, trade tends to fall off a bit. It revives spectacularly on the last Thursday in May. This is when the **Tan Hill Sheep Fair** takes place and, if only for a day, Tan Hill Inn becomes the centre of agricultural Yorkshire. 'It's the Royal Show for Swaledale Sheep is Tan Hill,' said one proud farmer scrutinising his flock, 'and I've got some princes and princesses here.' In cash terms the value of the prizes awarded at the Fair is negligible – just a few pounds for even a first class rosette. But at the auction that follows it's a different story. In 1990 one particularly prized Tupp Hogg (a young ram) was sold for £30,000.

GRINTON
1 mile S of Reeth on the B6270

🏛 Church of St Mary

Just to the south of Reeth lies the quiet village of Grinton whose parish **Church of St Andrew** served the whole of the dale for centuries. The building dates back to the 13th and 15th centuries, though there are still some Norman remains as well as a Leper's Squint (a small hole through which those afflicted by the disease could follow the service within). For those people living in the upper reaches of Swaledale who died, there was a long journey down the track to Grinton which became known as the Corpse Way.

Richmond

🏛 Castle 🏛 Culloden Tower 🏛 Easby Abbey

🏛 Green Howards Museum

🏛 Richmondshire Museum

🏛 🖌 Georgian Theatre Royal & Museum

The former county of Richmondshire (which still survives as a parliamentary constituency) once occupied a third of the North Riding of Yorkshire. Alan Rufus, the 1st Earl of Richmond, built the original **Richmond Castle** in 1071 and the site, 100 feet up on a rocky promontory with the River Swale passing below, is imposing and well chosen. The keep rises to 109 feet with walls 11 feet thick, while the other side is afforded an impregnable defence by means of the cliff and the river. Richmond Castle was the first Norman castle in the country to be built, right from the foundations, in stone. Additions were made over subsequent years but it reached its final form in the 14th century. Since then it has fallen into ruin though a considerable amount of the original Norman stonework remains intact.

With such an inspiring setting, it is hardly surprising that there is a legend suggesting that King Arthur himself is buried here, reputedly in a cave beneath the castle. The story goes that a simple potter called Thompson stumbled across an underground passage that led to a chamber where he discovered the king and his knights lying in an

FRENCHGATE GUEST HOUSE

66 Frenchgate, Richmond, North Yorkshire DL10 7AG
Tel/Fax: 01748 823421   mob: 07889 768696
e-mail: info@66frenchgate.co.uk
website: www.66frenchgate.co.uk

Standing on the ancient cobbled street from which it takes its name, **Frenchgate Guest House** is just a short stroll from Richmond's historic Market Place. Owner Ralph Doy and his staff have built up an enviable reputation for outstanding service, comfort and hospitality at this fine Victorian-era townhouse, bringing many repeat bookings and earning the accolade of 4 stars from the English Tourist Council – one of

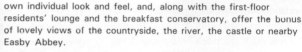

the few B&Bs so honoured in the region. Each of the   smartly decorated en-suite bedrooms, a twin and two doubles, has its own individual look and feel, and, along with the first-floor residents' lounge and the breakfast conservatory, offer the bonus of lovely views of the countryside, the river, the castle or nearby Easby Abbey.

Equally popular with business and leisure guests, Frenchgate combines traditional standards of hotel-keeping with up-to-date facilities and amenities, including internet access. The guest house is open all year round.

THE WIVES KITCHEN HEALTH & WHOLEFOOD

11 Finkle Street, Richmond, North Yorkshire DL10 4QA
Tel: 01748 822210

Leading off Richmond's vast Market square, pedestrianised Finkle Street is the home of Irene Wagstaffe and Pat Fava's **Wives Kitchen Health & Wholefood**.

This excellent shop sells a comprehensive range of supplements and remedies. They are stockists for Bioforce, Solgar, Weleda Homeopathic remedies, Tisseland Aromatherapy Products and many others, as well as their own label. They also stock a large and varied range of wholefoods, organic foods including dried fruit, cereals, nuts and seeds and flours. A wide selection of foods are available for those on special diets, for example, gluten-free and dairy free.

Since opening here in 1981, Irene and Pat have accumulated a wealth of experience in health and wholefood products and a loyal clientele from all over the region. They are on hand to offer friendly, personal service and helpful advice, and will do their best to track down any product not in stock. This busy, popular shop is open from 9 to 5 Monday to Saturday.

enchanted sleep, surrounded by priceless treasures. A voice warned him not to disturb the sleepers and he fled. Predictably, he was unable to locate the passage again. Another legend associated with the castle tells how a drummer boy was sent down the passageway. Beating his drum as he walked, the boy's progress was followed by the soldiers on the surface until, suddenly, the drumming stopped. Though the passageway was searched the boy was never seen again but, it is said, his drumming can still be heard.

Green Howards Museum, Richmond

In 1315, Edward II granted Richmond the right to protect the town by a stone wall after Scottish raiders had caused considerable damage in the surrounding area. By the 16th century, the walls were in a state of disrepair and little survives today. Two road bridges cross the River Swale in the town. The older of the two, Green Bridge, was erected in 1789 to the designs of John Carr after the existing bridge had been swept away by flood water. Its picturesque setting is enhanced by the massive cliff crowned by Richmond Castle that towers above it.

During the Middle Ages, the markets of Richmond gave the town much of its prosperity and its influence spread across Yorkshire to Lancashire. Also, like many North Yorkshire towns and villages, the textile industry played an important role in the continuation of the town's wealth and, for some time, Richmond became famous for its knitted stockings.

The **Green Howards Museum**, the regimental museum of the North Riding's infantry, is based in the old Trinity Church in the centre of the cobbled market square. The

regiment dates back to 1688, when it was founded, and the displays and collections illustrate its history with war relics, weapons, uniforms, medals, and regimental silver. Also housed in the museum is the town's silver. The church itself was founded in 1135 and, though it has been altered and rebuilt on more than one occasion, the original Norman tower and some other masonry have survived.

One of the grandest buildings in the town is the **Culloden Tower**, just off the town green. It was erected in 1747 by the Yorke family, one of whose members had fought at the Battle of Culloden the previous year. Unlike most follies, the interior of the three-storey tower is elaborately decorated in the rococo style and since it is now in the care of the Landmark Trust it is possible to stay there.

It is not surprising that a town steeped in history should have several museums. The **Richmondshire Museum** traces the history of this old place and its county. There is also a reconstruction of James Herriot's veterinary surgery taken from the popular television series as well as other period costumes and displays.

Richmond is also home to England's oldest theatre, the **Georgian Theatre Royal**, which originally formed part of a circuit that included Northallerton, Ripon, and Harrogate. Built in 1788 by the actor and manager Samuel Butler, it had at that time an audience capacity of 400. The connection with the theatrical Butler family ended in 1830 and from then until 1848 it was used, infrequently, by travelling companies. After the mid-19th century right up until the 1960s, the theatre saw a variety of uses, as a wine cellar and a corn chandler's among others, and it did not re-open as a theatre until 1963 and only then after much restoration work had been carried out. The **Georgian Theatre Royal Museum** was also opened and it contains a unique collection of original playbills as well as the oldest and largest complete set of painted scenery in Britain.

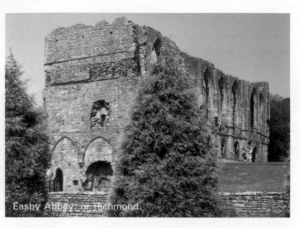
Easby Abbey, nr Richmond

About a mile east of the town lies **Easby Abbey**, a delightful monastic ruin that looks down to the River Swale. Founded in 1155 by Roald, Constable of Richmond Castle, its order of monks were of more modest leanings than the Cistercians, and the building certainly possesses none of the grandiose lines of Rievaulx and Fountains, although the riverside setting is a common feature. The Abbey's most notable feature is its replica of the Easby Cross, an Anglo-Saxon cross dating from the 9th century, and the extensive ruins can be reached by a pleasant riverside walk that is well signposted.

HUDSWELL
2 miles W of Richmond off the A6136

This ancient village, which was well established by the time it was recorded in the *Domesday Book*, stands high above the River Swale, and over the years it has gravitated to a more sheltered spot. The present St Michael's Church was built in the late 19th century on the site of an older building and the view from the churchyard is considered to be one of the finest in Richmondshire.

The walk from the village down to the river leads through pleasant woodland and takes in some 365 steps. About half way down, below a path leading off to an old lime kiln, can be found **King Arthur's Oven**, a horizontal crack in the limestone, which, it is claimed, has connections with Richmond Castle and the legend of King Arthur.

CATTERICK
5 miles SE of Richmond off the A1

🏠 Kiplin Hall

This is an ancient settlement with an attractive village green and a nearby racecourse that, every Sunday hosts the largest street market in England.

Ever since the time of the Romans, when the settlement was known as *Cataractonium*, Catterick has been associated with the armed forces. Located on the Roman highway between London and Hadrian's Wall, the garrison was also close to the place where Paulinus, Bishop of York, baptised 10,000 Christians in the River Swale. Today, the army garrison (the largest in Europe) is some three miles to the west. RAF Leeming lies just south of the village.

The connections with Nelson are not immediately obvious, but it was Alexander Scott, vicar of Catterick in 1816, who was at Nelson's side when he died at Trafalgar. Also, the Admiral's sister-in-law, Lady Tyrconnel, lived at nearby **Kiplin Hall**, a beautiful Jacobean country home famed for its wonderful interior plasterwork and medieval fishponds. The hall also contains many mementoes of Nelson and Lady Hamilton and, on display in the Blue Room, is a folding library chair from the Admiral's cabin on *HMS Victory*. The hall also has a strong American connection since it was built by the 1st Lord Baltimore, who was instrumental in founding the state of Maryland, whose capital city bears his name.

MOULTON
2 miles SE of Scotch Corner off the A1

🏛 Hall

This small village is home to two fine 17th-century manor houses that were built by members of the Smithson family. The Manor House, in the village centre, was originally built in the late-16th century and was improved greatly in the mid-17th century. Just to the south lies **Moulton Hall**, built by George Smithson following his marriage to Eleanor Fairfax in 1654. Similar in size to the original Smithson family home and somewhat resembling it, Moulton Hall is now in the hands of the National Trust.

MIDDLETON TYAS
1 mile E of Scotch Corner off the A1

Situated in a sheltered position yet close to the Great North Road, the position of the village church, away from the village centre and at the end of a long avenue of trees, seems strange. However, when the Church of St Michael was built it served not only Middleton Tyas but also Moulton and Kneeton (the latter no longer in existence), between which Middleton lay. During the 18th century, the village saw a period of prosperity when copper was found and mined from the fields near the church. Several grand houses were built including East Hall, which belonged to Leonard Hartley, who founded the industry, though his son, George, had a grander house on the outskirts of Middleton that was designed by John Carr of York.

KIRBY HILL
4 miles NW of Richmond off the A66

This quiet hamlet lies midway between London and Edinburgh on the old Great North Road, and in the days of the stagecoach it was a busy stopping place. The cellar of the Blue Bell Inn still retains the rings to which prisoners travelling between the two capitals were tethered overnight.

RAVENSWORTH
5 miles NW of Richmond on minor road off the A66

Lying in the small and little-known dale of Holmedale, the Methodist chapel here, built in 1822, is the oldest chapel on the Richmond circuit. To the southeast of the village are the remains of the Fitzhughs' Norman castle, which is believed to have been in existence in

WHASHTON SPRINGS FARMHOUSE B&B

Whashton, nr Richmond, North Yorkshire DL11 7JS
Tel: 01748 822884   Fax: 01748 826285
e-mail: whashtonsprings@btconnect.com
website: www.whashtonsprings.co.uk

For more than 30 years, the Turnbull family have been running their farmhouse Bed & Breakfast in secluded Holmedale close to the border with County Durham and just below the famous landmark of the Jockey Cap. Now with Jane and David at the helm the accommodation at **Whashton Springs** comprises nine spacious en-suite rooms – twins, doubles and one of family size - some on the ground floor and all commanding lovely views. Also set around the courtyard is a holiday cottage for four. A super breakfast, with free-range eggs, yoghurt and heather honey, gets the day off to a perfect start, and guests can take a stroll in the garden, walk round the farm or plan their day in the comfortable lounge. Whashton Springs lies three miles north of Richmond, and west of Scotch Corner (A1) off the A66. It offers easy access to many of the scenic and historic attractions of Yorkshire and County Durham, and the Lake District is only an hour's drive away.

1180. However, the present ruins suggest that the demolished building was of a 14th-century construction. The castle is privately owned with no public access.

EAST LAYTON
4 miles NW of Scotch Corner off the B6274

🌱 Miniature World

The summer of 1999 saw the opening of a major new visitor attraction in North Yorkshire. **Miniature World** offers families and school groups a wonderful day out, giving them the opportunity of meeting a wide range of small animals (including rare breeds), enjoying pony rides, honing their orienteering skills and much more. Miniature World is open by appointment only. Gill and Stephen Sims, who created this unique project, like to ensure that each visit is individually tailored to suit the party.

ALDBROUGH
4 miles N of Scotch Corner off the B6275

🏛 Stanwick Camp

To the west of the village lies the enormous complex of earthworks known as **Stanwick Camp**. The series of banks and ditches were excavated in the 1950s and their discovery also revealed that the constructions had been carried out in the 1st century. The site, open to the public, is now owned by English Heritage.

FORCETT
6 miles N of Scotch Corner on the B6274

The mainly Norman village Church of St Cuthbert underwent a drastic restoration programme in 1859 and the interior is now chiefly Victorian. Nearby Forcett Park, which is privately owned, is a particularly outstanding example of an early Georgian house, complete with stables, lodges, and a fine dovecote. The dovecote and the splendid east gate can be seen from the road leading to the park from the village.

Wensleydale

Wensleydale, perhaps above all the others, is the dale most people associate with the Yorkshire Dales. Charles Kingsley once described it as 'the richest spot in all England … a beautiful oasis in the mountains'. At some 40 miles long, it is certainly the longest dale and it is also softer and greener than many of its neighbours. The pasture land, grazed by flocks of Wensleydale sheep, is only broken by the long lines of dry stone walls and the dale is, of course, famous for its cheese whose fortunes have recently been given an additional boost by Wallace and Gromit who have declared it to be their favourite!

Wensleydale is the only major dale not to be named after its river, the Ure, although until fairly recent years most locals still referred to the area as Yoredale or Uredale. The dale's name comes from the once important town of Wensley where the lucrative trade in cheese began in the 13th century. Wensley prospered for many years until 1563 when the Black Death annihilated most of its people and Leyburn became the trading centre of the lower dale. Wensleydale is also recorded in the 12th century as Wandeleysleydale – 'Waendel's woodland clearing in the valley'. Waendel has disappeared into the mists of time, but undoubtedly his clearing was somewhere near this attractive little village.

At the western end of the dale is Hawes, derived from the Norse word *hals* meaning neck and, indeed, the town does lies on a neck of land between two hills. Home of the Dales Countryside Museum and the Wensleydale Creamery, Hawes is an ideal starting point for exploring the dale. It is widely believed that the medieval monks of Jervaulx Abbey were responsible for introducing the manufacture of cheese to the dale some 700 years ago (they were of French origin). It was first made from ewe's milk but by the 1600s the milk of shorthorn cows was used instead since the sheep were becoming increasingly important for their wool and mutton. Originally just a summer occupation, and mainly the task of the farmer's wife, the production of Wensleydale cheese was put on a commercial footing when the first cheese factory was established at Gayle Beck, near Hawes, in 1897.

Using Hawes as a base, visitors can also follow the Turner trail, which takes in the scenic sights that so impressed JMW Turner when he visited Wensleydale and neighbouring Swaledale in 1816.

As it flows down the dale, the Ure is fed by a series of smaller rivers and becks, many of which have their own charming dale. Among the better-known are Coverdale, the home of some of England's finest racehorse stables, and peaceful Bishopdale with its ancient farmhouses. Remote Cotterdale, with its striking waterfall, and the narrow valley of the River Waldern are also well worth exploring.

Wensleydale, along with Swaledale and the area around Thirsk, are commonly referred to as Herriot Country, since it was this region of fells and friendly villages that provided many locations for the BBC series *All Creatures Great and Small*. Based on the working life of the real life vet, Alf Wight (1916-95), the stories recount the working life of Dales-people between the 1930s and 1960s with humour and affection.

Hawes

🏛 Dales Countryside Museum

🏛 Wensleydale Experience ⚲ Hawes Ropeworkers

At 850 feet above sea level, Hawes is the highest market town in Yorkshire. The present town expanded greatly in the 1870s after the arrival of the railways but there's still plenty of evidence of the earlier settlement in street names relating to ancient trades: Dyer's Garth, Hatter's Yard and Printer's Square. Now the commercial and market centre of the upper dale, Hawes offers a good range of shopping, accommodation and visitor attractions.

Housed in the former railway station, **The Dales Countryside Museum** (see panel below) tells the story of how man's activities have helped to shape the Dales' landscape. Providing fascinating historical details on domestic life, the lead-mining industry, hand-knitting and other trades as well as archaeological material, the museum covers many aspects of Dales' life from as far back as 10,000 BC.

One of those local industries was rope-making and at **The Hawes Ropeworkers**, adjacent to the museum, visitors can still see it in operation, with experienced ropers twisting cotton and man-made fibres to make halters, hawsers, picture cords, dog leads, clothes lines and other 'rope' items. The gift shop here stocks a comprehensive range of rope-related items along with an extensive choice of other souvenirs of the dale.

THE DALES COUNTRYSIDE MUSEUM
National Park and Tourist Information Centre

Station Yard, Hawes, North Yorkshire DL8 3NT
Tel: 01969 666210
e-mail: hawes@yorkshiredales.org.uk
website: www.yorkshiredales.org.uk

In three main galleries in the station yard at Hawes, **The Dales Countryside Museum** tells in entertaining and fascinating detail the story of the people, the industry and the landscape of the Yorkshire Dales. Started over 60 years ago by local historian Marie Hartley, the museum has major permanent displays and an exciting annual programme of events and changing exhibitions. The largest gallery is housed in the old goods shed that once stored freight awaiting transportation by steam trains of the Midland Railway. It is now filled with displays on local industry, crafts and framing. There is a gift

shop, information centre, study rooms and an outside demonstration area. The Time Tunnel traces the history of the area from the earliest times, and a video shown in the old railway carriages is themed on Dales life, at work and play. At the eastern end of Hawes, just off the main A684, the Museum is open daily from 10 to 5. All areas are accessible to wheelchairs.

The Museum offers 2 for 1 entry for adults on presentation of this book (entry is always free for accompanied children under 16).

YORKSHIRE DALES
National Park Authority

THE BEE LYNE GIFT SHOP

Main Street, Hawes, North Yorkshire DL8 3QW
Tel: 01969 667261

For more than 20 years, Ron and Susan Hampshire have been running the **Bee Lyne Gift Shop**, which stands on a corner site in the centre of Hawes. This classic gift shop, with something to suit all pockets, ages and occasions, holds a wide and constantly changing stock – much of it with a local theme – that includes clothes (Joules and Junior Joules), hats, handbags and purses, sheepskin rugs and slippers, mittens, tea towels, Lilliput Lane miniatures, adorable Ewe & Me sheep, mugs, maps and guide books, pictures and prints, cards and coasters... a veritable browser's delight!

Wensleydale's most famous product (after its sheep) is its soft, mild cheese, and at the **Wensleydale Cheese Experience** not only can you sample this delicacy, but also learn about its history through a series of interesting displays. With a museum, viewing gallery of the production area, cheese shop, gift shop and licensed restaurant, there's plenty here for the cheese lover to enjoy.

Around Hawes

HARDRAW
1 mile N of Hawes off the A684

🦆 🚶 Hardraw Force

Located in a natural amphitheatre of limestone crags, **Hardraw Force** is the highest, unbroken waterfall in England above ground, a breathtaking cascade 98 feet high. The top ledge of hard rock projects so far beyond the softer stone beneath that it used to be possible to walk behind the falling water as JMW Turner and Wordsworth did. Sadly, for safety reasons this is no longer possible. The waterfall shows at its best after heavy rain as, generally, the quantity of water tumbling over the rocks is not great. On two separate occasions, in 1739 and 1881, the falls froze

solid into a 100-feet icicle.

In the 1870s, the French stuntman Blondin astounded spectators when, not content with crossing the falls on a tightrope, he paused halfway to cook an omelette.

The amphitheatre here provides superb acoustics, a feature which has been put to great effect in the annual brass band competitions that began here in 1885 and have recently resumed. Access to Hardraw Force is through the Green Dragon pub where a small fee is payable. The inn itself is pretty venerable with records of a hostelry on this site since at least the mid-13th century. At that time the land here was a grange belonging to the monks of Fountains Abbey who grazed their sheep nearby.

COTTERDALE
4 miles NW of Hawes off the A684

🦆 Cotter Force

The small valley of Cotter Beck lies below the vast bulk of Great Shunner Fell which separates the head of Wensleydale from Swaledale. **Cotter Force**, although smaller than Hardraw, is extremely attractive though often neglected in favour of its more famous neighbour.

BAINBRIDGE
4 miles E of Hawes on the A684

🏛 Grough Hall   🌿 Semer Water

Back in the Middle Ages this area of Upper Wensleydale was a hunting forest, known as the Forest and Manor of Bainbridge, and the village itself was established around the 12th century as a home for the foresters. One of their duties was to show travellers the way through the forest. If anyone was still out by nightfall a horn was blown to guide them home. The custom is still continued between the Feast of Holy Rood (September 27th) and Shrove Tuesday when the present horn is blown at 9pm.

Ancient stocks are still in place on the spacious village green, and on the eastern edge of the village the River Bain rushes over a small waterfall as it makes its way down from Semer Water.

Just to the east of Bainbridge is **Brough Hill** (private) where the Romans built a succession of forts known collectively as *Virosidum*. First excavated in the late 1920s, they now appear as overgrown grassy hummocks. Much easier to see is the Roman road that strikes southwestwards from Bainbridge, part of the trans-Pennine route to Lancaster. It passes close to the isolated lake of **Semer Water**, one of Yorkshire's only two natural lakes. (The other is Lake Gormire, near Thirsk.) Semer Water stretches half a mile in length and teems with wild fowl. To the north the lake is drained by the River Bain which, at little more than two miles long, is the shortest river in England.

An enduring legend claims that a town lies beneath the depths of Semer Water, cast under water by a curse. A poor traveller once sought shelter in the town but was turned away by the affluent inhabitants. The next day he stood on the hill above the town, pronounced a curse, and a great flood engulfed the town immediately. There's an intriguing postscript to this tale. During a severe drought the level of the lake dropped to reveal the remains of a Bronze Age town.

ASKRIGG
5 miles E of Hawes off the A684

Recorded in the *Domesday Book* as 'Ascric', this once-important market town became better known to TV viewers as Darrowby, a major location for the long-running series *All Creatures Great and Small*. The 18th-century Kings Arms often featured as 'The Drovers Arms' and Cringley House doubled as Skeldale House, the fictional home of the TV vets.

THE KINGS ARMS

Askrigg, nr Leyburn, North Yorkshire DL8 3HP
Tel: 01969 650817   Fax: 01969 650927

The Kings Arms is a much-loved country pub in the picturesque little town of Askrigg. In the traditionally furnished bar an exceptional range of cask ales is on tap, along with a good choice of wines and malts. Owner-chef Keith Deeks, who learnt his trade in top London restaurants, took over in 2006 and continues to make friends with his menus of superb, freshly prepared dishes. Askrigg is known to TV viewers as Darrowby in the popular series *All Creatures Great and Small* and the Kings Arms starred as the Drovers Arms in that popular, long-running show. There are numerous photographs and other related memorabilia on the walls of the cast.

🏛 historic building   🏛 museum and heritage   🏛 historic site   🌄 scenic attraction   🌿 flora and fauna

During the 18th century Askrigg was a thriving town with several prosperous industries. Cotton was spun in a nearby mill, dyeing and brewing took place here and it was also a centre for hand-knitting. However, the town is particularly famous for clock-making, introduced by John Ogden in 1681. The village has been popular with tourists since the days of Turner and Wordsworth when the chief attractions here were the two waterfalls, Whitfield Force and Mill Gill. Despite its olde worlde atmosphere Askrigg was one of the first places in the dales to be supplied with electricity. That was in 1908 when the local miller harnessed the power of Mill Gill Beck.

Askrigg is bountifully supplied with footpaths radiating out to other villages, river crossings and farmsteads. One of the most scenic takes little more than an hour and includes two impressive waterfalls,

Whitfield Gill Force and Mill Gill Force. The route is waymarked from Mill Lane alongside the church.

AYSGARTH
7 miles W of Leyburn on the A684

⌂ Church of St Andrew **♦** Aysgarth Falls

The village is famous for the spectacular **Aysgarth Falls** where the River Ure thunders through a rocky gorge and drops some 200 feet over three huge slabs of limestone, which divide this wonderful natural feature into the Upper, Middle and Lower Falls. They provided a perfect location for the battle between Robin Hood and Little John in Kevin Costner's film *Robin Hood, Prince of Thieves*.

Close to the falls stands the **Church of St Andrew**, home of the Jervaulx Treasures – a vicar's stall that is made from the beautifully carved bench ends salvaged from Jervaulx

THE PALMER FLATT HOTEL

Aysgarth, nr Leyburn, North Yorkshire DL8 3SR
Tel: 01969 663228
e-mail: stay@palmerflatthotel.co.uk
website: www.palmerflatthotel.co.uk

The Palmer Flatt Hotel in Aysgarth offers the best of both worlds. It's a wonderful place for getting away from it all but it's also within easy reach of the many sights of this picturesque part of North Yorkshire – the Aysgarth Falls, one of the region's top attractions, is just 300 yards away. This superb hotel, owned and run by the Blythe family, and set in beautifully maintained gardens, has nine comfortable en-suite bedrooms (single, twins, doubles and a family room), all commanding lovely views of the Dales. Each room has its own individual appeal and all have central heating, television and beverage tray; two feature luxurious four-poster beds. The bedrooms and the public rooms, including a delightful conservatory, wood-panelled lounge bar and guests' lounge, are made for comfort. In the à la carte restaurant guests choose from a menu of freshly prepared dishes featuring prime local produce

including outstanding lamb and beef; a good range of wines accompanies the fine food, and other drinks include Black Sheep.

THORNTON LODGE

Thornton Rust, Aysgarth, Wensleydale DL8 3AP
Tel: 01969 663375
e-mail: enquiries@thorntonlodgenorthyorkshire.co.uk website: www.thorntonlodgenorthyorkshire.co.uk

Set in the heart of the Yorkshire Dales National Park, **Thornton Lodge** is a luxurious country house that was built in 1909 as the summer home of a wealthy cotton baron. The Lodge is set within three acres of formal grounds, with magnificent mature trees flanking the boundaries, and with lawned gardens stretching into views of the surrounding hills. Home to the Kilvington family since 2004, The Lodge today provides a genteel retreat amid fine period features and antiques.

The family has undertaken a major restoration project and have striven to return the property to the elegance of the Edwardian era. The magnificent oak panelled staircase in the entrance hall has been complemented by a beautiful stair runner and brass rods, whilst the oak flooring is once again laid bare, as intended in 1909.

Thornton Lodge has 9 individually styled rooms. Tastefully decorated in keeping with the Edwardian era, the rooms have been furnished with period wardrobes and dressing tables, blending these antiques with modern sofas from which to watch TV in comfort. A hearty cooked breakfast—that all important start to the day, is served in the elegant surroundings of the beautiful oak panelled dining room. Packed lunches and evening meals are available on request.

Abbey. During the Middle Ages, Aysgarth enjoyed the distinction of being the largest parish in England though the parish has since been subdivided into more manageable areas. But it still has the largest churchyard in England.

The Dales National Park has a Visitor Information Centre located here, with a spacious car park and café located close to the Church and Falls.

THORALBY
8 miles W of Leyburn off the A684

Situated on the north slope of Bishopdale, opposite its sister village Newbiggin, Thoralby was once a centre for lead-mining, and, although lead is no longer extracted here the mine can still be found on maps of the area. A side dale of Wensleydale, Bishopdale was once covered by a glacial lake that has

given rise to its distinctive wide valley base. Here can be found many of Wensleydale's oldest houses.

NEWBIGGIN-IN-BISHOPDALE
9 miles SW of Leyburn on the B6160

As might be supposed, the name of this Bishopdale village means 'new buildings' and it is indeed a relatively new settlement having been first mentioned in 1230! There is only one road along Bishopdale, a beautiful unspoilt valley with hay meadows, stone barns, traditional Dales long houses and a fine old coaching inn.

WEST BURTON
7 miles SW of Leyburn off the B6160

🐾 Mill Force 🐾 Cat Pottery

One of the most picturesque villages in Wensleydale, West Burton developed around

COUNTRY HIDEAWAYS

Margarets Cottage, West Burton, nr Leyburn,
Wensleydale, North Yorkshire DL8 4JN
Tel: 01969 663559
e-mail: guide@countryhideaways.co.uk website: www.countryhideaways.co.uk

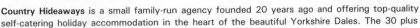

'Escape to the Yorkshire Dales.'

Country Hideaways is a small family-run agency founded 20 years ago and offering top-quality self-catering holiday accommodation in the heart of the beautiful Yorkshire Dales. The 30 plus properties, run by Nadine Bell and her staff for owners who

live in Wensleydale, Coverdale and Bishopdale, sleep from 2 to 10 and run from cosy little cottages to elegant houses and apartments in converted watermills. Each has its own individual appeal, but all are carefully selected for quality, comfort and location, earning the stamp of approval of Yorkshire Tourism and Quality in Tourism.

The properties are available for short-term, midweek, long weekend and longer stays and provide the perfect base for touring one of the country's most delightful and picturesque regions.

its large central green where a busy weekly market used to take place. A distinctive feature of the green is its market 'cross' - actually a modestly sized pyramid erected here in 1820. Just to the east of the village a path leads across a small packhorse bridge to **Mill Force**, perhaps the most photogenic of the Wensleydale waterfalls.

Cat lovers will enjoy the wide variety of felines on display at the **Cat Pottery**, overlooking the village green. This original collection of cats in ceramics and metallic or granite resin includes life-size stone cats for house or garden.

West Burton lies at the bottom of Walden, a narrow, steep-sided valley that provides a complete contrast to neighbouring

Bishopdale. Secluded and with a minimal scattering of houses and farms, Walden was one of the last places in Yorkshire where wild red deer were seen.

REDMIRE
4 miles W of Leyburn off the A684

Throughout its long history this village is thought to have occupied several sites in the vicinity. However, Redmire has been at its present location for many years and, on the village green, stands an old oak tree, supported by props, which is estimated to be at least 300 years old. When John Wesley preached in the village during his two visits in 1744 and 1774 it is believed that he stood in the shade of this very tree.

CASTLE BOLTON
5 miles W of Leyburn off the A684

🏛 Bolton Castle

Bolton Castle (see panel below) has dominated mid-Wensleydale for more than six centuries and is one of the major tourist attractions of the area. In 1379 the lord of the manor, Richard le Scrope, Lord Chancellor of England in the reign of Richard II, was granted permission to fortify his manor house and, using stone from a nearby quarry and oak beams from Lake District forests, the building was completed some 18 years later. Today, this luxurious fortified manor house is still occupied by a direct descendant of the 1st Lord Scrope and it remains an impressive sight with its four-square towers acting as a local landmark. The halls and galleries are remarkably well-preserved as are some of the private apartments used by Mary, Queen of Scots, when she was a reluctant visitor here between 1568-69. Indeed, modern day visitors can take tea in the grand room where she spent many melancholy days.

Vivid tableaux help bring history to life – the castle chaplain, the miller at work, the blacksmith at his forge – and there are regular living history events during the summer. If you climb to the battlements you will be rewarded with some breathtaking views along the dale.

The owner has restored two of the castle gardens as they would have been in medieval times – a Herb Garden and a Walled Garden.

To the north of the River Ure, and reached by, a footpath from Castle Bolton, is the isolated Apedale, named after its original owner, Api. Now a deserted valley with heather-clad moorland and wonderful views, Apedale still shows signs of former industry and activity when it was a busy lead-mining area.

WEST WITTON
4 miles W of Leyburn on the A684

Recorded in the *Domesday Book* as 'Witun', this village was then the largest in Wensleydale and exceptional in having stone rather than wooden houses. West Witton is well known

Bolton Castle

Castle Bolton, Leyburn, Yorkshire DL8 4ET
Tel: 01969 623981
website: www.boltoncastle.co.uk

Bolton Castle is a spectacular medieval fortress, situated in the heart of the beautiful Yorkshire Dales, on the boundary of the Yorkshire Dales National Park. It was built in 1399 by Richard le Scrope, 1st Lord Scrope of Bolton and Lord Chancellor of England. Bolton has never been sold, and remains in the private ownership of Lord Bolton, Richard le Scropes' descendant. Bolton is open daily throughout the year to visitors, and is also available for hire; it has a civil wedding license, and receptions grand or small can be held. Bolton is also available for use as a filming venue and has been used for scenes in *Ivanhoe*, *Elizabeth* (the film), *Heartbeat* and *'All Creatures Great and Small'*. There are also filming opportunities on other areas of the estate, whether it is moorland or forest you are looking for.

🏛 historic building 📷 museum and heritage 🏚 historic site 🜨 scenic attraction 🐾 flora and fauna

for its annual feast of St Bartholomew, patron saint of the parish church. The festival takes place on August 24th when an effigy of a man, known as the Bartle, is carried through the village. According to legend, Bartle was an 18th-century swine thief that was hunted over the surrounding fells before being captured and killed. The culmination of the three days of celebration is the burning of the effigy at Grassgill End.

CARLTON-IN-COVERDALE
4 miles SW of Leyburn on minor road off the A684

Carlton is Coverdale's principal village – with a population of less than 100. Nevertheless it has its own pub and is a wonderfully peaceful base for walking, hiking, fishing or touring the Dales National Park.

WENSLEY
1 mile W of Leyburn on the A684

🏠 Church of the Holy Trinity

🎨 White Rose Candles Factory

🚶 The Forbidden Corner

This peaceful little village beside the River Ure was once the main settlement in mid-Wensleydale and such was its importance it gave its name to the dale. However, in 1563,

the town was struck by plague and those who could, fled up the hill to Leyburn which was thought to be a healthier place.

The stately **Church of the Holy Trinity** is one of only two surviving medieval structures in Wensley (the other is the graceful bridge nearby) and it is thought to have been built on the site of an earlier Saxon church. Inside can be seen the unusual Bolton family pews which are actually a pair of opera boxes that were brought here from London during the 1700s when a theatre was being refurbished.

'Purveyors to the Military, Colonies, Overseas Missions, Churches and the Cinematograph Industries' runs the proud claim in the brochure for **White Rose Candles Workshop**. 'Patronised by the Nobility and Gentry' it continues; 'Cathedrals supplied include Ripon and Norwich'. One of Wensleydale's most popular attractions, the workshop is housed in a 19th-century water mill – the water wheel still exists and mills have been recorded on this site since 1203.

About a mile to the west of Wensley, on the Tupgill Park Estate, **The Forbidden Corner** is an unusual attraction. Strange and exotic buildings are scattered around the park, some of them underground, and visitors are given a list but must discover these fantastic

---

THE THREE HORSESHOES

Wensley, nr Leyburn, North Yorkshire DL8 4HJ
Tel: 01969 622327

The Three Horseshoes is located in the captivating village of Wensley, set beside the River Ure. This delightful old white-washed hostelry dates back to 1650 and is well-known locally for its excellent real ales - the pub was the Runner-up in CAMRA's Pub of the Year 2007 awards. Mine host, Nick Jones, takes great pride in the fact that the food served here is all home cooked from scratch using the best ingredients, locally sourced where possible. Other great attractions here are the regular live entertainment performances and the Curry and Italian nights.

---

constructions by themselves. 'In parts you might find your heart's delight,' says the brochure. 'In others you'll tremble with fear.' There's also a shop, refreshment room, and toilets, which are all accessible to the disabled, but some parts of the garden are only reached by way of steps. Admission is by pre-booked tickets only, which can be obtained at Leyburn Tourist Information Office.

Leyburn Market Square

Leyburn

🏛 Beech End Model Village 🏛 Wensleydale railway

🏞 🎵 The Shawl 🎻 Violin Making Workshop

🎵 The Teapottery 🎵 Longwool Sheepshop

The main market town and trading centre of mid-Wensleydale, Leyburn is an attractive town with a broad marketplace lined by handsome late-Georgian and Victorian stone buildings. Friday is market day when the little town is even busier than usual. There's an interesting mix of traditional family-run shops and surprisingly large supermarkets behind deceptively small frontages. Leyburn also boasts the only cinema, The Elite, to be found in the Dales.

The town has several interesting connections with famous people. Lord Nelson's surgeon, Peter Goldsmith, once lived in the Secret Garden House on Grove Square (and is buried in Wensley church, just a mile up the road). Flight Lieutenant Alan Broadley DSO, DFC, DFM, of Dam Busters fame, is named on the War Memorial in the main square, and just a few yards away is the birthplace of the 'Sweet Lass' of Richmond Hill. Many believe that the popular song refers to Richmond Hill in Surrey rather than Richmond, North Yorkshire. Not so. Frances

THE LITTLE CHOCOLATE SHOP

Leyburn Business Park, Leyburn, North Yorkshire DL8 5QA
Tel: 01969 625288   Fax: 01969 625027
e-mail: info@thelittlechocolateshop.co.uk
website: www.thelittlechocolateshop.co.uk

Clare Gardiner and her team are now making a splash at the Little Chocolate Shop in the heart of Wensleydale. Visitors to the factory are spoilt for choice - will they watch chocolates being made, watch a film, or choose from over 200 varieties of chocolates and confectionery, and seasonal specials? Shoppers can buy boxes and bags with ready-made selections or make up their own. You can even buy online for home delivery or for friends and family or join the online Chocolate Lovers Club. The factory hours are 9 to 5 Monday to Friday, and 10 to 4 on Saturday.

🏛 historic building 🏛 museum and heritage 🏛 historic site 🏞 scenic attraction 🍂 flora and fauna

I'Anson was born in her grandfather's house on Leyburn High Street and his initials, WIA, can still be seen above the door of what is now an interior decorator's shop. It was her husband-to-be, Leonard McNally, who composed the immortal song.

A fairly recent addition to Leyburn's attractions is **Beech End Model Village** in Commercial Square. Unique among model villages, this one is indoors. The scenery is finely detailed and there's plenty of hands-on fun to be had controlling the working models.

On the eastern edge of the town is Leyburn Station. Until five years ago you would have had a long wait here for a train – the last passenger train left some 50 years earlier. But an energetic group of railway enthusiasts have laboured for years to get the line re-opened and on July 4th 2003 their efforts were finally successful. The **Wensleydale Railway** now offers regular services to Bedale and Leeming Bar, a 12-mile route through pretty countryside. Normally, the train is driven by a vintage diesel locomotive but there are special steam train days. The Wensleydale Railway Company hopes to extend the service to the main line station at Northallerton and, even more ambitious, to extend westwards to meet up with the Settle to Carlisle railway.

The Shawl, to the west of the town, is a mile-long limestone scarp along which runs a footpath offering lovely panoramic views of the dale. A popular legend suggests that it gained its unusual name when Mary, Queen of Scots, dropped her shawl here during her unsuccessful attempt to escape from Bolton Castle. However, a more likely explanation is that Shawl is a corruption of the name given

to the ancient settlement here.

Leyburn Business Park is home to **The Violin Making Workshop.** Little has changed in the art of violin making over the centuries and the traditional tools and methods used by such master craftsmen as Stradivari are still employed today. Repairs and commissions are undertaken.

Close by, at **The Teapottery**, you can see other craftspeople at work – in this case creating a whole range of witty and unusual teapots, anything from a grand piano to a bathtub complete with yellow duck. The finished pots can be purchased in the showroom where there's also a tea room where your tea is served, naturally, in one of the astonishing teapots produced here.

Within the same business park are Tennant's of Yorkshire, the only major provincial auction house in England, which holds regular auctions throughout the year, and the Little Chocolate Shop (see panel on page 228) where visitors can watch hand-made chocolates being crafted and purchase the end product.

About two miles east of Leyburn, off the A684, the **Longwool Sheepshop** at Cross Lanes Farm in Garriston is a treat for anyone who appreciates good knitwear. Garments can be specially knitted to the customer's requirements. You can see the raw material grazing in the surrounding fields – rare Wensleydale longwool sheep. The Sheepshop also stocks an extensive range of hand knitting yarns and patterns for the enthusiast.

Around Leyburn

SPENNITHORNE
2 miles SE of Leyburn off the A684

This pleasant little village dates back many years. The present Church of St Michael and All Angels stands on the site of a Saxon church although the only remains of the ancient building to be seen are two ornamental stones set into the walls of the chancels and a Saxon monument in the vestry.

Two of Spennithorne's earlier residents are worth mentioning. John Hutchinson was born here in 1675 and went on to become steward to the 6th Duke of Somerset – and a rather controversial philosopher. He vehemently disagreed with Sir Isaac Newton's theory of gravity and was equally ardent in asserting that the earth was neither flat, nor a sphere, but a cube. Though there are no records mentioning that Hutchinson was ever considered as of unsound mind, another resident of Spennithorne, Richard Hatfield, was officially declared insane after he fired a gun at George III.

MIDDLEHAM
2 miles SE of Leyburn on the A6108

🏠 Castle

Middleham is an enchanting little town, which, despite having a population of fewer than 800, boasts its own Mayor, Corporation and quaint Town Hall. It is also the site of one of Yorkshire's most historic castles, several successful racing stables and not just one, but two, marketplaces. It is almost totally unspoilt, with a wealth of handsome Georgian houses and hostelries huddled together in perfect architectural harmony.

Rising high above the town are the magnificent ruins of **Middleham Castle** (English Heritage), a once-mighty fortress whose most glorious days came in the 15th century when most of northern England was ruled from here by the Neville family. The castle's most famous resident was the 'evil'

Middleham Castle

for the remains of **Coverham Abbey** (private). Built in the late 1200s, only some decorated arches remain, along with a Norman gateway. The nearby 17th-century manor house, Braithwaite Hall (National Trust), as well as other surrounding buildings, have clearly used the Abbey's stones in their construction – in some of the walls effigies from the old building can clearly be seen. The Hall can be visited by prior arrangement.

Richard III who was sent here as a lad of 13 to be trained in the 'arts of nobilitie'. Whatever crimes he committed later down in London, Richard was popular locally, ensuring the town's prosperity by granting it a fair and a twice-yearly market. The people of Middleham had good reason to mourn his death at the Battle of Bosworth in 1485.

Middleham is often referred to as the 'Newmarket of the North', a term you'll understand when you see the strings of thoroughbred racehorses clip-clopping through the town on their way to training runs on Low Moor. It was the monks of Jervaulx Abbey who founded this key industry. By the late 18th century races were being run across the moorland and the first stables established. Since then, the stables have produced a succession of classic race winners with one local trainer, Neville Crump, having three Grand National winners to his credit within the space of 12 years.

COVERHAM
4 miles S of Leyburn off the A6108

🏠 Hall

Lying beside the River Cover in little-visited Coverdale, this village is perhaps best known

Also in the village is the delightful walled Forbidden Garden, which includes a grotto with an underground labyrinth of chambers and passages. There is a shop and refreshment room; admission is by pre-booked tickets only. The garden is open daily from April until October and on Sundays until Christmas.

EAST WITTON
4 miles SE of Leyburn on the A6108

🏠 Jervaulx Abbey

An attractive village set beside the confluence of the rivers Cover and Ure, East Witton was almost entirely rebuilt after a great fire in 1796. The new buildings included the well-proportioned Church of St John although the old churchyard with its many interesting gravestones remains. Some two decades after that conflagration the village was struck by another calamity. In 1820, 20 miners perished in a coal mine accident at Witton Fell. They were all buried together in one grave in the new churchyard.

Just to the west of the village is **Jervaulx Abbey**, one of the great Cistercian sister houses to Fountains Abbey. The name Jervaulx is a French derivation of Yore (or

Ure), and Vale, just as Rievaulx is of Rye Vale. Before the Dissolution, the monks of Jervaulx Abbey owned huge tracts of Wensleydale and this now-solitary spot was once a busy trading and administrative centre. Despite its ruination, Jervaulx is among the most evocative of Yorkshire's many fine abbeys. The grounds have been transformed into beautiful gardens with the crumbling walls providing interesting backdrops for the sculptured trees and colourful plants and shrubs.

CONSTABLE BURTON
4 miles E of Leyburn on the A684

🌿 Hall Gardens

Surrounded by walled and wooded parkland, **Constable Burton Hall** is famous for its gardens (open March to October) and in particular its spacious, romantic terraces. The house itself is not open to the public, but its stately Georgian architecture provides a magnificent backdrop to the fine gardens, noble trees and colourful borders.

CRAKEHALL
10 miles E of Leyburn on the A684

🏛 Water Mill 🏛 Museum of Badges & Battledress

Crakehall has a huge village green with a small church and a huge former rectory overlooking it. Part of the green serves as the village's cricket pitch and is in regular use during the summer.

Sometime around AD 1090 the *Domesday Book* commissioners arrived in Crakehall and noted details of a mill on the beck that runs through this picturesque village. More than 900 years later there's still a mill on the very same spot. The present **Crakehall Water Mill** building dates from the 1600s; its mighty machinery from the 18th and 19th centuries. The Mill was still working until 2003 but at the time of writing it is up for sale and currently closed.

Housed in a former Methodist chapel dating back to 1840, the **Museum of Badges and Battledress** is a private collection displaying uniforms, equipment, cap badges, formation signs, trade badges and photographs of all branches of the Armed Forces. The exhibits include more than 60 mannequins dressed in various uniforms along with military equipment and ephemera dating from 1900 to the present day. The museum is open from Easter to September inclusive, but guided tours are available at any time by prior arrangement.

THE COUNTRYMANS INN

Hunton, nr Bedale, North Yorkshire DL8 1PY
Tel: 01679 450554
e-mail: tony@countrymaninn.co.uk
website: www.countrymaninn.co.uk

The Countrymans Inn is a classic country inn in mellow stone, standing on the main street of Hunton just north of the A684 Bedale to Leyburn road. In the cosy, inviting bar, with a cheerful log fire in the cooler months, four cask-conditioned ales are on tap, typically including Timothy Taylor Landlord, Black Sheep and a Dales brew. The Countrymans is much more than a cherished local. It also attracts lovers of good food with interesting fixed-price and à la carte menus, and a splendid meal is accompanied by well-chosen wines. Three en-suite bedrooms provide a comfortable base for exploring Wensleydale.

🏛 historic building 🏛 museum and heritage 🏛 historic site 🌿 scenic attraction 🌿 flora and fauna

BEDALE

12 miles E of Leyburn on the A684

🏛 Church of St Gregory 🏛 Bedale Hall

🐑 Big Sheep & Little Cow Farm

This pleasant little market town with its many fine Georgian buildings and old coaching inns, developed around the point where the Saxon track from Ripon joined the route from Northallerton to Wensleydale. Traders met here and in 1251 Henry III granted a charter for a weekly market every Tuesday that still flourishes today. The market cross still stands at the top of Emgate, a narrow street leading from the river to the marketplace. As commercial activity increased, water power was harnessed from the Bedale Beck for the processing of wool. Skinners and tanners worked down by the ford and the town was a lively hub of cottage industry.

The curving main street leads to the beautiful parish **Church of St Gregory** at the northern end. Recorded in the *Domesday Book* and incorporating architectural styles from the 12th to the 14th centuries, the building has a fine fortified tower and a striking medieval wall-painting of a left-handed St George. Just inside the churchyard is an old building dating from the mid-1600s, which served as a school in the 18th century.

Across the road from the church is **Bedale Hall**, a Palladian-style mansion with a superb ballroom. The Hall houses the library and local museum. The north front of the building is a particularly fine example of the Georgian architecture that gives Bedale its special character. Another building of interest is the 18th-century Leech House beside the beck, so called because it was once used by the local chemist to store his leeches.

A popular family attraction located just west of the town is **The Big Sheep and Little Cow Farm**. There are guided tours that include bottle-feeding the lambs, bathing George the pig, holding poultry and going into the fields to meet a menagerie of other animals. You don't have to take the tour – you can relax next to the old mill and sample the delicious Oakwoods Speciality Ice Cream, which is produced on the farm from the milk of ewes grazed on the old water meadows next to the watermill. Pony rides are available, there's an all-weather children's play area and a picnic area.

THE GOLDEN TORTOISE (BEDALE)

14 Sussex Street, Bedale, North Yorkshire DL8 2DS
Tel: 01677 423233

Established in Bedale in 2005, the **Golden Tortoise** is an Aladdin's Cave of giftware, arts and crafts, a great place to browse and a source of gifts, ornaments and novelties for all occasions and all ages. Famous names in stock include Anchor cottons and sewing materials, Airfix kits, Windsor & Newton artists' materials, limited edition animals from Gund, Lagoon wooden toys and puzzles, Nadal ceramic dolls, and soft toys and gifts from Russberry. Shop hours are 9.30 to 5 Tuesday to Saturday. There's another Golden Tortoise in Ripon (see page 242).

🎬 stories and anecdotes 🦢 famous people 🎨 art and craft 🎭 entertainment and sport 🚶 walks

SNAPE
13 miles SE of Leyburn off the B6268

🏛 Castle ⟆ Thorp Perrow Arboretum

⟆ Falcons of Thorp Perrow

The Falcons of Thorp Perrow, Snape

This quiet and unspoilt village, where the
original timber-framed cottages stand
side-by-side with their more modern
neighbours, is still dominated by its castle
as it has been for centuries. Reached via
an avenue of lime trees, **Snape Castle**
has a famous, if somewhat complicated,
royal connection as it was the home of
Lord Latimer of Snape (a member of the
Neville family), the first husband of Catherine
Parr, Henry VIII's last wife. The Nevilles
owned the castle for over 700 years and its
beautiful chapel, still used by the villagers, saw
the marriages of many Latimers and Nevilles.

Set in over 1,000 acres of parkland, **Thorp
Perrow Arboretum** is unique to Britain, if
not Europe, in that it was the creation of one
man, Col. Sir Leonard Ropner (1895-1977). Sir
Leonard travelled all over the world collecting
rare and unusual species for Thorp Perrow
and today the hundreds of trees he
enthusiastically collected are in their prime.
The arboretum was initially Sir Leonard's
private hobby but after his death his son, Sir
John Ropner, decided to open the 85-acre
garden to the public and the arboretum is now
one of the area's prime attractions. A treasure
trove of specimen trees, woodland walks,
nature trail, tree trails, a large lake, picnic area
and children's play area, the arboretum also
embraces the Milbank Pinetum, planted by
Lady Augusta Milbank in the mid-19th
century, and the medieval Spring Wood dating
back to the 16th century. Thorp Perrow
provides interest all year round, but perhaps
the most popular time is the spring when you

can witness one of the finest and most
extensive plantings of daffodils in the north
of England, among them some old and
unusual varieties. In addition to the fascinating
collection of trees, visitors will also find an
information centre, a tea room and a plant
sales area. An additional attraction at Thorp
Perrow, opened in the spring of 2000, is **The
Falcons of Thorp Perrow**, a bird-of-prey,
captive-breeding and conservation centre,
which has been created within a large,
formerly derelict walled garden. There are
more than 75 birds from all continents of the
world and regular flying demonstrations three
times a day, weather permitting.

WELL
*12 miles SE of Leyburn off the B6268
or B6267*

This pretty village takes its name from St
Michael's Well, which was being venerated long
before the Romans came here and built a
spacious villa near the well. Part of the
tessellated pavement of that villa is now on
display in the parish church, which is itself a
venerable building with foundations that date
back to Norman times. The church's greatest
treasure is a font cover dating from 1325, one

of the oldest in the country. It was a gift to the church from Ralph Neville, Lord of Middleham, who also founded the line of almshouses near the church, which were rebuilt by his descendants in 1758.

MASHAM
10 miles SE of Leyburn on the A6108

🏛 Sheep Fair   🎨 Arts Festival

🏛 Theakston's and Black Sheep Breweries

Set beside the River Ure, Masham (pronounced *Mazz-mm*) is a very picturesque place with a huge marketplace at its heart. The ancient Church of St Mary stands in one corner, a school founded in 1760 in another, while at the centre is the market cross surrounded by trees and flowers. The size of the marketplace reflects Masham's historical importance as a market town and its position, between the sheep-covered hills and the corn growing lowlands, certainly helped to support its flourishing trade. The sheep fairs held in the town in the 18th and 19th centuries were among the largest in the country and in September the **Masham Sheep Fair** revives those heady days, giving visitors the chance of seeing many rare breeds of sheep and goats as well as witnessing events such as dog agility and sheep racing.

The town is famed for its beer, boasting two celebrated breweries – Theakston's and Black Sheep. **Theakston's Brewery**, noted for its Old Peculier brew, was founded in 1827 by two brothers, Thomas and Robert. Adjoining

---

JOVENA CONFECTIONERY & FINE FOODS

7 Market Place, Masham, North Yorkshire HG4 4DZ
Tel: 01765 689021
e-mail: jovena@btconnect.com   website: www.jovena.com

Food and Confectionery lovers come from near and far to visit Joneva Confectionery & Fine Foods. John and Sandra Maughan have stocked their shop with over 4,000 top-quality items showcasing the best produce that Yorkshire has to offer: 16 flavours of Butter Fudge handmade on the premises; local cheese such as King Richard III Wensleydale and Mrs Bells Buffalo cheeses; Baibridge Tea Loafs and Celebration Fruit Cakes; Old-fashioned Boiled Sweets that you thought had stopped been made, and the finest selection of Handmade British and Continental Chocolates; locally made Rosebud Preserves; and the creamiest ice cream you will ever taste from Ryburns of Helmsley.

THROUGH THE LOOKING GLASS

1 Market Place, Masham, North Yorkshire HG4 4DZ
Tel: 01765 689223

Step **Through the Looking Glass** and into a wonderland for fashion-conscious ladies. On two floors of a classic stone building in the heart of Masham, Linda Burrows stocks a wide and ever-changing range of clothes, shoes, hats, belts, bags and jewellery in styles that combine classic and contemporary elements. Among the featured brands are Emreco, Oscar B, Olsen, Habella, Frank Lyman and Poppy (clothes); Oriano, Gionni and Dice (handbags) and Squadra Blu and Capiz (jewellery).

🎥 stories and anecdotes   🐉 famous people   🎨 art and craft   🎭 entertainment and sport   🚶 walks

Masham

Distance: *4.5 miles (7.2 kilometres)*
Typical time: *120 mins*
Height gain: *50 metres*
Map: *Explorer 302*
Walk: *www.walkingworld.com ID:2887*
Contributor: *Sam Roebuck*

DESCRIPTION:

The little market town of Masham (pronounced 'Mazz-mm') nestles in rolling countryside in Uredale, just outside the Yorkshire Dales, north of Ripon. Perhaps most famous for its connection with the Theakston brewing family, (being home to both the Theakston's and the Black Sheep breweries) it is also an excellent base for some splendid walking.

This walk starts in Masham's impressive market square and initially follows the route of the Ripon Rowel Walk (a local long-distance walk) along the banks of the River Ure. At the confluence of the Rivers Ure and Burn, we leave the Ure in favour of its tributary, which we follow for a few kilometres before striking away through pastureland. Soon, we pick up the Ripon Rowel once again and use this to return to Masham.

Dog-walkers please note that there are a number of dog-unfriendly stiles en route and a short, rocky scramble near water. There are also sheep aplenty, so please keep your pooch on a lead.

FEATURES:

River, Pub, Toilets, Church, Wildlife, Great Views, Café, Gift Shop, Food Shop, Mostly Flat, Public Transport, Restaurant, Tea Shop, Woodland, Ancient Monument

WALK DIRECTIONS:

1 | As you look towards the church from the Market Square, take the road in the left corner, which passes the school (on your left). Follow this slightly downhill. The road becomes a track, enters a grassy area and forks.

2 | Take the left-hand fork. Follow the track for 100m to a left-hand bend by a treatment plant. Continue ahead through a gate, to pass to the right of the treatment plant. Follow this path to the River Ure and continue along the riverbank for around 1.5km, to a wood at a right-hand bend in the path.

3 | Just around the bend, turn left into the woods. Follow the path as it turns right to follow the River Burn. In half a kilometre, the path emerges onto a road.

4 | Cross the road and continue ahead. The path can be vague here, but if you lose it, keep to the riverbank. The river bends right to meet a steep bank. Follow the path between the river and the bank until it crosses a stile into a field. Follow the right-hand side of the field to emerge onto a

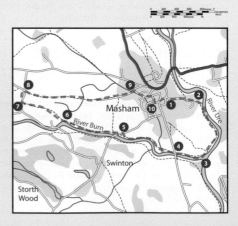

road. *In the unlikely event that this path is flooded, backtrack to the road and try a footpath on the opposite bank of the river.*

5 | Turn left onto the road and follow it for 50m to a golf club on the right. Turn into the golf club and follow the drive to the right of the clubhouse. Look for a small wooden structure with a green 'No Dogs' sign on it. Leave the drive to the right of the wooden structure to reach the riverbank. Turn right towards a footbridge. Cross the footbridge and turn right along the riverbank. *You are now on the golf course, so please be aware of golfers.* Keep close to the riverbank to pass a second footbridge and enter woodland. Continue as far as a third footbridge. Cross the footbridge, turn left and rise to a gate. Once through the gate, follow the track uphill as far as a farmyard.

6 | Pass to the right of the barn and continue through the farmyard. Once through, look for a small stile (ahead) in a wire fence. Cross the stile and continue ahead towards the right-hand side of a small copse at the far end of the field. Pass to the right of the copse and take the left-hand of a pair of staggered field-gates. Continue ahead on the right-hand side of the field to emerge onto a road.

7 | Turn right and follow the road for 150m to a left bend.

8 | Just onto a track (ahead), take a footpath on the right. This runs to the right of a hedge and to the bottom of the field. It then turns right to reach a stile. Cross the stile and follow this footpath (signed with the 'Ripon Rowel' symbol) over a number of fields. In 1.5km, emerge onto a factory forecourt. Keep ahead along the factory drive. This crosses a small bridge and joins a residential road.

9 | Turn right along the road and follow it to the brewery.

10 | Just after the brewery, turn left into an alley. Follow this until it emerges at the end of a short road. Turn right. Almost immediately, at the end of the road, turn left onto a main road that quickly leads you back to the square.

the brewery today is a modern visitor centre, which illustrates the process of brewing and the art of cooperage. Those taking the tour (which must be pre-booked) should be aware that there are two flights of steep steps along the route and the tour is not suitable for children under 10. Interestingly, the name of the famous brew derives from the fact that Masham in medieval times had its own Peculier Court (meaning special rather than odd) – an ecclesiastical body with wide-ranging powers.

The **Black Sheep Brewery** (see panel on page 239) is also well worth a visit. It is owned by another Theakston, Paul, who is the 6th generation of this famous brewing family. The vessels, plants and methods employed here are from a bygone era and currently produce five different ales, including a Monty Python ale thatwas specially commissioned to celebrate the 30th anniversary of the cult comedy series. The brewery also offers a guided tour and visitors get the chance to sample the traditionally made ales. In addition to the working brewery, the old Maltings building is home to a 'sheepy' shop and a popular bistro. Masham hosts an **Arts Festival** in October every two years (next one in 2009), offering a varied and exciting programme of talks, exhibitions, concerts, workshops, themed days, story telling and music.

ILTON

3 miles SW of Masham off the A6108

🏠 Druid's Temple

This village is close to one of the area's most interesting and unusual features – the **Druid's Temple**. Though the name suggests that this was an ancient meeting place for pagan worshippers, the charming folly was built in the 1820s by William Danby of the nearby

THE GALLERY

24 Market Square, Masham,
North Yorkshire HG4 4EB
Tel: 01765 689554 Fax: 01765 658599
website: www.mashamgallery.co.uk

Situated in the rolling hills of picturesque lower Wensleydale, Masham draws most of its visitors to the two well-known breweries, Theakston's and Black Sheep as well as its packed events calendar, including the annual sheep fair.

The Gallery is situated in a Georgian house overlooking the huge Market Place. It is a welcoming lively and colourful space, run by artist Josie Beszant. Her passion in finding unusual and exceptional art and craft shows itself in the range of work available here. Functional or fun ceramics, jewellery, glass and sculpture are displayed in 2 light rooms amongst contemporary paintings and prints. If you are looking to commission an artist to make or paint something, or if you want to buy or browse beautiful or unusual work, this has to be one of the best places to come.

The Gallery has a policy of selling only British or fairly traded products, and you will find Josie knows most of her 80 plus suppliers as many of them come from the local area. As well as the two gallery rooms there is also a children's room selling wooden toys and room accessories. Not surprisingly it has its own quirky style with a grass look floor and murals on the walls and ceiling. A play table, art materials and a children's gallery are also provided for younger visitors.

Varied exhibitions are held here three to four times a year either themed or featuring a particular artist, details are available on the website. Prices for artwork range from just £2 for an original piece of art from the unique Hayvend vending machine, to around £2000. Greetings cards and a gift-wrapping service are available. The Gallery has also been chosen to participate in the Arts Council 'own art' scheme, enabling customers to purchase work interest free over 10 months.

Every other year sees the Masham Arts Festival (next one 2009) a lively and eclectic mix of events and exhibitions, which Josie, along with the artistic community in Masham, helps to organise.

 historic building   museum and heritage   historic site   scenic attraction   flora and fauna

BLACK SHEEP BREWERY BISTRO AND VISITORS CENTRE

Wellgarth, Masham, Ripon, North Yorkshire, HG4 4EN
Tel: 01765 689227
website: www.blacksheepbrewery.co.uk

Established in the early 1990s by Paul Theakston, 6th generation of Masham's famous brewing family, the brewery has grown from strength to strength, and in early 2007 it was proud to be awarded Brewery of the Year by the Good Pub Guide for the second year running. In addition, Black Sheep Best Bitter was chosen as the North East's favourite cask ale in the recent Best of British Beer Awards hosted by Cask Marque and the *Daily Telegraph*.

The Black Sheep Brewery Visitor Centre is a major year-round attraction with regular 'shepherded' tours of the brewery involving a fascinating trip around the traditional brew house and fermenting room. Visitors experience the traditional brewing process and sample the award-winning ales.

The spacious split-level Bistro and Baa...r, with beautiful views over the river Ure, provides a variety of culinary delights throughout the day and into the evening. Also, if you're looking for that special gift, the Black Sheep Shop is full of 'ewe-nique' gifts for all occasions, including our full range of Black Sheep beers.

The Black Sheep Brewery Visitor Centre is great venue for corporate entertaining, product launches, parties and weddings, as well as hosting many special events throughout the year. Groups and parties are very welcome and a car and coach park is available on-site.

Swinton Estate. Resembling a miniature Stonehenge, the folly was inspired by a similar temple Danby saw on his travels in Europe and his building project was intended to provide work for local unemployed people. It is considered one of the best Druidic follies in the country. From Ilton village it can be reached by following part of the long-distance footpath known as the Ripon Rowel Walk.

WEST TANFIELD
16 miles SE of Leyburn on the A6108

Marmion Tower Thornborough Circles

This attractive village on the banks of the River Ure is home to a remarkable Tudor gatehouse known as the **Marmion Tower**. Overlooking the river and with a beautiful oriel window, the tower is open to the public.

For many years, West Tanfield was associated with the powerful Marmion family and the 14th-century Church of St Nicholas contains many effigies belonging to it.

Though the purpose of the **Thornborough Circles**, which lie just outside the village, remains a mystery, these late Neolithic or early Bronze Age oval earthworks are very impressive, especially from the air.

GREWELTHORPE
16 miles SE of Leyburn off the A6108

Hackfall Woods

It was long thought that the Romans had a camp to the north of this leafy village and the discovery in the early 1900s of the complete skeleton of a Roman soldier confirmed the

Marmion Tower, West Tanfield

with witchcraft. Apparently, the northeastern corner of the churchyard was favoured by practitioners of the black arts for conducting their strange rituals and charms. Black magic aside, the church has been pealing its bells for over 400 years and records show that in 1591 one of the bells was recast – the process taking place inside the church building.

This traditional Yorkshire village is also one of the few places in the country that can boast its own Sword Dance. Certainly a pagan ritual, thought to date back to prehistoric times, the performance of the dance is supposed to make the grass grow tall and to wake the earth from her winter's sleep.

Many of the farms around the village are dairy farms, and at Kirby Malzeard Dairy they still produce the traditionally-made Coverdale cheese. Very much a local speciality, it is one of the few remaining Dales' cheeses still made though, at one time, each dale had its own particular variety.

story. The remains were reburied in the churchyard at Kirkby Malzeard but the soldier's sandals are on view in the York Museum.

North of the village are the beautiful **Hackfall Woods** through which the River Ure flows. During the 19th century the Victorians developed the woodland, creating waterfalls and transforming the 18th-century follies that had been built here into splendid vantage points. Following a period of neglect, which began with the sale of the woodland in the 1930s, the Hackfall Woods are now in the care of the Woodland Trust and the area is being gradually restored to its 19th century condition.

KIRKBY MALZEARD
16 miles SE of Leyburn off the A6108

🏛 Church of St Andrew

Dating back to the 11th century, the **Church of St Andrew** is noted for its associations

NORTH STAINLEY
13 miles SE of Leyburn on the A6108

🐾 Lightwater Valley Theme Park

Just over 100 years ago, in 1895, excavations in a field just outside the village revealed the site of a Roman villa called Castle Dykes, though all that can be seen now are the grassed outlines of the foundations and the moat. However, the discovery does prove that there has been a settlement here for many centuries. The monks of Fountains Abbey also knew North Stainley. Slenningford Grange is thought to have been one of their many properties and a fishpond, dating from medieval times, is still in existence.

Just to the south of the village lies the **Lightwater Valley Theme Park** set in 175 acres of scenic grounds. The Park boasts

🏛 historic building 🏛 museum and heritage 🏛 historic site 🔱 scenic attraction 🌿 flora and fauna

Ultimate – the biggest roller-coaster in the world (authenticated by the *Guinness Book of Records*) - the Rat Ride, Falls of Terror, and the Viper to name just a few, and there are plenty of more appropriate activities for younger children. Also within the grounds is Lightwater Village, which offers a wide variety of retail and factory shops, a garden centre, restaurant and coffee shop.

WATH
14 miles SE of Leyburn off the A1

🏚 Norton Conyers

The stately home of **Norton Conyers** has been owned by the Graham family since 1624 though, undoubtedly, the house's main claim to fame is the visit made by Charlotte Brontë. During her stay here the novelist heard the story of Mad Mary, supposedly a Lady Graham. Apparently, Lady Graham had been locked up in an attic room, now tantalisingly inaccessible to the public. Charlotte eventually based the character of Mrs Rochester in her novel *Jane Eyre* on this unfortunate woman. Visitors to the hall will also see the famous painting of Sir Bellingham Graham on his bay horse, as Master of the Quorn hunt. It is rumoured that ownership of the painting was once decided on the throwing of a pair of dice. Other family pictures, furniture and costumes are on display and there's a lovely 18th-century walled garden within the grounds.

Ripon Cathedral

Ripon

🏚 Cathedral 🏚 Wakeman's House

🏚 Town Hall 🏚 Courthouse

🏚 🌹 Newby Hall & Gardens

🏛 Prison & Police Museum

🏛 Workhouse 🦋 🚶 Spa Gardens

This attractive cathedral city, on the banks of the Rivers Ure, Skell and Laver, dates from the 7th century when Alfrich, King of Northumbria granted an area of land, surrounding a new monastery to the Church. Later that century, in 672, St Wilfrid built a church on the high ground between the three rivers but, at the time of the demise of the Northern Kingdom in the mid-10th century, the monastery and church were destroyed, though the Saxon crypt survives to this day. By the time of the Norman Conquest, Ripon was a prosperous agricultural settlement

NORTH YORKSHIRE: COAST, MOORS AND DALES

THE GOLDEN TORTOISE (RIPON)

11a Westgate, Ripon, North Yorkshire HG4 2AT
Tel: 01765 608914

The **Golden Tortoise** has been here in Ripon for nearly 30 years, and has been in the current ownership since 2002. It's an Aladdin's Cave of giftware, arts and crafts, a great place to browse and a source of gifts, ornaments and novelties for all occasions and all ages. Famous names in stock include Anchor cottons and sewing materials, Airfix kits, Windsor & Newton artists' materials, limited edition animals from Gund, Lagoon wooden toys and puzzles, Nadal ceramic dolls, and soft toys and gifts from Russberry. Shop hours are 8.30 to 4.30 Monday to Saturday. There's another Golden Tortoise in Bedale (see page 233).

under ecclesiastical rule and it was at this time that a second St Wilfrid's Church was erected on the site of the Saxon building. On Christmas Day 1132, monks from York worshipped here while they were making a journey to found Fountains Abbey and, traditionally, the people of Ripon follow this ancient route on Boxing Day. Another centuries-old tradition enjoyed a recent revival, has, in 2008, become a victim or risk assessment and health and safety regulations. The pancake race, held on Shrove Tuesday, attracted local schools and businesses to race while tossing pancakes.

A striking survival of the Saxon cathedral is the 1,300-year-old crypt. At its northeast corner is a narrow passage known as The Needle. According to the 17th-century antiquary Thomas Fuller, women whose chastity was suspect were made to pass through it. If they were unable to do so, their reputations were irretrievably tarnished. 'They pricked their credit,' Fuller wrote, 'who could not thread the Needle.'

The crypt is all that remains of St Wilfrid's church, but the magnificent **Cathedral of St Peter and St Wilfrid**, which now stands on the site, is certainly well worth visiting. Begun in the mid-12th century by Archbishop Roger of York, it was originally

designed as a simple cruciform church; the west front was added in the mid-13th century and the east choir in 1286. Rebuilding work was begun in the 16th-century but the disruption of the Dissolution of the Monasteries caused the work to be abandoned and it was only the intervention of James I in the early 1600s that saved the building from ruin. Then established as a collegiate church, the diocese of Ripon was formed in 1836 and the church made a cathedral. Often referred to as the Cathedral of the Dales, the building, though one of the tallest cathedrals in England, is also the smallest. Discovered in 1976 close to the cathedral, the Ripon Jewel is the only surviving trace of the magnificence that was characteristic of the cathedral's early history. A small gold roundel inlaid with gemstones, the jewel's design suggests that it was made to embellish a relic casket or cross ordered by St Wilfrid.

Throughout the Middle Ages, the town prospered: its market charter had been granted by King Alfred in the 9th century and, at one time, Ripon produced more woollen cloth than Halifax and Leeds. The collapse of the woollen industry saw a rise in spur manufacture in the 16th century and their fame was such that

Ripon spurs were referred to in the old proverb: 'As true steel as a Ripon rowel'. As well as having three rivers, Ripon also had a canal built between 1767 and 1773 to improve the navigation of the River Ure. John Smeaton, builder of the Eddystone Lighthouse, was the designer. However, by 1820 the company running the canal had fallen into debt and it was little used after that time.

Fortunately, for today's visitor, the Industrial Revolution, and all its associated implications, by-passed Ripon and it was not until the early 20th century that the town flourished, though briefly, as a spa. However, many ancient customs and festivals have survived down the centuries. Perhaps the most famous is the sounding of the 'Wakeman's Horn' each night at 9pm in the marketplace. Dating back to the 9th century, the Wakeman was originally appointed to patrol the town after the nightly curfew had been blown and, in many ways, this was the first form of security patrol. The Wakeman was selected each year from the town's 12 aldermen and those choosing not to take office were fined heavily. Today, this old custom is revived in the Mayor-making Ceremony when the elected mayor shows great reluctance to take office and hides from his colleagues.

As might be expected, any walk around this ancient town reveals, in its buildings, its interesting and varied past. The heart of the town is the Market Place and here stands a tall obelisk, which was erected in 1702 to replace the market cross. Restored in 1781, at its summit are a horn and a rowel spur, symbolizing Ripon's crafts and customs. Situated at the edge of the square are the picturesque, half-timbered 14th-century **Wakeman's House** and the attractive Georgian **Town Hall**.

The Spa Baths building, opened in 1905 by the Princess of Battenberg, is a reminder of Ripon's attempt to become a fashionable spa resort. With no spring of its own, the town had to pipe in sulphur mineral water from Aldfield near Fountains Abbey. However, the scheme failed, though the building, which now houses the city's swimming pool, is a fine example of art nouveau architecture, and the Ripon Spa Gardens with its 18-hole putting course, flat green bowling, nine hole crazy golf, tennis courts, bandstand and café, is still a pleasant place for a stroll.

Near to the cathedral is Ripon's old **Courthouse** that was built in 1830 on the site of an earlier 17th-century Common Hall, used for the Quarter Sessions and the Court Military. Adjacent to this fine Georgian courthouse is a Tudor building that was part of the Archbishop of York's summer palace.

Also not far from the cathedral is the House of Correction, built in 1686, which served as the local prison between 1816 and 1878 and then became the police station until the late 1950s. This austere building is now home to the **Prison and Police Museum**, established in 1984, which depicts the history of the police force as well as giving visitors a real insight into the life of a prisoner in Victorian times. Almost as unfortunate as those prisoners were the inmates of **Ripon Workhouse**, the city's newest museum. The restored vagrants' wards of 1877 provide a chilling insight into the treatment of paupers in Yorkshire workhouses and the displays include a 'Victorian Hard Times Gallery'.

Horse racing at Ripon dates back to 1713, and the present course opened in 1900. Meetings are held between April and August and the course is widely regarded as one of the most beautiful in the country.

To the southeast of the city is one of the area's finest stately homes, **Newby Hall** (see advertisement on page 205). Built in the 18th century and designed by Robert Adam, much of the house is open to the public including the splendid Billiard Room with its fine portrait of Frederick Grantham Vyner. An ancestor of the family who have lived here from the mid-19th century, Frederick was murdered by Greek bandits after being kidnapped. The house is perhaps most famous for its superb tapestries and there is also a fine collection of Chippendale furniture.

It is, though, **Newby Hall Gardens** that draw most people to the house. Extensive and well designed, it was the present owner's father who transformed a nine hole golf course into the 25 acres of award-winning gardens that offer something for everyone whatever the time of year. Also found here is a wonderful Woodland Discovery Walk, a miniature railway, plenty of other attractions specially designed for children, a plant stall, shop and restaurant.

Around Ripon

STUDLEY ROGER
1 mile SW of Ripon off the B6265

🌿 Gardens 🏛 Fountains Abbey 🏛 Fountains Hall

The magnificent **Studley Royal Gardens** (see panel opposite) were created in the early 18th century before they were merged with nearby Fountains Abbey in 1768. Started by John Aislabie, Chancellor of the Exchequer and

---

ST GEORGES COURT B&B

Old Home Farm, Grantley, nr Ripon,
North Yorkshire HG4 3PJ
Tel: 01765 620618
e-mail: stgeorgescourt@bronco.co.uk
website: www.stgeorgescourt.co.uk

New owners are running **St Georges Court**, an oasis of peace and tranquillity on the edge of Wensleydale and close to the World Heritage site of Fountains Abbey. Guests can look forward to a warm, genuine welcome and a relaxed, comfortable stay in picturesque surroundings. Farm buildings round a courtyard have been sympathetically converted to provide five ground-floor guest bedrooms, all with spacious bathrooms with bath and fixed shower, king-size beds, smart pine furniture, television, beverage tray and hairdryer. One room is ideal for family use. Each room has its own front door and all enjoy lovely country views. The courtyard is surrounded by 20 acres of farmland that include a half-acre lake. It's an ideal spot for nature-lovers and bird-watchers, with abundant wildlife as well as the resident rare-breed pigs and sheep. Fresh local produce is used for the excellent breakfast served in the conservatory dining room.

🏛 historic building 🏛 museum and heritage 🏛 historic site ⚜ scenic attraction 🌿 flora and fauna

FOUNTAINS ABBEY & STUDLEY ROYAL

Nr Ripon, North Yorkshire HG4 3DY
Tel: 01765 608888
e-mail: fountainsenquiries@nationaltrust.org.uk   website: www.fountainsabbey.org.uk

Travel in time and visit nine centuries of history, landscape and architecture at the National Trust's Fountains Abbey and Studley Royal Water Garden. Awarded World Heritage Site status in 1986, the 'Wonder of the North' attracts visitors worldwide.

Founded in 1132 the Abbey ruins are today the most complete monastic ruins in Britain, displaying breathtaking medieval architecture. Just 13 monks founded the settlement at Fountains and by 1135 the small settlement was admitted into the rigorous Cistercian Order, with that came the introduction of the system of lay brothers. The lay brothers served as masons, tanners, shoemakers and smiths, but their chief role was to look after the Abbey's vast flocks of sheep, which lived on the huge estate. Henry VIII's Dissolution of the Monasteries in 1539 marked the end of the monks' tenure. Today, the Abbey oozes mystery, drawing you in to discover its secrets, held close for centuries.

Studley Royal Water Garden is a Georgian masterpiece of an ornamental green garden. Amazingly, the garden you see today, is little changed from the one that would have impressed Aislabie's visitors over 200 years ago. Neo-classical temples are elegantly reflected in formal geometric ponds and canals. Gentle cascades delight the ear and eye, while ancient trees and hedges fall away from secluded paths to reveal carefully arranged sweeping vistas.

John Aislabie inherited the estate in 1693 when he was Chancellor of the Exchequer. Expelled from public life in 1720 for his part in the South Sea Bubble scandal John turned his attention to transforming his wooded estate into one of England's most spectacular Georgian water gardens. No other site in Europe contains such a rich variety of historic monuments in such a beautiful landscape.

Fountains Abbey offers the visitor an unparalleled opportunity to appreciate the range of England's heritage.

🎭 stories and anecdotes 🐦 famous people 🎨 art and craft 🎟 entertainment and sport 🚶 walks

founder of the South Sea Company that spectacularly went bust in 1720, the landscaping took some 14 years. It then took a further 10 years to complete the construction of the buildings and follies found within the gardens. With a network of paths and the River Skell flowing through the grounds, it is well worth exploring these superb gardens.

A National Trust property, like the adjoining gardens, **Fountains Abbey** (see panel on page 245) is the pride of all the ecclesiastical ruins in Yorkshire and the only World Heritage Site in Yorkshire.

It is commonly thought that one of the Abbey's friars, renowned for his strength and skill as an archer, challenged Robin Hood to a sword fight. Forced to concede, the friar joined the Merry Men of Sherwood and became known as Friar Tuck. The Dissolution hit the abbey as it did all the powerful religious houses. The abbot was hanged, the monks scattered, and its treasures taken off or destroyed. The stonework, however, was left largely intact, possibly due to its remote location. In 1579, Sir Stephen Proctor pulled down some outbuildings in order to construct **Fountains Hall**, a magnificent Elizabethan mansion that still stands in the Abbey's grounds and part of which is open to the public.

Nidderdale

This typical Yorkshire dale with its dry stone walls, green fields, and pretty stone villages was christened 'Little Switzerland' by the Victorians. Indeed, the upper reaches of the valley of the River Nidd are steep and wooded with the river running through gorges, and with a covering of snow in winter, it is easy to see the resemblance. It is this natural beauty that draws many people to

the dale and there are also several remarkable features that are well worth exploring.

The history of the dale is similar to that of its neighbours. The Romans and Norsemen both settled here and there are also reminders that the dale was populated in prehistoric times. It was the all powerful Cistercian monks of Fountains and Byland Abbeys who began the business-like cultivation of the countryside to provide grazing for cattle and sheep and the space to grow food. This great farming tradition has survived and, though prosperity came and went with the lead-mining, a few of the textile mills established in the golden age of the Industrial Revolution can still be found here.

Best explored from Pateley Bridge, keen walkers will delight in the wide variety of landscape that can be covered within a reasonable amount of time. High up on the moorland, famed for its brilliant colour in late summer, there are several reservoirs, built to provide water for the growing population and industry in Bradford. This area is a must for bird watchers as there are excellent opportunities for spotting a number of species of duck as well as brent geese and whooper swans. Further down the valley, in the rich woodland, wildlife again abounds and the well-signposted footpaths help visitors reach the most spectacular sights.

The dry stone walls that are such a feature of the countryside in the Yorkshire Dales originated from the new demand for the scientific management of the land by enclosure following the Agricultural Revolution in the 18th century. The arrow-straight dividing walls sprang up high on the hillsides and the enclosures are still easily recognised by their geometric shapes. The walls are constructed by packing small stones on top of a firm foundation and tying these together with 'troughs' – stones spanning the width of the wall. The clumsy, irregular shaped stones require extremely skilful selection and placement and their mortarless construction remains a fascinating feature.

Pateley Bridge

Foster Beak Watermill   Nidderdale Museum

Panorama Walk

Considered one of the prettiest towns in the Dales, Pateley Bridge straggles up the hillside from its elegant 18th century bridge over the Nidd. Considering its compact size, the town is remarkably well connected by roads that have been here since the monastic orders established trade routes through the town for transporting

their goods. A street market, whose charter was granted in the 14th century, has however, been abandoned for some time, although sheep fairs and agricultural shows still take place here.

Pateley Bridge is more than just a market centre – the nearby lead mines, spinning and hand-loom weaving also provided employment for the local community. The construction of the turnpike road to Ripon in 1751, followed by the opening of a road to Knaresborough in 1756, gave the town a further economic boost. In the early 19th century, the brothers George and John Metcalfe moved their flax spinning business to nearby Glasshouses and they expanded rapidly. The lead mines, too, were expanding, due to the introduction of new machinery, and the town saw a real boom. The arrival of the railway in 1862 maintained this

THE OLD WORKHOUSE MUSEUM & CRAFT WORKSHOPS

King Street, Pateley Bridge, nr Harrogate, North Yorkshire HG3 5LE
Tel: 01423 714953
website: www.kingstreetworkshops.co.uk

Situated in an area of both natural and man-made beauty, the **Old Workhouse** is home to a number of workshops bringing together a small group of highly talented craftspeople.

Sanders & Wallace (Andrew and David) in Unit 4 (Tel: 01423 712570) are glassmakers, producing stunning contemporary pieces, all hand-made on the premises using traditional glass-blowing methods. Their repertoire includes drinking glasses, scent bottles, vases and paperweights.

Moxon & Simm (Debby and Ian) in Unit 1)Tel: 01423 712044) are outstanding jewellers, using precious metals and gemstones to produce a dazzling variety of wonderful, unique pieces, many of them inspired by old litho drawings of cell structures, such as shells and micro-organisms.

Crafty Tyke Productions in Unit 2 (Tel: 01423 715938) are specialists in all aspects of private and commercial digital photography and videography using state-of-the-art industrial standard equipment. Among the many ancillary services offered are restoring old or damaged photographs and remastering VHS videos to DVD.

Behind the workshops is the Nidderdale Museum (Tel: 01423 711225) telling the story of Dales life down the years. This development is supported by the Nidderdale Plus Partnership.

stories and anecdotes   famous people   art and craft   entertainment and sport   walks

flourishing economy, making the transportation of heavy goods cheaper and the carriage of perishable foods quicker.

Much of the Pateley Bridge seen today was built in those prosperous years. A town of quaint and pretty buildings, the oldest is St Mary's Church, a lovely ruin dating from 1320 from which there are some fine panoramic views. Another excellent vista can be viewed from the aptly named **Panorama Walk**, part of the main medieval route from Ripon to Skipton. The **Nidderdale Museum**, a winner of the National Heritage Museum of the Year, is housed in one of the town's original Victorian workhouses and presents a fascinating record of local folk history. The exhibits include a complete cobbler's shop, general store, Victorian parlour, kitchen and schoolroom, chemist's, haberdasher's, joiner's shop, solicitor's office as well as an agricultural, transport and industrial display.

The bridge at Pateley is a long established crossing, which was used by the monks of Fountains Abbey. The original ford was replaced by a wooden bridge in the 16th century and the present stone structure dates from the 18th century.

Just to the northwest of the town, up the river, is **Foster Beak Watermill**, a former flax mill that dates from the 18th century.

Around Pateley Bridge

RAMSGILL
5 miles NW of Pateley Bridge off the B6265

🐦 Gouthwaite Reservoir

This pleasant village, clustered around its well-kept green, was the birthplace of Eugene Aram in 1704. The son of a gardener at Newby Hall, Aram was arrested in 1758 in Kings Lynn for the murder of Daniel Clark in Knaresborough 13 years before. The trial took place in York and Aram caused a stir by conducting his own defence. However, he was convicted and later executed before his body was taken to Knaresborough where it was hung from a gibbet. The gruesome story has been the centre of many tales and songs including a very romantic version by Sir Bulwer Lytton.

Ramsgill is situated at the head of **Gouthwaite Reservoir**, built in the early 20th century by Bradford Corporation to satisfy the demand from the rapidly expanding town. Gouthwaite, along with the other two reservoirs in the Dale (Scar House and Angram), is now a popular and important site for wildfowl.

LOFTHOUSE
7 miles NW of Pateley Bridge off the B6265

🐦 How Stean Gorge

This is a small dales' village lying in the upper valley of the River Nidd and, unlike neighbouring Wharfedale, the stone walls and rocky outcrops are of millstone grit though the valley bottom consists of limestone. As a result, only in excessive weather is there water under the bridge here as, in normal conditions, the river drops down two sumps: Manchester Hole and Goydon Pot. The monks of Fountains Abbey certainly had a grange here but it is also probable that the village was first settled by Norsemen.

Nearby **How Stean Gorge** (see panel opposite), in the heart of Nidderdale, is often called Yorkshire's Little Switzerland and for good reason. This spectacular limestone gorge, which is up to 80 feet deep in places, through which the Stean Beck flows is a popular tourist attraction. A narrow path with

HOW STEAN GORGE

Lofthouse, Nidderdale, North Yorkshire HG3 5SF
Tel: 01423 755666
website: www.howstean.co.uk

How Stean Gorge is the exciting venue for a family day out, hidden at the head of the Nidderdale Area of Outstanding Natural Beauty near Harrogate.

North of Pateley Bridge the scenery changes into wild, unspoilt country with ever-changing views of hills and water at each bend in the road. It is this water that has carved the deep limestone ravine and caves of How Stean Gorge.

How Stean is not only a Special Site of Scientific Interest, but also a great place for walking. A fee is payable to enable you to enjoy a fantastic walk over narrow paths and footbridges down to the beck itself. An unlit cave is accessible for most, being straight forward walking. Bring a torch with you or buy one of our environmentally friendly LED torches to get the most out of the experience.

Bicycles are available to hire all year round with child tag-a-longs or a double buggy trailer, if required. A drop off can be arranged up to Scar House Reservoir, only 4 miles away, leaving an easy ride up to Angram Reservoir then, downhill all the way to Lofthouse and finally How Stean.

Our spacious campsite is available for tents, all year round for the brave, summer for the sensible!! A space is put aside for camp fires.

Our licensed restaurant produces home-cooked meals and cakes made with locally sourced ingredients.

Our gift shop attached to the restaurant stocks locally made crafts and gifts, featuring the talents of artists, photographers and wood turner.

Along with the Gorge, the restaurant and bar is open all year round, with the exception of Nidderdale Show day (usually 3rd Monday in September), Christmas Eve and Christmas Day. Visit our website above for more information.

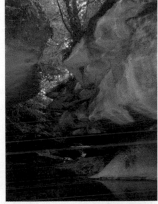

NORTH YORKSHIRE: COAST, MOORS AND DALES

footbridges guide the visitor along the gorge where the waters rush over the large boulders below. However, there are also many sheltered areas of calm water where fish hide under the rocks. As well as taking a stroll up this fascinating path, visitors can also step inside Tom Taylor's Cave and, along the walk, marvel at the wide variety of plant life that grows in this steep ravine.

MIDDLESMOOR
8 miles NW of Pateley Bridge off the B6265

This tucked away village of stone built cottages and houses lies at the head of Upper Nidderdale and is reached by a single, winding road. The existence of ancient settlers can be seen in the present 19th century Church of St Chad where an early 10th or 11th century preaching cross bearing the inscription *Cross of St Ceadda* can be seen.

BEWERLEY
1 mile SW of Pateley Bridge on the B6265

Recorded as *Bevrelie* (a clearing inhabited by badgers) in the *Domesday Book*, this is Nidderdale's oldest settlement. It was also the site of the earliest and most important of Fountains Abbey's many granges. Not only were they farming here, but lead was being extracted from the nearby moor. The recently restored Chapel, built here by one of the last abbots, Marmaduke Huby, acted for many years as the village school.

In the 17th century the Yorke family moved to the embellished hall at Bewerley following their purchase of the former lands of Byland Abbey in Nidderdale. During the subsequent years, the family laid out the parkland as well as rebuilding some of the village and, though the estate was sold in the 1920s and the hall demolished, the park remains and plays host to the annual Nidderdale Show. The name of the village's most influential family, however, is not forgotten as Yorke's Folly, two stone stoops, still stand on the hillside overlooking Bewerley.

WILSILL
1 mile E of Pateley Bridge on the B6165

🔗 Brimham Rocks

About two miles east of Wilsill are **Brimham Rocks** (National Trust), an extraordinary natural sculpture park. Formed into fantastic shapes by years of erosion, these great millstone grit boulders lie atop a steep hill amidst some 400 acres of heathland. Some of the shapes really do resemble their names – the 'Dancing Bear' in particular, but perhaps the most awe-inspiring is 'Idol Rock', a huge boulder weighing several tons thatrests on a base just a foot in diameter.

Brimham Rocks

🏠 historic building 🏛 museum and heritage 🏛 historic site 🏞 scenic attraction 🌿 flora and fauna

The National Trust has provided large scale maps for visitors to the rocks showing suggested itineraries and the positions and names of the major formations.

Wharfedale

The valley of the River Wharfe, Wharfedale, is the longest of the Yorkshire Dales following the river from its origins on Cam Fell for over 70 miles to Cawood, where it joins the River Ouse. At its source, almost 2,000 feet above sea level, the river

Barden Fell, Wharfedale

is nothing more than a moorland stream and, even in mid-Wharfedale, it is little more than a mountain river, broad, shallow, and peat brown in colour. The Romans named a local Goddess, Verbeia, after the river, and those who visit will understand why, as the goddess was known for her treachery as well as her beauty. Wharfedale is one of the most spectacular and most varied of the Yorkshire Dales, and no one who sees the river charging through the narrow gorge at The Strid, near Bolton Abbey, will deny that its power is to be respected.

For many years, Wharfedale has been the place to which those working in the grim industrial towns of Yorkshire came to for clean air and solitude. Today, it is probably the most popular of all Yorkshire's Dales and there is certainly a lot on offer to those who visit here. The chief towns of the dale are little more than villages and they have retained

much of their charm despite the various invasions of industry and tourism. Perhaps, this is because they were first invaded some 10,000 years ago by the hunter-gatherers of the Mesolithic age.

There is a lot to see in Wharfedale and, in keeping with much of the Yorkshire Dales National Park, there is a variety of landscape to discover. From the high moorland and fell, to the deep, eroded limestone gorges, the landscape varies almost, it seems, with every turn of the River Wharfe.

This section of Wharfedale has, over the years, inspired many of Britain's poets, writers, and painters. Both Coleridge and Wordsworth were taken with its beauty and, in the case of Wordsworth, with the local stories and legends. Ruskin enthused about its contrasts and Turner painted several scenes that also capture something of the dale's history and mystery.

Kettlewell

🏛 Church of St Mary

Kettlewell sits at the foot of Great Whernside on what may have been the course of the Roman road leading to Baunbridge Fort. The Anglo-Saxons farmed here and the terrace marks of later medieval strip-lynchet ploughing can still be seen.

Surrounded by the beautiful countryside of Upper Wharfedale, Kettlewell is a popular centre for tourists and walkers. At the meeting point of several old packhorse routes, which now serve as footpaths and bridleways, the village was a busy market centre and, at one time, the home of 13 public houses that catered to the needs of the crowds. The market charter, granted in 1320, is evidence that Kettlewell was once a more important

place than it is today, and the various local religious houses of Bolton Priory, Coverham Abbey and Fountains Abbey all owned land in the area.

Kettlewell is a conservation area, a charming place of chiefly 17th- and 18th-century houses and cottages. Its original 13th-century waterfall, later converted into a textile mill, has gone, though evidence of a local lead-mining industry remains. The late-19th century **Church of St Mary** attracts many visitors to its attractive churchyard and lychgate built on the site of a 12th-century building. The hills above Kettlewell are dotted with old mine shafts, and many of the cottages in the village were built to house the mine-workers of the 18th and 19th centuries. Care should be taken when exploring the area, and walkers should stay on the marked tracks.

LITTLEBECK BED & BREAKFAST

The Green, Kettlewell, North Yorkshire BD23 5RD
Tel: 01756 760378
e-mail: stay@little-beck.co.uk
website: www.little-beck.co.uk

After being charmed on a visit, Caroline and Paul Hatton moved to Kettlewell where they now run **Littlebeck**. This is a charming, detached Georgian house situated in the heart of Kettlewell overlooking the Dale to the front and a beck to the rear that flows into the River Wharfe. The house offers three tastefully furnished en-suite bedrooms with all those extra special touches, such as crisp white bed linen, fluffy towels and luxury toiletries. Each room also has a TV and refreshment tray.

For reading, relaxing or enjoying a drink there is a guest lounge where on chilly days you can snuggle up in front of an open fire and on warmer days you can sit on the pretty patio overlooking the beck.

From the front door there is the opportunity for either demanding fell walking or gentle strolling through meadows and along riverbanks. The area also offers exhilarating road and mountain bike routes, horse riding, fishing or rock climbing at the famous Kilnsey Crag.

Littlebeck can also provide private off road parking, safe storage for bikes and drying facilities.

🏛 historic building   📷 museum and heritage   🏚 historic site   ♤ scenic attraction   🌱 flora and fauna

Around Kettlewell

STARBOTTON
2 miles N of Kettlewell on the B6160

This quiet little Wharfedale village was the scene in 1686 of a disastrous flood when a huge head of water descended from the surrounding fells and swept away many of the houses and cottages. The damage was such that a national appeal was started and aid, in the form of money, was sent from as far afield as Cambridgeshire.

BUCKDEN
4 miles N of Kettlewell on the B6160

🦌 Langstrothdale Chase

Marking the beginning of Wharfedale proper, Buckden is the first full-sized village of the Dale and proudly boasts that it is also home to Wharfedale's first shop. Unusually for this area, the village was not settled by the Anglo-Saxons but, later, by the Normans, and it was the headquarters of the officers hunting in the forest of Langstrothdale. As the forest was cleared to make way for agriculture, Buckden became an important market town serving a large part of the surrounding area. Wool was one of the important sources of income for the dalesfolk and the local inn here still has some of the old weighing equipment from the days when the trade was conducted on the premises. The village is an excellent starting point for those wanting to climb Buckden Pike (2,302 feet), which lies to the east. The route to the summit takes in not only superb views but also several waterfalls.

Designated in Norman times as one of the feudal hunting forests, **Langstrothdale Chase** was governed by the strict forest laws. Just to the south of the village, which lies on the edge of the Chase, can be seen an old stone cross that was used to mark the forest boundary. Buckden's name means the 'valley of the bucks' but its last deer was hunted and killed here in the 17th century.

HUBBERHOLME
5 miles N of Kettlewell off the B6160

🏠 Hubberholme Parliament

This small village was originally two places: Hubberholme proper and Kirkgill, which takes its name from the nearby Church of St Michael and All Angels that was, at one time, a forest chapel. Each year, on New Year's Day, the villagers gather at the local pub for the **Hubberholme Parliament**. For that night, the public bar becomes the House of Commons, where the farmers congregate, while the room where the vicar and churchwardens meet is the House of Lords. Bidding then takes place between the farmers for the rent of a field behind the church and, encouraged by the vicar, the highest bidder gains the lease for the coming year.

LITTON
5 miles NW of Kettlewell off the B6160

This pretty village lends it name to the dale, Littondale, which is actually the valley of the River Skirfare. Once part of a Norman hunting forest, the dale was originally called Amerdale (meaning 'deep fork') and this ancient name is preserved in Amerdale Dub, where the River Skirfare joins the River Wharfe near Kilnsey.

YOCKENTHWAITE
6 miles NW of Kettlewell off the B6160

🪨 Giant's Grave

The unusual name of this small village is Viking in origin and, though once a prosperous place, Yockenthwaite is now a collection of old stone farms. On the surrounding fells lies a well-preserved Bronze Age stone circle and **Giant's Grave**, the remains of an Iron Age settlement.

ARNCLIFFE
3 miles W of Kettlewell off the B6160

🐦 Bridge End

Situated in Littondale, the village name dates back to Saxon times when the valley was referred to as Amerdale. This is a quiet, tranquil dale and life in this small village has remained the same for many years. Many of the buildings around the central village green are listed and, in its early years, the long running TV series *Emmerdale* was filmed here. Strongly recommended is a visit to the Falcon Inn where almost nothing has changed in half a century.

Near the village bridge, over the River Skirfare, stands a house, **Bridge End**, that was once the home of the Hammond family. While staying with the Hammonds, author Charles Kingsley was so taken with the village and Littondale that he incorporated the house and his hostess in his famous work, *The Water Babies*.

KILNSEY
3 miles S of Kettlewell on the B6160

🐦 🦌 Park & Trout Farm 🐏 Kilnsey Crag

This small hamlet, on the opposite bank of the River Wharfe from Conistone, is a great place from which many anglers fly fish and the Kilnsey Angling Club has its home in the village pub. This quiet and peaceful place is overlooked by the now uninhabited Old Hall, which was originally built as a grange for the monks of Fountains Abbey.

Kilnsey Park and Trout Farm is a popular place for family outings. Under-12s can enjoy their first experience of trout fishing, with all the tackle provided. Pony trekking is available, there's an estate shop selling dales' produce and fresh Kilnsey trout, a restaurant and a children's adventure centre, and visitors can also wander around the farm. Fly fishing, for those who like to indulge, is available in two well-stocked lakes.

The striking outline of **Kilnsey Crag** is unmistakable as one side of this limestone hill was gouged out by a passing glacier during the Ice Age. One of the most spectacular natural features in the dales, the crag has a huge 'lip' or overhang, which presents an irresistible challenge to adventurous climbers.

CONISTONE
4 miles S of Kettlewell off the B6160

This ancient settlement, whose name suggests that it once belonged to a king, is clustered around its maypole and village green. The village Church of St Mary is thought to have been founded in Saxon times and there are certainly two well-preserved Norman arches to be seen. The land surrounding Conistone is unusually flat and it was once the bottom of a lake formed by the melt water from the glacier that carved out Kilnsey Crag.

Grassington

🏛 Lea Green 🏛 Upper Wharfedale Folk Museum

🦌 Feast Sports and Festivals

One of the best loved villages within the Yorkshire Dales National Park, Grassington in many ways typifies the dales' settlement with its characteristic market square. Known as the capital of Upper Wharfedale, the historically

HARLEQUIN COUNTRY INTERIORS & GIFTS WITH THE UPSTAIRS GALLERY

2 Garrs Lane, Grassington, nr Skipton, North Yorkshire BD23 5AT
Tel: 01756 753099
e-mail: angela@harlequingrassington.co.uk

Located just off Grassington's cobbled main square, **Harlequin**, a stylish country interiors and gift shop, inspires its customers with its array cleverly displayed in three showrooms on two floors. Harlequin is the brainchild of the husband-and-wife team of Angela and Andrew Jackson. Having spent much of their time together visiting Europe's finest cities, not to mention some sleepy backwaters, in search of quaint curios to furnish their converted 18th-century barn, they have happily taken up the challenge of translating their talent for searching out the hidden treasures in their sourcing of unusual gift ideas to complement Harlequin's individual style. Rustic French and English country styles blend effortlessly with the range of bags, jewellery and scarves to offer the discerning buyer a chance to own something unique.

Added to all this, the building houses Grassington's new art gallery, The Gallery Upstairs, showcasing the work of 10 local artists ranging from ceramics, felt and rag-rugging work, to oils, watercolours and prints. All in all, Harlequin is well worth a visit. Interesting aromas, friendly staff and a willingness to please make for a pleasurable experience,

THE RUSTIC RABBIT

23 The Main Street, The Square, Grassington,
nr Skipton, North Yorkshire BD23 5AD
Tel: 01756 752772
Fax: 01756 730344

On the Square in Grassington, **The Rustic Rabbit** is filled with an eyecatching range of lovely things for the home. The mother-and-daughter team of Holly and Sandra Patrick have an unfailing eye for presentation, and their interesting and exciting displays complement the exposed beams and beautiful sweeping staircase in the light, airy premises. High-class household items include tableware, china, storage jars, linen, tea towels, aprons, oven gloves, candles and candle-holders, vases, chandeliers and lamps, wall-hangings and plaques, mirrors and frames in all styles and sizes. There are items of furniture from France and Scandinavia, bathroom accessories (Bath House Bathing Products, Burt's Bees), baby products and gifts (including huggable rabbits in smart costumes) and books on interior décor, gardens and cookery.

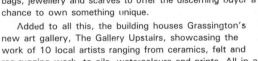
stories and anecdotes 🐦 famous people 🔎 art and craft ✍ entertainment and sport 🎿 walks

important valley roads meet here and the ancient monastic route from Malham to Fountains Abbey passes through the village.

Grassington's origins are rooted in ancient history; there was certainly a Bronze Age settlement here, the remains of an Iron Age village have been found, a Celtic field system lies on nearby **Lea Green**, and the village was mentioned in the *Domesday Book*. However, the settlement seen today is Anglian and, having passed through various families, is now part of the estate of the Dukes of Devonshire. With its narrow streets lined with attractive Georgian buildings, Grassington is a delightful place to wander around.

Housed in two 18th-century lead miners' cottages, in Grassington Square, is the **Upper Wharfedale Folk Museum**. Containing many exhibits and displays relating to the lives of those who have lived in the dale, the museum is open (afternoons only) at the weekend during the winter and daily throughout the summer. In the past, throughout the year, there were many festivals and holidays observed by the dales people and one, the **Feast Sports**, still takes place here on a Saturday in October. Among the many traditional events carried out, is the tea cake eating race, where children have to eat a tea cake, then race to the other end of the field. The winner is the first child who then whistles a tune. Other annual events include the Grassington Festival (2008 date 13 to 28 June) and the Dickensian Festival in December.

🏠 historic building 🏛 museum and heritage 🏚 historic site 🗺 scenic attraction 🌱 flora and fauna

Around Grassington

THRESHFIELD
1 mile W of Grassington on the B6160

Across the river from Grassington, Threshfield has at its heart a small village green called the Park, complete with the original village stocks and surrounded by charming 17th-century houses. Perhaps the most striking building is the Free Grammar School built in 1674. According to local people its porch is haunted by a fairy known as Old Pam the Fiddler. Threshfield was once famed for the production of *besoms* (birch brooms) but the last family to make them, the Ibbotsons, died out in the 1920s.

LINTON
1 mile SW of Grassington off the B6160

🏛 Church of St Michael & All Angels

This delightful and unspoilt village, that is more correctly called Linton-in-Craven, has grown up around its village green through which runs a small beck. This flat area of land was once a lake and around its edge was grown flax that the villagers spun into linen. The village is also the home of the **Church of St Michael and All Angels**, a wonderful building that is a fine example of rural medieval architecture. Probably built on the site of a pagan shrine, the church lies some way from the village centre though its handsome bell-cote is a suitable landmark. Among the 14th-century roof bosses can be seen the Green Man, an ancient fertility symbol of a man's head protruding through foliage, which was adopted by the Christian church.

Spanning Linton beck is a graceful 14th-century **Packhorse Bridge** that was repaired by Dame Elizabeth Redmayne in the late 17th century. During the repair work, Dame Elizabeth had a narrow parapet added to the bridge to prevent carts from crossing because, so it is said, the local farmers refused to contribute to the cost of the repairs.

CRACOE
3 miles SW of Grassington on the B6265

The village contains several 17th-century houses that are typical examples of the building style of the day. Constructed from stone quarried on nearby Cracoe and Rylstone Fell, the cavity between the three feet thick walls was filled with rubble. Above the village, on top of the fell, is a cairn built in memory of local men who died during the First World War. Construction of the cairn began in the early 1920s, but the professional masons experienced great difficulty as high winds tore down their work overnight. Eventually, a local man was hired for the task and, instead of coming down from the fell each night, he pitched his tent close to the cairn and remained on-site until it was completed.

14th-century Packhorse Bridge, Linton

🎞 stories and anecdotes 🦜 famous people 🎨 art and craft 🖉 entertainment and sport 🚶 walks

THORPE
2 miles SE of Grassington off the B6160

This small hamlet, the full name of which is Thorpe-sub-Montem (meaning 'below the hill'), lies in a secluded hollow between drumlins – long, low alluvial mounds. As well as taking advantage of its hidden position, ideal for secreting valuables and family members here during Scots' raids, the village was also known for its cobblers. Their fame was such that the monks of Fountains Abbey were among their regular customers. However, the influence of the monks did not prevent the high spirited cobblers from stealing nearby Burnsall's maypole and planting it on their own village green. The maypole did, eventually, return to its home village but not until the villagers of Burnsall had organised a rescue party.

HEBDEN
3 miles E of Grassington on the B6265

🏛 Stump Cross Caverns

From this quiet hamlet it is only a short distance to the wonderful 500,000-year-old cave at **Stump Cross Caverns**. The large show cave holds a fantastic collection of stalactites and stalagmites, which make it one of the most visited underground attractions in the area. During excavations, the remains of animals were found here and they can be seen on display at the visitor centre where there is also a gift shop and tea room.

BURNSALL
2 miles S of Grassington on the B6160

🏛 Church of St Wilfrid

The village is very dramatically situated on a bend in the River Wharfe with the slopes of Burnsall Fell as a backdrop. Of ancient origins, it is thought that, prior to the 8th

century, Wilfrid Bishop of York founded a wooden church on the site of which now stands the village's 12th-century church. The only remains of Wilfrid's building is the font, which can still be seen at the back of **St Wilfrid's Church**. The churchyard is entered via a unique lychgate and here can be seen two hogback tombstones and various other fragments that date back to the times of the Anglo-Saxons and the Danes.

However, it is not this sturdy dales' church that draws visitors to Burnsall, but its bridge. Today, this typical dales' bridge of five stone arches is the start of the annual Classic Fell Race, which takes place on a Saturday towards the end of August. Over the years, the flood waters of the River Wharfe have washed away the arches on several occasions but the villagers have always replaced them as this is the only crossing point for three miles in each direction.

APPLETREEWICK
4 miles SE of Grassington off the B6160

🏛 Barden Tower 🕭 Simon's Seat
🌿 Parcevall Hall Gardens 🏛 Trollers Gill

This peaceful village, which is known locally as Aptrick, lies between the banks of the River Wharfe and the bleak moorland, and is overlooked by the craggy expanse of **Simon's Seat**, one of Wharfedale's best-loved hilltops. Dating back to monastic times the northern slopes were the property of the monks of nearby Bolton Priory and lead has been mined on the surrounding moorland for many centuries. The village was also the home of William Craven, a Lord Mayor of London, who returned to spend much of his amassed wealth on improvements and additions to Appletreewick's fine old buildings. Known as the Dick Whittington of the Dale, William

Craven was born in 1548 and he moved to London when he became apprenticed to a mercer (a dealer in textiles and fine fabrics).

Just to the north of Appletreewick lie **Parcevall Hall Gardens**, a wonderful woodland garden that includes many varieties of unusual plants and shrubs. Though the 16-acre gardens are high above sea level (which provides the visitor with splendid views), many of the plants still flourish in these beautiful surroundings. The gardens, which are open between Easter and October, have a special quality of peace and tranquillity – appropriately enough since the lovely old Hall is now a Bradford Diocesan Retreat and Conference Centre.

The nearby gorge of **Trollers Gill** is said to be haunted by a fearsome ghost dog, with huge eyes and a shaggy coat, that drags a clanking chain. A local story, recorded in 1881, tells how a man, somewhat foolishly, went to the gorge in the middle of the night. He failed to return and his body, on which there were marks not made by a human, was later found by shepherds.

A little further down river is the stately ruin of **Barden Tower**, a former residence of Lord Henry Clifford, owner of Skipton

Castle. It was built in the 15th century but allowed to fall into decay and, despite repair in 1657, it is once more a ruin. Nearby is the attractive Barden Bridge, a 17th-century arch now designated as an ancient monument.

BOLTON ABBEY
7 miles S of Grassington on the B6160

Priory   The Strid

The village is actually a collection of small hamlets that have all been part of the estate of the Dukes of Devonshire since 1748. Bolton Abbey itself lies on the banks of the River Wharfe while the hamlets of Storiths, Hazelwood, Deerstones, and Halton East lie higher up.

The main attraction in the village is the substantial ruin of **Bolton Priory** (see panel on page 260), an Augustinian house that was founded in 1155 by monks from Embsay. In an idyllic situation on the banks of the River Wharfe, the ruins are well preserved while the nave of the priory church, first built in 1220, is now incorporated into the parish church.

After the Dissolution of the Monasteries the priory was sold to the 2nd Earl of Cumberland, Henry Clifford, and it has since passed into the hands of the Dukes of Devonshire, the Cavendish family. The 14th-century priory gatehouse, Bolton Hall, is the present duke's shooting lodge. Visitors walking to the priory ruins from the village pass through a hole in the wall, which frames one of the most splendid views of the romantic ruins. An attractive option when visiting the priory is to travel on the Embsay and Bolton Abbey Steam Railway

Barden Tower, Appletreewick

stories and anecdotes   famous people   art and craft   entertainment and sport   walks

Bolton Abbey

Estate Office, Bolton Abbey, Skipton,
North Yorkshire BD23 6EX
Tel: 01756 718009
website: www.boltonabbey.com

Bolton Abbey near Skipton is the Yorkshire Estate of the Duke and Duchess of Devonshire. Situated in Wharfedale, in the Yorkshire Dales National Park, this historic estate is a magnet for visitors drawn to its breathtaking landscapes and excellent facilities.

Visitors have flocked to Bolton Abbey for over one hundred years. On an August Bank Holiday in the 1890s the railway brought 40,000 people to Bolton Abbey; nearly as many people as now visit York in a week. After the First World War visitors arrived by train in their 'Sunday Best' with the children carrying buckets, spades and fishing nets. Some fathers never got much further than the Devonshire Arms' Refreshment Room, but many removed their boots and rolled up their trousers to paddle with their children by the sandy river bank. Little has changed over the years; visitors still come to see the landscape that inspired artists like Turner and Landseer, and poets such as Wordsworth.

As the name suggests, Bolton Abbey was originally a large monastic Estate, based around the 12th-century **Priory**. Legend has it that the Priory was established in 1120 by Cecily de Romille as an expression of her grief following the drowning of her son in the nearby Strid. Today, the ruins of the Priory set in an incomparable position overlooking the river Wharfe will evoke the past glories of the Estate, while the restored and thriving parish church shows that the Estate is still very much a living community.

whose station is about half a mile away, reached by a pleasant riverside footpath. Steam trains run every Sunday and most days in summer, and Thomas the Tank Engine is an occasional visitor.

In and around this beautiful village there are some 80 miles of footpaths and nature trails skirting the riverbanks and climbing up onto the high moorland. Upstream from the priory lies one of the most visited natural features in Wharfedale, a point where the wide river suddenly narrows into a confined channel of black rock through which the water thunders. This spectacular gorge is known as **The Strid** because, over the centuries, many heroic (or foolhardy) types have attempted to leap across it as a test of bravery.

Airedale

The 'Gateway to the Dales', Skipton has long been a starting point for any tour of the Yorkshire Dales and, though still a bustling centre for Airedale and its neighbour Malhamdale, the town's old industries have given way, to a large degree, to tourism. The source of the River Aire lies in Malhamdale, just to the north of Malham, and it flows through both dales before finally joining the River Ouse. For some of its length, in Airedale, the river lies side-by-side with the Leeds and Liverpool Canal. The construction of a navigable waterway, linking the two great industrial areas of Lancashire and Yorkshire, changed the lives of many living in the dales and certainly played a major part in establishing the textile mills in the area.

However, the importance of farming has never been lost and market day is a key event in the daily lives of the dalesfolk. As well as the sheep, other constant features of the countryside are the dry stone walls; a familiar sight to all those visiting the Yorkshire Dales.

Of the many and varied attractions in Airedale and the area surrounding Skipton, the most impressive feature is the beautiful limestone formations found to the north of Malham. The spectacular and enormous curved cliff of Malham Cove, created by glacial action during the last Ice Age, the limestone pavements above the cove, the deep gorge of Gordale Scar, and the remote natural lake, Malham Tarn, are all well worth a visit.

This dramatic scenic area has been designated a Site of Special Scientific Interest and, as well as the wonderful formations themselves, the area supports a wide range of animals, birds, and plant life. As there is a variety of terrain, from bleak, bracken strewn moorland to coniferous plantations, there is also a wide variety of flora and fauna.

Birdwatchers, particularly, will delight in the opportunity to catch sight of red grouse and short-eared owls on the moors while also having the chance to view the many wading birds that populate the lakes and reservoirs of the area.

Skipton

🏛 Castle 🏛 Public Library 🏛 The Black Horse Inn
🏛 Craven Museum 🏛 Leeds & Liverpool Canal

Often called the 'Gateway to the Dales', Skipton's origins can be traced back to the 7th century when Anglian farmers christened it Sheeptown. Featuring in the *Domesday Book*, the Normans decided to build a castle here to guard the entrance to Airedale and Skipton became a garrison town. **Skipton Castle**, home of the Cliffords, was begun in 1090 and the powerful stone structure seen today was devised in 1310 by Robert de Clifford, the 1st Earl of Skipton. The Cliffords were a fighting breed and, throughout the Middle Ages wherever there was trouble, a member of the family was sure to be found. The 8th Lord Clifford, Thomas, and his son John were both killed while fighting for the House of Lancaster during the War of the Roses. Later, George Clifford, Champion to Queen Elizabeth I and a renowned sailor, fought against the Spanish Armada and, as well as participating in many voyages of his own, he also lent a ship to Sir Walter Raleigh.

One of the most complete and well-preserved medieval castles in England, it is thanks to Lady Anne Clifford that visitors to Skipton can marvel at its buildings.

Springs Canal, Skipton

🎬 stories and anecdotes 🦅 famous people 🎨 art and craft 🎭 entertainment and sport 🚶 walks

APOTHECARY II

7 Craven Court, Skipton,
North Yorkshire BD23 1DG
Tel/Fax: 01756 700295
e-mail: info@apothecary2.co.uk
website: www.apothecary2.co.uk

Apothecary II is the top place in Skipton to shop for health, bath, skin and beauty products. Demand keeps some products in constant supply, but owner Emma Cox is always looking for interesting new stock. Among the leading brands always available are Burt's Bees – 95% natural skincare products rich in bees wax and essential oils and sold in environment-friendly packaging; Rose & Co Apothecary - beautiful bath and beauty products in pretty glass bottles, boxes and tins, and gorgeous gift sets in hat boxes and handbags that evoke vintage glamour and elegance; Crabtree & Evelyn's La Source, Gardeners' and Florals ranges; fabulously fragrant soaps and bath delights that are handmade locally; jewellery, compacts, make–up and toilet bags, perfume bottles, vintage style home accessories and linens. Also all kinds of keepsakes and collectables including Elvis, pin-up girl and Fifties' ladies themed items and bespoke gifts, which can be created, wrapped and mailed. It's always a treat to visit the shop in Craven Court, but customers can also browse the excellent website and order online.

BARBARA CUNNINGHAM AND MEZZO JEWELLERY

14 Craven Court, High Street, Skipton,
North Yorkshire BD23 1DG
Tel: 01756 7797597
e-mail: shop@gottohavediamonds.com.
website: www.gottohavediamonds.com

A stone building in a courtyard off Skipton's High Street is home to a unique jewellery emporium in two distinct sections. Owners Barbara and Gordon have invested many years of energy and passion into building up a business that offers quality, beauty and value and brings clients from overseas as well as all parts of the UK. **Barbara Cunningham Jewellery (BCJ)**, established in 1983, stocks new and exciting designer ranges in platinum, gold, silver, steel, palladium and titanium, with new products coming on line all the time. **Mezzo Jewellery**, established in 1992, is an extensive and constantly changing collection of highly desirable and impressive antique and pre-owned pieces, including rings and earrings, bracelets, bangles, brooches, chains, pendants and watches. A selection of the jewellery currently in stock can be seen on the excellent website. Personal specialist advice is always available, and other services provided by this outstanding enterprise include buying and selling gold, repairs and remodelling, ring sizing and stone replacement, and estimates and valuations.

Following the ravages of the Civil War, from which the castle did not escape, Lady Anne undertook a comprehensive restoration programme and, though little of the original Norman stonework remains, much of the work of the 1st Lord Clifford still stands.

As well as an enormous banqueting hall, a series of kitchens still remain with some of their original fittings, and a beautiful Tudor courtyard. There is also a rather unusually decorated room whose walls are lined with shells that were collected by George Clifford in the 19th century while he was travelling in the South Seas. However, the most striking feature of the castle is the impressive 14th-century gateway, which is visible from the High Street, and carries the Clifford family motto *Desormais* , which means 'Henceforth'.

Adjacent to the castle, at the top of the High Street, lies the parish **Church of the Holy Trinity,** which was originally built in the 12th century and replaced in the 1300s. There is much of interest inside the building, which has been topped by a beautiful oak roof since the 15th century. It is possible to spend many hours discovering the centuries of artefacts in the church and the various tombs and memorials that include the many tombs of the Clifford family. The church suffered damage during the Civil War and, again, Lady Anne Clifford came to the rescue, restoring the interior and rebuilding the steeple in 1655. Inside the church, among the many tombstones, you'll find is that of the Longfellow family, which included the uncle of the American poet, Henry Wadsworth

BUSY LITTLE BEES

Craven Court, Skipton, North Yorkshire BD23 1DG
Tel: 01756 700968
e-mail: shop@busylittlebees.co.uk   website: www.busylittlebees.co.uk

Candy Squire-Watts always wanted to run a business that
involved fashion and children, and in **Busy Little Bees** she has
turned her wishes into reality in fine style. In a handsome stone
building with large bay windows she has carefully chosen a
selection of high-quality branded children's wear from some of
the leading continental brands, including Catimini, Timberland,
Coco, Emile et Rose, Kaloo and Pampolina. In addition to the
clothes, the stock includes blankets, toys and big, bright reusable
calendars. Established as the top children's designer shop in the
Dales, Busy Little Bees attracts regular customers from far
and wide, and, with the stock constantly changing, every
visit reveals something new and desirable. The shop has a

relaxed atmosphere, and
Candy is always happy to
chat with her customers
about what is best for each
child, as well as being very
well informed about Skipton,
which was for many years a
centre of the textile industry.

THE BLUE BELL INN

Middle Lane, Skipton, North Yorkshire BD23 5QX
Tel: 01756 760230
e-mail: info@thebluebellinn.co.uk
website: www.thebluebellinn.co.uk

This 17th century coaching inn provides excellent food and
accommodation in the pretty village of Kettlewell. There is
an extensive range of dishes on the a la carte menu using
only the finest ingredients, including beef, lamb and trout
from the Dales, seafood from the east coast, fresh
seasonal vegetables and herbs. The menu always includes
a selection of vegetarian dishes and offers a variety of
weekly specials. The remarkably cosy bar at the Blue Bell
offers a fine selection of traditional hand-pulled cask ales
and an extensive wine list, or if you prefer, an enviable
range of single malt whiskies.

The Blue Bell has four en-suite double rooms and two
en-suite twin-bedded rooms.

All rooms have stunning views of Kettlewell and the
surrounding hills, are fully centrally heated and come
equipped with tea and coffee making facilities, remote control TV, radio alarm clock and hair
drier. All the rooms are non smoking.

Ample parking is available for residents at the rear of the building.

Skipton Castle

Longfellow. As well as the fine castle and church, the Normans also established Skipton as a market town and it received its first charter in 1204. The market today is still thriving and is very much an important part of daily life in the area.

For many years Skipton remained a market town, then, with the development of the factory system in the 19th century, the nature of the town began to change. Textile mills were built and cottages and terraced houses were constructed for the influx of mill workers. However, not all were happy with the changes that the Industrial Revolution brought about and, in 1842, a group of men, women, and children set out from the Pennine cotton towns and villages to protest at the mechanisation taking place. By the time the group had reached nearby Broughton, their number had grown to 3,000 and the Skipton magistrates urged them to turn back and return home. But the protesters continued, surging on Skipton, and the worried magistrates sent for military help. Moving from mill to mill, the mob stopped the looms and created panic among the townspeople. Special constables were quickly sworn in to help contain the situation and the Riot Act was read from the town hall steps. Though the

mob retreated to nearby Anne Hill, they refused to disperse and the soldiers were ordered to charge. During the ensuing violence, one soldier was killed and a magistrate blinded, but the mob, bar six of the leaders who were arrested, fled as the first shots were fired.

Skipton lies at the northernmost point of the 130-mile **Leeds and Liverpool Canal**, one of the earliest achievements of the Industrial Revolution. The Canal provided a cheap form of transport as well as linking Skipton with the major industrial centres of Yorkshire and Lancashire. The first of three trans-Pennine routes, the canal has 91 locks along the full length as well as two tunnels, one of which is over a mile long. Today, the canal basin behind the town centre, is busy with pleasure craft and boat journeys can be taken along a section in the direction of Gargrave. The towpath was also restored at the same time as the canal and there are a number of pleasant walks along the towpath, which includes a stretch along the cul de-sac Spring Branch beside the castle walls.

Before the days of the canal, travelling by road, particularly in winter, was often a hazardous business. One local tale tells how, one Christmas Eve, during a bad snow storm, a young waggoner set out from the town for Blubberhouses. Though an inn-keeper tried to dissuade him, the young man carried on into the night – thinking only of his betrothed, Ruth. He soon lost his way in a snow drift and chilled by the fierce northerly winds, fell to the ground in a comatose state. Safe in her cottage, Ruth suddenly awoke and ran out of the house crying that her John was lost. Two men hurried after her and by the time they had caught up with Ruth she was digging John out with her bare hands. He was none the worse for his misadventure and the couple married on New Year's Day.

A walk around the town is also worthwhile as there are many fascinating buildings to be found here. One in particular is the Town Hall which is now also the home of the **Craven Museum**. Dedicated to the surrounding area, there are many interesting displays relating to the geological and archaeological treasures that have been found locally, including a piece of Bronze Age cloth that is considered to be the oldest textile fragment in the country. Closer to the present day, there are displays of furniture illustrating the fine craftsmanship that went into even the most mundane household item, and also farming exhibits that reflect the changing lives of many of the people who lived off the surrounding countryside.

Almost opposite the Town Hall, on the High Street, are the premises of the Craven Herald, a newspaper that was established in 1874, although the publication had been produced for a short time in the 1850s. The building is fortunate in having retained its late-Victorian shop front, as well as the passageway to one side, and it was first occupied by William Chippendale in the late 18th century. A trader in textiles, Chippendale made his money by buying then selling on the cloth woven by the farmers in their own homes. Close to the newspaper's offices is the **Public Library,** which opened in 1910 and was funded by Andrew Carnegie. A large, ornate building, it is in contrast to the town's older buildings and stands as a reminder to the change in character that Skipton underwent in the late 19th century.

It seems fitting that, in a town which over many years has been dedicated to trade and commerce, Thomas Spencer, co-founder of

Marks & Spencer, should have been born here in 1851. Skipton, too, was the home of Sir Winston Churchill's physician, Lord Moran, who grew up here as the son of the local doctor.

As with many historic market towns, Skipton has its fair share of inns and public houses, which originally provided farmers with refreshment during the busy markets. The **Black Horse Inn** is one such pub and its date stone of 1676 is well worth a second look as it is carved with symbols of the butcher's trade: axes, animal heads and twisted fleeces. Originally called The King's Head, the inn was built by, not surprisingly, a butcher, Robert Goodgion. In the 19th century it served as a headquarters to Lord Ribblesdale's cavalry when they held their annual training in the town.

Around Skipton

EMBSAY
1 mile N of Skipton off the A59

🏠 Embsay & Bolton Abbey Steam Railway

🍃 Embsay Crag

The village is home to the **Embsay & Bolton Abbey Steam Railway**, which is based at the small country station. As well as taking a scenic steam train journey to the end of the line, a couple of miles away, there are over 20 locomotives, both steam and diesel, on display together with railway carriages. Special events are arranged throughout the year and opening times vary, though the trains run every Sunday.

Well before the days of railways, Embsay was home to an Augustinian priory, founded in 1130. However, for some reason the monks found life difficult here and, in 1145, they crossed Embsay Moor and moved to what is now Bolton Abbey. Those choosing to walk over the moor to the north of the village should take care as the area is peppered with old coal pits and disused shafts. However, the view from **Embsay Crag** (1,217 feet high) is well worth the effort of climbing.

RYLSTONE
5 miles N of Skipton on the B6265

🏛 Rylstone Cross

On Rylstone Fell, above this Pennine village, stands **Rylstone Cross**, which was, originally, a large stone that looked rather like a man. In 1885, a wooden cross was erected on top of the stone to commemorate peace with France and the initials DD and TB carved on the back of the cross refer to the Duke of Devonshire and his land agent, Mr T Broughton.

At the beginning of the 19th century, when Wordsworth was touring the area, he heard a local legend that became the basis for his poem *The White Doe of Rylstone*, published in 1815. The story, set in the 16th century, concerns the local Norton family and, in particular, Francis who gave his sister Emily a white doe before he went off to battle. Francis survived the conflict but he was murdered in Norton Tower on his return. Emily was struck down with grief and she was comforted by

the same white doe, returned from the wild, and which accompanied her on her visits to her brother's grave. Long after Emily's death, a white doe could still be seen lying on Francis's grave.

BROUGHTON
4 miles W of Skipton on the A59

🏛 Hall

The Tempest family has been associated with this farming community for the past 800 years and their family home, **Broughton Hall**, dates back to 1597, with additions made in the 18th and 19th centuries. The estate covers 3,000 acres and is now also home to a business park where many small businesses thrive. Those who visit on the last Sunday in June will also witness the Broughton Hall Game Fair, a well-attended event that covers all manner of country sports and pursuits. The building itself may seem familiar since it, as well as the grounds, have been used frequently by film crews as an historic location.

GARGRAVE
5 miles NW of Skipton on the A65

🏛 Kirk Sink

This picturesque small village in Upper Airedale was once a thriving market town and it also became a busy transport centre after the Leeds and Liverpool Canal was built. Lead from the nearby mines was loaded on to the barges at the five wharves here, while other goods were unloaded ready for distribution to the surrounding area. The village too played a part in the textile boom and there were two cotton mills in the village. Now no longer in commercial use (like the canal), some of the mills have been turned into residential

Site of Roman Villa, Gargrave

🎬 stories and anecdotes 🐦 famous people 🎨 art and craft 🖋 entertainment and sport 🚶 walks

R N MYERS & SON

Endsleigh House, High Street, Gargrave, Skipton,
North Yorkshire BD23 3LX
Tel: 01756 749587 Fax: 01756 749322
e-mail: rnmyersson@aol.com

Gargrave, a picturesque little village on the A65 in Upper
Airedale, was at one time a busy centre of canal
commerce and the cotton industry. The past is still very
much in evidence in many of the buildings, but the canal is
now used mainly for leisure pursuits and the cotton mills
are now private residences. More tangible evidence of
English heritage and traditional skills can be found in 18th-
century Endsleigh House, the main-street premises
occupied by the firm of **R N Myers & Son**, established in
1890 and now owned and run by Simon and Jean Myers.
Three showrooms are filled with top-quality antiques and
works of art. They deal principally in English oak,
mahogany and walnut furniture covering the period from
the 17th to the early 19th centuries. The frequently
changing stock also includes English and Chinese pottery
and porcelain, along with a hand-picked selection of
decorative items and collectables. The owners are always
ready with help and advice and undertake valuations of
customers' pieces. The showrooms are open from 9.30 to
5.30 Monday to Saturday.

accommodation while the canal is very much
alive with pleasure boats.

The remains of Celtic crosses found within
the village Church of St Andrew indicate that,
although the present building is chiefly
Victorian, there has been a church here for
centuries. The original church was destroyed
by the Scots during a raid in 1318. To the
south of the village, at **Kirk Sink**, is the site
of a Roman villa that was excavated in the
1970s. Relics recovered from the building can
be seen in Skipton and Cliffe Castle Museums;
the site itself has since been re-covered.

CONISTON COLD
7 miles NW of Skipton on the A65

Lying midway between Skipton and Settle, this
small village lies on the old route to the Lake
District. Like most places situated on once

busy routes, the village had its share of
coaching inns and one in particular was the
Punch Bowl Inn (until recently it acted as the
post office), which has an unusual circular
indentation on the front outside wall. In
days gone by the inn's patrons would stand
a few yards from the wall and try to kick a
ball to this mark.

AIRTON
8 miles NW of Skipton off the A65

🏠 Meeting House

This charming Airedale village is well known to
long-distance walkers as it lies on the Pennine
Way. Though small, there are a couple of
buildings of interest including a corn mill (now
converted into flats) that was first recorded in
1198. As sheep farming took over from corn,
the mill, like so many in the southern dales,

turned to cotton spinning though, with the advent of steam powered machinery, the industry moved to nearby Skipton.

At the beginning of the 18th century, Airton became a Quaker community and the **Meeting House**, which was built on land donated by the well-known Quaker weavers William and Alice Ellis, can still be seen by the village green. Another legacy of the village's Quaker community is the absence of a public house as the drinking of alcohol was strictly forbidden by the Friends.

Also found on the village green is a 17th-century Squatter's Cottage so called because, according to the law, any person building a house and having smoke rising from the chimney within 24 hours was granted the freehold of the property including the land within a stone's throw of the front door.

MALHAM
11 miles NW of Skipton off the A65

ⓐ Malham Cove ⓐ Gordale Scar ⓐ Malham Tarn

Malham village was originally two settlements, Malham East and Malham West, which were separated by the beck. Each came under the influence of a different religious house: Bolton Priory and Fountains Abbey respectively. United after the Dissolution of the Monasteries, the focal point of Malham became the village green where the annual sheep fairs were held. This pretty village of farms and cottages is one of the most visited places in the Yorkshire Dales though it is not the charming stone built dwellings that visitors come to admire, but the spectacular limestone scenery which lies just to the north. However, the two ancient stone bridges in the village centre are also worth a second glance. The New Bridge, which is also known as the Monks' Bridge, was built in the 17th century, while the Wash-Dub Bridge dates from the 16th century and is of a clapper design (limestone slabs placed on stone supports).

To the north of the village lies the ancient glacial grandeur of **Malham Cove**. Access is from the Langcliffe road beyond the last buildings of the village, down a path alongside the beck that leads through a scattering of trees. The 300-foot limestone amphitheatre is the most spectacular section of the mid-Craven fault and, as recently as the 1700s, a massive waterfall that was higher than Niagara Falls cascaded over its edge. A steep path leads to the limestone pavement at the top, with its characteristic clints and grykes, where water has carved a distinctive natural sculpture through the weaknesses in the limestone.

From here it is not too far to reach the

Malham Tarn

ⓝ stories and anecdotes ⓢ famous people ⓟ art and craft ⓔ entertainment and sport ⓚ walks

Kirkby Malham Circular

Distance: *4.0 miles (6.4 kilometres)*
Typical time: *120 mins*
Height gain: *130 metres*
Map: *Explorer OL 10*
Walk: *www.walkingworld.com ID:3239*
Contributor: *William Kembery*

Airton is situated on the unclassified road northwest of Skipton and southeast of Settle.

DESCRIPTION:

The walk rises over the saddle between the Thornber and Warber Hills. A stunning view of Kirkby Malham Church is seen before returning along the unusual limestone River Aire.

FEATURES:

Hills or Fells, River, Pub, Church, Birds, Flowers, Great Views, Food Shop, Good for Kids, Tea Shop

WALK DIRECTIONS:

1 | From Airton Village Green take the Otterburn and Hellifield road at the crossroads. At the village pump, turn right onto a stone track and as the stone track swings left carry straight on along the footpath signed Scosthrop. At the end of this narrow way cross straight over the first road and turn right along the second road.

2 | A café is to be found by walking to the end of this road and turning left for about 100m. Otherwise, after a few metres turn left through a little gate signed Malham Road. Walk past the house and down the left side of the garage to climb a stone stile into a field. Cross the field slightly right to pass through a further stile. Walk over the field to mount a ladder stile

,then cross straight over the next field to a wall with a stile that is **not** crossed. On reaching the wall turn left and follow it round the kink to a wall stile in the corner. Walk virtually straight across the next field passing an electricity pole, and continue on heading initially for a gate in the wall ahead.

3 | At a point between a stile by the farm buildings on the left and a large tree on the right horizon turn right to find another stone stile in the corner. Cross the stile and head away with the wall on the right, keep straight ahead as the wall turns away to climb a stile well right of the barn ahead. Carry on now with the wall again, over the stile and across the field to find a finger post. Follow it round to another finger post to the right of a barn. Follow the track round to the furthest gate on the left and walk up the hill on a good green track with a wire fence on the right. As the fence cuts away stick with the track and as that

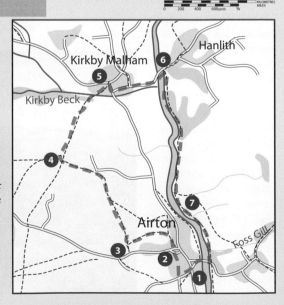

fades keep straight on to a finger post in the wall ahead.

4 | Through the kissing gate turn right with the pointer to Kirk Gate and Kirkby Malham. In a couple of hundred metres pass through a stile in the wall on the right. Proceed down the grassy bank and across the little stone bridge to a finger post. Then carefully follow the direction of the finger post left across a large field making for the centre of a copse. Pass through two gates, and, walking down the hill with a good view of the old stone church, cross a stile. Go down the narrow track across a stone stile, quickly followed, a few metres ahead, by a small gate on the left and crossing the stream arrive at the church.

5 | Turn right down the road trying hard to pass the pub and straight across at the crossroads following the sign to Hanlith. Eventually cross the River Aire by the stone bridge.

6 | Immediately turn right through a stone stile and walk down river on the left-hand bank. Follow the clear path to pass through two small gates, then follow the wall, which becomes a hedge, keeping it on your left.

7 | Just before an obvious footbridge takes the path off to the left, turn right across the field to a small gate stile in the wall. Through it, cross the river again and swing left for 40 metres, then turn left through a stone stile and kissing gate to carry on down with the river now on the left. Enter the wetland area and weave over bridges and dykes to pass to the right of the converted mill, through the carpark and onto the road. Turn right to find the village green.

equally inspiring **Gordale Scar**, a huge gorge carved by glacial melt water with an impressive waterfall leaping, in two stages, from a fissure in its face. Further on still is another waterfall known as Janet's Foss. Beside the waterfall is a cave that Janet, a friendly fairy, is reputed to inhabit. Three miles north of the scar is **Malham Tarn**, a glacial lake, which by way of an underground stream is the source of the River Aire, and Malham Tarn House, where such famous names as Ruskin, Darwin, and Charles Kingsley (author of *The Water Babies*) received inspiration.

ELSLACK
4 miles SW of Skipton off the A56

Overlooking the village is the 1,274 ft high Pinhaw Beacon from which there are some fine panoramic views over the heather covered moorland. During the Napoleonic Wars in the early 19th century, when there was great fear of an invasion from France, the beacon, one in a countrywide chain of communication beacons, was manned 24 hours a day. Unfortunately, during a raging blizzard on a January night in 1805, the lookout, Robert Wilkinson, died and was buried on the moor. His body was later exhumed and his grave can be seen in the parish churchyard to the northeast of the village.

THORNTON-IN-CRAVEN
5 miles SW of Skipton on the A56

This attractive village stands on the Pennine Way and from here there are magnificent views of Airedale and, towards, the west, Pendle Forest in Lancashire. Now a quiet place, during the Civil War the manor house was ruined by Royalist soldiers shortly after Cromwell had stayed here to attend a local wedding. The present house is situated opposite the original site. Past parish records associated with the 12th-century Church of St Mary are lost as they were accidentally burnt by the local rector.

EARBY
6 miles SW of Skipton on the A56

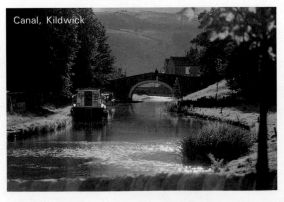

🏛 Museum of Yorkshire Dales Lead Mining

Though the Yorkshire Dales are thought of as a once thriving textile producer, lead-mining, for many centuries, was also a key industry. Housed in an old grammar school, that was founded in 1591 by Robert Windle, is the **Museum of Yorkshire Dales Lead Mining**, which was opened in 1971. The large collection, as well as the substantial documentation and indexing, has been put together by several local interest groups who began their work in 1945 when the Earby Mines Research Group was formed within the Earby Pothole Club. The museum, which has limited opening times, has many excellent displays including mine tubs, photographs, mine plans, small implements, mining machinery, and miners' personal belongings.

SILSDEN
4 miles SE of Skipton on the A6034

This well-contained stone built industrial town, which spreads uphill from the Leeds and Liverpool Canal, owes its development to the textile industry. Rows of terraced cottages and houses lie on the steep hillsides and there is newer housing on the outskirts of the town. It was the birthplace of Augustus Spencer, Principal of the Royal College of Art (1900 to 1920), whose

memorial can be seen in the 18th-century parish church.

Outside The King's Arms, in the centre of the village, stands an old mounting block, a survival from the days when this was a coaching and post house inn. The resident ghost probably dates back to that era as well.

LOTHERSDALE
7 miles NW of Keighley off the A629

A dramatic stretch of the Pennine Way passes through this village set in a deep valley in the heart of the moors. Charlotte Brontë knew the village well and in *Jane Eyre* the house she calls Gateshead is modelled on Lothersdale's Stonegappe, situated up on the hillside near the church.

KILDWICK
3 miles S of Skipton off the A629

🏛 Church of St Andrew

This picturesque little village, on the north bank of River Aire, is approached over a bridge that was built in the early 14th century by the canons of Bolton Priory. The village **Church of St Andrew** was also rebuilt around the 14th and 15th centuries, though the choir was extended to its unusually long

Canal, Kildwick

length sometime later, which gives the church is local name Lang Kirk o'Craven.

The River Aire is not the only waterway that passes through the village as it also lies on the banks of the Leeds and Liverpool Canal. Once a hive of industry with many spinning and weaving mills in the village and the surrounding area producing wool and silk yarn and cloth, the decline of the textile industry has caused many of the mills to close though some have now been converted to provide interesting accommodation or as offices for small business units. The canal, which until the 1930s was still in commercial use, is now the preserve of pleasure craft and Kildwick is a popular overnight mooring.

KEIGHLEY
10 miles NW of Bradford on the A650

- 🏛 Dalton Mill 🏛 🏛 Cliffe Castle & Museum
- 🏛 Keighley & Worth Valley Railway
- 🏛 Museum of Rail Travel

Lying at the junction of the Rivers Worth and Aire, this bustling textile and engineering town, despite its modern redevelopment, still retains a strangely nostalgic air of the Victorian Industrial Revolution. It was that era of rapid growth that created the town seen today, beginning at Low Mill in 1780, when cotton spinning on a factory scale was first introduced. Reminders of hardship endured by the many factory workers of that time can be seen in the labyrinth of ginnels and terraces that lie amid the many elaborately decorated mills. There are delightful carvings and on one early mill chimney are three heads, one wearing a top hat; in contrast is the classical French-styled **Dalton Mill** in Dalton Lane with its ornate viewing gallery.

The centre of Keighley is dominated by impressive Victorian civic buildings and a beautifully set out covered shopping precinct, where the statue of legendary local giant, Rombald, stands. The parish church, also in the centre, is famous as the site where Patrick Brontë often officiated at marriages. The graveyard contains 15th-century headstones, as well as a crude cross made from four carved heads, which is believed to be Saxon in origin. Above the town, by way of escaping the industrial past, one might enjoy a walk in Park Woods, taking the cobbled path to Thwaites Brow, which affords magnificent views of the town below.

Outside the town centre is **Cliffe Castle** which, despite its deceptive name, is in fact a grand late-19th-century mansion complete with a tower, battlements and parkland, which once belonged to local mill owners, the Butterfields. It now houses **Keighley Museum**, which concentrates on the fascinating local topography and geology of Airedale as well as the history of the town. Also housed in the museum is the hand loom, complete with unfinished cloth, that was used by Timmy Feather, the last hand loom weaver in England. Part of the building is still furnished and decorated in the lavish style of the 1880s.

To the south of Keighley the **Keighley and Worth Valley Railway** runs to Haworth and Oxenhope. This restored steam railway line, which is run completely by volunteers, passes through some attractive small villages and some notable stations complete with vintage advertising signs, gas lighting and coal fires in the waiting rooms. At Ingrow Station, **The Museum of Rail Travel** contains some fascinating items connected with Victorian travel, among them three small locomotives, coaches in various liveries, the clock from

Manchester's Mayfield Station, and an interesting collection of posters and other memorabilia from the golden age of steam.

HAINWORTH
1 miles SE of Keighley off the A650

⚹ Worth Way

The **Worth Way** is an interesting five mile walk from the heart of industrial Keighley to the eastern edge of the Worth Valley at Oxenhope. This landscape has changed little since the time when Mrs Gaskell wrote about the area while visiting Charlotte Brontë in 1856. En route, the Worth Way passes close to the village of Hainworth, which stands high on the hillside and commands some grand views of Harden Moor.

RIDDLESDEN
1 mile NE of Keighley off the A629

🏠 East Riddlesden Hall   ⚹ Three Peaks

Parts of **East Riddlesden Hall**, now a National Trust property, date back to Saxon times. The main building, however, was constructed in the 1630s by James Murgatroyd, a wealthy Halifax clothier and merchant. A fine example of a 17th-century manor house, the gabled hall is built of dark stone with mullioned windows, and it retains its original centre hall, superb period fireplaces, oak panelling, and plaster ceilings. The house is furnished in Jacobean style, which is complemented by carved likenesses of Charles Stuart and Henrietta Maria. East Riddlesden Hall also has one of the largest and most impressive timber framed barns in the North of England which now houses a collection of farm waggons and agricultural equipment. The hall is said to be haunted by the ghost of a

lady dressed in blue who wanders along the building's passageways and sets the child's cradle rocking.

Ribblesdale and the Three Peaks

The River Ribble, the source of which lies high up on bleak moorland to the northeast of Ingleton, passes through several ancient settlements before leaving the county of Yorkshire and flowing on into the mill town country of Lancashire. On opposite banks of the river, lie Settle and Giggleswick, which are overlooked by the towering white limestone cliffs of Castleberg Crag and Langcliffe Scar, parts of the mid-Craven fault.

Further north from these two market towns lies one of the most popular tourist centres in the dales, Ingleton, and high above the village are the famous **Three Peaks** of Ingleborough, Pen-y-ghent, and Whernside. The surrounding countryside is dominated by caves, potholes, and waterfalls and it is ideal country for all those who enjoy the outdoors.

The layer of limestone that lies across this whole area was laid down around 400 million years ago, when the shells of dead sea creatures and mud accumulated at the bottom of the

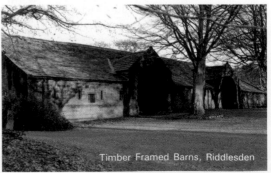
Timber Framed Barns, Riddlesden

🏠 historic building   📷 museum and heritage   🏛 historic site   ⚹ scenic attraction   🌱 flora and fauna

warm sea that covered a huge area of northern England. Much later, the layer of sandstone, known as millstone grit, was formed over the top. A lot is talked about the Craven Fault and, though it was formed by a series of mighty earthquakes, this all happened well over 30 million years ago so visitors need not worry about visiting the area. However, the line of the fault, where the land to the northwest was lifted up and the land to the southeast slipped down, is all too evident today. It was the action of water seeping into the limestone, which froze during the Ice Age, that has created the many caves and potholes of the area. Erosion, though this time on the surface, near Malham and elsewhere, formed the magnificent limestone pavements, while the Three Peaks, as they are capped by millstone grit, have stood the test of time and still stand proud.

This is farming country, and the traditional agricultural methods, along with the abundance of limestone, have given this region its own distinctive appeal. The high fells, composed of grits and sandstone, support heather moorlands and here can be found the only bird unique to Britain, the red grouse as well as several birds of prey. Meanwhile, the limestone areas support a much more varied plant life, though the woodlands are chiefly of ash. In these shaded places, among the wild garlic and lily of the valley, visitors might be lucky enough to come across roe deer, badgers and foxes.

Settle

🏛 Preston's Folly 📷 🚃 Settle to Carlisle Railway
🕳 Victoria Cave 🚃 Castleberg Crag

This small market town, which received its charter in 1249, still retains its thriving weekly market on Tuesdays. A busy stopping place in the days of the stagecoach, when travellers journeying between York and Lancaster and Kendal called here, Settle is now a popular place for visitors, walkers, and cyclists who stop in the town to take full advantage of the wide range of inns and hotels.

However, for most, Settle is best known for the famous **Settle to Carlisle Railway**, a proudly preserved memento of the glorious age of steam, although the regular daily services are now provided by diesel locomotives. The 72-mile line is still flanked by charming little signal boxes and stations that are a real tourist magnet. This attractive railway was built in the midst of great controversy and even greater cost, in both money and lives, earning it the dubious title of 'the line that should never have been built'. There is a churchyard at St Leonard's in Chapel-le-Dale where over 100 of the workers and miners, who laboured under the most adverse conditions, lie buried. Today, the trains still thunder over the 21 viaducts, through the 14 tunnels, and over the numerous bridges for which they gave their lives. Settle town itself is dominated by one of these huge viaducts as well as the towering limestone cliffs of **Castleberg Crag**, which offers spectacular views over the town. It can be reached by following the recently opened Tot Lord Woodland Trail.

Settle's architecture is very distinctive, in the main being Victorian sandstone buildings that all look as if they are born of the railway culture. Buildings of note include the arcaded Shambles, originally butchers' slaughter houses, the French-style Town Hall and the Victorian Music Hall. The town's oldest building is the 17th-century **Preston's Folly**, described as an extravaganza of mullioned windows and Tudor masonry. It is named after the man who created this anomalous fancy and impoverished himself in the process.

Apart from the grander structures on the main streets, there are charming little side streets, lined with Georgian and Jacobean cottages and criss-crossed with quirky little alleyways and ginnels with hidden courtyards and workshops of a time gone by.

Just outside the town, housed in an old cotton mill dating from the 1820s, is the Watershed Mill Visitor Centre. This charming place, on the banks of the River Ribble, offers a unique shopping experience.

The features of the surrounding countryside are equally interesting and, in particular, there is the fascinating **Victoria Cave**. Discovered in 1838 by Michael Horner, the cave has yielded finds of Roman relics, Stone Age artefacts, and even 120,000-year-old mammoth bones. Unfortunately, the instability of the rock in the area has caused the cave and the surrounding land to be closed to the public.

Around Settle

GIGGLESWICK
1 mile W of Settle off the A65

🏛 Church of St Alkelda 🏛 School

This ancient village, which lies below the limestone scar that is part of the Craven fault, is home to several interesting places including the 15th-century **Church of St Alkelda** and the well-known **Giggleswick School**. Alkelda is thought to have been a Saxon saint who was strangled for her faith, while the school, founded by James Carr, was granted a Royal Charter in 1553 by Edward VI. The school's fame stems from its observatory, which was used by the Astronomer Royal in 1927 to observe an eclipse of the sun. The school's chapel, the copper dome of which is a well-known local landmark, was built to

commemorate the Diamond Jubilee of Queen Victoria by Walter Morrison, a school governor who lived at Malham Tarn House.

Just to the north of Giggleswick can be found the famous Ebbing and Flowing Well, one of many in the area that owe their unusual name to the porous nature of the limestone of the area, which causes there sometimes to be water here and sometimes not.

RATHMELL
2 miles S of Settle off the A65

🐾 Horses Health Farm

From this small village, set beside the River Ribble, there are many footpaths along the riverbanks, through the nearby woods and up to Whelpstone Crag. An old farming community, the oldest farm here is dated 1689 and a little row of farm cottages called Cottage Fold are from around the same period.

Rathmell is also home to the **Horses Health Farm and Visitor Centre**, which was established in 1991 to provide a unique centre for the treatment of horses and ponies, and to put an edge on the fitness of performance animals. Within the centre are a hydrotherapy pool, solarium, an all-weather arena for schooling and a farrier's forge. The Visitor Centre was opened in 1998 in response to public interest in the work done here. Visitors can watch horses swimming in the pool and enjoying the solarium treatment, and cheer on the Racing Miniature Shetlands. The centre is only open on limited occasions - check before travelling.

LONG PRESTON
3 miles S of Settle on the A65

Hard to imagine today, but this pleasant village, which straddles the main road, was once larger than Leeds. Close to the pretty

Church of St Mary's, which dates back in part to the 12th century, the remains of a Roman encampment have been discovered. The other interesting building in Long Preston is Cromwell House which, so the legend goes, once gave refuge to the Puritan leader.

FEIZOR
3 miles NW of Settle off the A65

🐦 Yorkshire Dales Falconry & Conservation Centre

The village dates back to monastic times when it lay on the route from Kilnsey to the Lake District, which was much used by the monks of Fountains Abbey. Although both Fountains Abbey and Sawley Abbey had possessions in the area, there are few reminders of those times today. However, the **Yorkshire Dales Falconry & Conservation Centre** does bring visitors to this village. With demonstration flights held throughout the day, when the centre's wide range of birds of prey are seen flying free, and much else on offer it does make an interesting and unusual day out. The Centre was careful to re-create natural habitats, transporting 350 tons of limestone boulders to provide cliff-faced aviaries.

AUSTWICK
4 miles NW of Settle off the A65

🏛 Norber Boulders

This ancient village of stone cottages and crofts, dry stone walls, abandoned quarries, and patchwork hills was originally a Norse settlement: the name is Nordic for Eastern Settlement. The mostly 17th-century buildings, with their elaborately decorated stone lintels, flank what remains of the village green where the ancient cross stands as a reminder of when this was the head of a dozen neighbouring manors and the home of an annual cattle fair.

The most peculiar feature of the surrounding area has to be the **Norber Boulders**: a series of black boulders that stand on limestone pedestals, which, despite their contrived appearance, are a completely natural feature. They are also known locally as the Norber Erratics because they are anomalous – the grey silurian slate they are composed of usually occurs beneath limestone rather than on top. The mystery of their existence is explained by the fact that these huge rocks were originally deposited by glacial action at the end of the last Ice Age. Another distinctive local feature is the clapper bridge, a medieval structure made from large slabs of rock that span the local becks.

CLAPHAM
6 miles NW of Settle off the A65

🏛 Ingleborough Hall 🏛 Ingleborough Cave
🏛 Eldon Hall Cavern 🏛 Gaping Gill
🐦 🚶 Reginald Farrer Nature Trail

By far the largest building in the village is **Ingleborough Hall**, once the home of the Farrer family and now a centre for outdoor education. One member of the family, Reginald Farrer, was an internationally-renowned botanist and he was responsible for introducing many new plant species into the country. Many examples of his finds still exist in the older gardens of the village and in the hall's grounds and there is a particularly pleasant walk, the **Reginald Farrer Nature Trail**, which leads from Clapham to nearby Ingleborough Cave.

Though the whereabouts of **Ingleborough Cave** was known for centuries, it was not until the 19th century that its exploration was begun. One of the explorers, geologist Adam Sedgwick, is quoted as saying, 'we were forced to use our abdominal muscles as sledges and our mouths as candlesticks', which gives an excellent indication of the conditions the early potholers had to endure. However, their work proved worthwhile and the system is extremely extensive. Those visiting the caves today see only a small part of the five miles of caverns and tunnels though, fortunately, this easily accessible portion is spectacular. As well as exotic cave formations and illuminated pools, there is **Eldon Hall Cavern**, home to a vast mushroom bed.

This is an area that has a great abundance of natural waterfalls, but the waterfall seen near the village church is one of the very few that owes its existence to man. In the 1830s the Farrer family created a large lake, covering some seven acres of land, and the waterfall is the lake's overflow. As well as providing water for the village, a turbine was placed at the bottom of the waterfall and, with the help of the electrical power, Clapham was one of the first villages in the country to have street lighting. This is perhaps not as surprising as it might seem as Michael Faraday, the distinguished 19th-century scientist, was the son of the village blacksmith.

Overlooked by Ingleborough, close to the village, is the giant pothole known as **Gaping Gill**. Some 340 feet deep, the hole is part of the same underground limestone cave system as Ingleborough Cave and the main chamber is similar in size to York Minster. Twice a year, the public can gain access via a bosun's chair on a winch that is operated by local caving clubs.

NEWBY
7 miles NW of Settle off the A65

This tiny hamlet was originally situated about a mile south of its present position because, in the 17th century, the Great Plague decimated the village's population. The survivors moved away and rebuilt Newby and many of the buildings date from this time.

The village came under the direction of the monks of Furness Abbey and the remains of their walled garden can still be seen. By the Victorian era, Newby had become a thriving weaving community. However, the cottage industry was soon overtaken by the new factory systems and, by 1871, the village had once again returned to peace and quiet.

Ingleton

| 🏛 White Scar Caves 🏃 Waterfalls |
| 🐾 🏃 Ingleborough |

Mentioned in the *Domesday Book* – the name means 'beacon town' – Ingleton is certainly one of the most visited villages in the dales. As a gateway to the Three Peaks, it is also popular with walkers. From as long ago as the late 1700s, Ingleton has been famous for the splendid scenery and numerous caves that lie within a short distance, though some are harder to find and even harder to reach. The coming of the railway, which gave those working in the towns easy and cheap access to the countryside, greatly increased the numbers of visitors looking for clean, country air. Though Ingleton is no longer served by trains, the village is still dominated by the railway viaduct that spans the River Greta. The river, which is formed here by the meeting of the Rivers Twiss and Doe, is famous for its salmon leaps.

Discovered in 1865 by Joseph Carr, the **Ingleton Waterfalls**, which were not immediately made accessible to the public, have been delighting visitors since 1885. Along the four miles of scenic walks, the stretch of waterfalls includes those with such interesting names as Pecca Twin Falls, Holly Bush Spout, Thornton Force, and Baxengill Gorge.

🏠 historic building   🏛 museum and heritage   🏛 historic site   🐾 scenic attraction   🌿 flora and fauna

Dating from the Ice Age, **White Scar Caves** were only discovered in 1923 by an adventurous student named Christopher Long. Though he saw only by the light of a torch, standing alone in the vast underground cave now known as Battlefield Cavern must have been an awesome experience. It stretches for more than 330 feet, soaring in places to 100 feet high, with thousands of oddly-shaped stalactites dripping from its roof. The 80-minute guided tour of the longest show caves in Britain covers one mile and passes cascading waterfalls and curious cave formations such as the Devil's Tongue, the Arum Lily and the remarkably lifelike Judge's Head. The temperature inside the cave stays constant all year round at a cool 8°C (46°F) so don't forget to bring something warm. The caves lie a mile and a half from Ingleton on the B6255 road to Hawes.

Ingleborough, at 2,375 feet, is the middle summit of the Three Peaks. For over 2,000 years, the peak has been used as a beacon and a fortress and, as a result, it is perhaps the most interesting. A distinctive feature of the horizon for miles around as it is made of several layers of rock of differing hardness, there are several paths to the summit most of which begin their journey in Ingleton. As well as the fine views on a clear day, there are also several interesting features on top of the peak. The most recent of these are the remains of a tower that was built by a local mill owner, Mr Hornby Roughsedge. Though the intended use of the building is not known, its short history is well-documented. A grand opening was arranged on the summit and the celebrations, probably helped by a supply of ale, got a little out of hand when a group of men began tearing down the structure.

At the highest point is a triangulation point while, close by, a cross-shaped shelter has

been built that offers protection from the elements whatever their direction. The shelter acts as a reminder that the weather can change quickly in this area and a walk to the summit, however nice the day is at lower levels, should not be undertaken without careful thought as to suitable clothing.

To the east, on the edge of the summit plateau, are the remains of several ancient hut circles and, beyond, the remains of a wall. The Romans are known to have used Ingleborough as a signal station, but the wall may have been built by the Brigantes whose settlement on the mountain was called *Rigodunum*.

Around Ingleton

THORNTON-IN-LONSDALE
1 mile NW of Ingleton off the A65

🏛 Church of St Oswald

This small village of a few houses, an inn and an interesting church dates back to at least the 12th century and is probably much older. The 13th-century **Church of St Oswald** was unfortunately burnt almost to the ground in 1933 and only the tower remains of the original building. The rest of the church was rebuilt to resemble the extensive restoration work that was undertaken here in 1870. On an outside wall of the tower is an unusual carving of a rose, a thistle and a shamrock, which is believed to commemorate the union of England and Wales with Scotland and Ireland in 1801.

CHAPEL-LE-DALE
6 miles N of Ingleton on the B6255

⌘ ⚡ Whernside

Whernside, to the north of the village, is the highest of the Three Peaks, at 2,418 feet, and also the least popular of the mountains – consequently there are few paths to the summit. Just below the top are a number of tarns. Here, in 1917, it was noticed that they were frequented by black-headed gulls. Those walking to the top of the peak today will also see the birds, a reminder that the northwest coast is not so far away.

KEASDEN
4 miles S of Ingleton off the A65

Today, Keasden is a scattered farming community that is easily missed, but evidence from the 17th-century church records tell a different story. At that time there were some 40 farms here (now there are around 15) as well as many associated trades and craftsmen. The name Keasden comes from the Old English for 'cheese valley' and some of the farms still retain the vast stone weights of the cheese presses though, unfortunately, the recipe for the local cheese has been lost.

LOW BENTHAM
3 miles S of Ingleton on the B6480

Lying close to the county border with Lancashire and on the slopes of the Pennines, this village is pleasantly situated in the valley of the River Wenning, a tributary of the River Lune. Like many Pennine villages in the late 17th and early 18th centuries, Low Bentham was taken over by the textile industry and there was a linen mill here. After a time, the mill changed hands, and also direction, taking on the specialised task of spinning silk before that, too, ceased in the 1960s as a result of the increasing use of man-made fibres.

The growth in textiles in the area coincided with an increase in Quakerism within the parish and, in 1680, a meeting house was set up in the village. Established as a place of non-conformist worship, the village was also well-known as a place of Wesleyan Methodism by 1800.

LANGCLIFFE
1 mile N of Settle on the B6479

As its name suggests, Langcliffe lies in the shelter of the long cliff of the Craven fault where the millstone grit sandstone meets the silver grey of the limestone. Although the majority of the houses and cottages surrounding the central village green are built from the limestone, some sandstone has also been used, which gives this pretty village an added charm. The Victorian urn on the top of the Langcliffe Fountain was replaced by a stone cross, after the First World War, in memory of those villagers who died in the conflict.

STAINFORTH
1 mile N of Settle on the B6479

⚄ 杏 Catrigg and Stainforth Forces

This sheltered sheep-farming village owes its existence to the Cistercian monks who brought those animals to this area. The monks were also responsible for building the 14th-century stone packhorse bridge, which carries the road over the local beck, a tributary of the River Ribble.

Horton-in-Ribblesdale

Although the village is certainly old, there are few buildings that date beyond the days of the Civil War: during those turbulent times, much of Stainforth was destroyed.

Catrigg Force, found along a track known as Goat Scar Lane, is a fine waterfall that drops some 60 feet into a wooded pool, while to the west is **Stainforth Force** flowing over a series of rock shelves.

HORTON-IN-RIBBLESDALE
6 miles N of Settle on the B6479

🏛 St Oswald's Church ⚘ 🏃 Pen-y-ghent

First mentioned in the *Domesday Book*, the village, whose name means literally the settlement on the muddy land or marsh, was probably in existence long before the 11th century. The oldest building here is the 12th-century **St Oswald's Church**, which still shows signs of its Norman origins in the chevron designs over the south door. Inside, peculiarly, all the pillars lean to the south and, in the west window, there is an ancient piece of stained glass showing Thomas à Becket wearing his bishop's mitre.

This village is the ideal place from which to explore the limestone landscapes and green hills of Upper Ribblesdale. To the east lies **Pen-y-ghent** (2,273 feet high), one of the famous Three Peaks. For particularly energetic visitors to Horton, there is the demanding Three Peaks Challenge, which is organised by the Pen-y-ghent Café. The 24-mile hike takes in not only Pen-y-ghent but the other two peaks, Ingleborough and Whernside, and those completing the trek within 12 hours qualify for membership of the Three Peaks of Yorkshire Club. Less energetic walkers will be glad to hear that the café not only supplies well-earned refreshments, but also has copious local

information and runs a highly efficient safety service.

The whole of this area has been designated as being of Special Scientific Interest, mainly due to the need to conserve the swiftly eroding hillsides and paths. This is an ancient landscape, well worth the efforts to preserve its ash woodlands, primitive earthworks, and rare birdlife including the peregrine falcon, ring ouzel, curlew and golden plover. There are also a great many caves in the area, which add to the sense of romance and adventure one feels in this place.

There are several listed buildings in the area including Lodge Hall, which was formerly known as Ingman Lodge. Before the 20th century, a judge would travel around the countryside on horseback stopping to try cases rather than villagers commuting to major towns for their trials. Here, if anyone was found guilty of a capital crime, they were brought to Ingman Lodge to be hanged.

RIBBLEHEAD
10 miles N of Settle on the B6479

🏛 ⚘ Viaduct 🏛 Station & Visitor Centre

Lying close to the source of the River Ribble is an impressive structure, the **Ribblehead Viaduct**, which was built to carry the Settle to Carlisle Railway 165feet above the valley floor. Opened in 1876, after taking five years and 6,000 men to construct, its 24 arches span the dark moorland and it is overlooked by Whernside. A bleak and exposed site, the viaduct is often battered by strong winds, which, on occasion, can literally stop a train in its tracks. The **Ribblehead Station and Visitor Centre**, housed in former station buildings, presents an interpretive display showing the history of the line with special emphasis on the Ribblehead locality.

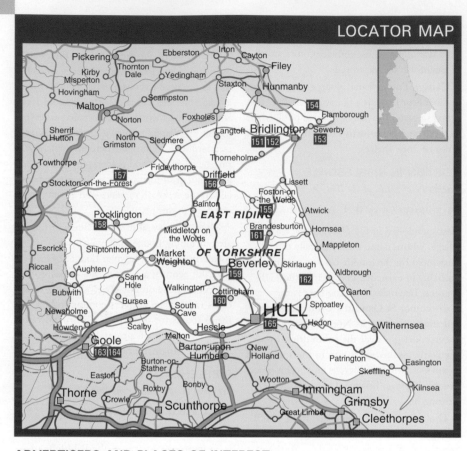

LOCATOR MAP

ADVERTISERS AND PLACES OF INTEREST

🏛 historic building   🏛 museum and heritage   🏛 historic site   ♧ scenic attraction   🌱 flora and fauna

5 | East Riding and the Wolds

'Fold upon fold of encircling hills, piled rich and golden' – such was the author Winifred Holtby's fond memory of the Wolds landscape. She was born in 1898 in Rudston on the northern edge of the Wolds, a village dominated by the prehistoric Rudston Monolith. This colossal block of stone, a daunting symbol of some misty pagan belief, stands challengingly close to Rudston's Christian parish church. Twenty-five feet (7.6m) high, it is the tallest standing stone in Britain. Winifred Holtby left the village and became a leading figure in London literary circles, editor of the influential magazine *Time and Tide*, but in her own books it was those 'rich and golden hills' that still enthralled her. In her most successful novel, *South Riding*, the fictional Riding is unmistakably recognisable as the Wolds among whose gently rolling acres she had spent her childhood.

Flamborough Head

The Wolds are a great crescent of chalk hills that sweep round from the coast near Flamborough Head to the outskirts of Hull. There were settlers here some 10,000 years ago – but never very many. In the early 1700s, Daniel Defoe described the area as 'very thin of towns and people' and also noted the 'great number of sheep'. Little has changed: the Wolds remain an unspoilt tract of scattered farmsteads and somnolent villages with one of the lowest population densities in the country. Artists remark on the striking quality of the light and air, and on the long views that open up, perhaps across undulating hills to the twin towers of Beverley Minster or to the great towers of the Minster at York. The Wolds never rise above 800 feet, but the open landscape makes them particularly vulnerable to winter snowstorms: children have been marooned in their schools; the dipping and twisting country roads, even in recent years, have been blocked for weeks at a time.

The southeastern corner of Yorkshire tends to be overlooked by many visitors. If only they knew what they were missing. Beverley is one of the most beguiling of Yorkshire towns and its Minster one of the greatest glories of Gothic architecture. Its parish church, built by a medieval guild, rivals the Minster in its grandeur and in its colourful interior. The whole town has the indefinable dignity you might expect from a community that was a capital of the East Riding in former days when Hull, just six miles to the south, was still a rather scruffy little port.

To the east and south of Beverley lies the old Land of Holderness, its character quite different from anywhere else in Yorkshire. A wide plain, it stretches to the coast where for aeons the land has been fighting an incessant, and losing, battle against the onslaught of North Sea billows. The whole length of the Holderness coast is being eroded at an average rate of three inches a year, but in some locations up to three feet or more gets gnawed away. At its southernmost tip, Spurn Point curls around the mouth of the Humber estuary, a cruelly exposed tip of land whose contours get re-arranged after every winter storm.

Withernsea Lighthouse

The coastal towns and villages have a bleached and scoured look to them, perhaps a little forbidding at first. It doesn't take long however for visitors to succumb to the appeal of this region of wide vistas, secluded villages and lonely shores.

Selby is the most southerly of the eight districts that make up the vast, sprawling county of North Yorkshire. Here, the level plains of the Vale of York stretch for miles – rich, agricultural land watered by the four great Yorkshire rivers, Ouse, Wharfe, Derwent and Aire, and by the Selby Canal. It is ideal country for walking and cycling, or for exploring the waterways on which a wide variety of rivercraft is available for hire. Just a few miles away, on the other side of the River Aire, traffic on the M62 hurtles between Leeds and Hull, but here you can still find quiet villages, inviting hostelries, and one of the country's most flamboyant stately homes, Carlton Towers.

Bridlington

- 🏛 Priory 🏛 Sewerby Hall 🏛 Bayle Museum
- 🏛 Old Penny Memories Museum
- 🏛 Beside the Seaside 🏛 Bondville Miniature Village

Bridlington lies at the northern tip of the crescent of hills that form the Wolds. The old town lies a mile inland from the bustling seaside resort with its manifold visitor amusements and attractions that has been understandably popular since early Victorian times. The attractions of a vast, 10-mile stretch of sandy beach distract most visitors from the less obvious beauties of **Bridlington Priory** in the old town. The Priory was once one of the wealthiest in England, but it was ruthlessly pillaged during

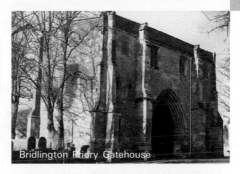

Bridlington Priory Gatehouse

the Reformation. Externally it is somewhat unprepossessing, but step inside and the majestic 13th-century nave is unforgettably impressive. A corner of the Priory churchyard recalls one of the most tragic days in the town's history. During a fearsome gale in January 1871, a whole fleet of ships

GALLERY 49

1 Market Place, Old Town, Bridlington,
East Yorkshire YO16 4QJ
Tel: 01262 679472
e-mail: GalleryForty-Nine@unicombox.co.uk
website: www.galleryforty-nine.com

A mile inland from the sandy beaches of the popular holiday resort lies the old town of Bridlington with its impressive priory and two fascinating museums. It is also gaining a name as a centre of high-quality shops and galleries, and prominent among the latter is **Gallery 49,** a double-fronted property at the top of the old town. Liz Hillman opened her gallery at the end of 2007, celebrating originality and seeking to promote work by East Riding and other regional artists. Ever-changing displays, supplemented by four annual exhibitions, showcase the work of contemporary artists and printmakers, jewellers, ceramicists, photographers and workers in textiles, glass and wood. Among the artists and makers who have featured here are artists Jill Carter, George Hainsworth, Jackie Stonehouse and Elaine Turnbull; jewellers Laura Alexander, Julie Folds and Jacqueline Warrington; ceramicists Michelle Freemantle, Jess Ball and Robert Goldsmith; printmaker Margaret Hockney; worker in wood Sue Harker; textile designer Corinne Young and

photographer of local and coastal scenes Nick Railer. The gallery is open Thursday, Friday and Saturday from 10.30 to 4.30, also Mondays in summer. Other times by arrangement.

📖 stories and anecdotes 🐦 famous people 🎨 art and craft 🎭 entertainment and sport 🚶 walks

EASTFIELD GARDEN CENTRE AND THE POTTING SHED CAFE

Easton Road, Bridlington, East Yorkshire YO16 4XF
Tel: 01262 676285
website: www.eastfield-gardencentre.co.uk

Eastfield Garden Centre and the Potting Shed Café has been run as a family business for the past 30 years, building up a loyal local clientele in the process. The Centre is stocked with a wide range of bulbs and plants, seeds, garden tools, pots, gravel, stone and fencing for landscaping, outdoor furniture, aquatic products and coldwater fish, as well as seasonal items for Christmas. Gift ideas include chinaware, paintings, sweets and preserves, and the staff are always ready to give advice on gardening matters. In the coffee shop anything from a light snack to a full meal is available.

foundered along the coast. Bridlington's lifeboat was launched but within minutes it was 'smashed to matchwood': most of its crew perished. Twenty bodies were washed ashore and later buried in the Priory churchyard: it was estimated that 10 times as many souls found a watery grave. This awesome tragedy is still recalled each year with a solemn service of remembrance when the lifeboat is drawn through the town.

Queen Henrietta Maria's visit to Bridlington was not as tragic, but it was certainly quite exciting. In February 1643, she landed here on a Dutch ship laden with arms and aid for her beleaguered husband, Charles I. Parliamentary naval vessels were in hot pursuit and having failed to capture their quarry, bombarded the town. Their cannon balls actually hit the Queen's lodging. Henrietta was forced to take cover in a ditch where, as she reported in a letter to her husband, 'the balls sang merrily over our heads, and a sergeant was killed not 20 paces from me'. At this point Her Majesty deemed it prudent to retreat to the safety of Boynton Hall, three miles inland and well beyond the range of the Parliamentary cannons.

These stirring events, and many others in the long history of Bridlington and its people, are vividly brought to life with the help of evocative old paintings, photographs and artefacts in the **Bayle Museum**. Quite apart from its fascinating exhibits, the museum is well worth visiting for its setting inside the old gatehouse to the town, built around 1390.

Penny arcades were once an indispensable feature of seaside resorts. At the **Old Penny Memories Museum** you can see 'What the Butler Saw', have your fortune told, test your strength on the Minigrip, discover your matrimonial prospects, pit your skills against a pinball machine, and enjoy a host of other entertainments on the extensive collection of antique slot machines – and all for just one old penny each. There's also a Sixties' café with lots of colourful memorabilia of the period.

A more recent attraction, opened at Easter 1999, is **Beside the Seaside**, an all-weather venue where visitors can take a promenade through Bridlington's heyday as a resort, sampling the sights, sounds and characters of a seaside town. Film shows and period amusements such as antique coin-in-the-slot games and a Punch & Judy Show, displays reconstructing a 1950s boarding house as well as the town's maritime history – the museum

Sewerby Hall and Gardens

Church Lane, Sewerby, Bridlington,
East Riding of Yorkshire YO15 1EA
Tel: 01262 673769
e-mail: sewerby.hall@eastriding.gov.uk
website: www.eastriding.gov.uk/sewerby/hall

Sewerby Hall is situated 2 miles north of the seaside resort of Bridlington, on the East Yorkshire coast. The grade I listed country house is set in 50 acres of landscaped gardens in a cliff top location on the outskirts of Sewerby village.

The house was built 1714-1720 by John Greame; bow wings and a portico were added in 1808-1811. Later additions include an Orangery and dining room. These days the magnificent ground floor Orangery and Swinton Rooms provide wonderful settings for civil marriage ceremonies, concerts and piano recitals, meetings, seminars, educational activities, art workshops and tea dances.

The Amy Johnson Room opened in 1959. The original collection was a gift from Amy's father in October 1958, and consisted of various souvenirs and mementoes presented to Amy and her husband, Jim Mollison. Since then, additional material received from other sources has further enhanced the Amy Johnson Collection.

The Lovely Gardens of Sewerby extend some 50 acres and offer magnificent views over Bridlington Bay, from Flamborough headland to the northeast, down to Spurn Point looking south. The gardens are a skilful blend of art and nature, with formal walks, terraces and contrasting woodland. The magnificent monkey puzzle trees of the pleasure gardens are reputed to be amongst the oldest in England, and there are many more fine specimen trees over 200 years old.

provides a satisfying experience for both the nostalgic and those with a general curiosity about the town's past.

On the northern outskirts of Bridlington is **Sewerby Hall** (see panel above), a monumental mansion built on the cusp of the Queen Anne and early Georgian years, between 1714 and 1720. Set in 50 acres of garden and parkland (where there's also a small zoo), the house was first opened to the public in 1936 by Amy Johnson, the dashing, Yorkshire-born pilot who had captured the public imagination by her daring solo flights to South Africa and Australia. The Museum of East Yorkshire here houses some fascinating memorabilia of Amy's pioneering feats along with displays of motor vehicles, archaeological finds and some remarkable paintings among which is perhaps the most famous portrait of Queen Henrietta Maria, wife of Charles I. Queen Henrietta loved this romantic image of herself as a young, carefree

stories and anecdotes 　 famous people 　 art and craft 　 entertainment and sport 　 walks

woman, but during the dark days of the Civil War she felt compelled to sell it to raise funds for the doomed Royalist cause that ended with her husband's execution. After passing through several hands, this haunting portrait of a queen touched by tragedy found its last resting place at Sewerby Hall.

Close by is **Bondville Miniature Village**, one of the finest model villages in the country. The display includes more than 1,000 handmade and painted characters, over 200 individual and unique villages, and carefully crafted scenes of everyday life, all set in a beautifully landscaped one-acre site. The Village is naturally popular with children who are fascinated by features such as the steam train crossing the tiny river and passing the harbour with its fishing boats and cruisers.

Flamborough Head

Around Bridlington

FLAMBOROUGH
4 miles NE of Bridlington on the B1255.

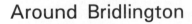
Flamborough Head   Danes Dyke

At **Flamborough Head**, sea and land are locked in an unremitting battle. At the North Landing, huge foam-spumed waves roll in between gigantic cliffs, slowly but remorselessly washing away the shoreline. Paradoxically, the outcome of this elemental conflict is to produce one of the most picturesque locations on the Yorkshire coast, much visited and much photographed.

Flamborough has a long and lively maritime history, not least for being the site of one of the most stubborn naval battles in British history, which occured off Flamborough Head between the American squadron led by John Paul Jones and two British ships of war. Taking place during the War of Independence in 1777, watchers on the coast were transfixed by this intense battle that eventually led to the defeat of the British, when British Captain Pearson surrendered his sword to John Paul Jones.

Victorian travel writers, also came to appreciate and honour Flamborough, not just for its dramatic setting but also for its people. They were so clannish and believed in such strange superstitions. No boat would ever set sail on a Sunday, wool could not be wound in lamplight, anyone who mentioned a hare or a pig while baiting the fishing lines was inviting doom. No fisherman would leave harbour unless he was wearing a navy-blue jersey, knitted by his wife in a cable diamond mesh peculiar to the village and still worn today. Every year the villagers would slash their way through Flamborough in a sword-dancing frenzy introduced here in the 8th century by the Vikings. Eventually, local fishermen grew weary of this primitive role, so although the sword dance still takes place it is now performed by boys from the primary school, wearing white trousers, red caps and the traditional navy-blue jerseys.

Flamborough's parish church contains two particularly interesting monuments. One is the tomb of Sir Marmaduke Constable, which shows him with his chest cut open to reveal his heart being devoured by a toad. The knight's death in 1518 had been caused, the story goes, by his swallowing the toad that had been drowsing in Sir Marmaduke's lunchtime pint of ale. The creature then devoured his heart. The other notable monument is a statue of St Oswald, patron saint of fishermen. This fishing connection is renewed every year, on the second Sunday in October, by a service dedicated to the Harvest of the Sea, when the area's seafarers gather together in a church decorated with crab pots and fishing nets.

Flamborough Head's first, and England's oldest surviving lighthouse, is the octagonal chalk tower on the landward side of the present lighthouse. Built in 1674, its beacon was a basket of burning coal. The lighthouse that is still in use was built in 1806. Originally signalling four white flashes, developments over the years have included a fog horn in 1859 and, in more recent years, a signal of radio bleeps. Until it was automated in 1995, it was the last manned lighthouse on the east coast.

Just to the north of Flamborough is **Danes Dyke**, a huge rampart four miles long designed to cut off the headland from hostile invaders. The Danes had nothing to do with it, the dyke was in place long before they arrived. Sometime during the Bronze or Stone Age, early Britons constructed this extraordinary defensive ditch. A mile and a quarter of its southern length is open to the public as a Nature Trail.

BEMPTON
3 miles N of Bridlington on the B1229

🦅 Bempton Cliffs

Bempton Cliffs, 400 feet high, mark the northernmost tip of the great belt of chalk that runs diagonally across England from the Isle of Wight to Flamborough Head. The sheer cliffs at Bempton provide an ideal nesting place for huge colonies of fulmars, guillemots, puffins and Britain's largest seabird, the gannet, with a wingspan six feet wide. In Victorian times, a popular holiday sport was to shoot the birds from boats. Above them, crowds gathered to watch gangs of 'climmers' make a hair-raising descent by rope down the cliffs to gather the birds' eggs. Most were sold for food, but many went to egg collectors. The climmers also massacred kittiwakes in their thousands: kittiwake feathers

Danes Dyke

RSPB's Bempton Cliffs Nature Reserve

RSPB North of England Office,
4 Benton Terrace, Sandyford Road,
Newcastle upon Tyne NE2 1QU
Tel: 01912 813366

The chalk cliffs at Bempton form part of England's largest seabird colony between Flamborough Head and Bempton. Over 200,000 seabirds breed on the reserve alone. As well as managing reserves such as this, the RSPB also works for the better protection of the marine environment.

For much of the year, the cliffs at Bempton are relatively quiet, but during the breeding season, between April and August, they are crammed with birds. The spectacle, noise, activity and smell all contribute to an overwhelming and memorable experience. As many seabird colonies are on remote islands, Bempton offers a rare opportunity to watch breeding seabirds at close quarters.

Both puffins and gannets breed at Bempton. About 2,000 pairs of puffins return to the cliffs to breed and each pair lays a single egg in a crevice in the rock face. Between May and the end of July they regularly visit their young with small fish, but by August, the young puffins have left the cliffs to spend the winter on the North Sea. Bempton has the largest mainland gannet colony (gannetry) in Britain. Over 2,500 pairs nest on the cliffs and can be seen here from January to November, but are most active between April and August when they are breeding. They will travel up to 60 miles to find food. When fishing, gannets can dive from heights of up to 130 feet, entering the water at up to 60 mph.

Six other species of seabirds nest at Bempton Cliffs.

were highly prized as accessories for hats and for stuffing mattresses. The first Bird Protection Act of 1869 was specifically designed to protect the kittiwakes at Bempton. A ban on collecting eggs here didn't come into force until 1954. Bempton Cliffs are now an **RSPB bird sanctuary** (see panel above), a refuge during the April to August breeding season for more than 200,000 seabirds making this the largest colony in England. The RSPB provides safe viewpoints allowing close-up watching, plus there's also a visitor centre, shop and refreshments.

BARMSTON
5 miles S of Bridlington off the A165

The road leading from Barmston village to the sands is just over half a mile long: in Viking times it stretched twice as far. The whole of this coast is being eroded at an average rate of three inches every year, and as much as three feet a year in the most vulnerable locations.

🏚 historic building   🏛 museum and heritage   🏚 historic site   ⚜ scenic attraction   🌱 flora and fauna

Fortunately, that still leaves plenty of time to visit Barmston's village pub before it tumbles into the sea!

CARNABY
2 miles SW of Bridlington on the A614

🏛 John Bull – World of Rock

Leaving Bridlington on the A166 will soon bring you to **John Bull – World of Rock**, which has become a premier tourist attraction in this part of East Yorkshire and really is a great day out. Whether you are young or old, you will be fascinated to discover the history and delights of making rock. The older generation will particularly revel in the smell of the old-fashioned way of making toffee and the interesting bygone displays. Animation and taped conversation accompany you as you explore the exhibition which is described as a total sensory experience. You can even try your hand at making a personalised stick of rock.

BURTON AGNES
5 miles SW of Bridlington on the A166

🏛 Manor House 🏛 Hall

The overwhelming attraction in this unspoilt village is the sublime Elizabethan mansion, Burton Agnes Hall, but visitors should not ignore **Burton Agnes Manor House** (English Heritage), a rare example of a Norman house, a building of great historical importance but burdened with a grimly functional architecture, almost 800 years old, that chills one's soul. As Lloyd Grossman might say, 'How could anyone live in a house like this?'

Burton Agnes Hall

Burton Agnes Hall is much more appealing. An outstanding Elizabethan house, built between 1598 and 1610 and little altered, Burton Agnes is particularly famous for its splendid Jacobean gatehouse, wondrously decorated ceilings and overmantels carved in oak, plaster and alabaster. It also has a valuable collection of paintings and furniture from between the 17th and 19th centuries – including a portrait of Oliver Cromwell 'warts and all' – and a large collection of Impressionist paintings. The gardens are extensive with more than 2,000 plants, a maze and giant board games in the Coloured Gardens. Other visitor facilities include an ice cream parlour, a dried-flower and herb shop, a children's animal corner, and an artists' studio. A very popular addition is the plant sales where numerous uncommon varieties can be obtained. The Impressionist Café, open throughout the Hall's season, seats 64 inside and, in good weather, 56 outside. Non-smoking, but licensed and offering only the very best in home cooking, the café serves some particularly delicious scones.

CRUCKLEY ANIMAL FARM

Foston on the Wolds, nr Driffield,
East Yorkshire YO25 8BS
Tel: 01262 488837
website: www.cruckley.co.uk

Cruckley Animal Farm nestles in the heart of rural
East Yorkshire, in a beautiful setting a world away
from the hustle and bustle of town life. Sue and
John Johnston's farm, established 20 years ago,
supports many different varieties of cattle, sheep,
pigs, horses, donkeys and poultry. Some breeds,
such as the Greyfaced Dartmoor and the Boreray (St Kilda)
sheep, are endangered, and the farm also safeguards six rare
breeds of British pigs. The farm has been approved by the
Rare Breeds Survival Trust since 1994 and is the only farm in
East Yorkshire to achieve this accolade – showing that
conservation is high on the list of priorities. Enormously
popular with families and children, the farm is home to more
than 40 varieties of farm animal. It stages daily milking
demonstrations and seasonal events such as harvesting and
sheep-clipping. The children's paddock, with its hand-reared
small animals, is a sure-fire winner with the youngsters. Hot

and cold drinks, ices, sweets, home-made cakes and themed gifts are sold in the tea room and
shop, and the farm has indoor and outdoor picnic areas and a children's play area. A 1½-mile
walkway meanders through the farm, revealing all kinds of wildlife, insects and wild flowers.
Cruckley Farm is open from Easter to the end of September.

FOSTON ON THE WOLDS

7 miles SW of Bridlington off the B1249 or
A165

🐾 Cruckley Animal Farm

If you can't tell a Gloucester Old Spot from a
Saddleback, or a Belted Galloway from a
Belgian Blue, then take a trip to **Cruckley
Animal Farm** (see panel above) where all will
become clear. Cruckley Farm is open daily
from the end of April until early October and
is clearly signposted.

Driffield

Located on the edge of the Wolds, Driffield is a
busy little market town at the heart of an
important corn-growing area. A cattle market is
held here every Thursday; a general market on
both Thursday and Saturday, and the annual
agricultural show has been going strong since
1854. All Saints Parish Church, dating back to
the 12th century has one of the highest towers
in the county and some lovely stained glass
windows portraying local nobility.

Driffield was once the capital of the Saxon
Kingdom of Dear, a vast domain extending
over the whole of Northumbria and
Yorkshire. It was a King of Dear who, for
administrative convenience, divided the
southern part of his realm into three parts,
'thriddings', a word that gradually evolved into
the famous 'Ridings' of Yorkshire.

Driffield has expanded westwards to meet
up with its smaller neighbour, Little Driffield.
A tablet in the church here claims that, in the
Saxon monastery that stood on this site,
Aldred, King of Northumbria, was buried in

KELLEYTHORPE FARM SHOP

Kelleythorpe Roundabout, Market Weighton Road, Driffield,
East Yorkshire YO25 9DW
Tel: 01377 256627
e-mail: hoppertiffy@hotmail.com
website: www.kelleythorpefarmshop.co.uk

At **Kelleythorpe Farm Shop** James and Tiffy Hopper and their
well-informed staff sell a wide selection of the best food,
almost all of it home or locally produced. Aberdeen Angus beef is home-reared and butchered on
site, and other goods include Berkshire and local pork, lamb from the Wolds, seasonal fruit and
vegetables, cheese, ice cream from Mr Moo and Cream of the Wolds, fresh baking daily, apple
juice and cordials. In the deli section are sausage rolls, pies, soups, and smoked and frozen fish.

AD 705 after being wounded in a battle
against the Danes.

Around Driffield

KIRKBURN

3 miles SW of Driffield on the A614

🏛 St Mary's Church

The architectural guru Nikolaus Pevsner
considered **St Mary's Church** in Kirkburn to
be one of the two best Norman parish
churches in the East Riding. Dating from 1119,
the church has an unusual tower staircase, a
richly carved and decorated Victorian screen,
and a spectacular early Norman font covered
with carved symbolic figures.

SLEDMERE

7 miles NW of Driffield on the B1252/B1253

🏛 Sledmere House 🏛 Eleanor Cross

🏛 Wagoners Memorial

Sledmere House is a noble Georgian
mansion built by the Sykes family in the 1750s
when this area was still a wilderness infested
with packs of marauding wolves. Inside, there
is fine furniture by Chippendale and Sheraton,
and decorated plasterwork by Joseph Rose.
The copy of a naked, and well-endowed,

Apollo Belvedere in the landing alcove must
have caused many a maidenly blush in
Victorian times, and the Turkish Room –
inspired by the Sultan's salon in Istanbul's
Valideh Mosque – is a dazzling example of
oriental opulence. Outside, the gardens and
the 220 acres of parkland were landscaped by
Capability Brown.

The Sykes family set a shining example to
other landowners in the Wolds by agricultural
improvements that transformed a 'blank and
barren tract of land' into one of the most
productive and best cultivated districts in the
county. They founded the famous Sledmere
Stud, and the second Sir Tatton Sykes spent
nearly two million pounds on building and
restoring churches in the area. Sledmere
House itself was ravaged by fire in 1911. Sir
Tatton was enjoying his favourite lunchtime
dessert of rice pudding when a servant rushed
in with news of the fire and urged him to
leave the house. 'First, I must finish my
pudding, finish my pudding,' he declared, and
did so. An armchair was set up for him on the
lawn and Sir Tatton, then 85 years old,
'followed the progress of the conflagration' as
the household staff laboured to rescue the
house's many treasures. After the fire,
Sledmere was quickly restored and the Sykes
family is still in residence. The house is open

to the public and music lovers should make sure they visit between 2 and 4pm when the enormous pipe organ is being played.

Across the road from Sledmere House are two remarkable, elaborately detailed, monuments. The **Eleanor Cross** – modelled on those set up by Edward I in memory of his Queen, was erected by Sir Tatton Sykes in 1900; the **Wagoners Memorial** designed by Sir Mark Sykes, commemorates the 1,000-strong company of men he raised from the Wolds during the First World War. Their knowledge of horses was invaluable in their role as members of the Army Service Corps. The finely-carved monument is like a 'storyboard', its panels depicting the Wagoners' varied duties during the war. In the main house itself, a recently redesigned exhibit tells the story of the Wagoners Special Reserve through old photographs, memorabilia and some of the medals they were awarded.

WEST LUTTON
10 miles NW of Driffield off the A64 or B1253

West Lutton Church is yet another of the

many repaired or restored by Sir Tatton Sykes in this corner of the East Riding. It stands overlooking the village green and pond, its lych gate reached by a tiny bridge.

WHARRAM PERCY
11 miles W of Driffield off the B1248

🏚 Deserted Medieval Village

A minor road off the B1248 leads to one of the most haunting sights in the county – the **Deserted Medieval Village** of Wharram Percy (English Heritage; free). There had been a settlement here for some 5,000 years, but by the late 1400s the village stood abandoned. For a while the church continued to serve the surrounding hamlets but, in time, that too became a ruin. The manor house of the Percy family who gave the village its name, peasant houses dating back to the 13th century, a corn mill, a cemetery complete with exposed skeletons – these sad memorials of a once thriving community stand windswept and desolate. Until fairly recently it was assumed that the villagers had been driven from their homes by the plague, but scholars are now certain that the cause was simple economics: the lords of the manor, the Percys, turned their lands from labour-intensive crop cultivation to sheep farming, which needed only a handful of shepherds. Unable to find work, the villagers drifted elsewhere.

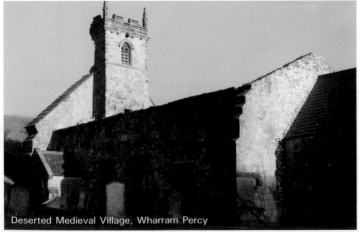
Deserted Medieval Village, Wharram Percy

🏛 historic building   🏚 museum and heritage   🏛 historic site   ♨ scenic attraction   🌿 flora and fauna

THE ROBERT FULLER GALLERY

Fotherdale Farm, Thixendale, nr Malton,
North Yorkshire YO17 9LS
Tel: 01759 368355
e-mail: mail@robertefuller.com
website: www.robertefuller.com

The **Robert Fuller Gallery** is located in picturesque countryside in the heart of the Yorkshire Wolds, just outside the village of Thixendale between Pocklington and Malton. Renowned wildlife artist Robert E Fuller invites visitors into his gallery of wildlife art originals, prints, bronzes and greetings cards. Robert has travelled the world to paint and photograph some of nature's best-loved creatures. He has visited many parts of Africa and India, and a recent trip took him to Antarctica, South Georgia and the Falklands. Although his paintings of British animals and birds are Robert's main speciality. The gallery, which Robert designed himself, is open from 11 am to 4.30 pm Monday to Saturday, & closed on Sundays. Occasionally Robert is away on field trips,

so it is always worth checking the website or ringing ahead if you are travelling from afar. If you are unable to visit the gallery itself, Robert's work can also be seen on the gallery's excellent website or by requesting a free colour catalogue.

HUGGATE

10 miles W of Great Driffield off the B1246 or B1248

🌿 Kipling Cotes Derby

Huggate is tucked away deep in the heart of the Wolds with two long-distance walks, the Minster Way and the Wolds Way, skirting it to the north and south. The village clusters around a large green with a well, which is claimed to be the deepest in England.

The pretty village of Warter, about four miles south of Huggate, is where the 'oldest horse race in the world' has its winning post. The post is inscribed with the date 1519, the year in which the **Kipling Cotes Derby** was first run. This demanding steeple chase, which passes through several parishes, is still held annually on the third Thursday in March.

POCKLINGTON

14 miles SW of Great Driffield off the A1079

🏛 Kilnwick Percy Hall 🎢 Penny Arcadia

🌱 Burnby Hall & Gardens 🎋 Londesborough Park

Set amidst rich agricultural land with the Wolds rising to the east, Pocklington is a lively market town with an unusual layout of twisting alleys running off the marketplace. Its splendid church, mostly 15th century but with fragments of an earlier Norman building, certainly justifies its title as the Cathedral of the Wolds (although strictly speaking, Pocklington is just outside the Wolds). William Wilberforce went to the old grammar school here and, a more dubious claim to fame, the last burning of a witch in England took place in Pocklington in 1630.

Founded in Anglo-Saxon times by 'Pocela's

POPPY'S CRAFT & WORKSHOP

20 Market Place, Pocklington,
York YO42 2AR
Tel/Fax: 01759 303120
website: www.craftypoppycanknit.com

Ever since she can remember Trisha Brant has been a compulsive knitter. So when she grew wiser and looked into possible career oportunities it made perfect sense for her to open her own shop and turn a passion into a business.

Fellow knitters come from near and far to **Poppy's Crafts & Workshop** in the heart of Pocklington to browse and buy. All the leading brands of wool are in stock, including Patons, Stylecraft, Wendy, Twilleys, King Cole, Debbie Bliss, Rowan and Mirasol. A wide selection of patterns is also always available.

Knitting is just one part of the business, which also sells a range of needles, buttons, ribbonsand cross-stitch and tapestry kits, together with various paper-crafting supplies (Kay & Co, Artoz, Provocraft) and jewellery and beading kits.

Trisha and her staff are always ready with expert help and advice on knitting and any related topic, and they also hold regular demonstrations and courses, either one-to-one or in small groups.

There's plenty to see in the lively market town of Pocklington, including the splendid mostly 15th century church and the world-famous gardens at Burnby Hall. But for anyone with an interest in knitting and associated crafts Poppy's is definitely the place to head for.

And for those who can't visit the shop itself, Poppy's offers an online shopping service – the goods can then be posted or customers can collect them at a time to suit them from the store. If you require more information on the online shopping service please visit the website for more details.

people', by the time the *Domesday Book* was compiled Pocklington was recorded as one of the only two boroughs in the East Riding. A market followed in the 13th century, but it was the building in 1815 of a canal linking the town to the River Ouse, and the later arrival of the railway, that set the seal on the town's prosperity.

A popular and unusual attraction in Pocklington is the **Penny Arcadia** housed in the Ritz Cinema in the marketplace. 'Not so much a museum as a fun palace', it contains a wonderful collection of penny-in-the-slot amusement machines ranging from 'What the Butler Saw' to fortune-telling and pinball machines.

Burnby Hall Gardens, Pocklington

The people of Pocklington have good reason to be grateful to Major PM Stewart who, on his death in 1962, bequeathed **Burnby Hall and Gardens** to the town. The eight acres of gardens are world-famous for the rare collection of water-lilies planted in the two large lakes. There are some 50 varieties and in the main flowering season from July to early September they present a dazzling spectacle. The Major and his wife had travelled extensively before settling down at Burnby and there's a small museum in the Hall displaying his collection of sporting trophies.

A mile outside the town is **Kilnwick Percy Hall**, a magnificent Georgian mansion built in 1784 for the Lord of the Manor of Pocklington. It now houses the Madhyamaka Centre, the largest Buddhist settlement in the western world. Visitors can stay in converted stables at the Hall, either to take part in one of the residential courses or to use as a base for exploring the area. There's a modest charge for full board; smoking and drinking alcohol are not allowed.

A few miles to the south of Pocklington is **Londesborough Park**, a 400-acre estate that was once owned by the legendary railway entrepreneur, George Hudson. He had the York to Market Weighton railway diverted here so that he could build himself a comfortable private station. The railway has now disappeared but part of its route is included in the popular long-distance footpath, the Wolds Way.

GOODMANHAM
14 miles SW of Driffield off the A1079

Goodmanham is always mentioned in accounts of early Christianity in northern England. During Saxon times, according to the Venerable Bede, there was a pagan temple at Goodmanham. In AD 627 its priest, Coifu, was converted to the Christian faith and with his own hands destroyed the heathen shrine. Coifu's conversion so impressed Edwin, King of Northumbria, that he also was baptised and made Christianity the official religion of his kingdom. Other versions of the story attribute King Edwin's conversion to a different cause. They say he was hopelessly enamoured of the beautiful Princess Aethelburh, daughter of the King of Kent. Aethelburh, however, was a Christian and she refused to marry Edwin until he had adopted her faith.

MARKET WEIGHTON
16 miles SW of Driffield on the A614/A1069

Market Weighton is a busy little town where mellow 18th-century houses cluster around an early Norman church. Buried somewhere in the churchyard is William Bradley, who was born at Market Weighton in 1787 and grew up to become the tallest man in England. He stood 7 feet 8 inches high and weighed 27 stone. William made a fortune by travelling the country and placing himself on display. He was even received at Court by George III who, taking a fancy to the giant, gave him a huge gold watch to wear across his chest.

SOUTH DALTON
13 miles SW of Driffield off the B1248

🏛 St Mary's Church

The most prominent church in East Yorkshire, **St Mary's Church**, has a soaring spire more than 200 feet high, an unmistakable landmark for miles around. Built in 1861 by Lord Beaumont Hotham, the church was designed by the famous Victorian architect JL Pearson and the elaborate internal and external decorations are well worth looking at.

Beverley

🏛 Minster	🏛 St Mary's Church	🏛 Market Cross
🏛 North Bar	🏛 Guildhall	🖎 Art Gallery
🏛 East Yorkshire Regimental Museum		
🖎 Picture Playhouse	🛦 Hudson Way	

'For those who do not know this town, there is a great surprise in store ... Beverley is made for walking and living in'. Such was the considered opinion of the late Poet Laureate, John Betjeman. In medieval times, Beverley was one of England's most prosperous towns and it remains one of the most gracious. Its greatest glory is the **Minster** whose twin towers, built in glowing magnesian limestone, soar above this, the oldest town in East Yorkshire. More than two centuries in the making, from around 1220 to 1450, the Minster provides a textbook demonstration of the evolving architectural styles of those years. Among its many treasures are superb, fine wood carvings from the Ripon school, and a 1,000 year old fridstol, or sanctuary seat. Carved from a single block of stone, the fridstol is a relic from the earlier Saxon church on this site. Under Saxon law, the fridstol provided refuge for any offender who managed to reach it. The canons would then try to resolve the dispute between the fugitive and his pursuer. If after 30 days no solution had been found, the seeker of sanctuary was given safe escort to the county boundary or the nearest port. The custom survived right up until Henry VIII's closure of the monasteries.

Unlike the plain-cut fridstol, the canopy of the 14th-century Percy Shrine is prodigal in its ornamentation – 'the finest piece of work of the finest craftsmen of the finest period in British building'. The behaviour of some

THE POPPY SEED COFFEE SHOP

13 North Bar Within, Beverley,
North Yorkshire HU17 8AP
Tel: 01482 871598

Just down the road from Beverley's medieval gateway, **The Poppy Seed Coffee Shop** offers excellent home-cooked fare.

Owned and run by mother-and-daughter team Rita Jones and Kate Johnson, who came here in 2001 after some years' cooking for weddings at a stately home, in the ground-floor delicatessen you will find a wholesome choice of quiches, patisseries, traditional puddings, sandwiches to take away and picnic 'kits'.

These are also served in the first-floor restaurant together with light lunches. The poppy Seed is licensed so alcoholic beverages along with superb coffees, teas and other beverages are all available.

The coffee shop is close to a good selection of fashionable shops with easy on-street parking nearby and is open from 9.00am to 5.00pm Monday to Saturday.

visitors to this glorious Shrine was not, it seems, always as reverent as it might have been. When Celia Fiennes toured the Minster in 1697 she recorded that the tomb of 'Great Percy, Earle of Northumberland was a little fallen in and a hole so bigg as many put their hands in and touch'd the body which was much of it entire.' Great Percy's remains are now decently concealed once again.

As well as the incomparable stone carvings on the shrine, the Minster also has a wealth of wonderful carvings in wood. Seek out those representing Stomach Ache, Toothache, Sciatica and Lumbago – four afflictions probably almost as fearsome to medieval people as the Four Riders of the Apocalypse.

Close by is the **North Bar,** the only one of the town's five medieval gatehouses to have survived. Unlike many towns in the Middle

Ages, Beverley did not have an encircling wall. Instead, the town fathers had a deep ditch excavated around it so that all goods had to pass through one of the gates and pay a toll. North Bar was built in 1409 and, with headroom of little more than 10 feet, is something of a traffic hazard, albeit a very attractive one. Next door is Bar House, in which Charles I and his sons stayed in the 1630s. Another visitor to the town, famous for very different reasons, was the highwayman Dick Turpin who, in 1739, was brought before a magistrates' hearing conducted at one of the town's inns. That inn has long since gone and its site is now occupied by the Beverley Arms.

St Mary's Church, just across the road from the Beverley Arms, tends to be overshadowed by the glories of Beverley Minster. But this is another superb medieval building, richly endowed with fine carvings, many brightly coloured, and striking sculptures. A series of ceiling panels depicts all the Kings of England from Sigebert (623-37) to Henry VI. Originally, four legendary kings were also included, but one of them was replaced in recent times by a portrait of George VI. Lewis Carroll visited St Mary's when he stayed with friends in the town and was very taken with a stone carving of a rabbit – the inspiration, it is believed, for the March Hare in *Alice in Wonderland*. Certainly the carving bears an uncanny resemblance to Tenniel's famous drawing of the Mad Hatter.

The wide market square in the heart of the town is graced by an elegant **Market Cross**, a circular pillared building rather like a small Greek temple. It bears the arms of Queen Anne in whose reign it was built at the expense of the town's two Members of Parliament. At that time, of course, parliamentary elections were flagrantly corrupt but at Beverley the tradition continued longer than in most places – in 1868 the author Anthony Trollope stood as a candidate here but was defeated in what was acknowledged as a breathtakingly fraudulent election.

The **Guildhall** nearby was built in 1762 and is still used as a courtroom. The impressive courtroom has an ornate plasterwork ceiling on which there is an imposing Royal Coat of Arms and also the familiar figure of Justice holding a pair of scales. Unusually, she is not wearing a blindfold. When an 18th-century town clerk was asked the reason for this departure from tradition, he replied, 'In Beverley, Justice is not blind.'

Just around the corner from the Guildhall was one of the oldest working cinemas in the country. The **Picture Playhouse** was built in

1866 and an inscription on its pediment still advertises its original function as the town's Corn Exchange.

Beverley boasts two separate museums and galleries. The **Beverley Art Gallery** contains an impressive collection of local works including those by Frederick Elwell RA and the **East Yorkshire Regimental Museum** has six rooms of exhibits chronicling the area's long association with the regiment.

From Beverley, serious walkers might care to follow some or all of the 15-mile **Hudson Way**, a level route that follows the track of the old railway from Beverley to Market Weighton. The Hudson Way wanders through the Wolds, sometimes deep in a cutting, sometimes high on an embankment, past an old windmill near Etton and through eerily abandoned stations.

Skidby Mill

ANN AT ELIZABETH FASHIONS

52 Finkle Street, Cottingham, nr Beverley,
East Yorkshire HU16 4AZ
Tel: 01482 841246

Ann Rhodes has been a successful retailer in the pleasant village of Cottingham since 2002, attracting clients from all over Yorkshire and the South for a range of clothes aimed mainly at the 30 + age group and spanning sizes 10 to 20. Among the brands stocked by **Ann at Elizabeth Fashions** are Chianti, Emreco, Poppy, Oscar B, Viz a Viz, Slimma and Lewinger. Located just off the Market Green, with free parking outside (1 hour), the shop is open from 9.30 to 4.30 Monday to Saturday.

Around Beverley

SKIDBY

6 miles S of Beverley off the A164

Mill   Museum of Rural Life

In the 1800s more than 200 windmills were scattered across the Wolds. Today, **Skidby Mill** is the only one still grinding grain and producing its own wholemeal flour. Built in 1821, it has three pairs of millstones powered by four 12-metre sails, each weighing more than 1.25 tonnes. Weather permitting, the mill is working every weekend, Bank Holidays and, during the school summer holidays, Wednesday to Sunday.

At the same location is the **Museum of East Riding Rural Life** where the farming year is chronicled using historic implements and fascinating photographs. The displays feature the Thompson family, who owned Skidby Mill for more than a century, and other local characters.

Holderness

'Lordings, there is in Yorkshire, as I guess/A marshy country called Holdernesse.'

With these words Chaucer begins the Summoner's story in *The Canterbury Tales*. It's not surprising that this area was then largely marshland since most of the land lies at less than 10 metres above sea level. The name Holderness comes from Viking times: a 'hold' was a man of high rank in the Danelaw, 'ness' has stayed in the language with its meaning of promontory. The precise boundaries of the Land of Holderness are clear enough to the east where it runs to the coast, and to the south where Holderness ends with Yorkshire itself at Spurn Point. They are less well-defined to the north and west where they run somewhere close to the great crescent of the Wolds. For the purposes of this book, we have taken as the northern limit of Holderness the village of Skipsea, where, as you'll discover in the next entry, some early Norman Lords of Holderness showed a remarkable lack of loyalty to their King.

Hornsea

Museum   Hornsea Mere   Butterfly World

This small coastal town can boast not only one of the most popular visitor attraction in Humberside, Freeport Hornsea, but also Yorkshire's largest freshwater lake, Hornsea Mere. **Hornsea Mere**, two miles long and one mile wide, provides a refuge for over 170 species of birds and a peaceful setting for many varieties of rare flowers. Human visitors are well provided for, too, with facilities for fishing, boating and sailing. Hornsea is also the home of the excellent sands, a church built with cobbles gathered from the shore, well-tended public gardens and a breezy, mile-long promenade all adding to the town's popularity.

The excellent **Hornsea Museum**, established in 1978, is a folk museum that has won numerous national awards over the years, as well as being featured several times on television. The museum occupies a Grade II listed building, a former farmhouse where successive generations of the Burn family lived for 300 years up until 1952. Their way of life, the personalities and characters who influenced the development of the town or found fame in other ways, are explored in meticulously restored rooms brimming with furniture, decorations, utensils and tools of the Victorian period. The kitchen, parlour and bedroom have fascinating displays of authentic contemporary artefacts, and the museum complex also includes a laundry, workshop, blacksmith's shop and a barn stocked with vintage agricultural implements.

In Swallow Cottage next door, children can undergo the Victorian school experience under the tutelage of 'Miss Grim' – writing on slates, having good deportment instilled and, above all, observing the maxim 'Silence is Golden'. The cottage also houses a comprehensive and varied display of early Hornsea pottery, various temporary exhibitions, and, in summer, a refreshment room for visitors. Remarkably, this outstanding museum is staffed entirely by volunteers.

For a satisfying shop-till-you-drop experience, Hornsea Freeport – the 'Independent State of Low Prices' – is hard to beat. There are discounts of up to 50 per cent or more on everything from designerwear, childrenswear and sportswear to chinaware, kitchenware and glassware. There are themed leisure attractions and bright, fun-filled play areas to keep the children amused.

Butterfly World is home to more than 200 species of colourful butterflies.

Around Hornsea

ATWICK
2 miles NW of Hornsea on the B1242

Like Hornsea, Atwick once had its own mere. Some years ago, excavations in its dried-up bed revealed fossilised remains of a huge Irish elk and the tusk of an ancient elephant, clear proof of the tropical climate East Yorkshire enjoyed in those far-off days. Atwick is a picturesque village on the coast, just two miles north of Hornsea. It has been a regular winner of local – and, in 1997, county – awards in the Britain in Bloom competition.

SKIPSEA
5 miles NW of Hornsea on the B1242

🏚 Skipsea Mere

When William the Conqueror granted Drogo de Bevrere the Lordship of Holderness, Drogo decided to raise his castle on an island in the shallow lake known as **Skipsea Mere**. Built mostly of timber, the castle had not long been completed when Drogo made the foolish mistake of murdering his wife. In the normal course of events, a Norman lord could murder whomever he wished, but Drogo's action was foolish because his wife

CHARTER'S BUTCHERS

30 Main Street, Brandesburton, nr Driffield,
East Yorkshire YO25 8RL
Tel: 01964 542232   Fax: 01964 502799

On the main street of Brandesburton, a short drive from Beverley, **Charter's Butchers** has been serving the local community since 1896. Kevan and Sarah Vickers are maintaining the shop's lofty and well-earned reputation for outstanding quality, service and product knowledge. Prime pork, beef, lamb and poultry are mainly locally sourced, and Charter's is also well-known for its cooked meats, pies and sausages – these come in some 15 tempting varieties, including pork & apple, sweet chilli, Stilton & chive and ham & tomato. The shop also sells bread and cakes, cheese, eggs, chutneys and preserves.

was a kinswoman of the Conqueror himself. Drogo was banished and his lands granted to a succession of other royal relatives, most of whom also came to a sticky end after becoming involved in rebellions and treasonable acts. The castle was finally abandoned in the mid-13th century and all that remains now is the great motte, or mound, on which it was built and the earth ramparts surrounding it.

WEST NEWTON

5 miles S of Hornsea off the B1238

🏠 Burton Constable Hall

Just outside the village of West Newton is **Burton Constable Hall** (see panel on page 304), named after Sir John Constable who in 1570 built a stately mansion here which incorporated parts of an even older house, dating back to the reign of King Stephen in the 1100s. The Hall was again remodelled, on Jacobean lines, in the 18th century and contains some fine work by Chippendale, Adam and James Wyatt. In the famous Long Gallery with its 15th-century Flemish stained glass, hangs a remarkable collection of paintings, among them Holbein's portraits of Sir Thomas Cranmer and Sir Thomas More, and Zucchero's Mary, Queen of Scots. Dragons abound in the dazzling Chinese Room, an exercise in oriental

exotica that long pre-dates the Prince Regent's similar extravaganza at the Brighton Pavilion. Thomas Chippendale himself designed the fantastical Dragon Chair, fit for a Ming Emperor. Outside, there are extensive parklands designed by Capability Brown, and apparently inspired by the gardens at Versailles. Perhaps it was this connection that motivated the Constable family to suggest loaning the Hall to Louis XVIII of France during his years of exile after the Revolution. (Louis politely declined the offer, preferring to settle rather closer to London, at Hartwell in Buckinghamshire.) Also in the grounds of the Hall are collections of agricultural machinery, horse-drawn carriages and 18th century scientific apparatus.

The descendants of the Constable family still bear the title 'Lords of Holderness' and along with it the rights to any flotsam and jetsam washed ashore on the Holderness peninsula. Many years ago, when the late Brigadier Chichester Constable was congratulated on enjoying such a privilege, he retorted, 'I also have to pay for burying, or otherwise disposing of, any whale grounded on the Holderness shore – and it costs me about £20 a time!' The huge bones of one such whale are still on show in the grounds of the Hall.

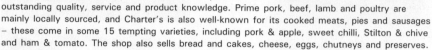

🎬 stories and anecdotes   🦜 famous people   🎨 art and craft   🖊 entertainment and sport   🚶 walks

Burton Constable Hall

Burton Constable, Hull,
East Yorkshire HU11 4LN
Tel: 01964 562400
website: www.burtonconstable.com

Burton Constable is a large Elizabethan mansion set in a 300-acre park with nearly 30 rooms open to the public. The interiors of faded splendour are filled with fine furniture, paintings and sculpture, a library of 5,000 books and a remarkable 18th century 'cabinet of curiosities', which contains fossils, natural history specimens and the most important collections of scientific instruments to be found in any country house. Occupied by the Constable family for over 400 years, the house still maintains the atmosphere of a home.

The superb 18th and 19th century interiors include a Gallery, Dining and Drawing Rooms, Bedrooms, Chapel and Chinese Room. A total of 30 rooms are open to view and these include some fascinating 'below stairs' areas such as an intriguing Lamp Room. Outside the house there are gardens with statues, a delightful orangery ornamented with coade stone, a stable block and wild fowl lakes set in 300 acres of parkland landscaped by 'Capability' Brown in the 1770s.

Withernsea

Lighthouse Spurn Point

The next place of interest down the Holderness coast is Withernsea. Long, golden sandy beaches stretch for miles both north and south, albeit a mile further inland than they were in the days of William the Conqueror. The old **Lighthouse** is a striking feature of the town and those energetic enough to climb the 127-foot tower are rewarded by some marvellous views from the lamp room. The lighthouse was decommissioned in 1976 and now houses two small museums. One is dedicated to the history of the Royal National Lifeboat Institution; the other to the actress Kay Kendall. Her grandfather helped build the lighthouse in 1892 and was the last coxswain of the deep sea lifeboat. Kay was born in Withernsea and later achieved great success in the London theatre as a sophisticated comedienne, but she is probably best remembered for the rousing trumpet solo she delivered in the Ealing Studios hit film *Genevieve*.

South of Withernsea stretches a desolate spit of flat windswept dunes. This is **Spurn Point**, which leads to Spurn Head, the narrow hook of ever-shifting sands that curls around the mouth of the Humber estuary. This bleak but curiously invigorating tag end of

Yorkshire is nevertheless heavily populated – by hundreds of species of rare and solitary wild fowl, by playful seals, and also by the small contingent of lifeboatmen who operate the only permanently manned lifeboat station in Britain. Please note that a toll is payable beyond the village of Kilnsea, and there is no car park. Access to Spurn Head is only on foot.

Around Withernsea

HALSHAM
4 miles W of Withernsea off the B1362

Halsham was once the seat of the Constable family, Lords of Holderness, before they moved to their new mansion at Burton Constable. On the edge of Halsham village, they left behind their imposing, domed mausoleum built in the late 1700s to house ancestors going back to the 12th century. The mausoleum is not open to the public but is clearly visible from the B1362 Hull to Withernsea road.

PATRINGTON
4 miles SW of Withernsea on the A1033

🏛 St Patrick's Church

Shortly after it was built, **St Patrick's Church** at Patrington was dubbed 'Queen of Holderness', and Queen it remains. This sublime church took more than 100 years to build, from around 1310 to 1420, and it is one of the most glorious examples of the eye-pleasing style known as English Decorated. Its spire soars almost 180 feet into the sky making it the most distinctive feature in the flat plains of Holderness. St Patrick's has the presence and proportions of a cathedral although only enjoying the status of a parish church. A parish church, nevertheless, which

St Patrick's Church, Patrington

experts consider among the finest dozen churches in Britain noted for architectural beauty. Patrington's parish council go further: a notice displayed inside St Patrick's states unequivocally, 'This is England's finest village Church.' Clustering around it, picturesque Dutch-style cottages complete an entrancing picture, and just to the east of the village, the Dutch theme continues in a fine old windmill.

HEDON
10 miles W of Withernsea off the A1033

🏛 Town Hall

Founded around AD 1130 by William le Gros, Lord of Holderness, Hedon quickly became a port and market town of great importance. A market still takes place every Wednesday in the square with its row of Georgian shops and early 19th-century dwellings. Nearby, in St Augustine's Gate, is the handsome **Town Hall,** built in 1692. From time to time, the town's Civic Silver Collection is on display

📷 stories and anecdotes 🐦 famous people 🎨 art and craft 🎭 entertainment and sport 🚶 walks

Hedon Haven

Distance: *4.2 miles (6.7 kilometres)*

Typical time: *120 mins*

Height gain: *10 metres*

Map: *Explorer 292 and 293*

Walk: *www.walkingworld.com ID:2582*

Contributor: *Sam Roebuck*

The walk is on well defined footpaths, tracks, country lanes, and town streets. There are toilet facilities at the start/end. There is a pub (The Haven Inn) at Hedon Haven, and a number of pubs in Hedon centre. The best picnic opportunities were the bridge at Waymark 10, or on a low wall just after Waymark 10, which offered a more comfortable place to sit, but a less scenic location.

DESCRIPTION:

The pretty little market town of Hedon, just to the east of Hull is worth a visit if you're in the area, having a number of little independent or specialist shops. The church, with its impressive tower, forms the start of the walk, and is visible much of the way round.

From here the walk takes us out to the outskirts of Hedon, and around a series of footpaths, tracks and lanes that circle around the outside of much of the town. This includes the last stretch, which is along the disused Hull to Withernsea railway line.

FEATURES:

Pub, Toilets, Play Area, Church, Cafe, Gift Shop, Food Shop, Mostly Flat, Public Transport, Restaurant, Tea Shop

WALK DIRECTIONS:

1 | From the market place, continue slightly up hill and along Souttergate, passing the church on your left. In 400m, take Twyers Lane on the left. Follow this 100m to a minor road.

2 | Cross, and continue ahead until the footpath forks by a footbridge. Do not cross the footbridge, but take either fork, as both paths run parallel, before rejoining. Continue for 500m as far as a kissing gate.

3 | Do not go through the gate, but turn sharp left to follow the ditch on your left. Follow this path for 50m until it swings sharp right at a footbridge. Cross the footbridge, and turn right. Follow the ditch on your right to a road. Cross the road, and continue in the same direction (along a wall) to a more major road (New Road).

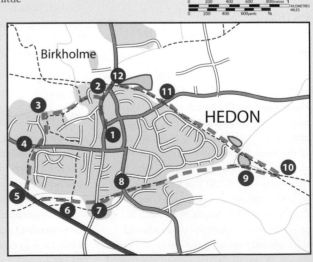

4 | Cross the road, and follow the ditch for 500m, until you are close to a main A-road.

5 | Cross an earth bridge on the right, to approach the main road. Just before the path climbs to the road, turn sharp left to parallel the road. Follow this path 20m to a footbridge. Cross the footbridge, and continue ahead, bearing slightly away from the main road, onto a track. The track leads to the Haven Inn.

6 | Continue ahead onto a lane. Follow it until it ends at a T-junction.

7 | Continue ahead onto a footpath that runs to the left of a garden. Follow this to a road.

8 | Cross the road, and continue in the original direction along a footpath. Follow this for 100m to a T-junction. Turn left to cross a footbridge, and then turn right. Continue along the bank for 100m, until the path turns left into a residential area. Do not turn left with the path, but continue ahead, following the bank. The path eventually runs into open country, and ends at a field.

9 | Go through the gate into the field, and continue in the same direction to the end of the field.

10 | At the end of the field, continue a few metres to a narrow track and turn sharp left. This is the disused Hull to Withernsea line. Follow it just over 1km to a road.

11 | Cross the road, and continue ahead on the railway path.

12 | At the next road, turn left. In a few metres, ignore a road that forks left, and continue along this road to the market place, and the start.

here. It includes the oldest civic mace in the country, dating back to 1415. Hedon Museum (free) has displays of maps, photographs and artefacts relating to the history of Hedon and Holderness; these are changed regularly. Limited opening times.

PAULL
12 miles W of Withernsea off the A1033

🏛 Fort Paull

Fort Paull's role as a frontier landing and watch point goes back to at least Viking times. Henry VIII built a fortress here in the mid-1500s; a second fort was added at the time of the Napoleonic wars. Charles I based himself at Fort Paull for some time during the Civil War; Winston Churchill visited its anti-aircraft installations during the Second World War.

Today, the spacious 10-acre site offers a wide variety of attractions for all the family. In addition to the historical displays, including rare period and contemporary artillery, there are classic military vehicles, an array of waxwork creations, a parade ground where re-enactments take place, an assault course for youngsters, a Bird of Prey Centre, museum, gift shop, bar and restaurant. The fort is open seven days a week, all year.

Selby

🏛 Abbey

In 1069 a young monk named Benedict, from Auxerre in France, had a vision. It's not known exactly what the vision was but it inspired him to set sail for York. As his ship was sailing up the Ouse near Selby, three swans flew in formation across its bows. (Three swans, incidentally, still form part of the town's coat of arms.) Interpreting this as a sign of the Holy Trinity, Benedict promptly went ashore and set

Selby Abbey

up a preaching cross under a great oak called the Stirhac. The small religious community he established went from strength to strength, acquiring many grants of land and, in 1100, permission to build a monastery. Over the course of the next 120 years, the great **Selby Abbey** slowly took shape, the massively heavy Norman style of the earlier building gradually modulating into the much more delicate early English style. All of the Abbey was built using a lovely cream-coloured stone.

Over the centuries this sublime church has suffered more than most. During the Civil War it was severely damaged by Cromwell's troops who destroyed many of its statues and smashed much of its stained glass. Then in 1690 the central tower collapsed. For years after that the Abbey was neglected and by the middle of the 18th century a wall had been built across the chancel so that the nave could

be used as a warehouse. That wall was removed during a major restoration during the 19th century, but in 1906 there was another calamity when a disastrous fire swept through the Abbey. Visiting this serene and peaceful church today it's difficult to believe that it has endured so many misfortunes and yet remains so beautiful. Throughout all the Abbey's troubles one particular feature survived intact – the famous Washington Window, which depicts the coat of arms of John de Washington, Prior of the Abbey around 1415 and a direct ancestor of George Washington. Prominently displayed in this heraldic device is the stars and stripes motif later adapted for the national flag of the United States. Guided tours of the cathedral are available.

Devotees of railway history will want to pay their respects to Selby's old railway station. Built at the incredibly early date of 1834 it is the oldest surviving station in Britain. From Selby the railway track runs straight as a ruler for 18 miles to Hull – the longest such stretch in Britain.

Around Selby

SOUTH MILFORD
9 miles W of Selby off the A162

🏛 Steeton Hall Gatehouse

About nine miles west of Selby, near the village of South Milford, is the imposing 14th century **Steeton Hall Gatehouse**, all that remains of a medieval castle once owned by the Fairfax family. A forebear of the famous Cromwellian general is said to have ridden out from here on his way to carry off one of the nuns at Nun Appleton Priory to make her his bride. He was Sir William Fairfax; she was Isabel Thwaites, a wealthy heiress.

SHERBURN-IN-ELMET

10 miles W of Selby on the A162

🏛 All Saints' Church

This attractive village was once the capital of
the Celtic Kingdom of Elmete. Well worth
visiting is **All Saints' Church**, which stands on
a hill to the west and dates from about 1120. Its
great glory is the nave with its mighty Norman
pillars and arcades. A curiosity here is a 15th
century Janus cross that was discovered in the
churchyard during the 1770s. The vicar and
churchwarden of the time both claimed it as
their own. Unable to resolve their dispute, they
had the cross sawn in half: the two beautifully
carved segments are displayed on opposite
sides of the south aisle.

RICCALL

4 miles N of Selby on the A19

🌿 Skipwith Common Nature Reserve

The ancient village of Riccall was mentioned
in the *Domesday Book* and has a church that
was built not long after. The south doorway
of the church dates back to about 1160 and
its fine details have been wellpreserved by a
porch added in the 15th century. The village's
great moment in history came in 1066 when
the King Harold Hardrada of Norway and
Earl Tostig sailed this far up the Ouse with
some 300 ships. They had come to claim
Northumbria from Tostig's half-brother King
Harold of England but they were
comprehensively defeated at the Battle of
Stamford Bridge.

Riccall is popular with walkers: from the
village you can either go southwards alongside
the River Ouse to Selby, or strike northwards
towards Bishopthorpe on the outskirts of
York following the track of the dismantled
York to Selby railway. This latter path is part
of the 150-mile-long Trans Pennine Trail

linking Liverpool and Hull.

Just to the south of Skipwith, the Yorkshire
Wildlife Trust maintains the **Skipwith
Common Nature Reserve.** This 500 acres
of lowland heath is one of the last such areas
remaining in the north of England and is of
national importance. The principal interest is
the variety of insect and birdlife, but the
reserve also contains a number of ancient
burial sites.

WEST HADDLESEY

5 miles SW of Selby on the A19

🌿 Yorkshire Garden World

At **Yorkshire Garden World** gardeners will
find endless inspiration in its six acres of
beautiful display and nursery gardens.
Organically grown herbs, heathers,
ornamental perennials, wild flowers and
climbers are all on sale; the gift shop has a
huge variety of home-made crafts, herbal
products, Leeds pottery and garden products;
and the many different gardens include a
Heather and Conifer Garden, an
Aromatherapy Garden, an Open Air Herb
Museum, a Lovers' Garden, and the Hall Owl
Maze for children.

CARLTON

6 miles S of Selby on the A1041

🏛 Carlton Towers

A mile or so south of Camblesforth, off the
A1041, is **Carlton Towers**, a stately home that
should on no account be missed. This
extraordinary building, 'something between
the Houses of Parliament and St Pancras
Station', was created in the 1870s by two
young English eccentrics, Henry, 9th Lord
Beaumont, and Edward Welby Pugin, son of
the eminent Victorian architect, AG Pugin.
Together, they transformed a traditional

Jacobean house into an exuberant mock medieval fantasy in stone, abounding with turrets, towers, gargoyles and heraldic shields. The richly-decorated High Victorian interior, designed in the manner of medieval banqueting halls, contains a minstrels' gallery and a vast Venetian-style drawing room. Both Beaumont and Pugin died in their forties, both bankrupt. Carlton Towers is now the Yorkshire home of the Duke of Norfolk and is open to the public during the summer months.

In Carlton village the Comus Inn is the only licensed premises in the country to bear that name. It is believed to have been named after the Greek god of sensual pleasure, Comus, the son of Bacchus.

About three miles northeast of Carlton is the village of Drax, which, as well as providing Ian Fleming with a sinister-sounding name for one of the villains in his James Bond thrillers, is also home to the largest coal-fired power station in Europe. Drax's vast cooling towers dominate the low-lying ground between the rivers Ouse and Aire. The power station has found an unusual way of harnessing its waste heat - by channelling some of it to a huge complex of glasshouses covering 20 acres; part of the heat goes to specially constructed ponds in which young eels are bred for the export market. Guided tours of the power station are available by prior arrangement.

GOOLE
10 miles SE of Selby on the A614

🏛 Waterways Museum   🏛 Museum & Art Gallery

Britain's most inland port, some 50 miles from the sea, Goole lies at the hub of a waterways

CHUCKS AND CHEESE

79 Pasture Road, Goole, East Yorkshire DN14 6BP
Tel: 01405 768748
e-mail: chucksncheese@yahoo.co.uk   website: www.chucksandcheese.co.uk

Chucks and Cheese is a highly respected specialist food and drink shop on Goole's top shopping street. Up to 80 cheeses, most of them British, are on display, along with Mrs Darlington's

chutneys, preserves and local honey, Longley Farm yoghurts and Brymor ice cream from Masham. All the eggs come from their own hens, which they rear from day-old chicks. They lay in barns at their poultry farm at nearby Pollington.

Waterways Museum, Goole

network that includes the River Ouse, the River Don (known here as the Dutch River), the River Aire and the Aire & Calder Navigation. The **Waterways Museum**, located on the dockside, tells the story of Goole's development as a canal terminus and also as a port connecting to the North Sea. The museum displays model ships and many photographs dating from 1905 to the present day, and visitors can explore an original Humber Keel, *Sobriety*, and watch crafts people at work. There are also occasional short boat trips available.

More of the town's history is in evidence at **Goole Museum and Art Gallery** which displays ship models, marine paintings and a changing programme of exhibitions. Other attractions in the town include its refurbished

Victorian Market Hall, open all year Wednesday to Saturday, and a well-equipped Leisure Centre, which provides a wide range of facilities for all ages.

HEMINGBROUGH
4 miles E of Selby off the A63

🏛 St Mary's Church

Anyone interested in remarkable churches should seek out **St Mary's Church** at Hemingbrough. Built in a pale rose-coloured brick, it has an extraordinarily lofty and elegant spire soaring 190 feet high and, inside, what is believed to be Britain's oldest misericord. Misericords are hinged wooden seats for the choir that can be folded back when they stand to sing. Medieval woodcarvers delighted in adorning the underside of the seat with intricate carvings. The misericord at Hemingbrough dates back to around AD 1200.

HOWDEN
9 miles E of Selby on the A63

🏛 Minster   🏛 Wressle Castle

🏛 Real Aeroplane Museum

Despite the fact that its chancel collapsed in 1696 and has not been used for worship ever

Howden Minster

Barnes Wallis knew Howden well: he lived here while working on the R100 airship, which was built at Hedon airfield nearby. It made its maiden flight in 1929 and successfully crossed the Atlantic. At the nearby Breighton Aerodrome is the **Real Aeroplane Museum**, which illustrates the history of flight through the work of Yorkshire aviation pioneers.

About four miles northwest of Howden are the striking remains of **Wressle Castle**, built in 1380 for Sir Henry Percy and the only surviving example in East Yorkshire of a medieval fortified house. At the end of the Civil War, three of the castle's sides were pulled down and much of the rest was destroyed by fire in 1796. But two massive towers with walls six feet thick, the hall and kitchens remain. The castle is not open to the public, but there are excellent views from the village road and from a footpath that runs alongside the River Derwent. A fine old windmill nearby provides an extra visual bonus.

since, **Howden Minster** is still one of the largest parish churches in East Yorkshire and also one of its most impressive, cathedral-like in size. From the top of its soaring tower, 135 feet high, there are wonderful views of the surrounding countryside – but it's not for the faint-hearted. The ruined chapter house, lavishly decorated with a wealth of carved mouldings, has been described as one of the most exquisite small buildings in England.

When the medieval Prince-Bishops of Durham held sway over most of northern England, they built a palace at Howden which they used as a pied-à-terre during their semi-royal progresses and as a summer residence. The Hall of that 14th-century palace still stands, although much altered now.

Howden town is a pleasing jumble of narrow, flagged and setted streets with a picturesque stone and brick Market Hall in the marketplace. The celebrated aircraft designer

Hull

🏛 Wilberforce House Museum	🏛 Maritime Museum
🏛 Spurn Lightship	🏛 Streetlife Transport Museum
🐾 The Deep	🌿 Ferens Art Gallery

During the Second World War, Hull was mercilessly battered by the Luftwaffe: 7,000 of its people were killed and 92 per cent of its houses suffered bomb damage. Then in the post-war years its once huge fishing fleet steadily dwindled. But Hull has risen phoenix-like from those ashes and is today the fastest-growing port in England. The port area extends for seven miles along the Humber with 10 miles of quays servicing a constant flow of commercial traffic arriving from, or departing for, every quarter of the globe. Every day, a succession of vehicle ferries link the city to the

European gateways of Zeebrugge and Rotterdam. Hull is unmistakably part of Yorkshire, but it also has the freewheeling, open-minded character of a cosmopolitan port.

Hull's history as an important port goes back to 1293 when Edward I, travelling north on his way to fight the Scots, stopped off here and immediately recognised the potential of the muddy junction where the River Hull flows into the Humber. The king bought the land from the monks of Meaux Abbey (at the usual royal discount) and the settlement thenceforth was known as 'Kinges town upon Hull'.

The port grew steadily through the centuries and at one time had the largest fishing fleet of any port in the country with more than 300 trawlers on its register. The port's rather primitive facilities were greatly improved by the construction of a state-of-the-art dock in 1778. Now superseded, that dock has been converted into the handsome Queen's Gardens, one of the many attractive open spaces created by this flower-conscious city which also loves lining its streets with trees, setting up fountains here and there, and planting flower beds in any available space. And waymarked walks such as the **Maritime Heritage Trail** and the Fish Pavement Trail make the most of the city's dramatic waterfront.

A visit to Hull is an exhilarating experience at any time of the year but especially so in October. Back in the late 1200s the city was granted a charter to hold an autumn fair. This began as a fairly modest cattle and sheep mart but over the centuries it burgeoned into the largest gathering of its kind in Europe. Hull Fair is now a nine day extravaganza occupying a 14-acre site and offering every imaginable variety of entertainment. That takes care of October, but Hull also hosts an Easter Festival, an International Festival (some 300 events from mid-June to late July), a Jazz on the Waterfront celebration (August), an International Sea Shanty Festival (September) and a Literature Festival in November.

Throughout the rest of the year, Hull's tourism office modestly suggests you explore its 'Marvellous Museums – Fabulous and Free' – a quite remarkable collection of eight historic houses, art galleries and museums. Perhaps the most evocative is the **Wilberforce House Museum** in the old High Street. William Wilberforce was born here in 1759 and, later, it was from here that he and his father lavished thousands of pounds in bribes to get William elected as Hull's Member of Parliament. Nothing unusual about that kind of corruption at the time, but William then redeemed himself by his resolute opposition to slavery. His campaign took more than 30 years and William was already on his deathbed before a reluctant Parliament finally outlawed the despicable trade. The museum presents a shaming history of the slave trade along with a more uplifting story of Wilberforce's efforts to eliminate it for ever.

Other stars of the 'Magnificent Eight' are **The Ferens Art Gallery** which houses a sumptuous collection of paintings and sculpture that ranges from European Old Masters (including some Canalettos and works by Franz Hals), to challenging contemporary art; the **Hull Maritime Museum**, which celebrates seven centuries of Hull's maritime heritage and includes a fine collection of scrimshaw. A more unusual museum is the **Spurn Lightship.** Once stationed on active duty 4.5 miles east of Spurn Point, the 200-ton, 33-metre long craft is now moored in Hull's vibrant Marina. Visitors can explore the 75-year-old vessel with the help of its knowledgeable crew. The city's noisiest museum is the **Streetlife Transport Museum**, which traces 200 years of transport history. Visitors are transported back to the days of horse-drawn carriages, steam trains, trams and penny-farthing cycles. There are curiosities such as the 'Velocipede', the Automobile à Vapeur (an early steam-driven car), and Lady Chesterfield's ornamental sleigh, decorated with a swan, rearing unicorn and a panoply of bells to herald her approach.

The Deep (see panel below) advertises itself as the World's Only Submarium. Its huge main tank contains 2.5 million litres of water, 87 tonnes of salt – and some fearsome Sand Tiger and Leopard sharks. Visitors can walk the ocean floor in the world's deepest viewing tunnel, pilot a submarine in the futuristic research station, Deep Blue One, and ride in the underwater lift surrounded by sharks, rays, potato grouper, golden trevally, Napoleon wrasse, and hundreds of other sea creatures.

Before leaving the city, make sure you see two of its more unusual features. Firstly, visitors to Hull soon become aware of its unique public telephones. They are still the traditional, curvy-topped, heavily-barred boxes, but with the distinctive difference that Hull's are all painted a gleaming white. What isn't apparent is that by some bureaucratic quirk, Hull remained the only municipally owned telephone company in Britain until it was floated on the Stock Exchange, as Kingston Communications, early in 2000. The sale brought the City Council a huge windfall. The second unusual feature of Hull is found in Nelson Street where you can avail yourself of award-winning loos. These spotless conveniences, complete with hanging baskets of flowers, have become a tourist attraction in their own right. The poet Philip Larkin was the librarian of Hull University from 1955 until his death in 1985. His funeral was held in the Church of St Mary the Virgin, the University Church, and he is buried at Cottingham under a simple white gravestone inscribed ' writer'.

The Deep

Hull, East Yorkshire HU1 4DP
Tel: 01482 381000
website: www.thedeep.co.uk

Welcome to The Deep, one of the most spectacular aquariums in the world. This award-winning Yorkshire family attraction is home to 40 sharks and over 3,500 fish. The dramatic building designed by Sir Terry Farrell is located in Hull on the Humber Estuary, just an hour from York. The Deep is operated as a charity dedicated to increasing enjoyment and understanding of the world's oceans.

Behind the scenes a team of dedicated marine biologists care for all of the animals at The Deep as well as carrying out vital research into the marine environment. It first opened its doors in March 2002 and so far has welcomed over 2 million visitors from the UK and abroad.

Using a combination of hands on interactives, audiovisual presentations and living exhibits it tells the story of the world's oceans. Visitors will be taken on a journey from the beginning of time through to the present day oceans and the icy darkness of a futuristic Deep-Sea research lab, Deep Blue one.

🏛 historic building 🏛 museum and heritage 🏛 historic site ⚘ scenic attraction 🌿 flora and fauna

Around Hull

HESSLE
5 miles W of Hull off the A63

🏛 Humber Bridge 🚶 Humber Bridge Country Park

At Hessle the River Humber narrows and it was here that the Romans maintained a ferry, the *Transitus Maximus*, a vital link in the route between Lincoln and York. The ferry remained in operation for almost 2000 years until it was replaced in 1981 by the **Humber Bridge** whose mighty pylons soar more than 500 feet above the village.

It is undoubtedly one of the most impressive bridges on earth, and also one of the least used – someone described it as the least likely place in Britain to find a traffic jam. With an overall length of 2,428 yards (2,220m), it is one of the world's longest single-span bridges. For more than a third of a mile only four concrete pillars, two at each end, are saving you from a watery death. From these huge pylons, 510 feet (155m) high, gossamer cables of thin-wired steel support a gently curving roadway. Both sets of pylons rise vertically, but because of the curvature of the earth they actually lean away from each other by several inches. The bridge is particularly striking at night when the vast structure is floodlit.

The great bridge dwarfs Cliff Mill, built in 1810 to mill the local chalk. It remained wind-driven until 1925 when a gas engine was installed. Although it is no longer working, the mill provides a scenic feature within the **Humber Bridge Country Park**. This well laid out park gives visitors a true back-to-nature tour a short distance from one of modern man's greatest feats of engineering. The former chalk quarry has been attractively landscaped, providing a nature trail, extensive walks through woodlands and meadows, picnic and play areas, and picturesque water features.

WELTON
10 miles W of Hull off the A63

A little further south is the pretty village of Welton where a stream flows past the green, under bridges and into a tree-encircled duck pond. It has a church dating from Norman times, which boasts a striking 13th-century doorway and Pre-Raphaelite windows made by William Morris' company of craftsmen. In the graveyard stands a memorial to Jeremiah Found, a resilient local reputed to have outlived eight wives.

The notorious highwayman Dick Turpin was not a local but his villainous career came to an end at Welton village when he was apprehended inside the Green Dragon Inn. Local legend has it that this establishment gave him hospitality before he was taken off to the magistrates at Beverley who committed him to the Assizes at York where he was found guilty and hanged in 1739.

BRANTINGHAM
11 miles W of Hull off the A63

🏛 War Memorial

The village of Brantingham, just off the A63, is worth a short diversion to see its remarkable **War Memorial**, once described as 'lovingly awful'. Conceived on a monumental scale, the memorial was built using masonry recycled from Hull's old Guildhall when that was being reconstructed in 1914. Various stone urns placed around the village came from the same source.

LOCATOR MAP

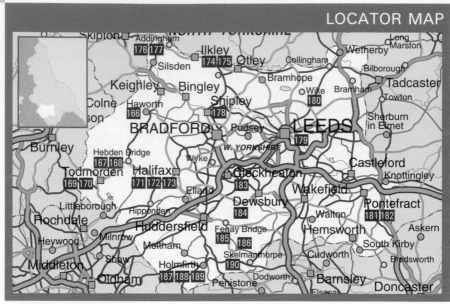

ADVERTISERS AND PLACES OF INTEREST

🏛 historic building   🏛 museum and heritage   🏛 historic site   🌳 scenic attraction   🌿 flora and fauna

6| West Yorkshire

West Yorkshire, while having the scenery of the Pennines, is still dominated by the effects of the Industrial Revolution that turned this region into one of the world's great wool manufacturing areas. The land had been farmed, mainly with sheep, since the Middle Ages and, in order to supplement their wages, the cottagers took to hand loom weaving in a room of their home. However, the advances in technology, beginning in the 18th century, replaced the single man-powered looms with water-powered machinery that was housed in the large mill buildings in the valley bottom and close to the source of power – the fast flowing streams and rivers coming down from the surroundings hills and moors.

During the 19th century there was an explosion of building and the quiet riverside villages grew into towns and the South Pennine textile boom was in full flow. At first the conditions in the mills were grim as, indeed, were the living conditions for the mill workers but, with the reduction in the hours of the working day, people were able to take the opportunity to discover, and in some cases rediscover, the beauty of the surrounding moorland. Not all the villages were completely taken over by the mills and, in many, the old stone built weavers' cottages, with their deep windows to let in light for the worker within, survive.

Although the Yorkshire woollen textile industry is now almost a thing of the past, the heritage of those prosperous days can be seen in almost any town or village of the region.

The wealthy mill owners built grand villas for themselves and also contributed to the construction of the marvellous array of opulent civic buildings that are such a feature of West Yorkshire towns. Today, however, many of the mills, which have remained redundant for decades are now being put to other uses while places such as Bradford, Leeds, Huddersfield and Wakefield are finding new industries to take the place of the old. There is a wealth of interesting museums here that concentrate on the wool industry, but there are also others such as the National Museum of Photography, Film and Television in Bradford, that look towards the future. Coal mining, too, was a feature of West Yorkshire and the National Coal Mining Museum, near Wakefield, provides visitors with the opportunity to go down a real mine shaft.

However, despite there being several grand stately homes in the area, such as Temple Newsam near Leeds, East Riddlesden Hall near Bradford and Harewood House, the foremost residence that most people make a pilgrimage to in West Yorkshire is The Parsonage at Howarth. It was here that the Brontë family moved to in 1820 and, surrounded by the wild Pennine landscape, the three sisters, Charlotte, Anne and Emily, became inspired by their surroundings and wrote some of the most famous novels in the English language. Now a museum dedicated to the tragic sisters, this fine Georgian house is a starting point for a 40-mile footpath that takes in many of the places that feature in the Brontë novels.

Brontë Country

This area of West Yorkshire, surrounding the Brontë family home at Haworth, is dominated by the textile towns and villages along the valley bottom and the wild and bleak moorland above. The land has been farmed, mainly with sheep, since the Middle Ages. In order to supplement their wages, the cottagers took to hand loom weaving in a room of their home. The advances in technology, beginning in the 18th century, replaced the single man-powered looms with water-powered machinery that were housed in the large mill buildings in the valley bottom and close to the source of power.

During the 19th century there was an explosion of building and the quiet riverside villages grew into towns; the South Pennine textile boom was in full flow. At first the conditions in the mills were grim as, indeed, were the living conditions for the mill workers but, with the reduction in the hours of the working day, people were able to take the opportunity to discover, and in some cases rediscover, the beauty of the surrounding moorland.

Not all the villages were completely taken over by the mills. In many, the old stone-built weavers cottages, with their deep windows to let in light for the worker within, survive. This, then, was the landscape of the area to which the Brontë family moved in 1820 when their father, Patrick, took up the position of rector of Haworth. Within five years, both Maria Brontë (the mother) and two of the five girls died; the unhealthy climate having begun to take its toll. Though all the remaining children did receive an education, it was in a somewhat haphazard way and they spent much of their time with each other isolated at the parsonage. After various attempts at working, generally as teachers, the girls, and their brother Branwell, all returned to the parsonage in the mid-1840s and this is when their writing began in earnest.

Haworth

🏛	Brontë Parsonage Museum
🏛	Keighley & Worth Valley Railway
🗘	Top Withins 🚶 Brontë Way

Once a bleak moorland town in a dramatic setting that fired the romantic imaginations of the Brontë sisters, Haworth has been transformed into a lively, attractive place with wonderful tea houses, street theatre, and antique and craft shops, very different to how it must have been in the Brontë's days. It was then a thriving industrial town, squalid amidst the smoke from its chimneys, filled with the noise of the clattering looms, which were rarely still. It is worth exploring the ginnels and back roads off the steeply rising high street, to get a feeling of what the place was

Brontë Parsonage Museum

AITCHES GUEST HOUSE

11 West Lane, Haworth,
West Yorkshire BD22 8DU
Tel: 01535 642501
e-mail: aitches@talk21.com
website: www.aitches.co.uk

Philomena and David Evans greet guests with genuine warmth at **Aitches Guest House**, an elegant Victorian house at the top of the Brontë village. The house overlooks the Brontë Parsonage and is a two-minute stroll from the centre of the village with its interesting shops, tea rooms, restaurants and pubs. The guest rooms in this stylish home from home are individually and comfortably furnished and all have en-suite facilities, central heating, TV/DVD, clock radio and beverage tray.

A sumptious five-course Yorkshire breakfast is a special feature of a stay at Aitches and is taken in the elegant period dining room. Guests also have use of a cosy lounge, well stocked with books and games. There are four double rooms and one twin. Rates are competitive and there are special terms for mid-week and 5-night stays. Families and dogs are welcome.

like in the days of the Brontës.

The Parsonage, built in 1777, is the focus of most Brontë pilgrimages and is now given over to the **Brontë Parsonage Museum**. The Brontë Society has restored the interior to resemble as closely as possible the house in which the sisters lived with their father and brother. There are exhibitions and displays of contemporary material, personal belongings, letters and portraits, as well as a priceless collection of manuscripts, first editions and memorabilia in the newer extension

Taking their inspiration from the surrounding bleak and lonely Haworth Moor, and from the stories they made up as children, the three sisters, Anne, Charlotte, and Emily, under male *noms de plume*, all became published authors while Branwell, though by all accounts a scholar, sought refuge in the beer at the local

inn. Then the tuberculosis that had attacked the family earlier returned and, one by one, Patrick Brontë's children succumbed to the terrible disease. The story of the Brontë family is one of tragedy, but the circumstances of their deaths were all too common in the 19th century and graphically illustrate the harshness of life some 150 years ago.

Many visitors are drawn to the area by the story of the family and the **Brontë Way**, a 40-mile linear footpath with a series of four guided walks, which links the places that provided inspiration to the sisters. The most exhilarating and popular excursion is that to **Top Withins**, a favourite place of Emily's and the inspiration for the 'Wuthering Heights' of the novel. The route also takes into account a great variety of scenery, from wild moorlands to pastoral countryside.

Brontë enthusiasts can also sit in the Black Bull, where Branwell sent himself to an early grave on a mixture of strong Yorkshire ale, opium and despair (although the last two are not available here these days). The Post Office, from where the sisters sent their manuscripts to London publishers, is still as it was, as is the Sunday School at which they all taught. Sadly, the church that they all attended no longer exists, although Charlotte, Emily, and Branwell (Anne is buried in Scarborough) all lie in a vault in the new church, which dates from 1879.

As well as devotees of the Brontë legend, Haworth is popular with steam railway fans. The town is the headquarters of the **Keighley and Worth Valley Railway**, a thriving volunteer-run railway that serves six stations (most of them gas-lit) in the course of its 4¾-mile length. The railway owns an extensive and varied collection of locomotives and everything combines to re-create the atmosphere of the days of steam. There are daily services during July and August and intermittent services throughout the rest of the year. To listen to the talking timetable, telephone 01535 643629.

The countryside around Haworth inspires the modern visitor as much as it did the Brontës. This is excellent walking country and it is worth taking a trip through the Penistone Hill Country Park, following the rough track by old moorland farms to the Brontë Falls and stone footbridge. For the energetic, the path eventually leads to the deserted ruins of Top Withins Farm, said to have been the inspiration for the setting of *Wuthering Heights*. It is said that the ghost of Emily Brontë has been seen walking, with her head bowed, between the Parsonage and Top Withins Farm.

Around Haworth

OAKWORTH
1 mile N of Haworth on the B6143

Those visiting Oakworth may find its Edwardian station, on the Keighley and Worth Valley Railway line somewhat familiar. In fact, not only did it feature in the classic film *The Railway Children*, but also in episodes of the TV series *Sherlock Holmes*.

STANBURY
4 miles S of Keighley off the B6143

🏠 Ponden Mill

Close to the village lies **Ponden Mill**, which was, in the heyday of Yorkshire's textile industry, one of the largest working mills in the country. At the height of production, cloth from Ponden Mill was exported around the world. Though the vast majority of the mills have now closed and the Yorkshire textile industry is virtually a thing of the past, Ponden Mill is still open, this time as a retail centre selling all manner of textiles from home furnishings and linens to country clothing. To round off your visit, have a look in the clog shop where traditional methods of manufacture are still on show.

OXENHOPE
9 miles W of Bradford on the A6033

This village contains more than 70 listed buildings, including a Donkey Bridge, two milestones, a mounting block, a cowshed, and a pigsty. The early farmhouses had narrow mullioned windows, which gave maximum light for weaving, and some had a door at first-storey level so that the pieces could be taken out. The first mill here was built in 1792 and, during the 19th century, there were up to

20 mills producing worsted.

Many scenes for *The Railway Children* were set here in 1970 using local views and local people. A station on the Keighley and Worth Valley Railway also serves the village.

HEBDEN BRIDGE
5 miles NW of Halifax on the A646

🏭 Mill 🏯 Rochdale Canal

🦅 🎨 Land Farm Sculpture Garden

This mill town is characterised by the stepped formation of its houses, which were stacked one on top of the other up the steep sides of the Calder valley. There has been a village here for many years, centred around the crossing-point of the River Calder. When the first bridge was built is not known, but as early as the beginning of the 16th century its state of repair was causing concern and, in a style typical of this area of Yorkshire, a stone bridge was erected close by. Found in St George's Square in the heart of the town, the historic **Hebden Bridge Mill** has, for almost 700 years now, been powered by the fast-flowing waters of the River Hebden. For over four centuries this was a manorial corn mill before it was converted into a textile mill that was finally abandoned in the 1950s. Now lovingly restored, the mill is home to various stylish shops, restaurants and craft workshops.

The **Rochdale Canal**, which slices through the town, was completed in 1798. It was constructed to link the Calder and Hebble Navigation with the Bridgewater and Ashton canals from Lancashire. Used by commercial traffic since 1939, the canal has been repaired

SPIRALS

11-13 Market Street, Hebden Bridge,
West Yorkshire HX7 6EU
Tel: 01422 847462
e-mail: taspirlas@btconnect.com
website: www.spiralsofhebden.co.uk

Spirals is a well-established Fairtrade retail business located in Hebden Bridge, a picturesque mill town in the South Pennines. Owners Sarah and Helen have filled their shop with a wide variety of fairtrade and eco-friendly goods large and small, from home furnishings and accessories to clothing, jewellery, toys, local artwork, world music, home furnishings and gifts for any occasion. The shop is attractively laid out over two floors, providing a feast for the eyes and ever-changing delights for browsers and anyone looking for something to enhance the home, a personal treat or a special gift. The shop, whose décor includes a lot of attractive natural wood, is open seven days a week. Hebden Bridge is generously supplied with interesting shops, and Spirals should definitely be at the head of every visitor's list.

📖 stories and anecdotes 🐦 famous people 🎨 art and craft 🏃 entertainment and sport 🚶 walks

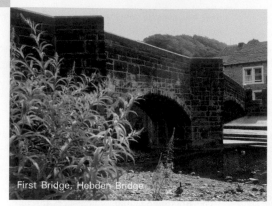
First Bridge, Hebden Bridge

One of the first purpose-built industrial towns in the world, Hebden Bridge grew rapidly as the demand for textiles boomed. Over the years, the town has seen many changes of fortune and, today, with the textile industry now gone, it is a place of bookshops, antique shops, restaurants, and a market.

To the northwest of Hebden Bridge lies the **Land Farm Sculpture Garden and Gallery**, a delightful woodland garden created over some 30 years from a barren Pennine hillside that faces north and lies some 1,000 feet above sea level. Attached to the house is an art gallery; both are open at weekends and Bank Holiday Mondays from May to the end of August.

and sections of it, including that between Hebden Bridge and Todmorden, are now open to traffic though, now, it consists mainly of pleasure craft. Motor boat cruises are available from the marina.

HEART GALLERY

The Arts Centre, 4a Market Street, Hebden Bridge, West Yorkshire HX7 6AA
Tel: 01422 845845
e-mail: alison@heartgallery.co.uk
websites: www.heartgallery.co.uk
   or www.heartgalleryblog.wordpress.com
   or www.flickr.com/photos/heartgallery

Heart Gallery is a unique contemporary jewellery and craft gallery featuring an eclectic mix of ever-changing work by around 60 emerging and established designers and makers, with quality and originality guaranteed.

Heart Gallery is passionate about all things beautiful and sells the very best of inspirational work including fresh, innovative and exciting contemporary jewellery, ceramics, glass, textiles, wood, furniture, accessories and stationery. Heart Gallery ensures that there is something for everyone's taste and budget and is constantly evolving and reinventing itself.

Heart Gallery prides itself on showcasing classic pieces for today's modern living alongside the more quirky and challenging accent pieces, and brings unusual and unique sumptuous gifts and design-led interior and lifestyle products together in one beautiful and inviting space, offering a haven from the predictability of the High Street. Once discovered, never forgotten. Opening times: Wednesday, Thursday, Friday 10:30–5, Saturday 10:30–5:30, Sunday 12–4:30.

🏚 historic building   🏛 museum and heritage   🏛 historic site   🛶 scenic attraction   🌱 flora and fauna

ECHOES

650a Halifax Road, Eastwood,
Todmorden OL14 6DW
Tel: 01706 817505

Specialising in antique and vintage costume, textiles and jewellery, **Echoes** is highly respected in the world of vintage retailing for evening wear. Owners Patricia and Richard Oldman have been at their present shop since 1987, but Patricia has been passionate about antique and vintage costume since she was 10 years old. Today, their customers include stylists, collectors, and costume designers such as the award-winning Anthony Powell. The interior of their shop provides a glorious display of colourful and elegant vintage garments that once adorned past generations, along with some beautiful jewellery. Amongst these gems are biqs cut evening dresses and 1920s beaded dresses. Desirable and stylish, they are all affordable, prices are remarkably reasonable.

Echoes is located on the A646, midway between Hebden Bridge and Todmorden.

HEPTONSTALL
7 miles NW of Halifax off the A646

🌳 Hardcastle Crags 🎭 Paceggers Play

The village, one of the main tourist centres in Calderdale, overlooks Hebden Bridge and **Hardcastle Crags**. This beautiful wooded valley is protected and cared for by the National Trust and, from the crags, there are several interesting walks along the purpose-built footpaths. It is also one of only three places in Britain where two churches occupy the same churchyard. In this case, the original church, which dates from 1256, was struck by lightning in the 1830s and a new church was built next to the ruin.

Every year, on Good Friday, the **Paceggers Play** takes place in Weavers Square. It's an ancient method of storytelling with actors dressed in elaborate costumes recounting the legend of St George.

TODMORDEN
4 miles W of Hebden Bridge on the A646

🏛 Town Hall

This is another typical mill town that grew with the expansion of the textile industry. Before the 19th century, Todmorden had been a spartan place with many of the villagers eking out frugal lives by hand loom weaving. Following the building of the first mill here, Todmorden began to grow and the highly ornate and flamboyant public buildings were, in the main, built by the mill owners. Though many towns which owe their existence to industry also bear the scars, Todmorden has retained all its charm and character and is an excellent place to visit for those interested in architecture. It boasts a magnificent **Town Hall** designed by John Gibson and opened in 1875. One of the finest municipal buildings of its size in the country, the grand old

MAKEPIECE

2 Dale Street, Todmorden, Lancashire OL14 5PX
Tel: 01706 815888
e-mail: info@makepiece.co.uk
website: www.makepiece.co.uk

The partners behind the **Makepiece** studio shop in Todmorden have a clear vision of what they want to do: 'Make beautiful clothes with ethics; use natural yarns from sustainable farming; observe fair employment practices and work to be carbon neutral.' For hundreds of years, farmer makers in this Pennine valley have produced wool, spun it and created fabric pieces.

Makepiece has taken their legacy and created a collection of desirable contemporary clothes for the future. Co-founder, Beate Kubitz, keeps a small flock of sheep to supply them with a naturally coloured undyed Shetland yarn, and buys luxurious alpaca and lustrous mohair from other UK farms. Much of the wool is spun into yarn in Yorkshire within 20 miles of the studio.

Designed in the studio in Todmorden by co-founder Nicola Sherlock, small runs of the exclusive knitwear range are knitted by craft knitters in the area. Complementary woven garments are made in Lancashire - some using fabric woven locally in Delph.

Makepiece is a small gem, drawing on its heritage on the border or Yorkshire and Lancashire and well worth a visit for gorgeous clothes and accessories.

---

building stands half in Yorkshire and half in Lancashire. So the ornate carving in the pediment represents the farming and iron trades of Yorkshire in the right panel; the cotton trade of Lancashire in the left.

MYTHOLMROYD

5 miles W of Halifax on the A646

🌿 World Dock Pudding Championships

Prior to the 1600s, the valley bottom in what is now Mytholmroyd was marshy and of little use as foundations for a village, though some of the outlying farms in the area date from the late 14th century. However, with the need to build more mills close to a supply of water, the land was improved and Mytholmroyd joined the age of the Industrial Revolution.

Each spring the town is host to the **World Dock Pudding Championships**. Dock Pudding is unique to this corner of the county and is made from the weed *Polygonum Bistorta* or sweet dock (which should never be confused with the larger docks that are commonly used for easing nettle stings). In spring, the plant grows profusely and local people pick it by the bagful. The docks are then mixed with young nettles and other essential ingredients and cooked to produce a green and slimy delicacy the appearance of which is found by many to be rather off-putting. It is usually served with bacon after having been fried in bacon fat, and is believed to cure acne and cleanse the blood.

Halifax

| 🏛 Piece Hall | 🏛 Town Hall | 🏛 🏛 Shibden Hall |
| 🏛 St John's Church | 🏛 Eureka! | 🏛 Bankfield Museum |
| 🏛 Calderdale Industrial Museum |

Halifax boasts one of Yorkshire's most impressive examples of municipal architecture, the glorious 18th-century **Piece Hall**. It possesses a large quadrangle where regular markets are held on Fridays and Saturdays, surrounded by colonnades and balconies behind which are some 40 specialist shops. On Thursdays, a flea market is held here and there's a lively and varied programme of events for all the family throughout the season. There's also an art gallery with a varied programme of contemporary exhibitions and workshops, a museum and tea room.

The **Town Hall** is another notable building, designed by Sir Charles Barry, architect of the Houses of Parliament, and there's an attractive Borough Market, constructed in cast iron and glass with an ornate central clock.

In Gibbet Street stands a grisly reminder of the past – a replica of a guillotine, the original blade being kept in the Piece Hall Museum. There are many hidden places in old Halifax to explore: from Shear's Inn, an old weavers' inn near the town centre, one can walk up the cobbled Boy's Lane, very little changed from Victorian times, or trace out the ancient *Magna Via*, a medieval path to the summit of Breacon Hill.

Halifax also boasts the largest parish church

🎬 stories and anecdotes 🐟 famous people 🎨 art and craft 🎭 entertainment and sport 🚶 walks

DELI-CIOUS

14 Westgate, Halifax,
West Yorkshire HX1 1DS
Tel/Fax: 01422 384477

Andrea the New Proprietor of **Deli-cious** has been inspired to venture into the business world and share with the public her high-class licensed deli/coffee shop – a member of the Guild of Fine Foods – in a covered arcade in the town centre on the historic main street, opposite the Borough Market. In rustic modern surroundings, with plenty of natural light and a warm, friendly ambience, the shop sells a fine selection of local, British and Continental produce along with wines and spirits from around the world. Everything on display is available to take away, but can also be enjoyed inside at a table for 4 or outside when the sun shines. Trading hours are 9 to 5 Monday to Saturday.

in England, **St John's Church**. Of almost cathedral-sized proportions, it dates from the 12th and 13th centuries although most of the present building is from the 1400s. It has a lovely wooden ceiling, constructed in 1635, a magnificent William & Mary altar rail and modern reredos by 'Mouseman' Thompson. Visitors should also look out for Old Tristram, a life-sized wooden effigy of a beggar, reputedly based on a local character who haunted the precincts collecting for the poor. It was designed to serve as the church poor box – and still does.

Right next door to Piece Hall, the **Calderdale Industrial Museum** houses still-working looms and mill machinery, hand textile demonstrations and among the many displays one celebrating the town's greatest contribution to modern travel, the Catseye!

From the Great Wheel to the Spinning Jenny, from mining to moquette, from steam engines (in live steam) to toffee, the museum provides a riveting insight into Halifax's industrial heritage.

Situated next to Halifax railway station, **Eureka!** is Britain's first and only interactive museum designed especially for children between three and 12-years-old funded by the Duffield and Clore foundations. With more than 400 larger-than-life exhibits and exciting activities available, Eureka! opens up a fascinating world of hands-on exploration. A team of 'enablers' help children make the most of their visit, there are regular temporary exhibitions, and the complex includes a café and gift shop.

Now a vibrant complex of businesses, galleries, theatre, café and design and book

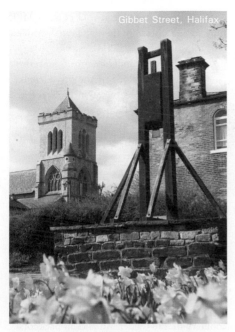

Gibbet Street, Halifax

Shibden Hall and Park (see panel below), about a mile out of town, is somewhere very special that should not be missed. The Old Hall itself lies in a valley on the outskirts of the town and is situated in 90 acres of parkland. The distinctive timber-framed house dates from 1420 and has been carefully furnished to reflect the various periods of its history. The 17th-century barn behind the Hall houses a fine collection of horse-drawn vehicles and the original buildings have been transformed into a 19th-century village centre with a pub, estate worker's cottage, saddler's, blacksmith's, wheelwright's and potter's workshop.

Also on the outskirts of the town is the **Bankfield Museum**, the home between 1837 and 1886 of Edward Akroyd, the largest wool manufacturer in Britain. He lavished money and attention on the building, transforming it from a modest town house into a magnificent Italianate mansion with elaborate ceilings, staircases and plasterwork. After his death, his sumptuous home became a museum and now houses an internationally important collection of textiles and costumes from around the world. Contemporary crafts are also featured and the museum hosts an interesting

shops, Dean Clough is housed in a magnificent Victorian carpet mill that is a reminder of Halifax's textile heritage. Built between 1840 and 1870 by the Crossley family, this mill was once home to one of the world's leading carpet factories, which ceased production in 1982.

Shibden Hall

Lister's Road, Halifax, West Yorkshire HX3 6XG

For over 300 years this was the Lister's family home, but **Shibden Hall** itself is even older, built in 1420. Generations have lived and worked here and today the hall reflects this continual development. The rooms, ranging from the 17th century to the 20th century, are set out as if someone has just slipped out for a moment.

There is the 17th-century barn with its display of carriages and the Folk Museum that shows how craftsmen worked in the 19th century. Open from March to November, 11-5 Monday to Saturday, 12-5 Sunday. December to February, 11-4 Monday to Saturday, 12-4 Sunday.

programme of temporary exhibitions, workshops, seminars, master classes and gallery demonstrations. Here, too, is a Toy Gallery, the Duke of Wellington's Regimental Museum and the Marble Gallery that sells contemporary crafts. Surrounding his house, Akroyd built a model village called Akroydon that, with its terraced houses, allotments, park and church was the first 'urban' village. The **Bankfield Museum** is open all year round from Tuesday to Sunday and on Bank Holiday Mondays.

Around Halifax

SOWERBY BRIDGE
2m SW of Halifax on the A58

🏠 Greenups Mill

Sowerby Bridge has a rather odd connection with the Brontës. For a while, Branwell Brontë worked as a booking clerk at the railway station here. He was dismissed in March 1842 when discrepancies were found in his accounts. Branwell also worked in the same role at nearby Luddenden Foot where he was a member of the library at the White Swan Inn. (At that time, several hostelries provided this amenity for their patrons.) A condition of membership of the library stipulated 'sobriety and decorous conduct' on pain of a fine of 2d (0.8p) for each offence. This requirement must have caused Branwell some difficulty as he was a scandalously heavy drinker.

An important crossing of both the Rivers Ryburn and Calder in medieval times, and possibly as far back as the Roman occupation, Sowerby Bridge first had water-powered mills as early as the 14th century. The mills, first used for grinding corn, moved into textile production and by the

1850s were all steam-driven. **Greenups Mill**, built in 1792, was the first integrated woollen mill in Yorkshire with all the textile processes brought under one roof. Sowerby Bridge also boasted one of the first turnpike roads in Britain, constructed in 1735. Just a short time later, the Calder and Hebble Navigation, surveyed by John Smeaton, the designer of the Eddystone Lighthouse, was opened in 1770, followed by the Rochdale Canal in 1804. A reminder of the busy days of the canal is Tuel Lane Lock and Tunnel, which joined the two man-made waterways. It re-opened in 1996 and it is a grand sight to watch the narrowboats negotiating what is the deepest lock in the country.

RIPPONDEN
5 miles SW of Halifax on the A58

Ripponden lies in the valley of the Ryburn, a tributary of the Calder. An ancient packhorse bridge crosses the river and, right beside it, the Old Bridge Inn, which is one of the oldest inns in Yorkshire. It was already in existence in 1313 and its interior, with its sloping floors and different levels, has been compared to a funfair crazy house.

THORNTON
4 miles W of Bradford on the B6145

🏠 Brontë Birthplace

Thornton is an essential stopping place on the Brontë trail for it was here that the three sisters were born, at No 74 Market Street, now open to the public as the **Brontë Birthplace**. Their father was the vicar of Thornton and one of the treasures of his parish church is a font, inscribed with the date 1687, in which Charlotte, Emily and Anne were all baptised. Charlotte was only four years old, her two sisters still toddlers,

Norwood Bottoms, nr Thornton

in the town's museum are altars carved in gritstone, dedicated to the Roman gods.

The spring at White Wells brought more visitors to the town in the 18th century. A small bath house was built where genteel and elderly patients were encouraged to take a dip in the healing waters of the heather spa. Early Victorian times saw the development of the Hydros – hydropathic treatment hotels – providing hot and cold treatments based on the idea of Dr Preissnitz of Austria who, in 1843, became the director of Britain's first Hydro at nearby Ben Rhydding.

The coming of the railways from Leeds and Bradford in the 1860s and '70s, during a period of growth in the Yorkshire woollen industry, saw the town

when the family moved a few miles northwest to Haworth where their father had been appointed rector.

Ilkley

🏛 ✑	Manor House Art Gallery & Museum
🚶	Riverside Gardens 🚶 Ilkley Moor
🚶	Cow & Calf Rocks

Originally an Iron Age settlement, Ilkley was eventually occupied by the Romans who built a camp here to protect their crossing of the River Wharfe. They named their town *Olicana*, so giving rise to the present name with the addition of the familiar *ley* (Anglo-Saxon for 'pasture'). Behind the medieval church is a grassy mound where a little fort was built and

take on a new role as a fashionable commuter town. Wool manufacturers and their better-paid employees came, not only to enjoy the superb amenities, but to build handsome villas. If Bradford and Leeds were where people made their brass, so it was said at the time, then it was usually at Ilkley that it was spent. Even today, Ilkley sports some remarkable and opulent Victorian architecture as proof of this.

Ilkley's patrons and well-to-do citizens gave the town a splendid Town Hall, Library, Winter Gardens and King's Hall and a sense of elegance is still present along The Grove. It is a delight to have morning coffee in the famous Betty's coffee house, and discerning shoppers will find a wealth of choice, some in a perfectly preserved Victorian arcade

---

🎞 stories and anecdotes ✑ famous people ✑ art and craft ✐ entertainment and sport 🚶 walks

RAMUS SEAFOOD EMPORIUM

2 Victorian Mews, South Hawksworth Street, Ilkley West Yorkshire LS29 9DX
Tel: 01943 600388
website: www.ramus.co.uk

"Nobody's pickier about Seafood"

Opened in August 2007 this, the second **Ramus Seafood Emporium**, has become an immediate hit with both residents and visitors to this famous spa town. It is cornucopia with the finest that the sea has to offer displayed in gleaming stainless steel counters. This is like no fish shop you have ever seen, unless you have visited the big brother to this shop in Harrogate, hence the reason it attracts visitors from miles around.

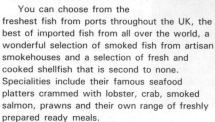

You can choose from the freshest fish from ports throughout the UK, the best of imported fish from all over the world, a wonderful selection of smoked fish from artisan smokehouses and a selection of fresh and cooked shellfish that is second to none. Specialities include their famous seafood platters crammed with lobster, crab, smoked salmon, prawns and their own range of freshly prepared ready meals.

Sold alongside the range of seafood are other varieties of fine food from smoked meats and fresh olives to fresh fish sauces and homemade flavoured butters. There is also a selection of fine food hampers and seafood cooking utensils such as oyster knives and claw crackers.

Although this shop is new, the team behind it have 35 years of experience of the seafood industry and have developed one of the most respected businesses of its kind in the country. Seafish, the industry governing body, has twice voted Ramus Seafoods Independent Seafood Retailer of the Year.

Come in and meet the friendly knowledgeable team who will help you choose the from the best selection of fish in the North.

For more information on Ramus Seafoods visit www.ramus.co.uk.

complete with potted palms and balconies.

Between the remains of the Roman fort and the River Wharfe lie the **Riverside Gardens**, a favourite place for a stroll that might lead over a 17th century packhorse bridge across the river. On the side of this bridge, beside the stone steps, the flood levels of the river have been marked, along with the dates. On the opposite side of the river is The Lido, one of the few surviving outdoor swimming pools in Yorkshire. Its idyllic surroundings and extensive terraces make it a popular place in summer while, next to the Lido, is an indoor pool open all year round. From the Lido a footpath leads up to Middleton Woods, in May a sea of bluebells.

Housed in a building that dates from the 15th, 16th and 17th centuries, complete with mullioned windows, carved beams and an interesting wall privy, the **Manor House Art Gallery and Museum** tells the history of Ilkley from its prehistoric roots through to its development as a Victorian spa town; upstairs is an art gallery hosting a programme of temporary exhibitions throughout the year.

One of the most famous West Yorkshire attractions has to be **Ilkley Moor**, immortalised in the well-known song. Like any of the Yorkshire moors, Ilkley Moor can look inviting and attractive on a sunny day, but ominous and forbidding when the weather takes a turn for the worse. The River Wharfe runs along the edge of the moor and through the town of Ilkley, which is clustered within a narrow section of the valley in the midst of heather moorland, craggy gritstone and

THE OLIVE BRANCH

140 Main Street, Addingham, nr Ilkley, West Yorkshire LS29 0LY
Tel: 01943 830123

The wonderful Yorkshire village of Addingham has a friendly
community feel that extends through the streets, the public areas,
the pubs, the cafés and speciality shops like **The Olive Branch**.
Owner Jill Atkinson, her sister-in-law Jane and Jane's mum Wendy,
have a love of country living style, and their close links to rural life
through their farming families is reflected in the hand-picked
selection of home and gift ware. You'll also find baby-related
products and cards and gifts for most occasions. The owners pride
themselves on sourcing, unusual, high-quality goods. They are
stockists of Emma Bridgewater pottery, Cath Kidston homeware,
bedding and towels by Lulu Guinness and Annie Tempest's
'Tottering by Gently' artwork on mugs and other products, as well
as designer yarns and some unique vintage finds. They offer a
warm welcome to all who pass through the door into a shop that
retains all the original fittings from its days as a milliners at the turn
of the last century. These include a beautiful long counter and
wonderful glass cupboards and pristine shelving beautifully lit by

period fittings. The front of the shop has a French feel, painted in
Farrow & Ball green with soft grey. A pretty Georgian handrail leads to the door, above which
the figures 140 are gilded in true period style. The shop is open from 9.30 to 5 Tuesday to
Friday, 9.30 to 5.30 Saturday, closed Sunday and Monday.

LIME KILN FURNITURE

3b Town Head Trading Estate, Main Street, Addingham,
West Yorkshire LS29 0PD
Tel: 01943 830099
e-mail: info@limekilnfurniture.com
website: www.limekilnfurniture.com

Quality is the keynote throughout the range of furniture
handmade by expert craftsmen at **Lime Kiln Furniture**. In
a small warehouse-style building on Addingham's small
business estate they offer a complete, bespoke service
for any item required, including sideboards, dressers, tables, beds,
bookcases, blanket boxes,
television and hi-fi cabinets and any
other item. The main raw materials

are hardwoods, mainly oak, walnut,
mahogany, cherry, ash and poplar,
and the wood is obtained from
sustainable sources, traded in
friendly, ethical style. Customers
can visit the showroom and
adjacent workshop, which are open
for browsing, buying and
discussing their requirements.

wooded hillside. Few places in the north can equal Ilkley Moor or, more correctly, Rombalds Moor. The moorland, much of it still covered in heather, is also an area of national importance for its archaeology. There is a series of mysteriously marked cup and ring stones dating from the Bronze Age. Almost in the centre of the moor is an ancient stone circle, no doubt a site of some religious importance. Only the keen walker is likely to find these, located high up on the moor, but there is a fine example of a cup and ring stone in the lower part of St Margaret's churchyard in Queen's Road.

Looking at a map of the area, many people's attention is drawn to the curiously-named **Cow and Calf Rocks**, which form a striking moor-edge landmark above Ben Rhydding. The Cow is a great gritstone outcrop concealing an old quarry, popular with climbers, while the free-standing Calf is a giant boulder.

Around Ilkley

ADDINGHAM
3 miles W of Ilkley off the A65

Although Addingham dates back to Saxon times (it was named after a Saxon chieftain, Adda), the village enjoyed its greatest prosperity in the 18th century when no fewer than five water mills lined the banks of the Wharfe. Four of them were textile mills and no longer operate, but the fifth, a timber mill, is still working.

BEN RHYDDING
1 mile E of Ilkley off the A65

'A few weeks spent at Ben Rhydding seem to effect a complete change in the system,' wrote one Victorian visitor to the spa. 'I have seen delicate women, scarcely able to walk feebly round the garden on their first arrival, become strong enough to walk to the Hunting-tower, a lovely point in the heart of the moor at some distance from the house.'

The original Ben Rhydding Hydropathic Hotel, opened in 1844 by a consortium of Leeds businessmen, was built in the Scottish baronial style so popular at the time. By 1908, interest in hydropathy had declined and the exuberant building became the Ben Rhydding Golf Hotel. Later it was turned into flats but finally demolished in 1955.

Athough the name suggests some Scottish connection – and the surrounding scenery certainly has a Caledonian grandeur – 'Ben Rhydding' is actually derived from nearby Bean Rhydding, or bean clearing.

BURLEY IN WHARFEDALE
3 miles SE of Ilkley on the A65

Mentioned in the Anglo-Saxon Chronicle in AD 972 as Burhleg and in the *Domesday Book* as Burghelai, it remained a small riverside settlement until the 1790s when the Industrial Revolution reached the village. Many of the terraces of stone-built cottages, designed for the mill workers, have survived and are now highly desirable residences. Burley's population has doubled since the 1920s but the Main Street is still lined with Yorkshire stone cottages and houses, and the surrounding hills frame every view.

OTLEY
5 miles SE of Ilkley on the A660

🏛 Parish Church	🏫 Prince Henry's Grammar School
🌱 Wharfedale Agricultural Show	
🚶 The Chevin Forest Park	

Although it now forms part of the Leeds Metropolitan District, Otley has retained its distinctive character, still boasting a busy cobbled marketplace and many little alleyways and courtyards. Each May the **Wharfedale Agricultural Show**, founded in 1799 and the oldest show of its kind in England, is held in a nearby field.

Even older is **Prince Henry's Grammar School**, founded in 1602 by James I and named after his eldest son. In front of the building in Manor Square is a statue of Thomas Chippendale, the great furniture maker who was born in Otley in 1718. In 1754 Chippendale published *The Gentleman and Cabinet-Maker's Director*, which was immensely influential in both Britain and the USA. His own workshop produced a comparatively small number of pieces, but he gave his name to a style that dominated a generation and is still highly prized.

In addition to the statue on the front of the Grammar School, Otley's most famous son is commemorated by a plaque on the wall of Browns Gallery, which records that Thomas Chippendale was born in 1718 in a cottage that stood on this spot.

Otley's parish church dates from Saxon times although the main body was constructed in the 11th century. An unusual memorial, close by, is a stone model of Bramhope Railway Tunnel with its impressive crenellated entrance portals. It was built in the 1830s on the Leeds-Thirsk railway line and more than 30 labourers died during its construction – a tragic loss of life which, the model commemorates.

An attractive feature of the town is **The Chevin Forest Park,** a forested ridge above the town which can be reached by a delightful walk that starts in the town. There are also pleasant walks along the River Wharfe.

Bradford

🏛 Cathedral	🏛 Lister's Mill
🏛 Undercliffe Cemetery	🏛 Museum of Colour
🏛 National Museum of Photography, Film & Television	
🏛 Industrial Museum	🖈 Cartwright Hall Art Gallery

Bradford is a city with much to offer the visitor. In terms of numbers, the most popular attraction is undoubtedly the **National Museum of Photography, Film and Television**, which houses IMAX, one of the largest cinema screens in the world. If you suffer from vertigo you'll need to close your eyes as the huge, wrap-around screen shows such heart-stopping scenes as roller-coaster rides and Alpine mountaineering. There's plenty to keep you occupied here for hours – virtual reality exhibits, the Kodak

National Museum of Photography, Film and Television

Gallery, which leads you on a journey through the history of popular photography, an extensive TV display that ranges from the world's first TV pictures to the very latest, and much, much more. A vast space presents world-class exhibitions on photography, film, TV and new media.

Of related interest is Britain's only **Museum of Colour**. 'The World of Colour' gallery looks at the concept of colour, how it is perceived and its importance. Visitors can see how the world looks to other animals, mix coloured lights and experience strange colour illusions. In the 'Colour and Textiles' gallery you can discover the fascinating story of dyeing and textile printing from Ancient Egypt to the present day. Computerised technology allows you to take charge of a dye-making factory and decorate a room. The museum is open Tuesday to Saturday all year round.

Found in Lister Park, the collections at the **Cartwright Hall Art Gallery** reflect the diverse cultural mix that helps to make Bradford the vibrant and unique city it has become in the 21st century. From Victorian paintings and sumptuous Indian silks, to the challenges of contemporary art, this gallery is as interesting and far-reaching as the city itself.

The **Bradford Industrial Museum and Horses at Work** celebrates the city's industrial heritage. It is housed in an original worsted spinning mill complex built in 1875 and re-creates life in Bradford in late Victorian times. Open all year, the museum also offers horse-bus and tram rides, a shire horse centre, a reconstructed mill owner's house and the working men's back-to-back cottages. The complex also includes a café, shop and picnic area.

Architecturally, the most striking building in Bradford must be **Lister's Mill**. Its huge ornate chimney in the style of an Italian *campanile* dominates the city skyline and it's claimed that it is wide enough at the top to drive a horse and cart around. A rather quirkier sign of the city's former riches is **Undercliffe Cemetery**. Here the wool barons were buried, each in a more opulent Gothic mausoleum than the last. It is easy to spend an hour here admiring the Victorian funereal art on show with the cityscape laid out before you.

The fact that the city has a **Cathedral** is an indication of its importance. The parish church became the Cathedral when Bradford was made an Anglican diocese in 1919. The first evidence of worship on the site is provided by the remains of a Saxon preaching cross. Today, the Cathedral contains many items of interest, including beautiful stained glass windows, some of which were designed by William Morris, carvings and statuary.

Around Bradford

SHIPLEY
4 miles N of Bradford on the A6037

🏠 Shipley Glen

Although Shipley town is mainly industrial, **Shipley Glen** (see panel on page 336) is a very popular area for tourists. Within the grounds is a narrow gauge, cable hauled tramway, built in 1895, that carries passengers a quarter of a mile up the side of a steep hill, passing en route through Walker Wood, famous for its bluebells.

SALTAIRE
4 miles NW of Bradford off the A657

🏠 Model Village   ✏ 1853 David Hockney Gallery

🏠 Museum of Victorian Reed Organs

Saltaire is the **Model Village** on the River

🎬 stories and anecdotes 🐦 famous people ✏ art and craft 🎵 entertainment and sport 🚶 walks

Shipley Glen Cable Tramway

95 Frizinghall Road, Bradford,
West Yorkshire BD9 4LU
Tel: 01274 492026
website: www.glentramway.co.uk

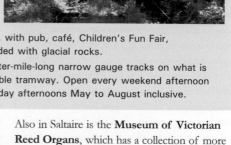

The Tramway, built in 1895, is situated near the World Heritage Site of Saltaire, and runs up the wooded hillside to enable visitors to reach the delights of Shipley Glen. The area is a popular visitor attraction, with pub, café, Children's Fun Fair, Countryside Centre and wooded valley studded with glacial rocks.

The trams trundle up and down the quarter-mile-long narrow gauge tracks on what is considered to be Britain's oldest working cable tramway. Open every weekend afternoon (Sundays only Nov, Jan and Feb) plus weekday afternoons May to August inclusive.

Aire created by Sir Titus Salt for the workers at his spinning and weaving mills. Salt was a very benevolent employer and determined to provide his workers with everything essential for a decent standard of living. Built between 1851 and 1876, the facilities in the village were designed to cater for all their needs – health, leisure and education, but there were no public houses. The spiritual needs of the work force were attended to by the elegant and sumptuously furnished Congregational Church, which has been described as the most beautiful Free Church in the north of England.

A bust of Sir Titus stands in the porch and a statue in nearby Robert's Park (where swearing and gambling were banned) above the figures of a llama and an alpaca whose wool he imported for spinning in his mills.

The Victoria Boat House was built in 1871 and has been beautifully restored, with an open fire, pianola and wind-up gramophone, all re-creating a traditional parlour atmosphere where you can enjoy cream teas and attend special Victorian Evenings in the dress of that time.

Also in Saltaire is the **Museum of Victorian Reed Organs**, which has a collection of more than 45 instruments, including harmonicas and an American organ, which are demonstrated from time to time, and some of which are available for visitors to try.

Saltaire isn't completely locked in the past. The former Salt's Mill has been converted into the **1853 David Hockney Gallery**, which displays the world's largest collection of paintings by the internationally acclaimed artist who was born in Bradford in 1937.

A couple of miles northeast of Baildon, at Guiseley, is the most famous fish and chip shop in the world, Harry Ramsden's. Harry's career as the world's most successful fish frier began in Bradford where he was the first to offer a sit-down fish and chip meal. He moved to Guiseley in 1928 and the original white-painted wooden hut, 10 feet by 6 feet, in which he started business is still on the site today. The present building holds its place in the *Guinness Book of Records* as the world's busiest fish and chip restaurant, serving nearly one million customers each year.

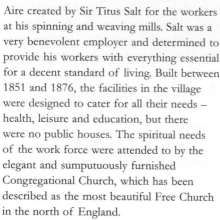

🏛 historic building 🏛 museum and heritage 🏛 historic site ⚘ scenic attraction 🌱 flora and fauna

Leeds

🏛 Kirkstall Abbey	🏛 Temple Newsam House
🏛 Aire & Calder Navigation	🐑 Home Farm
🏛 Thackray Medical Museum	🐠 Tropical World
🎨 City Gallery	🎨 Henry Moore Institute

In recent years, the city of Leeds has seen
something of a renaissance. Its waterfront,
neglected and derelict for so long, is now
buzzing with new developments. Abandoned
warehouses have been imaginatively
transformed into fashionable bars, restaurants
and tourist attractions, all less than 15 minutes
walk from the shopping centre. Debenhams
has a flagship store in the heart of the city and
other high profile stores are also flocking
here. Perhaps the most talked about is Harvey
Nichols, whose Knightsbridge emporium
enjoyed a heightened reputation in the 1990s
thanks to the BBC series *Absolutely Fabulous*. In
parallel with these developments the **Aire and
Calder Navigation**, is being transformed to
enable leisure traffic to use the waterway as
well as freight.

The city is also a major European cultural
centre with its own opera and ballet companies,
Northern Ballet Theatre and Opera North,
while the West Yorkshire Playhouse, regarded
as the 'National Theatre of the North',
provides a showcase for classic British and
European drama as well as work by new
Yorkshire writers. The Leeds International Film
Festival, held every October since 1986, has
hosted major world premieres for films such as
Brassed Off. The Leeds International Piano
Competition was established in 1963 and has
produced many outstanding winners including
Radu Lupu and Murray Perahia.

The city also boasts some outstanding
galleries and museums. Located right next to
the monumental Town Hall, the **Leeds City
Art Gallery**, founded in 1888, showcases an
exceptional collection of Victorian and
French Post-Impressionist paintings along
with major works by Courbet, Lowry, Sickert,
Stanley Spencer and Bridget Riley. Linked to
the gallery is the **Henry Moore Institute** (see
panel opposite), the first centre in Europe
devoted to the display and study of sculpture
of all periods. There's also a Craft & Design
shop selling cards, jewellery and pottery, and
an art library.

The **Thackray Medical Museum**, one of
the largest museums of its kind in Europe,
possesses more than 25,000 extraordinary
objects in its collection. They range from a
surgical chain saw and Prince Albert's Medical
Chest, through to a 17th-century correction
frame. Visitors can listen in to the thoughts
and feelings of a surgeon, his assistants and
Hannah Dyson, an 11-year-old girl whose leg
has been crushed in a factory accident, as they
prepare for the amputation of Hannah's leg.
Or you might prefer to walk through a giant
gut in Bodyworks and find out exactly why
your tummy rumbles.

Opened by Queen Elizabeth II in 1998, the
Royal Armouries trace the development of
arms and armour from the 5th century BC to
modern times. The museum utilises interactive
computer displays, videos, films, music and
poetry to tell the story of arms and armour in
battle, self-defence, sport and fashion. Outside,
the Tiltyard features jousting and hunting
tournaments daily from April to September,
while a bustling Menagerie Court includes
displays of falcons, hunting dogs and horses.

To the northwest of the city, **Kirkstall
Abbey** is one of the most complete ruins in
this part of Yorkshire. Building started in 1152
by the Cistercians and was completed within a

Henry Moore Institute

74 The Headrow, Leeds,
West Yorkshire LS1 3AH
General enquiries: 0113 246 7467
Information line: 0113 234 3158
Fax: 0113 246 1481
website: www.henry-moore-fdn.co.uk

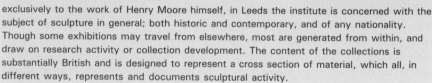

The **Henry Moore Institute** in Leeds is a unique resource devoted exclusively to sculpture, with a programme comprising exhibitions, collections and research. The centre was established by the Henry Moore foundation as a partnership with Leeds City Council in 1982. In 1993 it moved from Leeds City Art Gallery to the newly converted Henry Moore Institute next door.

Whereas the Henry Moore foundation at Moore's home in Perry Green in Hertfordshire devotes its activities exclusively to the work of Henry Moore himself, in Leeds the institute is concerned with the subject of sculpture in general; both historic and contemporary, and of any nationality. Though some exhibitions may travel from elsewhere, most are generated from within, and draw on research activity or collection development. The content of the collections is substantially British and is designed to represent a cross section of material, which all, in different ways, represents and documents sculptural activity.

generation, so Kirkstall is regarded by many as representing Cistercian architecture at its most monumental. It was executed with typical early Cistercian austerity as can be seen in the simplicity of the outer domestic buildings. The bell tower, a 16th-century addition, was in contravention of the rule of the Order that there were to be no stone bell towers as they were considered an unnecessary vanity.

A few miles north of Leeds city centre is one of the UK's most popular garden tourist attractions and home to the largest collection of tropical plants outside Kew Gardens – **Tropical World**. Visitors can follow the 'Tropical Trail' into an Amazonian rainforest where waterfalls tumble into jungle pools and

birds of every hue fly through the trees. There's also a Desert World and a Nocturnal House where fruit bats, monkeys, bush babies and rock cavies reside – animals that can normally only be seen during twilight hours.

A couple of miles southwest of the city is **Temple Newsam House**, often referred to as the 'Hampton Court of the North'. Set in 1,200 acres of parkland (entry to which is free), this Tudor-Jacobean gem boasts extensive collections of decorative arts displayed in their original room settings. Among them is one of the largest collections of Chippendale furniture in the country. Adjacent to Temple Newsam House is the country's largest approved Rare Breeds Centre

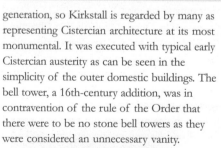

– Home Farm. Visitors to this working farm will see pigs, goats, horses and poultry alongside interesting displays of vintage farm machinery and past farming methods.

Around Leeds

HAREWOOD
8 miles N of Leeds on the A61

🏛 Harewood House

One of the grandest stately homes in the country, **Harewood House** was built at a time when many of the most illustrious names in the history of English architecture, interior decoration, furniture making and landscape gardening were at the peak of their powers.

For the creation of Harewood in the mid-1700s, Edwin Lascelles was able to employ the dazzling talents of Robert Adam, John Carr, Thomas Chippendale and Capability Brown. Edwin's son, Edward, was one of the first to patronise a young artist named JMW Turner and many of Turner's paintings are still here along with hundreds by other distinguished painters collected by later generations of the family.

Many of the finest of them are displayed in a superb gallery that extends along the whole west end of the house. Among the masterpieces on show are works by Bellini, Titian, Veronese, El Greco and Tintoretto, while family portraits by Reynolds, Hoppner and Gainsborough look down from the silk-covered walls of the opulent drawing rooms. Along with superb gardens, charming walks, a bird garden, which is home to some 120 exotic species, an adventure playground, boat trips on the lake, and an extensive events and exhibitions programme, Harewood House is

WIKE RIDGE FARM B&B
Wike, nr Shadwell, Leeds LS17 9JF
Tel: 0113 266 1190

Since 1993 Jill McCandlish has been welcoming guests from near and far to **Wike Ridge**, a tastefully renovated and extended stone farmhouse set in 13 acres of farmland on a high ridge that commands marvellous views. The setting is delightful, and the whole place has a relaxed, friendly feel that makes guests feel instantly at home. The accommodation comprises 5 rooms – 3 single, a double and a twin/family room – with TV and a selection of drinks; washing and ironing facilities and hairdryer are available on request. Interesting artwork is dotted throughout the bedrooms and day rooms. An excellent breakfast with plenty of choice is served from 6.30 in the dining room overlooking the beautiful gardens.

This is excellent walking country, and there are many match play golf courses nearby. Harewood House, one of the grandest stately homes in the country, is just two miles away, and the farm is easily reached from the M1, A1 and M62.

🏛 stories and anecdotes 🐿 famous people 🎨 art and craft 🎭 entertainment and sport 🚶 walks

indisputably one of Yorkshire's must-see visitor attractions.

BRAMHAM
8 miles NE of Leeds off the A1

🏛 Bramham Park

Bramham Park is one of Yorkshire's most exquisite country houses and is special for a number of reasons. The house itself dates from the Queen Anne era. It was built for Robert Benson, Lord Bingley, between 1698 and 1710, and is superbly proportioned in an elegant and restrained classical style. The final effect is more French than English and indeed the gardens were modelled on Louis XIV's Versailles, with ornamental canals and ponds, beech groves, statues, long avenues and an arboretum with an impressive collection of rare and unusual trees. The interior contains elegant furniture and paintings by major artists such as Kneller and Sir Joshua Reynolds.

BOSTON SPA
11 miles NW of Leeds on the A659

Set beside the broad-flowing River Wharfe, this attractive little town enjoyed many years of prosperity after a Mr John Shires discovered a mineral spring here in 1744. The spa activities have long since ceased. There's a pleasant riverside walk that can be continued along the track of a dismantled railway as far as Tadcaster in one direction, Wetherby in the other. The town's impressive 19th-century church is notable for its stately tower and the 36 stone angels supporting the nave and aisles.

WETHERBY
11 miles NW of Leeds off the A1

🏛 Bramham Park

Situated on the Great North Road, at a point midway between Edinburgh and London,

Wetherby was renowned for its coaching inns, of which the two most famous were The Angel and The Swan & Talbot. It is rumoured that serving positions at these inns were considered so lucrative that employees had to pay for the privilege of employment in them!

The town has remained unspoilt and has a quaint appearance with a central marketplace that was first granted to the Knights Templar. Many of the houses in the town are Georgian, Regency, or early Victorian. Apart from its shops, galleries, old pubs, and cafés, there is also a popular racecourse nearby. Another feature is the renowned 18th-century bridge with a long weir, which once provided power for Wetherby's corn mill and possibly dates from medieval times. The bridge once carried traffic along the Great North Road; the A1 now bypasses the town.

About five miles south of Wetherby, **Bramham Park** is noted for its magnificent gardens, 66 acres of them, and its pleasure grounds, which cover a further 100 acres. They are the only example of a formal, early 18th-century landscape in Britain. Temples, ornamental ponds, cascades, a two-mile long avenue of beech trees and one of the best wildflower gardens in the country, are just some of the attractions. In early June, the park hosts the Bramham Horse Trials. The house itself, an attractive Queen Anne building, is open to groups of six or more by appointment only.

ABERFORD
13 miles E of Leeds on the B1217

🏛 Lotherton Estate & Gardens

To the southeast of this village lies an elegant Edwardian mansion, **Lotherton Estate and Gardens**, providing a fascinating insight into

🏛 historic building   🏛 museum and heritage   🏛 historic site   🍃 scenic attraction   🌿 flora and fauna

life in those serene days before the First World War. It was once the home of the Gascoigne family who were local land and coal mine owners. They were also enthusiastic travellers and collectors with a discriminating taste that is evident in the family paintings, furnishings and works of art on display.

The house, gardens and estate were given to the citizens of Leeds in 1968 by Sir Alvary and Lady Gascoigne. Since then their collections have been added to and now include superb 19th- and 20th-century decorative art as well as costume and Oriental art. Other attractions include the Edwardian formal gardens, a walled garden with some quirky spiral topiary, a bird garden with more than 200 species of rare and endangered birds, a 12th-century Chapel of Ease, deer park and café. The estate and gardens are open Tuesday to Sunday and Bank Holiday Mondays March to December.

PONTEFRACT
9 miles SE of Leeds off the M62/A1

🏰 Castle   🏮 Liquorice Fayre

Shakespeare alluded to the town in his plays as 'Pomfret' – a place of influence and power,

often visited by kings and their retinues. The great shattered towers of **Pontefract Castle** (see panel below) stand on a crag to the east of the town. Built by Ilbert de Lacy in the 11th century, it was one of the most formidable fortresses in Norman England. In medieval times it passed to the House of Lancaster and became a Royal Castle. Richard II was imprisoned here and tragically murdered in its dungeons on the orders of Henry Bolingbroke who then assumed the crown as Henry IV.

The castle was a major Royalist stronghold during the Civil War, after which it was destroyed by Cromwell's troops. Today it remains as a gaunt ruin with only sections of the inner bailey and the lower part of the keep surviving intact. There is an underground chamber, part of the dungeons where prisoners carved their names so that they might not be utterly forgotten. The unfortunate Richard II may have been incarcerated in this very chamber.

Many of the streets of Pontefract evoke memories of its medieval past with names such as Micklegate, Beast Fair, Shoe Market,

Pontefract Castle

Castle Chain, Pontefract, Yorkshire WF8 1QH
Tel: 01977 723440
website: www.wakefield.gov.uk

In the Middle Ages, **Pontefract Castle** was one of the most important fortresses in the country. It became a royal castle in 1399, upon the accession of Henry Bolinbroke to the throne. Richard II subsequently died in the castle the following year after being one of many important prisoners to be lodged there.

During the English Civil War the castle was held by the King's supporters throughout three sieges, but as a result, after 1649, it was largely demolished. The remains of the castle, and the underground magazine chamber, are open to visitors. There is also a working blacksmith on site.

FARMER COPLEY'S FARM SHOP

Ravensknowle Farm, Pontefract Road, Purston, nr Pontefract, West Yorkshire WF7 5AF
Tel: 01977 600200   Fax: 0845 2992209
e-mail: info@farmercopleys.co.uk
website: www.farmercopleys.co.uk

Located on the A645 Pontefract-Wakefield road at Purston, **Farmer Copley's Farm Shop** specialises in quality home and locally produced foods, including well matured grass-fed beef, pies, breads, fruit and vegetables, dairy products, preserves and much more. Owners Heather and Robert Copley offer the very best of foods from the region – 80% comes from their own farm (which also grows the famous Pontefract licorice) or from sources within a 30-mile radius, guaranteeing quality, consistency and full traceability. The farm has a full butchery department on site.

A host of awards testifies to the quality of Farmer Copleys: Best Farm Shop at the Great Yorkshire Show, Harvey Nichols Taste Award for its Aberdeen Angus beef, and Best Farm Shop of the Year and Most Innovative Business Awards at the Butchers Shop of the Year Awards 2007-2008 held at Claridge's Hotel in London.

The farm shop is open from 10 to 5.30 (Sunday 10 to 4) 7 days a week.

Salter Row and Ropergate. Modern development has masked much of old Pontefract but there are still many Georgian buildings and old winding streets.

The town's most famous products, of course, are Pontefract Cakes. Liquorice root has been grown here since monastic times and there's even a small planting of liquorice in the local park. The town celebrates this unique heritage with the five-day **Pontefract Liquorice Fayre** in mid-August, which includes two days of jousting, archery and battle re-enactments at Pontefract Castle.

BIRSTALL
6 miles SW of Leeds on the A653

🏛 Oakwell Hall

This town is home to **Oakwell Hall**, an Elizabethan manor house that dates from 1583 and is one of England's most charming historic houses. Now set out as a 17th-century home, the panelled rooms contain a fine collection of oak furniture, reproduction soft furnishings and items of domestic life. The gardens contain period plants, including culinary and medicinal herbs, while the grounds are now Oakwell Hall Country Park. Charlotte Brontë visited the Hall in the 19th century and it appears as Fieldhead in her 1849 novel *Shirley*.

DEWSBURY
8 miles SW of Leeds on the A653

🏛 Minster 🏛 Museum

Dewsbury is an extremely old town, which once had considerable influence. It has one of the region's oldest town centres with an

METCALFES

28 Northgate, Cleckheaton, West Yorkshire BD19 5AE
Tel: 01274 874373

Metcalfes is a traditional family butcher, well-known in the area for the consistently high quality of everything it sells. It was established more than 40 years ago by the Metcalfe family, and with John Metcalfe at the helm, it continues to provide an outstanding service to Cleckheaton and the surrounding district. Behind the classic façade with its distinctive red-and white striped awning, the various meats and meat

products are shown in a spotless, well laid-out display. The cuts and joints, the poultry and the game are all of the very best quality, and the skilled butchers also make use of the same top-notch ingredients to produce the home-cured hams and bacon, pies and pastries, sausages and black puddings for which Metcalfes is renowned and has won many awards and prizes. Quality, consistency and excellent service are watchwords at this outstanding purveyor of meat, whose opening hours are 8 to , Saturday 8 to 4, closed Sunday.

imposing Town Hall designed by Henry Ashton and George Fox. It also has a number of other notable public and commercial buildings, a substantial shopping area (with some 443,500 square feet of retail floorspace) and a famous open market.

According to legend, **Dewsbury Minster** is situated at the very spot where, in AD 627, St Paulinus baptised converts to Christianity in the River Calder. The church dates from the 12th century, although the tower was erected in 1767 to a design by the eminent York architect, John Carr. The interior has some interesting features, among them fragments of an Anglo-Saxon cross and coffin lids. The Minster is perhaps best known for its custom of tolling the 'Devil's Knell' on Christmas Eve to ward off evil spirits, with a bell known as Black Tom. There are Brontë connections here. Patrick Brontë was curate of Dewsbury

between 1809 and 1811, and Charlotte taught at Wealds House School nearby. The school was run by a Miss Wooler who later gave Charlotte away when she was married.

Dewsbury Museum is dedicated to childhood and, open all year, it takes visitors on a fascinating journey right back to the first decades of the 20th century, as seen through the eyes of a child.

Wakefield

🏛 Cathedral 🏛 Sandal Castle 🏛 Nostell Priory

🏛 Museums ✎ Art Gallery ✐ Mystery Plays

One of the oldest towns in Yorkshire, Wakefield stands on a hill guarding an important crossing of the River Calder. Its defensive position has always been importa~ and it was the Battle of Wakefield in 146⁶

FABWORKS MILL SHOP

Providence Mills, Bradford SE, Dewsbury,
West Yorkshire WF13 1EN
Tel: 01924 466031   Fax: 01924 466029
e-mail: sales@fabworks.co.uk
website: www.fabworks.co.uk

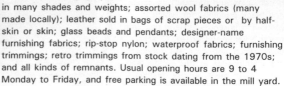

Fabworks was established in 1996 primarily as a textile resource for schools and colleges, involving fashion and dance as well as creative textiles and furnishings. It has grown steadily as a retail outlet, with new types of fabrics added on a regular basis. The stock includes 100% cotton –

plain colours, glazed colours, curtain lining, T-shirting, stripes, checks and printed curtaining; polyester in many shades and weights; assorted wool fabrics (many made locally); leather sold in bags of scrap pieces or by half-skin or skin; glass beads and pendants; designer-name furnishing fabrics; rip-stop nylon; waterproof fabrics; furnishing trimmings; retro trimmings from stock dating from the 1970s; and all kinds of remnants. Usual opening hours are 9 to 4 Monday to Friday, and free parking is available in the mill yard.

when the Duke of York was defeated, that gave rise to the mocking song *The Grand Old Duke of York*.

Many students of the Robin Hood legends claim that the famous outlaw had his origins in Wakefield. As evidence they cite the Court Rolls in which one Robin Hode is noted as living here in the 14th century with his wife Matilda. Also medieval in origin are the **Wakefield Mystery Plays**, which explore Old and New Testament stories in vivid language.

There are four main streets in the city, Westgate, Northgate, Warrengate and Kirkgate, which still preserve the medieval city plan. One of the most striking surviving buildings of that time is the tiny **Chantry Chapel** on Chantry Bridge, which dates from the mid-1300s and is the best of only four ~~s~~uch examples of bridge chapels in England. ~~It~~ is believed to have been built by Edward IV ~~to co~~mmemorate the brutal murder of his ~~broth~~er Edmund. Grandest of all though is

Wakefield Cathedral, which was begun in Norman times, rebuilt in 1329 and refashioned in 1470 when its magnificent 247-foot high spire – the highest in Yorkshire – was added. The eastern extension was added in 1905, which was considered necessary after the church became a Cathedral in 1888. Other interesting buildings in the town include the stately Town Hall, the huge County Hall, the recently restored Victorian Theatre Royal and many fine Georgian and Regency terraces and squares.

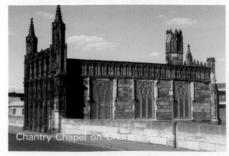

Chantry Chapel on Chantry Bridge

historic building 🏛 museum and heritage 🏚 historic site 🏛 scenic attraction ⚜ flora and fauna

Wakefield's cultural attractions include **Wakefield Art Gallery**, housed in an attractive former Victorian vicarage just a short stroll from the town centre. Collections include many early works by locally born sculptors Henry Moore and Barbara Hepworth, along with important work by many other major British modern artists. **Wakefield Museum**, located in an 1820s building next to the Town Hall, was originally a music saloon and then a Mechanics' Institute. It now houses collections illustrating the history and archaeology of Wakefield and its people from prehistoric times to the present day. There is also a permanent display of exotic birds and animals garnered by the noted 19th-century traveller, naturalist and eccentric, Charles Waterton, who lived at nearby Walton Hall where he created the world's first nature reserve. Also of interest is the **Stephen G Beaumont Museum**, which houses an unusual exhibition of medical memorabilia and exhibits telling the story of the local lunatic asylum that was founded in 1818 and only closed in 1995. The museum, which has a scale model of the early 19th-century building, is only open on Wednesdays.

Just south of the city centre stands **Sandal Castle**, a 12th-century motte-and-bailey fortress that was later replaced by a stone structure. It overlooks the site of the Battle of Wakefield in 1460. Such was this castle's importance that Richard III was planning to make Sandal his permanent northern stronghold when he was killed at Bosworth Field. Today, all that remains are ruins as the castle was destroyed by Cromwell's troops after a siege in 1645. From the castle there are magnificent views across the Calder Valley. Discoveries made during recent excavations of the site can be found in Wakefield's new Interpretive Centre.

A visit to the **National Coal Mining**

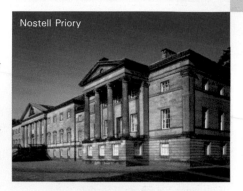

Nostell Priory

Museum for England at Caphouse Colliery in Overton, a few miles southwest of Wakefield, includes a guided tour 450 feet underground, indoor exhibitions and videos, outdoor machine displays, a working steam winder, train rides and, for children, an adventure playground and some friendly pit ponies.

Over to the southeast from Wakefield, **Nostell Priory** is one of the most popular tourist venues in this area. The word 'priory' is misleading since it evokes the picture of an ecclesiastical structure. But Nostell is in fact a large Palladian building erected on the site of an old Augustinian priory. It was in 1733 that the owner, Sir Rowland Winn, commissioned James Paine to build a grand mansion here. Paine was only 19 at the time and this was his first major project. Thirty years later, only half the state rooms were constructed and Sir Rowland's son, also named Rowland, engaged an up-and-coming young designer to complete the decoration. The young man's name was Robert Adam, and between 1766 and 1776 his dazzling designs produced an incomparable sequence of interiors.

There was a third man of genius involved in the story of Nostell Priory – the cabinet maker Thomas Chippendale. What is believed to be his 'apprentice piece', made around 1735, is on display here – an extraordinary doll's house six

Newmillerdam

Distance: *3.7 miles (5.9 kilometres)*

Typical time: *90 mins*

Height gain: *100 metres*

Map: *Explorer 278*

Walk: *www.walkingworld.com ID:2083*

Contributor: *Graham Wilson*

ACCESS INFORMATION:

Buses come here from Wakefield and Barnsley. There is a pay and display car park at the start of the walk.

ADDITIONAL INFORMATION:

Newmillerdam boasts three pubs with food, one restaurant (next to the car park) and one café. You can also guarantee ice cream vans at most times of the year. The car park is pay and display and is situated opposite the Fox and Hounds pub.

DESCRIPTION:

This circular walk passes through five separately named woods. Long Bank Plantation, Bushcliff Wood and Kings Wood are old mixed broadleaf woodlands, together with some stands of conifers, which comprise Newmillerdam Country Park. These woods are striking when the leaves are in fall, in bud, when the rhododendrons are in flower and when the bluebells carpet the ground.

Seckar Wood and Patch Wood are predominately silver birch and oak. These woods are renowned for the variety of fungi which can

be found on the rotting dead wood. It is within the heart of these woods that the land tops out and the heather-clad sandy moorland provides glorious views across West Yorkshire.

FEATURES:

Pub, Toilets, Cafe, Public Transport, Restaurant, Woodland

WALK DIRECTIONS:

1 | Leave the car park opposite the Fox and Hounds and turn right on the Barnsley Road. Cross over the lake.

2 | Next to The Dam pub, take the steep road up the hill, alongside the wall of the park. At the top of the hill turn right and walk to the end of Hill Top Road.

3 | Where Hill Top Road takes a 90 degree bend, carry straight on into the field and take the footpath across the field to where it meets the woods. Enter the woods and go straight on down the wide track until the bottom of

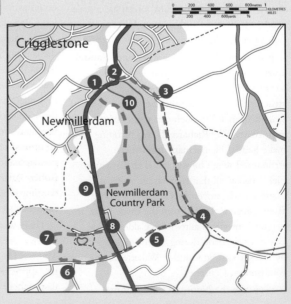

the hill. The path carries straight on as the slope levels out but you will see a 45 degree fork to your right, which only stretches for a hundred yards or so.

4 | At this fork turn right and then right again, onto the main track. Follow this track over the stream and up the hill.

5 | At the top of the hill, there is the first bridge over the disused railway on your left. Take this track to the left and follow it until reaching the Barnsley Road. Cross the road and go up Seckar Lane until reaching a footpath sign to the right.

6 | At this footpath, follow the path into the woods. It is narrow and takes you down to the bottom of the valley, across boardwalks and up the other side. On the ascent, there is a fork with a waymarker sign; take the left fork which goes straight up the hill and comes out at a wide track in open country.

7 | At this wide track you will turn right and follow the track back to the Barnsley Road. Before doing this though, detour left onto the heathland and enjoy the views.

8 | At the road turn left and walk until crossing the disused railway. After this there is a lay-by on the right-hand side, with a double gate leading back into the woods.

9 | Go through this gate and quickly pick up a trail off to the left. The trail is within the woods, but you can see the fence of the lodge house on your left. The trail winds its way through these woods until meeting a better trodden path. There are a few, don't worry which one you take, so long as you are eventually travelling with the field wall parallel to your path.

10 | When the field wall turns 90 degrees left, your path goes diagonally to the left and down the hill, back into the car park.

feet high and replete with the most elaborate detail, every minuscule door, window or desk drawer functioning perfectly. Today, Nostell Priory can boast the most comprehensive collection of Chippendale's work in the world.

Around Wakefield

WINTERSETT
6 miles SE of Wakefield off the A638

🐦 Heronry & Countryside Discovery Centre

Found on the historic estate of Walton Hall, once the home of the famous 19th-century naturalist Charles Waterton, is the **Heronry and Waterton Countryside Discovery Centre**, which provides information and exhibitions about the surrounding country park, which includes two reservoirs and woodland that was once part of the ancient Don Forest.

WOOLLEY
6 miles S of Wakefield off the A61

🐦 🦌 Newmillerdam Country Park & Boathouse

Despite being surrounded by industrial towns, Woolley has managed to retain its rural air and its old hall, now a course and conference centre, standing on land that was originally enclosed as a hunting park during the reign of Henry VII. Just to the northeast lies **Newmillerdam Country Park and Boathouse**, which was, in the 19th century, part of the Chevet Estate and a playground for the local Pilkington family. The boathouse, built in the 1820s, has been restored as a visitors' centre (open Sundays and Bank Holiday Mondays), while the rest of the 240-acre park offers ample opportunity for walking and viewing wildlife at close quarters. Just to the northwest lies Woolley Edge, from where there are wonderful views out across

ORIGIN

86 Fenay Bridge Road,
Fenay Bridge, Huddersfield,
West Yorkshire HD8 0AY
Tel: 01484 431461
e-mail: info@origin-gifts.co.uk
website: origin-gifts.co.uk

With a background in design and an
awareness of the very limited choice of
gifts and cards in the area, the owner
of **Origin** found the perfect answer!
That was in 1985, and her first Origin
was in Halifax's historic Piece Hall;
since then she has moved twice, and the present premises in Fenay
Bridge Road were acquired in 1990.

This is a redbrick country-style building under a recycled blue slate
mill roof built to her own design, and she has had to extend the
building three times to accommodate the ever-increasing range of
products. To call this an Aladdin's Cave does it scant justice. The
owner tried to provide an ever-changing range of lovely gifts,
greetings cards and packaging for all tastes and occasions. Every
space (even the ceiling!) is filled with an eyecatching display of
beautiful things priced to suit all pockets.

Prominent on show is a fine variety of health care and toiletry
products, including the ranges of top producers Nougat skincare,
Crabtree & Evelyn, which is highly desirable, Bath House for men and
women, and Bach Flower Remedies. Senses are enlivened through
ranges of aromatherapy products by Tisserand and Natural by Nature oils, Colony Candles and
the highly practical range of the Natural Wheatbag Company. There are cards for every
conceivable occasion, jewellery for young and old, and children will love their own little part of
the shop, where the Jellycat and Jelly Kitten, Think Pink and Humphrey's Corner ranges are

guaranteed to delight. Origin is open from 9.30
to 5.30 Tuesday to Saturday (and other days on
the run up to Christmas). Free parking is
available outside the shop.

Emley Moor and, on a clear day, all the way to Barnsley. The discovery of a flint axe as well as flints and scrapers from the Iron Age suggest that there have been settlements here since prehistoric times.

NORMANTON
4 miles E of Wakefield off the A655

A former mining town, Normanton has a spacious park, a moat round a hill where the Romans built a camp, and a large, mostly 15th-century church with a fine 500-year-old font. The stained glass windows here are something of an oddity since none of them originally belonged to the church. They were part of a collection amassed by a 19th-century resident of the town who was himself a glass painter and bequeathed the unrelated pieces to the church. The most striking is a 15th-century *Pietà* in the east window, which has been identified as Flemish in origin.

Huddersfield

| 📷 Canals 📷 Tolson Memorial Museum |
| 📷 Standedge Visitor Centre 🎨 Art Gallery |

Huddersfield's earliest roots can be found on the 1,000-foot high Castle Hill, which has been occupied as a defence since the Stone Age. Simple tools, flints, bone needles, combs and pottery, dating back to 2000 BC have been unearthed here. The much later ramparts of an Iron Age fort, built here around 600 BC can still be seen. In 1147 the Normans repaired the earthworks and built a motte and bailey castle, which was apparently used as a base for hunting. The hill was also used as a beacon when England was threatened by the Spanish Armada, and again during the Napoleonic wars. The lofty Jubilee Tower, built in 1897 to celebrate Queen Victoria's Diamond Jubilee, is

the most recent structure on the summit and was funded by public subscription. Inside the tower there's a museum that traces the hill's 4,000 years of history.

With its steep, often cobbled streets, millstone grit cottages and larger Victorian dwellings, Huddersfield has a very distinctive character all its own. The town flourished in Victorian times and its most impressive buildings date from that era. The stately railway station was designed by James Pigott of York and built between 1846-50, to be followed by the Italianate Town Hall.

Back in the town, the **Tolson Memorial Museum** has displays that range from the tools of the earliest settlers in the area to modern day collections contributed by local people. One of the most popular exhibits is the collection of vintage vehicles and motoring memorabilia in the 'Going Places' collection. Other displays trace the story of the Industrial Revolution, so important to the growth of the town, and the political protests it engendered.

Huddersfield Art Gallery holds the Kirklees Collection of British Art covering the past 150 years, with a lively programme of exhibitions that showcase contemporary works from regional, national and international artists.

The town is also home to two canals that helped to link Huddersfield not only with the national canal network, but also with other industrial towns. Completed in 1780 and paid for by the Ramsden family, the **Huddersfield Broad Canal** was constructed to link the town with the Calder and Hebble Navigation. The canal's Aspley Basin is today home to a marina. In 1794, work began on the **Huddersfield Narrow Canal**, linking the town with Ashton-under-Lyne. Its centrepiece, the Standedge Tunnel, took 17

THORNCLIFFE FARM SHOP

Westfield Lane, Emley Moor, nr Huddersfield, West Yorkshire HD8 9SZ
Tel: 01924 848171
Fax: 01924 848593
e-mail: craddockjnjnc@aol.com

Located at Emley Moor, off the A642 east of Huddersfield, **Thorncliffe Farm Shop** specialises in traditionally-hung home-fed beef, pork, lamb, chicken and fresh fruit and vegetables.

The shop is owned and run full-time by Rosemary and Mat Craddock; Rosemary is the 6th generation of the family who first farmed here in 1827 and Mat trained as an agricultural engineer. Stone-built, slate-roofed buildings were converted into a shop whose reputation extends far beyond the locality, but it started in a small way. When the shop opened in 1999 in a pig stye up the road from the family farm, the staff consisted of Rosemary and a part-time butcher.

Twice extended, in 2001 and 2004, it comprises a butchery counter, a delicatessen area, a fruit and vegetable area and a large bakery. It now employs 37 staff full or part time, including seven qualified butchers and six in the kitchen producing the dishes and meals that would grace the kitchen of any restaurant, entirely additive-free and bearing no relation to the mass-produced meals that rightly attract so much scorn. The home-reared meat is the mainstay of the business, but the ready-meals also bring customers from many miles around. They include the likes of beef in Guinness, lasagne, moussaka and ham shanks, along with outstanding sausages and pies – steak, steak & kidney, meat & potato, chicken - all made using the farm's produce. The shop sells a huge selection of prime cheeses, bread, cakes and pastries, preserves and pickles.

Thorncliffe has won many awards, including NFU Best Farm Shop Yorkshire and the Northeast, Farm Retail Association's Best UK Newcomer and BPEX gold awards 2006-2007 for their pies, sausages and ready-meals. There's plenty to see in the area, including Bretton Sculpture Park at West Bretton, the National Coalmining Museum at Middlestown and the Kirklees Light Railway at Clayton West. But for lovers of top-quality food a trip to this wonderful village shop must be high on the list of places to visit. It is open from 8.30 to 6 Monday to Friday, 8.30 to 4 Saturday, and 10 to 1 Sunday.

years to complete and is the longest, highest and deepest canal tunnel in the country. The **Standedge Visitor Centre** at Marsden houses an exciting and interactive exhibition telling the story of the canal and the tunnel. The surrounding countryside offers a wide range of activities including walking, cycling and fishing, and this area of outstanding natural beauty is also a haven for wildlife. Not far from Huddersfield, Kirklees is traditionally the place where Robin Hood died, bled to death by the wicked prioress. With his dying breath he shot an arrow and asked his Merry Men to bury him at the spot where it fell. A stone tablet marks that spot in a wood above the River Calder.

Around Huddersfield

SCAPEGOAT HILL
3 miles W of Huddersfield off the A62 or A640

Colne Valley Museum

About a mile south of the oddly-named Scapegoat Hill, the **Colne Valley Museum** is housed in three 19th-century weavers' cottages near the parish church. Visitors can see a loom chamber with working hand looms and a Spinning Jenny; a weavers' living room of 1850 and a gas-lit clogger's shop of 1910. On two weekends a year, a craft weekend is held when many different skills are demonstrated. Light refreshments are available and there's also a museum shop. Run entirely by its members, the museum has featured many times on TV and is open weekends and Bank Holidays throughout the year, but party visits can be arranged at other times.

MELTHAM
5 miles SW of Huddersfield on the B6107/B6108

A typical Pennine mill town, Meltham is

mostly Victorian but with a handsome Georgian parish church dating from 1786, which is challenged in size by the spacious Baptist Chapel, rebuilt in 1864. Only two mills have survived, but the Meltham Mills Band, founded in 1845, is still thriving and has won many competitions throughout the country, including the British Championship.

Some customs of the past have also managed to survive. On Collap Monday (the day before Shrove Tuesday) the town's shopkeepers distribute free sweets to children; there is carol singing on Christmas Eve in the centre of the village; and on Whit Monday the different congregations of churches and chapels join in the Whitsuntide Walk around the town accompanied by the brass band.

HOLMBRIDGE
7 miles SW of Huddersfield on the A6024

This charming village stands at the head of a steep-sided valley and enjoys picture-postcard views of the Pennines and the Holme valley. There are cottages here dating from the 1700s and the area is known for its unusual style of architecture, four-decker cottages dug into the hillside. The lower cottage is approached from the front, the upper cottage is reached by a steep flight of stone steps leading round the back.

HONLEY
3 miles S of Huddersfield off the A616

The centre of this delightful little Pennine village has been designated as a site of historic interest. There are charming terraces of weavers' cottages and lots of interesting alleyways, and the old village stocks still stand in the churchyard of St Mary's. The Coach and Horses Inn has strong connections with the Luddite movement of the early 1800s. It was

SHADES OF CHINA

23 Hollowgate, Holmfirth, West Yorkshire HD9 2DG
Tel/Fax: 01484 687596

There has been a china shop on these premises for more
than 20 years. The current owner is Karen Keighley, who
took over the business in 2007.

Shades Of China is the leading local supplier of china,
glassware and collectables. Most of the top names are
represented which includes Border Fine Arts (both classic
and studio ranges), Royal Doulton, Royal Worcester and
Spode. Emma Bridgewater, Poole Pottery and Royal Scot Crystal are also available.

There is also a good selection of baby and christening gifts, many
of which can be personalised with the baby's name. Celebration
giftware is also on sale for events such as ruby and golden weddings.
The delightful range of collectables includes Beatrix Potter, Winnie the

Pooh and Wallace and Gromit. The
attractive village of Holmfirth is a
beautiful place for a stroll, with
courtyards, alleyways, weavers' cottages
and a lovely Georgian church – and of
course the *Last of the Summer Wine*
connection. But it's also an excellent
place to find a special gift, as Shades of
China proves.

BEATTIES DELI & COFFEE SHOP

6 Towngate, Holmfirth, West Yorkshire HD9 1HA
Tel: 01484 689006
website: www.beattiesdeli.co.uk

Visitors to the pretty town of Holmfirth will fine plenty of
interesting things to see, but it would be really batty not to find
time to look in at **Beatties Deli & Coffee Shop**. Frank Westerby
has filled his shop with all kinds of good things to eat and drink.
The delicatessen range includes speciality cheeses, quiches,
pâtés, cooked and preserved meats, roasted vegetables, olives
and olive oils, balsamic vinegar, wine vinegar and pesto. There
are made-to-order sandwiches, baguettes and panini, jacket
potatoes, soups, salads, savoury and sweet pastries, chilli jam,
Thai jelly, onion marmalade and Rosebud preserves, jams, jellies
and pickles hand-
made in Yorkshire.
Beatties stocks a fine
range of freshly
ground coffees and
speciality teas. This
excellent shop is
open from 9.30 to 5
seven days a week.

ATKINSONS BUTCHERS

Sheffield Road, New Mill, Holmfirth, West Yorkshire HD9 7JT
Tel: 01484 683288
Email: atkinsons.butchers@hotmail.co.uk

Quality and personal service are bywords at **Atkinsons**, a high-class family butcher, poulterer and licensed game dealer in the heart of *Summer Wine* country. The butcher's bike with its basket propped against the wall sets the tone for this traditional but modern shop, which has been owned and run by brothers John and Paul Mallinson since 1991. All the meat comes from locally reared animals, many of which are sourced at the Holmfirth auction mart. From the delicatessen counter come pies and pasties, cooked and cured meats, freshly-cut sandwiches, English and Continental cheeses, olive oil on tap, pickles and preserves.

here, in 1812, that two Luddites, Benjamin Walker and Thomas Smith, spent the night drinking after murdering a mill owner at nearby Marsden. They were later arrested, convicted and executed at York. Not far from the inn is another interesting feature – an old well dated 1796 whose date stone warns passers-by they will be fined 10 shillings (50p) if found to be 'defouling' the water.

THONGSBRIDGE
5 miles S of Huddersfield on the A616

Upperthong, Netherthong and Thongsbridge derive the common element of their names from the Danish word 'thing', meaning an assembly or council. Thongsbridge is set beside a tributary of the River Holme and is very much a part of the *Last of the Summer Wine* country.

HOLMFIRTH
6 miles S of Huddersfield on the A6024/A635

  🖉 Picturedrome

BBC-TV's longest-running situation comedy, *Last of the Summer Wine*, has made the little Pennine town of Holmfirth familiar to viewers around the world. Visitors can enjoy an authentic bacon buttie in the real Sid's Café, gaze at Nora Batty's cottage, and sit in the famous pub. The rest of the town offers a network of side lanes, courts and alleyways while the terraces of weavers' cottages are typical of a town famous for its production of wool textiles.

As with so many of these moorland villages, there is a lot of surrounding water, and in its time Holmfirth has suffered three major floods. The worse occurred in 1852 when the nearby Bilberry Reservoir burst its

Last of the Summer Wine, Exhibition

🖺 stories and anecdotes 🐦 famous people 🎨 art and craft 🖉 entertainment and sport 🚶 walks

banks, destroying mills, cottages and farms, killing 81 people. A pillar near the church records the height the waters reached.

Holmfirth has a lovely Georgian church, built in 1777-8 in neo-classical style to the designs of Joseph Jagger. The gable faces the street and the tower is constructed at the eastern end against a steep hillside.

During the first half of the 20th century, a comprehensive range of traditional saucy seaside postcards was produced by Bamforths of Holmfirth. The company also printed hymn sheets and, rather surprisingly, made many early silent movies. Bamforths also owned a cinema in the town, which has recently been restored as **Picturedrome**. The re-instated building now hosts a wide range of film events and other entertainment, and there is also a selection of the vintage postcards on display.

HEPWORTH
7 miles S of Huddersfield on the A616

What is one to make of a village that lies on the River Jordan, has a house that has always been known as Solomon's Temple (although no one knows why), and a parcel of land called Paradise, the only place it is said where fruit trees will grow? There are some other curious names here, including Meal Hill, where the Romans brought their hand-mill stones to grind corn, and Barracks Fold where, during the plague, the healthy barricaded themselves in against the

---

THINKING OF YOU

10B Commercial Road, Skelmanthorpe,
Huddersfield, HD8 9DA
Tel: 01484 865553
website: www.thinking-of-you.org

Thinking of You was opened by Melinda in 1999. Nine years and five expansions later, the shop consists of 10 rooms situated on three floors filled with beautiful cards, gifts and jewellery for every occasion. Of our hundreds of cards on offer, many are handmade, beautiful works of art in themselves. Most of our rooms are themed. We have one room entirely dedicated to jewellery to suit all tastes, styles and pockets, another for children's gifts, another for weddings and so on. We are a happy, friendly shop and are always on hand to give help and advice (and make cups of tea!). We understand the importance of finding exactly the right card and/or gift to suit the person/occasion. It's very easy to spend a pleasurable hour or two exploring all our rooms and perusing our vast range of quality and tasteful stock covering all price ranges (hence the cups of tea!). We also have a

free gift-wrapping service, and if you spend more than £15 on a gift, the wrapping paper comes free, too. Situated on the main road in Skelmanthorpe, which is a large, busy, friendly village, convenient for Huddersfield, Barnsley and Wakefield and close to junctions 38 and 39 off the M1, we are open six days a week (longer at Christmas) and look forward to your visit.

🏠 historic building   🏛 museum and heritage   🏚 historic site   🍃 scenic attraction   🌱 flora and fauna

infected. There are still some triangular patches of land in the village that are believed to contain the common graves of the plague victims.

FARNLEY TYAS
3 miles SE of Huddersfield off the A626 or A629

Farnley Tyas is another attractive Pennine village with scattered stone farmhouses and barns, and 18th- and 19th-century workers' cottages grouped around the crossroads. It is mentioned in the *Domesday Book* as 'Fereleia': the Tyas part of its name comes from the Le Teyeis family which owned much of the land hereabouts from the 13th century.

DENBY DALE
8 miles SE of Huddersfield on the A635/A636

Denby Dale is famous for its gigantic meat pies. The first of these Desperate Dan-sized dishes was baked in 1788 to celebrate George III's return to sanity and later ones marked the victory of Waterloo and Queen Victoria's Jubilee. The 1928 monster meal was organised to raise funds for the Huddersfield Royal Infirmary, but the festivities were almost cancelled when the organisers discovered that a large part of the pie had gone bad. Four barrowloads of stinking meat were secretly spirited away.

Perhaps because of that mishap, no more great pies were attempted until 1964 when it was decided to commemorate the four royal births of that year. On this occasion, two walls of Mr Hector Buckley's barn, in which the pie had been baked, had to be demolished to get it out. The most recent pie was made in 2000 as part of the town's Millennium celebrations. It weighed a hearty 12 tonnes.

CLAYTON WEST
8 miles SE of Huddersfield on the A636

🏛 Kirklees Light Railway   🎨 Yorkshire Sculpture Park

A popular attraction at Clayton West is the **Kirklees Light Railway**, a 15 inch gauge steam railway that runs along the old Lancashire and Yorkshire Clayton West branch line. The track runs through gently rolling farmland for about four miles with a quarter-mile long tunnel adding to the thrill. The large station/visitor centre at Clayton West provides passengers with comfortable, spacious surroundings to await their train or take advantage of the light refreshment café and the souvenir shop. The railway operates daily during the season and every weekend throughout the year. For train times and other information, telephone 01484 865727.

One of the leading attractions of the area is found about three miles northeast of Clayton West, conveniently close to Junction 38 of the M1. The **Yorkshire Sculpture Park** draws in some 200,000 visitors a year and since you only pay a small charge for parking it represents amazing value for money. Changing exhibitions of sculpture are set in the beautiful 18th-century parkland of Bretton Hall, 200 acres of historic landscape providing a wonderful setting for some of the best sculpture to be seen in Britain today by artists from around the world.

Alongside the programme of indoor and outdoor exhibitions, more permanent features include the YSP collection of works in many different styles (from 19th-century bronzes by Rodin to contemporary sculptures), and a display of monumental bronzes by Henry Moore sited within the adjacent 100-acre Bretton Country Park.

LOCATOR MAP

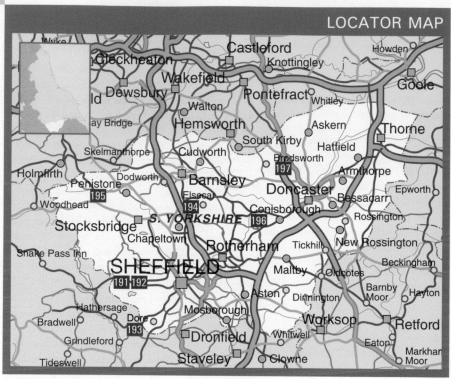

ADVERTISERS AND PLACES OF INTEREST

7| South Yorkshire

South Yorkshire tends to be overlooked as a tourist venue, but this is a region of great age and antiquity and, in many places, real beauty, both natural and man-made. Sheffield claims to be England's greenest city, and the wild open spaces of the Pennine moorlands of the Peak District National Park roll right up to its western boundaries.

Sheffield's prosperity is founded on steel and, in particular, cutlery, and though there are few ancient buildings in England's fourth-largest city to explore, there is a wealth of museums and galleries on offer to the visitor. To the north of Sheffield is Barnsley, whose prosperity comes from the rich seams of coal that have been exploited in the local area. Meanwhile, to the east lies Rotherham, where iron ore has been mined and smelted since the 12th century. While its wealth is certainly based upon metal, Rotherham is also the home of Rockingham Pottery, which was was once favoured by royalty.

Further east again is the busy riverside town of Doncaster, which was established by the Romans and today has the air of a pleasant market town. However, this was once one of the country's most important centres of steam locomotive manufacture

Whirlow Brook Park, Sheffield

and it is famous for having built *Mallard*, which still holds the record for the top speed attained by a steam train. Today, though, Doncaster is best known as the home of the St Leger, Britain's oldest classic horse race, first run in 1776.

Elsewhere in the county visitors can discover the delights of Roche Abbey, a 12th-century Cistercian house, Conisbrough Castle, which boasts the oldest stone keep in England, and the faded Victorian grandeur of Brodsworth Hall.

Sheffield

- 🏛 City Museum & Art Gallery 🖼 Graves Art Gallery
- 🏛 Kelham Island Museum 🖼 Millennium Galleries
- 🏛 Bishop's House Museum 🖼 Site Gallery
- 🏛 Traditional Heritage Museum
- 🏛 Turner Museum of Glass 🌿 Botanical Gardens
- 🏛 Sheffield Bus Museum
- 🏛 South Yorkshire Railway

In recent years, Sheffield has reinvented itself. England's fourth-largest city, it is still busy with its steel, cutlery, engineering and tool-making industries, but is also a vibrant, international, multi-cultural city and a world-class centre for sport, headquarters of the government-backed UK Sports Institute with an impressive array of international venues. There are facilities for iceskating, dry skiing and two indoor climbing centres. It is perhaps the fastest-growing city in Yorkshire, thanks to a forward-looking programme of new housing and public spaces and a university that continues to draw students in their thousands, many of whom choose to stay on in Sheffield after they've finished their studies. It was well placed for the development of the steel industry, with local iron ore, stone for grinding and plentiful supplies of water rushing down from the Pennines. Thomas Boulsover was a pioneer in the development of Sheffield plate and Henry Bessemer, who developed his process for simplifying the process of making steel, he set up his works in Sheffield. It is appropriate that the Town Hall, built in Renaissance style in 1897, is crowned with a statue of Vulcan, the Roman god of metal and fire. Notable among the city's many museums is the **Kelham Island Museum**, a living museum that tells the story of Sheffield. Visitors can see the mighty River Don Engine

in steam – the most powerful working steam engine in Europe; reconstructed workshops; the Little Mesters working cutler; and craftspeople demonstrating traditional Made in Sheffield skills. For children up to nine years old, The Melting Shop provides an interactive experience where they can 'clock on' to become a piece of steel – including being rolled and hammered!

Sheffield's industrial heritage is celebrated at the **City Museum and Mappin Art Gallery** in Weston Park. The museum houses the city's collection of cutlery, metalwork, ceramics, coins, archaeology and natural history. The Mappin Art Gallery has a permanent display of Victorian paintings and organises an imaginative programme of temporary exhibitions.

Sheffield Cathedral

Bishops' House

Norton Lees Lane, Sheffield, Yorkshire S8 9BE
Tel: 0114 278 2600

Bishops' House is the best preserved timber-framed house in Sheffield. It was built around 1500 and is tucked away at the top of Meersbrook Park. Bishops' House typifies the development of the smaller English domestic house in the 16th and 17th centuries. Inside, the house retains many of its original features and looks just as it would have done in the 17th century, giving a tantalising flavour of Stuart England. The Great Parlour is restored as a typical dining room and the first floor chamber contains the original bedroom furniture and fittings listed in a 17th-century inventory of contents.

Many different families have lived in the house over the years, but the first owners remain a mystery. There is a story that the house was built for two brothers, John and Geoffrey Blythe, who went on to become Bishops, but there is no evidence that Bishops' House was their home.

In 1886, the property passed to the Corporation (now Sheffield City Council) and until 1974 Recreation Department employees lived in the house. In 1976 Bishops' House was restored and opened as a museum.

Sheffield has several outstanding galleries devoted to the visual arts. The **Millennium Galleries** have helped to establish the city as a cultural force in the north of England. A remarkable building of white columns and striking glass arches, it holds four unique galleries that showcase not only Sheffield's impressive metalware collection, but also provide space to show the city's wonderful collection of paintings, drawings and natural history exhibits. One gallery hosts visiting installations from the Victoria and Albert Museum and other distinguished collections from throughout the country; another features the very best of contemporary design and technology, while a third houses the fascinating collection formed for the people of Sheffield in 1875 by the Victorian artist,

critic and sage, John Ruskin. It includes paintings, watercolours and drawings, minerals, plaster casts and architectural details, illuminated manuscripts and books.

Nearby, the **Graves Art Gallery**, given in the 1930s by a businessman who established the country's first mail-order firm, displays a wide-ranging collection of British art from the 16th century to the present, along with European paintings and a fine collection of watercolours, drawings and prints. One of its major treasures is the Grice Collection of Chinese ivories, which forms the centrepiece of a display of non-European artefacts.

Another gallery of interest, the **Site Gallery**, is devoted to photographic and new media exhibitions and events. One of the largest contemporary visual art and media centres in the country, the gallery also offers darkroom and digital imaging facilities, as well as photographic and digital courses in the recently created education suite.

Sheffield's most picturesque museum is undoubtedly the **Bishop's House Museum** (see panel on page 359), which dates from around 1500 and is the earliest timber-framed house still standing in the city. Many original features survive and the bedchamber and great parlour are furnished in the style of the home of a prosperous 17th-century yeoman. There are also displays on Sheffield in Tudor and Stuart times, and changing exhibitions on local history themes.

The **Traditional Heritage Museum** offers a unique collection of displays on life and work in the city between the 1850s and 1950s while, at the University of Sheffield, the **Turner Museum of Glass** contains over 300 items of contemporary and art glass from Europe and the United States along with a unique collection of over 100 drinking glasses.

A museum of a very different nature, the **Sheffield Bus Museum**, is housed in the Tinsley Tram sheds on Sheffield Road. The collection includes many types of bus and other transport-related exhibits such as destination blinds, old timetables and models. The museum also houses the Tinsley Model Railway layout.

Of related interest is the **South Yorkshire Railway** in Meadowbank. As well as displaying more than 60 locomotives, there are vintage carriages and wagons, and a signal box. Plans are underway to run a steam-hauled passenger

---

INSIDE

261 Sharrow Vale Road, Sheffield,
South Yorkshire S11 8ZE
Tel/Fax: 0114 268 6838
e-mail: insidesheffield@hotmail.co.uk
website: www.inside-interiors.uk.com

Deborah Hunt returned from a career in London to her home city of Sheffield to open **Inside** in 2001. Elizabeth Parker, a trained illustrator and graphic artist, has been managing the shop alongside her since 2007. The word eclectic could have been coined for this splendid enterprise, where every visit brings new things to discover for home and gift ideas. The stock includes a combination of vintage items and salvaged finds with contemporary design from around the world, and an intriguing variety of furniture and gifts sourced from European markets and international suppliers. The exterior retains the traditional look of its days as a butchers shop, and the red door, flanked by handsome box trees, tempts browsers and buyers into a treasure trove of gift ideas and lovely things for the home. The shop has an intimate boutique style, with the warmth and welcoming feel of a real home – slate floor, hand-crafted kitchen area, exposed brick, chandeliers, and original old-fashioned counters. The shop stands just off the main shopping area of Ecclesall Road, five minutes from the city centre and a quick drive from the Derbyshire countryside. Shop hours are 10 to 5.30 Monday to Saturday, also Sundays on the run-up to Christmas.

Sheffield Botanic Gardens

Botanical Gardens, with collections of shrubs, trees and plantings sheltered in a historic landscape first opened in 1836.

Around Sheffield

CROSSPOOL

4 miles W of Sheffield on the A57

The Bell Hagg Inn

Intriguingly, it was a fit of pique that led to the building of **The Bell Hagg Inn**. Back in the 1830s a certain Dr Hodgson offered the vicar of Stannington (a village across the River Rivel from Crosspool) a large donation for the church funds. But Hodgson was well known as

service on the three-and-a-half miles line from Meadowhall to Chapeltown.

Nor is Sheffield all hustle and bustle. The city's most peaceful spot has to be the

---

DORE DELICATESSEN

40 High Street, Dore, nr Sheffield, South Yorkshire S17 3GU
Tel: 0114 236 8574
e-mail: info@catherines-choice.com
website: www.catherines-choice.com

Behind the blue-shuttered frontage on the main street of Dore, David and Catherine Trickett's **Dore Delicatessen** is filled with good things to eat. Food is a passion here, as demonstrated by the aphorism printed on the menu: 'If more of us valued food and cheer and song above hoarded gold, it would be a merrier world.' Priding itself as Sheffield's premier producer of home cooking, it offers a super choice that runs from bites and nibbles to sandwiches and wraps, jacket potatoes, quiches, chicken liver pâté, fish pies, cottage pies, apple pie, carrot cake, chocolate cake and tarte au citron.

The shop also sells a fine selection of prime cheeses, local cooked meats, ice cream, mincemeat and top-quality bottled goods. Personalised picnic hampers provide a wonderful variety of savoury delights and scrumptious desserts, and hand-chosen packed lunches are perfect for hikers and cyclists. The Dore Delicatessen caters for all sorts of occasions, from meetings and conferences to dinner parties and champagne breakfasts.

---

stories and anecdotes 　 famous people 　 art and craft 　 entertainment and sport 　 walks

Bradfield

Distance: *3.7 miles (5.9 kilometres)*

Typical time: *120 mins*

Height gain: *140 metres*

Map: *Explorer OL 1*

Walk: *www.walkingworld.com ID:2469*

Contributor: *Graham Wilson*

Buses run to Bradfield from Sheffield; refer to
local bus companies in South Yorkshire.
Car parking is in Bradfield.

DESCRIPTION:

This walk provides a lovely way to spend an
afternoon in picturesque South Yorkshire. The
village of Bradfield is deservedly popular, as it
is a delightful place with a fantastically-sited
church up the hill. The circular route is easy
but takes in waterside woods, broadleaf
woods, a nature reserve famed for its frog
sub-species, coniferous woods and open fields
affording good views across to the Pennines.
As the walk crosses into two different dales, it
provides differing aspects of this area of the
country.

FEATURES:

Lake/Loch, Pub, Toilets,
Church, Birds, Great Views,
Food Shop, Public Transport,
Tea Shop, Woodland

WALK DIRECTIONS:

1 | Park your car either on the
roadside near the cricket
pitch, or in the car park at
the rear. Wherever you have
parked, effectively walk anti-
clockwise around the walled

pitch until reaching the corner near the shop.
At this corner, take the left-hand road off the
main road until it becomes a track.

2 | As the road becomes a track, follow it for a
few yards until it goes off to the right. Turn
right at this point and ascend the hill using
these old steps. Carry on up the hill until
meeting the road.

3 | At the road, turn left.

4 | After passing the reservoir, there is a gate
on the left marked 'Agden Reservoir'. Turn
left through the gate and follow the waterside
track. The track follows the reservoir edges
until being routed slightly uphill to a gate. Go
through this gate and turn left.

5 | Follow this track and when it meets a wall
where the wooded area thins out with a track
off to the right, follow the main path straight
on. Follow the path until it turns sharp left and
crosses the river. Carry on with this track up
the other side of the valley.

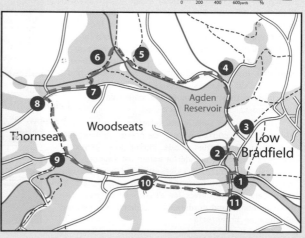

6 | The track meets a crossroads of paths here. Go straight on over this crossroads. Again the track winds its way up through the woods until turning back on itself over a river-bridge. At this point follow the track until meeting the road.

7 | At the road, turn right up the hill until the next road junction.

8 | At the road junction, turn left until meeting the first bridleway sign off to the left. At this sign, turn left into the fields and head along this track until dropping down to the next road.

9 | At the road, turn left and walk along it until meeting a smaller road coming in from the right.

10 | Turn right down this smaller road to the bottom of the valley. Shortly after ascending again, there is a path off to the left. Cross the stile to the left and follow this footpath through the fields until emerging at the road.

11 | At the road, turn left and head back into Bradfield.

a gambler and frequenter of pubs, so the vicar declined the generous offer. Incensed by this rebuff, Hodgson bought the land directly opposite the church and built the pub there, a monument to drinking that no one attending Divine Service at Stannington church could possibly overlook. It clings to the cliffside, a defiant piece of architecture obviously intended to make a statement. Amazingly, the pub survived Dr Hodgson and today it's owned and run by John and Genine Chidlaw who offer their customers excellent food, well-maintained ales, varied entertainment and comfortable accommodation.

OUGHTIBRIDGE
5 miles NW of Sheffield on the A6102

This pleasing village is set on the west bank of the River Don looking across to the tree-covered slopes of Wharncliffe Wood. The settlement dates back to Saxon times at least, but surprisingly there is no church and no evidence of there ever having been one.

WHARNCLIFFE SIDE
5 miles NW of Sheffield on the A6102

Nestling in the valley below Wharncliffe Crags, Wharncliffe Side is a community of some 2,000 people and a popular location for commuters to Sheffield and Stocksbridge. An old tradition in the village tells of the Dragon of Wantly, which lurked in the recesses of the crags and terrorised the local people until a knight by the name of More did battle with the monster and killed it. A cave up on the crags is still called the Dragon's Den and local children experience an enjoyable frisson of terror by shouting into its depths. Another ancient tradition in the village is the Whitsuntide walk when Sunday school children process around Wharncliffe Side stopping at various points to sing hymns.

RENISHAW

9 miles SE of Sheffield on the A616

🏚 Renishaw Hall

This sizeable village gives its name to **Renishaw Hall**, located about a mile to the northwest. The beautiful formal Italian gardens and 300 acres of wooded park are open to visitors, along with a nature trail and a Sitwell family museum, an art gallery, a display of Fiori de Henriques sculptures in the Georgian stables, and a café. The Hall itself is open to group and connoisseur tours by special arrangement only.

WALES

9 miles SE of Sheffield on the B6059

👣 Rother Valley Country Park

A mile or so to the west of Wales the **Rother Valley Country Park** provides excellent facilities for water sports including sailing, windsurfing, canoeing and jet skiing, as well as a cable water ski tow. Visitors can hire equipment or use their own, and training courses from beginner to instructor level are available in various water sports. Other attractions include a lakeside golf course, a Craft Centre with craftspeople at work, cycle hire, gift shop, cafeteria – and Playdales, a 'mega play area' for children under 14.

ROTHERHAM

7 miles NE of Sheffield on the A630/A631

🏚 Church of All Saints	🏚 Roche Abbey
🏚 Wentworth Woodhouse	🏛 Clifton Park Museum
🏛 York & Lancaster Regimental Museum	🏛 Magna

The town's most striking building is undoubtedly the **Church of All Saints**. With

Rother Valley Country Park

its soaring crocketed tower, pinnacled buttresses and battlements, and imposing porch, it is one of the finest examples of Perpendicular architecture in Yorkshire. It dates mainly from the 15th century, although there is evidence of an earlier Saxon church on the site.

A church here was listed in the *Domesday Book* and in 1161 the monks of Rufford Abbey were granted the right to prospect for and to smelt iron, and to plant an orchard, and from that day industry has existed side-by-side with agriculture.

Seventy-five per cent of the Borough of Rotherham is actually rural but it was heavy industry that put the town on the map. From the mid-18th century, the Walker Company of

Rotherham was famous for cannons, their products serving to lethal effect in the American War of Independence and at the Battle of Trafalgar. They also built bridges, among them Southwark Bridge in London and the bridge at Sunderland. Another famous bridge builder was born here in 1901. Sir Donald Coleman Bailey invented the Bailey Bridge, which proved to be of great military value, especially during the Second World War.

The town also had lighter industries. Rockingham Pottery, produced here in the late 18th and early 19th century, is now highly prized by collectors. There's a fine collection at the **Clifton Park Museum**, a stately building whose interior has changed little since it was built in 1783 for the Rotherham ironmaster, Joshua Walker. The most breathtaking piece is the spectacular Rhinoceros Vase, which stands almost four feet high. In addition, the museum houses a collection of other Yorkshire pottery, English glass, silver and British oil paintings and watercolours. The grounds around Clifton House form the largest urban park in the Borough, which has 10 urban parks altogether, along with three country parks, seven golf courses, 10 swimming pools and a leisure centre.

Another museum of interest is the **York and Lancaster Regimental Museum** in the Central Library. The regiment had strong ties with South Yorkshire, its recruits drawn mainly from Barnsley, Sheffield and Rotherham. The displays include historic uniforms, campaign relics and more than 1,000 medals, among them nine Victoria Cross groups. There are also sections on local militia, rifle volunteers and territorials.

Dramatically set within the former Templeborough steelworks, **Magna** was the UK's first science adventure park. This imaginative exploration of the power of the four natural elements – earth, air, fire and water – offers visitors the opportunity of experiencing the full power of lightning, firing a water cannon, manoeuvring a real JCB digger, getting close to a tornado or blowing up a virtual rock face. In the Living Robots Show, predator robots pursue each other in an epic struggle to survive and breed. In the Power Pavilion, after donning overalls and cap for your 'shift', you can shed a few pounds by creating electricity on a giant treadmill, test your strength in a self-lifting chair, attack a target with a giant catapult and discover how much you would weigh on the planets Mars or Jupiter. The site also has a restaurant, cafeteria, picnic areas and shops.

To the northwest of the town, the palatial 18th-century mansion **Wentworth Woodhouse** boasts the longest frontage in England, some 600 feet long. The house is not open to the public, but is clearly visible from its Park. Also visible are a number of follies and monuments dating from the 1700s. The most curious of these is the Needle's Eye, which consists of a tower with a stone urn on top and is pierced by a carriageway. Legend says it was built in response to a wager by the Marquis of Rockingham, owner of Wentworth Woodhouse, that he could drive through the eye of a needle. One structure which *is* open (on Sunday afternoons during the season), is the Wentworth Mausoleum, which was built in 1788 in memory of the 2nd Marquis.

A little further afield, near the village of Maltby, are the dramatic ruins of **Roche Abbey** (English Heritage). The abbey dates from the 12th century and takes its name from the rocky limestone of the riverside site. The majestic remains of this great abbey stand in a

Roche Abbey, nr Maltby

throughout the year as well as housing a fine permanent collection.

The town's most impressive museum is actually located a few miles to the west, in the village of Cawthorne. **Cannon Hall** is a magnificent 18th-century country house set in formal gardens and historic parkland. It offers unique collections of pottery, furniture, glassware and paintings, along with the 'Charge Gallery', which documents the story of the 13th/18th Royal Hussars.

About a mile to the south of Barnsley is the **Worsbrough Mill Museum and Country Park**. The Grade II listed mill dates from around 1625. A steam mill was added in the 19th century and both have been restored to full working order to form the centrepiece of an industrial museum. Wholemeal flour, ground at the mills, can be bought here. The mill is set within a beautiful 200-acre country park, whose reservoir attracts a great variety of birds including heron.

landscape fashioned by Capability Brown in the 1770s as part of the grounds of Sandbeck Park, home of the Earls of Scarborough.

BARNSLEY

10 miles N of Sheffield on the A61

| 🏠 Cannon Hall 🏛 Worsborough Mill Museum |
| 🏛 Elsecar Heritage Centre 🕸 Cooper Gallery |

The county town of South Yorkshire, Barnsley stands on the River Dearne and derived its Victorian prosperity from the rich seams of coal hereabouts. It has an appropriately imposing Town Hall although the building is comparatively recent, completed in 1933. Nearby, the **Cooper Gallery** is a lively centre for the arts, which hosts a varied programme of exhibitions

Another three miles to the southeast, situated in attractive South Yorkshire countryside just off the M1 (J36), the **Elsecar Heritage Centre** (see panel opposite) is an imaginative science and history centre which is fun and educational for all the family. Visitors can discover hands-on science in the Power House; nostalgic travel on the Elsecar Steam Railway; the history of South Yorkshire in the Elsecar People exhibition; and interactive multi-media in the Newcomen Beam Engine Centre. The centre is also the base for several working craftspeople who make and sell their products here. Special events include a Friends of Thomas the Tank Engine day.

SILKSTONE

4 miles W of Barnsley off the A628

The travel writer Arthur Mee dubbed Silkstone's parish church the Minster of the Moors, and it is indeed a striking building. Parts of the church date back to Norman times but most of it was built during the golden age of English ecclesiastical architecture, the 15th century. Outside, there are graceful flying buttresses and wonderfully weird gargoyles. Inside, the ancient oak roofs sprout floral bosses on moulded beams, and old box-pews and lovely medieval screens all add to the charm. The old stocks just outside The Ring o' Bells are another sign of the antiquity of this former mining village.

THURLSTONE

9 miles SW of Barnsley off the A628

Thurlstone developed when the first settlers realised that the nearby moors provided extensive grazing for sheep and the lime-free waters of the River Don were ideal for the washing of wool. Today the village still has some fine examples of the weavers' cottages, which sprang up during the early 19th century, the best of which can be seen on Tenter Hill.

Elsecar Heritage Centre

Wath Road, Elsecar, Barnsley, S74 8HJ
Telephone: 01226 740203
e-mail: elsecarheritagecentre@Barnsley.gov.uk
website: www.Barnsley.gov.uk/leisure

The **Elsecar Heritage Centre** nestles within the beautiful South Yorkshire countryside and dates from the early 1800's when it was originally owned by the local Earls Fitzwilliam as their main industrial workshops, producing everything needed for their industrial empire. Many of the buildings and facilities have been restored and preserved, with several being used again as workshops for local crafts people. Activities include traditional printers, woodwork shop, jewellery making and flower arranging.

As well as a large selection of Craft Workshops, the Centre also has an Antiques Centre, a Bottle Museum, 'Playmania' children's activity centre, the Elsecar Preservation Group Steam Railway Line and the world-famous Newcomen Beam Engine, the only remaining Beam Engine in its original location. Our on-site 'Brambles Tea-rooms' can provide light refreshments as well as a full and varied menu of main meals throughout the day.

The Heritage Centre also holds regular special events within its multi-purpose exhibition hall all year round, from concerts, antique fairs, championship dog shows, and natural health festivals to Japanese Koi Fish shows.

Here the finished cloth would have been dried and stretched on 'tenters' – large wooden frames placed outside on the street, which gave the road its name.

The village's most famous son was Nicholas Saunderson, born in 1682, who was blinded by smallpox at the age of two. He taught himself to read by passing his fingers over the tombstones in Penistone churchyard – 150 years before the introduction of Braille. Nicholas went on to attend grammar school and rose to become Professor of Mathematics at Cambridge University.

PENISTONE
15 miles NW of Sheffield on the A628

Perched 700 feet above sea level, Penistone forms a gateway to the Peak District National Park, which extends for some 30 miles to the south of the town. Penistone's oldest building

is the 15th-century tower of its parish church, which overlooks a graveyard where ancestors of the poet William Wordsworth are buried. Later centuries added an elegant Dissenters' Chapel (in the 1600s) and a graceful Cloth Hall in the 1700s.

DUNFORD BRIDGE
15 miles SW of Barnsley off the A628

The hamlet of Dunford Bridge is only shown on very large scale maps, but if you are travelling westwards from Barnsley on the A628, after 13 miles or so you will see a sign for the Stanhope Arms off to the right. It's well worth seeking out this grand old inn, built in the 1800s as a shooting lodge for the Cannon Hall Estate. It stands beside the entrance to the Woodhead railway tunnel, which runs beneath the moors for more than three miles. When the tunnel opened in 1852 it was twice as long as

---

HAZLEHEAD HALL FARM SHOP

Lee Lane, Millhouse Green, Sheffield,
South Yorkshire S36 9NN
Tel: 01226 764800/07866 779638
e-mail: shop@hazlehead.co.uk
website: www.hazlehead-hall.co.uk

Anyone who appreciates the finest seasonal food will have their appetites aroused and their taste buds stimulated at **Hazlehead Hall Farm Shop**. It stands on the A628 west of Barnsley, in the picturesque valley of Penistone, just above the gateway to the Peak District National Park.

In this most pleasant of settings, owner Sarah Booth has stocked her shop with a wide range of artisan and specialist foods. Meats include top-quality farm-reared, traditionally matured beef, pork and lamb; home-produced ham, bacon, sausages, game and meat pies, ready-made meals, cakes and pastries.

In the coffee shop, visitors can relax and enjoy a wide range of sandwiches, snacks, light meals, daily fresh baking and a selection of hot and cold drinks.

---

any other in the world. There's an interesting display of memorabilia erected for the Tunnel Tigers (the men who built it), in the snug of the Stanhope Arms.

CONISBROUGH

5 miles SW of Doncaster on the A630

🏰 Castle

The town is best known for the 11th-century **Conisbrough Castle** (English Heritage), which features prominently in one of the most dramatic scenes in Sir Walter Scott's novel *Ivanhoe*. The most impressive medieval building in South Yorkshire, Conisbrough Castle boasts the oldest circular keep in England. Rising some 90 feet and more than 50 feet wide, the keep stands on a man-made hill raised in Saxon times. Six huge buttresses some six feet thick support walls that in places are 15 feet deep. Visitors can walk through the remains of several rooms, including the first floor chamber where the huge open fireplaces give one a fascinating insight into the lifestyle of Norman times. The castle also offers a visual presentation, a visitor centre and a tea room.

Conisbrough Castle

CADEBY

4 miles SW of Doncaster off the A630

Listed in the *Domesday Book* as Catebi, this pleasant little village is surrounded by prime agricultural land. For centuries Cadeby had no church of its own; parishioners had to travel some two miles to the parish church in Sprotbrough. Then in 1856, the owners of the huge Sprotbrough estate, the Copley family, paid for a church to be built in Cadeby. It was designed by Sir George Gilbert Scott, the architect of St Pancras Station in London, and resembles a medieval estate barn with its steeply pitched roofs and lofty south porch. A century and a half later, Cadeby is again without a church since Sir George's attractive church has been declared redundant.

📖 stories and anecdotes 🕊 famous people 🎨 art and craft 🎭 entertainment and sport 🚶 walks

Doncaster

🏛 Brodsworth Hall   🏛 Doncaster Museum

🏛 KOYLI Regimental Museum

🏛 Museum of South Yorkshire Life

The Romans named their riverside settlement beside the River Don *Danum*, and a well-preserved stretch of the road they built here can be seen just west of Adwick le Street. The modern town boasts some impressive buildings, notably the Mansion House built in 1748 and designed by James Paine. The Minster of St George was rebuilt in 1858 by Sir George Gilbert Scott and it's an outstanding example of Gothic revival architecture with its lofty tower, 170 feet high and crowned with pinnacles. The lively shopping centre is enhanced by a stately Corn Exchange building and a market that takes place every Tuesday, Friday and Saturday. Doncaster was once one of the most important centres for the building of steam engines. Thousands were built here, including both *The Flying Scotsman* and *Mallard*. The latter, a streamlined Pacific (4-6-2 wheel arrangement) designed by Sir Nigel Gresley, holds the record for the fastest steam train in the world, achieving a top speed of 125mph in July 1938. For a further insight into the history of the town and surrounding area, **Doncaster Museum** contains several exciting and informative exhibitions on the various aspects of natural history, local history and archaeology. Housed in the same building is the **Regimental Museum of the King's Own Yorkshire Light Infantry**, which reflects the history of this famous local regiment.

Whether or not you're connected with the racing fraternity most people will have heard of the St Leger, the oldest of the five classic races, which is run over a distance of a mile and three-quarters on a Saturday in September. It was founded by Colonel Barry St Leger in 1776. Doncaster Racecourse provides a magnet for all horse-racing enthusiasts, with top-class racing under both Flat and National Hunt rules.

On the northwestern outskirts of the town, **Cusworth Hall** is home to the **Museum of South Yorkshire Life**. The Hall is a splendid Georgian mansion built in the 1740s and set in a landscaped park. The interior features varied displays on the social history, industry, agriculture and transport in the area.

Another three miles or so to the northwest of Doncaster, **Brodsworth Hall** (English Heritage - see panel opposite) is a remarkable example of a Victorian mansion that has survived with many of its original furnishings and decorations intact. When Charles and Georgiana Thellusson, their six children and 15 servants moved into the new hall in 1863 the house must have seemed the last word in both grandeur and utility. A gasworks in the grounds supplied the lighting and no fewer than eight water closets were distributed around the house, although rather surprisingly, only two bathrooms were installed.

More immediately impressive to visitors were the opulent furnishings, paintings, statuary and decoration. The sumptuous reception rooms have now a rather faded grandeur and English Heritage has deliberately left it so, preserving the patina of time throughout the house to produce an interior that is both fascinating and evocative. A vanished way of life is also brought to life in the huge kitchen and the cluttered servants' wing. The Hall stands in 15 acres of beautifully restored Victorian gardens, complete with a summer house in the form of a classical temple, a target range where the family practised its archery, and a pets cemetery where the family dogs - and a prized parrot with the unimaginative name of Polly - were buried between 1894 and 1988. There is also a fascinating exhibition illustrating the family's obsession – yachting.

Around Doncaster

NORTON
8 miles N of Doncaster off the A19

 Church of St Mary Magdalene

This sizeable village is located close to the borders with North and West Yorkshire and was once busy with farming, mining and quarrying. Nowadays it's a peaceful place, a tranquil base for commuters to Doncaster and Pontefract. Its most impressive building is the ancient parish **Church of St Mary Magdalene** whose splendid 14th-century west tower is considered by many to be the finest in Yorkshire. Once there was also a priory here, standing beside the River Went, but now only a fragment of wall remains. However, the old water mill has survived.

STAINFORTH
7 miles NE of Doncaster off the A18 or A614

Stainforth and Keady Canal

Stainforth was once an important trading centre and inland port on the River Don. It also stands on the banks of the **Stainforth and Keadby Canal**, which still has a well-preserved dry dock and a 19th-century blacksmith's shop. This area of low, marshy ground was drained by Dutch engineers in the 1600s to produce rich, peaty farmland. The place has retained the air of a quiet backwater, a little-explored area of narrow lands and pretty hamlets, the fields drained by slow-flowing dykes and canals. The rich peat resources are commercially exploited in part, but also provide a congenial home for a great deal of natural wildlife.

Brodsworth Hall and Gardens

Brodsworth, Nr Doncaster, South Yorkshire DN5 7XJ
Tel: 01302 722598
website: www.english-heritage.org.uk

One of England's most complete Victorian country houses, **Brodsworth Hall** was opened to the public in 1995 following a major programme of restoration and conservation by English Heritage. English Heritage decided to conserve rather than restore the interior, retaining the original furnishings and finishes, so preserving the patina that only time and family use can bring. Hence Brodsworth today is the story of a once brashly opulent house now having grown comfortably old and inviting to all.

The gardens complemented the house when laid out in the 1860's and are now well on their way to being restored to their appearance at the time of their maturity. Beyond the terrace and croquet lawns, bordered by clipped evergreen shrubs, lies the formal flower garden now superbly laid out with spring and summer bedding appropriate to the period. Beyond can be found the romantic quarry garden, an enchantment of paths, bridges and vistas, with its newly resorted rock garden and fern dell.

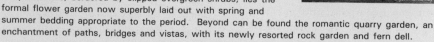 stories and anecdotes · famous people · art and craft · entertainment and sport · walks

FISHLAKE

10 miles NE of Doncaster off the A614

Set along the banks of the River Don, which is known here as the Dutch River, Fishlake is effectively an island since it is surrounded by rivers and canals and can only be entered by crossing a bridge. It's a charming village with a striking medieval church famous for its elaborately carved Norman doorway, an ancient windmill and a welcoming traditional inn.

THORNE

10 miles NE of Doncaster on the A614

This ancient market town on the River Don has been a port since at least 1500 with ships sailing from here to York, Hull, London and Europe. The waterfront was once busy with boat-builder's yards where vessels of up to 400 tons were built. In 1802, Thorne gained a second waterfront, on the newly constructed Stainforth and Keadby Canal, which attracted most of the water traffic from the unpredictable River Don. As late as 1987 there were still boat-building yards at work here, but in that year they finally closed and the area is being carefully developed in a way that will commemorate the town's heritage.

BRANTON

4½ miles E of Doncaster off the B1396

🐦 🐾 Brockhole Riding & Visitor Centre

Surrounded by agricultural land, Brockholes Farm has been a working farm since 1759 and one where the traditional farming skills have been passed down from one generation to the next. Today, at **Brockhole Riding and Visitor Centre**, visitors can watch demonstrations of those same skills, such as those employed by the farrier and the shepherd, as well as seeing many animals

associated with traditional free-range farming. The riding centre here caters for complete beginners through to experienced riders and, along with professional instructors, has a range of horses and ponies to suit all ages and abilities.

FINNINGLEY

7 miles SE of Doncaster on the A614

A unique feature of this pleasant village close to the Nottinghamshire border is its five village greens, the main one having a duck pond complete with weeping willows. Finningley is a living village with a well-used Village Hall, originally a barn but which later served as the village school. Finningley has a beautiful Norman church with a rectors' list dating back to 1293 and a post office that has been in the same family for five generations. The year 2004 saw the opening of Robin Hood Airport outside the village, which utilised the runways from the old RAF base, built just before the Second World War. This has led to increased development and investment in the area while not disturbing Finningley's traditional appeal.

BAWTRY

9 miles SE of Doncaster on the A614

This pleasant little market town stands close to the Nottinghamshire border and in medieval times it was customary for the Sheriff of South Yorkshire to welcome visiting kings and queens here. In the mid-1500s the then Sheriff, Sir Robert Bowes, accompanied by 200 gentlemen dressed in velvet and 4,000 yeomen on horseback, greeted Henry VIII and – in the name of Yorkshire – presented him with a purse containing the huge sum of £900 in gold.

Today's Bawtry is an upmarket and exciting

town with a brand new airport (see above), very good shopping in select boutiques, and an impressive selection of excellent and stylish restaurants. As befits a place that can trace its traditions and heritage back to its days as a bustling 12th-century port on the River Idle with strong connections to the founding fathers of the United States, it has managed to maintain its sense of history and distinct character while keeping up with the times. A happy mix of stunning buildings, small boutiques and sophisticated restaurants, it remains the quintessential English town. Many of the buildings are grand three-storey Georgian affairs that help the town maintain a tranquil and restrained appearance, and shoppers will find everything from clothes and accessories to furniture, soft furnishings and general items for the home. Long a coaching stagepost along the old Great North Road, Bawtry continues its proud tradition of offering great food and drink to visitors with a range of elegant eateries that are justly popular, so that the town has become a regular evening hot spot, particularly at the weekend. The airport has led to increased investment in the area and Bawtry is set to see more changes and improvements in goods and services on offer, while maintaining the traditional attractions that make it stand out.

NORTH ANSTON
12 miles S of Doncaster on the A57

🐦 Tropical Butterfly House, Wildlife & Falconry Centre

This village, separated from its neighbour South Anston by the main road, is home to the **Tropical Butterfly House, Wildlife and Falconry Centre** where not only can visitors see the exotic butterflies, birds, snakes and crocodiles in a tropical jungle setting, but also enjoy outdoor falconry displays and, at the baby farm animal area, bottle-feed lambs (depending on the season). This centre, open all year, also has a nocturnal reptile room, nature trail and children's outdoor play area.

TOURIST INFORMATION CENTRES

County Durham

BARNARD CASTLE
Woodleigh, Flatts Road, Barnard Castle,
County Durham, DL12 8AA
e-mail: tourism@teesdale.gov.uk
Tel: 01833 690909

BISHOP AUCKLAND
Town Hall, Ground Floor,
Market Place, Bishop Auckland,
County Durham, DL14 7NP
e-mail: bishopauckland.touristinfo
*　　　　@durham.gov.uk*
Tel: 01388 604922

DARLINGTON
13 Horsemarket,
Darlington, DL1 5PW
e-mail: tic@darlington.gov.uk
Tel: 01325 388666

DURHAM
2 Millennium Place,
Durham City, DH1 1WA
e-mail: touristinfo@durhamcity.gov.uk
Tel: 0191 384 3720

GUISBOROUGH
Priory Grounds, Church Street,
Guisborough,TS14 6HG
e-mail: guisborough_tic
*　　　　@redcar-cleveland.gov.uk*
Tel: 01287 633801

HARTLEPOOL
Hartlepool Art Gallery, Church Square,
Hartlepool, TS24 7EQ
e-mail: hpooltic@hartlepool.gov.uk
Tel: 01429 869706

MIDDLESBROUGH
(PO Box 69), Middlesbrough Info. Centre &
Box Office, Albert Road,
Middlesbrough, TS1 2QQ
e-mail: middlesbrough_tic
*　　　　@middlesbrough.gov.uk*
Tel: 01642 729700

MIDDLETON-IN-TEESDALE
10 Market Place, Middleton-in-Teesdale,
County Durham, DL12 0QG
e-mail: middletonplus@compuserve.com
Tel: 01833 641001

PETERLEE
4 Upper Yoden Way, Peterlee,
County Durham, SR8 1AX
e-mail: touristinfo@peterlee.gov.uk
Tel: 0191 586 4450

REDCAR
West Terrace, Esplanade, Redcar,
Cleveland, TS10 3AE
e-mail: redcar_tic
*　　　　@redcar-cleveland.gov.uk*
Tel: 01642 471921

SALTBURN-BY-SEA
3 Station Buildings, Station Square,
Saltburn-by-Sea,
Cleveland, TS12 1AQ
e-mail: saltburn_tic
*　　　　@redcar-cleveland.gov.uk*
Tel: 01287 622422

STANHOPE
Durham Dales Centre, Castle Gardens,
Stanhope, County Durham, DL13 2FJ
e-mail: durham.dales.centre
*　　　　@durham.gov.uk*
Tel: 01388 527650

STOCKTON-ON-TEES
Stockton Central Library, Church Road,
Stockton-on-Tees, TS18 1TU
e-mail: touristinformation
*　　　　@stockton.gov.uk*
Tel: 01642 528130

East Yorkshire

BEVERLEY
34 Butcher Row, Beverley,
East Yorkshire, HU17 0AB
e-mail: beverley.tic@eastriding.gov.uk
Tel: 01482 867430

BRIDLINGTON
25 Prince Street, Bridlington,
East Riding of Yorkshire, YO15 2NP
e-mail: bridlington.tic@eastriding.gov.uk
Tel: 01262 673474

HORNSEA
120 Newbegin, Hornsea, HU18 1PB
e-mail: hornsea.tic@eastriding.gov.uk
Tel: 01964 536404

HULL
1 Paragon Street, Hull,
East Yorkshire, HU1 3NA
e-mail: tourist.information
*　　　　@hullcc.gov.uk*
Tel: 01482 223559

HUMBER BRIDGE
North Bank Viewing Area,
Ferriby Road, Hessle,
East Yorkshire, HU13 0LN
e-mail: humberbridge.tic
*　　　　@eastriding.gov.uk*
Tel: 01482 640852

WITHERNSEA
131 Queen Street,
Withernsea, HU19 2DJ
e-mail: withernsea.tic@eastriding.gov.uk
Tel: 01964 615683

North Yorkshire

AYSGARTH FALLS
Aysgarth Falls National Park Centre,
Aysgarth Falls, Leyburn,
North Yorkshire, DL8 3TH
e-mail: aysgarth@ytbtic.co.uk
Tel: 01969 662910

DANBY
The Moors Centre, Danby Lodge,
Lodge Lane, Danby, Whitby,
North Yorkshire, YO21 2NB
e-mail: moorscentre
*　　　　@northyorkmoors-npa.gov.uk*
Tel: 01439 772737

TOURIST INFORMATION CENTRES

TOURIST INFORMATION CENTRES

FILEY

The Evron Centre, John Street, Filey,
North Yorkshire, YO14 9DW
e-mail: fileytic@scarborough.gov.uk
Tel: 01723 383637

GRASSINGTON

National Park Centre, Colvend,
Hebden Road, Grassington,
North Yorkshire, BD23 5LB
e-mail: grassington@ytbtic.co.uk
Tel: 01756 752774

HARROGATE

Royal Baths, Crescent Road, Harrogate,
North Yorkshire, HG1 2RR
e-mail: tic@harrogate.gov.uk
Tel: 0845 389 3223

HELMSLEY

The Visitor Centre, Helmsley Castle,
Castlegate, North Yorkshire, YO62 5AB
e-mail: helmsley@ytbtic.co.uk
Tel: 01439 770173

HORTON-IN-RIBBLESDALE

Pen-y-ghent Cafe,
Horton-in-Ribblesdale, Settle,
North Yorkshire, BD24 0HE
e-mail: horton@ytbtic.co.uk
Tel: 01729 860333

INGLETON

The Community Centre Car Park, Ingleton,
North Yorkshire, LA6 3HG
e-mail: ingleton@ytbtic.co.uk
Tel: 015242 41049

KNARESBOROUGH

9 Castle Courtyard,
Market Place, Knaresborough,
North Yorkshire, HG5 8AE
e-mail: kntic@harrogate.gov.uk
Tel: 0845 389 0177

LEEMING BAR

The Yorkshire Maid,
The Great North Road, Leeming Bar,
Bedale, North Yorkshire, DL8 1DT
e-mail: leeming@ytbtic.co.uk
Tel: 01677 424262

LEYBURN

4 Central Chambers, Railway Street,
Leyburn, North Yorkshire, DL8 5BB
e-mail: TIC.Leyburn
    @Richmondshire.gov.uk
Tel: 01969 623069

MALHAM

National Park Centre, Malham, Skipton,
North Yorkshire, BD23 4DA
e-mail: malham@ytbtic.co.uk
Tel: 01969 652380

MALTON

58 Market Place, Malton,
North Yorkshire, YO17 7LW
e-mail: maltontic@btconnect.com
Tel: 01653 600048

PATELEY BRIDGE

18 High Street, Pateley Bridge,
North Yorkshire, HG3 5AW
e-mail: pbtic@harrogate.gov.uk
Tel: 0845 389 0179

PICKERING

Ropery House, The Ropery, Pickering,
North Yorkshire, YO18 8DY
e-mail: pickering@ytbtic.co.uk
Tel: 01751 473791

REETH

Hudson House, The Green, Reeth,
Richmond, North Yorkshire, DL11 6TB
e-mail: reeth@ytbtic.co.uk
Tel: 01748 884059

RICHMOND

Friary Gardens,
Victoria Road, Richmond,
North Yorkshire, DL10 4AJ
e-mail: richmond@ytbtic.co.uk
Tel: 01748 850252

RIPON

Minster Road, Ripon,
North Yorkshire, HG4 1QT
e-mail: ripontic@harrogate.gov.uk
Tel: 0845 389 0178

SCARBOROUGH

Brunswick Shopping Centre, Westborough,
Scarborough, North Yorkshire, YO11 1UE
e-mail: tourismbureau
    @scarborough.gov.uk
Tel: 01723 383636

SCARBOROUGH
(HARBOURSIDE)

Harbourside TIC, Sandside, Scarborough,
North Yorkshire, YO11 1PP
e-mail: harboursidetic
    @scarborough.gov.uk
Tel: 01723 383636

SELBY

Visitor Information Centre, 52 Micklegate,
Selby, North Yorkshire, YO8 4EQ
e-mail: selby@ytbtic.co.uk
Tel: 01757 212181

SETTLE

Town Hall, Cheapside, Settle,
North Yorkshire, BD24 9EJ
e-mail: settle@ytbtic.co.uk
Tel: 01729 825192

SKIPTON

35 Coach Street, Skipton,
North Yorkshire, BD23 1LQ
e-mail: skipton@ytbtic.co.uk
Tel: 01756 792809

SUTTON BANK

Sutton Bank Visitor Centre,
Sutton Bank, Thirsk,
North Yorkshire, YO7 2EH
e-mail: suttonbank@ytbtic.co.uk
Tel: 01845 597426

THIRSK

Thirsk Tourist Information Centre,
49 Market Place, Thirsk,
North Yorkshire, YO7 1HA
e-mail: thirsktic@hambleton.gov.uk
Tel: 01845 522755

TOURIST INFORMATION CENTRES

WHITBY
Langborne Road, Whitby,
North Yorkshire, YO21 1YN
e-mail: whitbytic@scarborough.gov.uk
Tel: 01723 383636

YORK
Outer Concourse, Railway Station,
Station Road, York,
North Yorkshire, YO24 1AY
e-mail: kg@ytbyork.swiftserve.net
Tel: 01904 550099

YORK
Exhibition Square, York,
North Yorkshire, YO1 7HB
e-mail: tic@york-tourism.co.uk
Tel: 01904 550099

Northumberland

ADDERSTONE
Adderstone Services, Adderstone Garage,
Belford, Northumberland, NE70 7JU
e-mail: adderstone@hotmail.com
Tel: 01668 213678

ALNWICK
2 The Shambles, Alnwick,
Northumberland, NE66 1TN
e-mail: alnwicktic@alnwick.gov.uk
Tel: 01665 510665

AMBLE
Queen Street Car Park, Amble,
Northumberland, NE65 0DQ
e-mail: ambletic@alnwick.gov.uk
Tel:01665 712313

BELLINGHAM
Fountain Cottage, Main Street,
Bellingham, Near Hexham,
Northumberland, NE48 2BQ
e-mail: bellinghamtic@btconnect.com
Tel: 01434 220616

BERWICK-UPON-TWEED
106 Marygate, Berwick upon Tweed,
Northumberland, TD15 1BN
e-mail: tourism
@berwick-upon-tweed.gov.uk
Tel: 01289 330733

CORBRIDGE
Hill Street, Corbridge,
Northumberland, NE45 5AA
e-mail: corbridgetic@btconnect.com
Tel: 01434 632815

CRASTER
Craster Car Park, Craster, Alnwick,
Northumberland, NE66 3TW
e-mail: crastertic@alnwick.gov.uk
Tel: 01665 576007

HALTWHISTLE
Railway Station, Station Road, Haltwhistle,
Northumberland, NE49 9HN
e-mail: haltwhistletic@btconnect.com
Tel: 01434 322002

HEXHAM
Wentworth Car Park, Hexham,
Northumberland, NE46 1QE
e-mail: hexham.tic@tynedale.gov.uk
Tel: 01434 652220

MORPETH
The Chantry, Bridge Street, Morpeth,
Northumberland, NE61 1PD
e-mail: tourism@castlemorpeth.gov.uk
Tel: 01670 500700

ONCE BREWED
Northumberland National Park Centre,
Military Road, Bardon Mill, Hexham,
Northumberland, NE47 7AN
e-mail: tic.oncebrewed@nnpa.org.uk
Tel: 01434 344396

OTTERBURN
Otterburn Mill, Otterburn,
Northumberland, NE19 1JT
e-mail:tic@otterburnmill.co.uk
Tel: 01830 520093

ROTHBURY
Northumberland National Park Centre,
Church House, Church Street, Rothbury,
Northumberland, NE65 7UP
e-mail: tic.rothbury@nnpa.org.uk
Tel: 01669 620887

SEAHOUSES
Seafield Car Park, Seafield Road, Seahouses,
Northumberland, NE68 7SW
e-mail: seahousesTIC
@berwick-upon-tweed.gov.uk
Tel: 01665 720884

WOOLER
Wooler TIC, The Cheviot Centre,
12 Padgepool Place, Wooler,
Northumberland, NE71 6BL
e-mail: woolerTIC
@berwick-upon-tweed.gov.uk
Tel: 01668 282123

SouthYorkshire

BARNSLEY
Central Library, Shambles Street,
Barnsley, South Yorkshire, S70 2JF
e-mail: barnsley@ytbtic.co.uk
Tel: 01226 206757

DONCASTER
38-40 High Street, Doncaster,
South Yorkshire, DN1 1DE
e-mail: tourist.information
@doncaster.gov.uk
Tel: 01302 734309

ROTHERHAM
40 Bridgegate, Rotherham,
South Yorkshire, S60 1PQ
e-mail: tic@rotherham.gov.uk
Tel: 01709 835904

SHEFFIELD
Visitor Information Point,
14 Norfolk Row, Sheffield, S1 2PA
e-mail: visitor@sheffield.gov.uk
Tel: 0114 2211900

Tyne and Wear

GATESHEAD
Central Library, Prince Consort Road,
Gateshead, Tyne & Wear, NE8 4LN
e-mail: tic@gateshead.gov.uk
Tel: 0191 433 8420

GATESHEAD
Gateshead Visitor Centre, St Mary's Church,
Gateshead, NE8 2AU
e-mail: tourism@gateshead.gov.uk
Tel: 0191 478 4222

NEWCASTLE AIRPORT
Tourist Information Desk, Newcastle Airport,
Newcastle upon Tyne,
Tyne & Wear, NE13 8BZ
e-mail: niatic@hotmail.com
Tel: 0191 214 4422

NEWCASTLE-UPON-TYNE
Newcastle Information Centre,
8-9 Central Arcade, Newcastle upon Tyne,
Tyne & Wear, NE1 5AF
e-mail: tourist.info@newcastle.gov.uk
Tel: 0191 277 8000

NORTH SHIELDS
Unit 18, Royal Quays Outlet Shopping,
North Shields, Tyne & Wear, NE29 6DW
e-mail: ticns@northtyneside.gov.uk
Tel: 0191 2005895

SOUTH SHIELDS
South Shields Museum & Gallery,
Ocean Road, South Shields,
Tyne & Wear, NE33 2HZ
e-mail: museum.tic@s-tyneside-mbc.gov.uk
Tel: 0191 454 6612

SOUTH SHIELDS
(AMPHITHEATRE)
Sea Road, South Shields, NE33 2LD
e-mail: foreshore.tic
            @s-tyneside-mbc.gov.uk
Tel: 0191 455 7411

SUNDERLAND
50 Fawcett Street, Sunderland,
Tyne & Wear, SR1 1RF
e-mail: tourist.info@sunderland.gov.uk
Tel: 0191 553 2000

WHITLEY BAY
Park Road, Whitley Bay,
Tyne & Wear, NE26 1EJ
e-mail: ticwb@northtyneside.gov.uk
Tel: 0191 2008535

West Yorkshire

BATLEY
The Mill Discount Department Store,
Bradford Road, Batley,
West Yorkshire, WF17 5LZ
e-mail: batley@ytbtic.co.uk
Tel: 01924 426670

BRADFORD
City Hall, Centenary Square, Bradford,
West Yorkshire, BD1 1HY
e-mail: tourist.information
            @bradford.gov.uk
Tel: 01274 433678

HALIFAX
Piece Hall, Halifax,
West Yorkshire, HX1 1RE
e-mail: halifax@ytbtic.co.uk
Tel: 01422 368725

HAWORTH
2/4 West Lane, Haworth,
Near Keighley, West Yorkshire, BD22 8EF
e-mail: haworth@ytbtic.co.uk
Tel: 01535 642329

HEBDEN BRIDGE
Visitor and Canal Centre, New Road,
Hebden Bridge, West Yorkshire, HX7 8AF
e-mail: hebdenbridge@ytbtic.co.uk
Tel: 01422 843831

HOLMFIRTH
49-51 Huddersfield Road, Holmfirth,
West Yorkshire, HD9 3JP
e-mail: holmfirth.tic@kirklees.gov.uk
Tel: 01484 222444

HUDDERSFIELD
3 Albion Street, Huddersfield,
West Yorkshire, HD1 2NW
e-mail: huddersfield.tic@kirklees.gov.uk
Tel: 01484 223200

ILKLEY
Town Hall, Station Rd, Ilkley,
West Yorkshire, LS29 8HB
e-mail: ilkley@ytbtic.c.uk
Tel: 01943 602319

LEEDS
Gateway Yorkshire, PO Box 244,
The Arcade, City Station, Leeds,
West Yorkshire, LS1 1PL
e-mail: tourinfo@leeds.gov.uk
Tel: 0113 242 5242

OTLEY
Otley Library & Tourist Information,
Nelson Street, Otley,
West Yorkshire, LS21 1EZ
e-mail: otleytic@leedslearning.net
Tel: 0113 247 7707

TODMORDEN
15 Burnley Road, Todmorden,
West Yorkshire, OL14 7BU
e-mail: todmorden@ytbtic.co.uk
Tel: 01706 818181

WAKEFIELD
9 The Bull Ring, Wakefield,
West Yorkshire, WF1 1HB
e-mail: tic@wakefield.gov.uk
Tel: 0845 601 8353

WETHERBY
Wetherby Library & Tourist Info. Centre,
17 Westgate, Wetherby,
West Yorkshire, LS22 6LL
e-mail: wetherbytic@leedslearning.net
Tel: 01937 582151

INDEX OF ADVERTISERS

INDEX OF ADVERTISERS

INDEX OF ADVERTISERS

SPECIALIST SHOPS

Looking for more walks?

The walks in this book have been gleaned from Britain's largest online walking guide, to be found at *www.walkingworld.com*.

The site contains over 2000 walks from all over England, Scotland and Wales so there are plenty more to choose from in this book's region as well as further afield - ideal if you are taking a short break as you can plan your walks in advance. There are walks of every length and type to suit all tastes.

Want more detail for the walks in this book? Next to every walk in this book you will see a Walk ID. You can enter this ID number on Walkingworld's 'Find a Walk' page and you will be taken straight to the details of that walk.

- Over **2000** walks across Britain

- **Print routes out as you need them**

- **No bulky guidebook to carry**

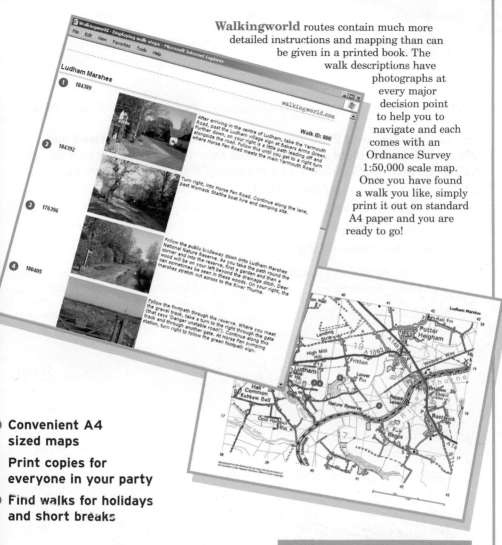

Walkingworld routes contain much more detailed instructions and mapping than can be given in a printed book. The walk descriptions have photographs at every major decision point to help you to navigate and each comes with an Ordnance Survey 1:50,000 scale map. Once you have found a walk you like, simply print it out on standard A4 paper and you are ready to go!

- Convenient A4 sized maps
- Print copies for everyone in your party
- Find walks for holidays and short breaks

A modest annual subscription gives you access to over 2000 walks, all in Walkingworld's easy to follow format. The database of walks is growing all the time and as a subscriber you gain access to new routes as soon as they are published.

Visit the Walkingworld website at *www.walkingworld.com*

INDEX OF WALKS

READER REACTION FORM

The **Travel Publishing** *research team would like to receive readers' comments on any visitor attractions or places reviewed in the book and also recommendations for suitable entries to be included in the next edition. This will help ensure that the* **Country Living series of Rural Guides** *continues to provide its readers with useful information on the more interesting, unusual or unique features of each attraction or place ensuring that their visit to the local area is an enjoyable and stimulating experience. To provide your comments or recommendations would you please complete the forms below and overleaf as indicated and send to:*

The Research Department, Travel Publishing Ltd, 7a Apollo House, Calleva Park, Aldermaston, Reading, RG7 8TN

YOUR NAME:

YOUR ADDRESS:

YOUR TEL NO:

Please tick as appropriate: COMMENTS ☐   RECOMMENDATION ☐

ESTABLISHMENT:

ADDRESS:

TEL NO:

CONTACT NAME:

PLEASE COMPLETE FORM OVERLEAF

READER REACTION FORM

COMMENT OR REASON FOR RECOMMENDATION:

....

....

....

....

....

....

....

....

....

....

....

ORDER FORM

To order any of our publications just fill in the payment details below and complete the order form. For orders of less than 4 copies please add £1 per book for postage and packing. Orders over 4 copies are P & P free.

Please Complete Either:

I enclose a cheque for £ [ ] *made payable to Travel Publishing Ltd*

Or:

CARD NO: [ ] EXPIRY DATE: [ ]

SIGNATURE: [ ]

NAME: [ ]

ADDRESS: [ ]

TEL NO: [ ]

Please either send, telephone, fax or e-mail your order to:

Travel Publishing Ltd, 64-66 Ebrington Street, Plymouth, Devon PL4 9AQ
Tel: 01752 276660 Fax: 01752 276699 e-mail: info@travelpublishing.co.uk

	Price	Quantity		Price	Quantity
Hidden Places Regional Titles			**Country Living Rural Guides**		
Cornwall	£8.99	....	East Anglia	£10.99	....
Devon	£8.99	....	Heart of England	£10.99	....
Dorset, Hants & Isle of Wight	£8.99	....	Ireland	£11.99	....
East Anglia	£8.99	....	North East of England	£10.99	....
Lake District & Cumbria	£8.99	....	North West of England	£10.99	....
Northumberland & Durham	£8.99	....	Scotland	£11.99	....
Peak District and Derbyshire	£8.99	....	South of England	£10.99	....
Yorkshire	£8.99	....	South East of England	£10.99	....
Hidden Places National Titles			Wales	£11.99	....
England	£11.99	....	West Country	£10.99	....
Ireland	£11.99	....	**Other Titles**		
Scotland	£11.99	....	Off The Motorway	£11.99	....
Wales	£11.99	....	Garden Centres and Nurseries	£11.99	....
Country Pubs and Inns Titles			of Britain		
Cornwall	£5.99	....			
Devon	£7.99	....			
Sussex	£5.99	....	**TOTAL QUANTITY** [ ]		
Wales	£8.99	....			
Yorkshire	£7.99	....	**TOTAL VALUE** [ ]		

TOWNS, VILLAGES AND PLACES OF INTEREST

TOWNS, VILLAGES AND PLACES OF INTEREST

TOWNS, VILLAGES AND PLACES OF INTEREST

TOWNS, VILLAGES AND PLACES OF INTEREST

TOWNS, VILLAGES AND PLACES OF INTEREST

TOWNS, VILLAGES AND PLACES OF INTEREST

TOWNS, VILLAGES AND PLACES OF INTEREST